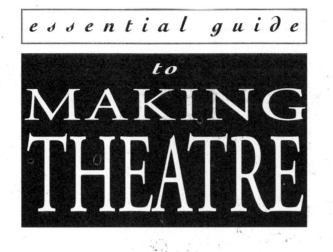

essential guide

to

MAKING
THEATRE

Richard Fredman • *Ian Reade*

ISBN 0 340 655143

First published 1996
Impression number   10   9   8   7   6   5   4   3   2   1
Year   2000   1999   1998   1997   1996

Typeset by Fakenham Photosetting Ltd, Fakenham, Norfolk NR21 9NL.
Printed in Great Britain for Hodder & Stoughton Educational, a
division of Hodder Headline Plc, 338 Euston Road, London NW1 3BH
by The Bath Press

CONTENTS

✳ 3 ✳

ACKNOWLEDGEMENTS

The authors wish to thank the following people:

Text: Jon Churchill, Sue Auty, Claire Marshall, Tim Etchells, Les Moore, Perry Horner, Ralph Oswick, David Humpage, David Robert.

Photos and drawings: Ben Pedlar (p 273); Rick Fiore (pp 47, 51–53, 55, 57–59, 125, 126,); Andy Sharp (pp 170, 185, 186); Ralph Oswick (pp 181–183); Kelvin Rogers (p 13); Forced Entertainment/Hugo Glendinning (pp 37, 279); IOU Theatre Company, Meecham/Wheeler (p 35); Richard Kalina (p 144); The Whalley Range All Stars/Peter Walsh (p 17); Scarlet Theatre/Lietta Granato (p 84); Sonia Maria Reade (pp 9, 24, 26, 27).

Interviews: Ralph Oswick, Ewan Marshall, Pavel Douglas, Hilary Strong, Gregory Ripley-Duggan, Elyse Dodgson, Mark Rylance, Grainne Byrne, Debbie Isitt, Claire Marshall, Andy O'Hanlon.

Workshops and rehearsals: James Dandridge, Georgina Penning, Rachel Middleton-Evans, Jessica Cooper, Darren Johnston, Louisa Colvill, Emma Woolley, Michelle Taylor, Steven Goodchild, Maria Mitchell, Andrew Newman, Darren Daly, Sarah Binder, Sarah Shea, Gareth Thomas, Meredith Guerrini, Julie Ford, Emily Dunn, Nicole Frith, Danielle Colley, Caroline Thorne.

BTEC First Diploma In Performing Arts 95/96 South East Essex College.

BTEC National In Performing Arts Year 1 95/96 South East Essex College (Gilbert & George).

Natural Theatre Company Workshoppers 1996.

Research: Stella Paine, Sonia Maria Reade.

INTRODUCTION

The *Essential Guide To Making Theatre* has an extremely wide remit: to serve as an educational resource and practical handbook, and also to provide an insight into the professional theatre world.

We have chosen the most significant points of each part of the theatrical process, and discussed these points in as much detail as the space allowed. There are a plethora of other valuable publications which will provide a great deal more in-depth material, and where relevant we have referred to these works so that follow-up study can be carried out. Our main objective was to provide as much appropriate detail as possible, within the restriction of compiling a *portable* work.

We have a strong inclination towards the practical aspects of theatre, and have attempted to produce a book which would reinforce active explorations of text and techniques. The manual is intended for those people who *do* want to get on with the work in hand, and to provide as many insights as possible into the multiplicity of directions into which practical work can lead you.

In addition, all of the sections are backed-up by interviews with working professionals who provide you with an up-to-date perspective on a variety of roles and methods undertaken in contemporary theatre.

How to use this book

There are six main sections to this book, with each section cross-referring in various ways to the others. For instance, Stanislavski is discussed from an historical perspective in Chapter 6, History Of Theatre, as part of Chapter 4, Directing Techniques and also in Chapter 2, Acting Techniques. In this manner we are attempting to realise the original aim of combining the values of education with useful, working perspectives on practical work and the professional theatre.

chapter one
DEVISING TECHNIQUES

The three main areas of devising that we'll be concentrating on in this chapter are:

- Street/intervention theatre
- Character-based drama
- Issue-based/community theatre

An additional section at the end of the chapter is entitled Experimental devising companies.

Figure 1.1 below gives a rough idea of our method. Whatever form of devising you have decided on, you will need to warm up – loosen up the mind and the body, ready to create. Before you actually begin improvising, you will need to do one of three things:

1 Observe characters and situations as source material (street theatre and character-based drama).
2 Introduce a stimulus, e.g. a social problem (issue-based/community theatre).
3 Brainstorm: all throw in ideas, then pick the best or the most appropriate. This is a method of group decision-making that can be used with any of the above forms.

Figure 1.1 *Methods of devising*

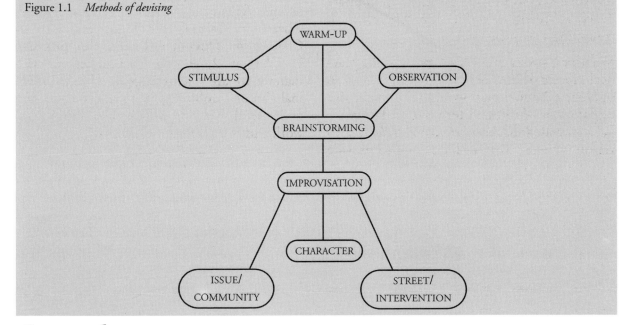

Street theatre

Theatre is happening all of the time, in every location that you might find yourself in. On the street, for example, you can often find passers-by simply staring at window cleaners or cars being towed away. What makes apparently mundane scenes like this interesting to the public?

The minimum requirement to make theatre happen is:

- a point of focus (could be a character or an action)
- an audience.

You might want to develop this work into a full-blown street theatre extravaganza, or perhaps you just want to dip your toes in the water. There are a few simple ideas for small projects in the next activities which might give

TASK

- Think of yourselves as scientists. The street and the outside world make up your laboratory. Go out and find some of your own examples of 'real' theatre.
- Get tooled up! All scientists need the right equipment to record their observations accurately. Select a few items from the tool box below.

> - Notepad and pen
> - Video camera
> - An open mind
> - Tape recorder
> - Camera

- Report back with your findings. Share your discoveries with the rest of the group. Discuss the scenes that took place. Are there any common factors?

TASK

Below are three examples of street theatre in action which you could try out.

1 *Film Noir Spies*: You have been watching far too many old black and white movies. You decide that the rest of the population also need to share your obsession, so dress up accordingly: long macs and hats (as near identical as possible – we got ours from the Lost and Found desk at the train station, but you can buy them cheaply from rag traders), black shoes and trousers, shirts, ties, shades and newspapers. Spy on the locals as inconspicuously as possible – you will soon become noticed. Remember, less is more! (See Figure 1.2.)

2 *Coarse drain fishing*: A day out for the Honourable Society of Drain Anglers. Try and make sure that your costumes are completely accurate, otherwise people will simply assume that you are students on an exercise rather than drain anglers. You must give some thought to your character, because passers-by will stop for a chat!

3 *The cleaners*: Definitely time for a spring clean! Create a group of crazy cleaners who really want to scrub that town and all its inhabitants. Great opportunity to work on character and engage with the general public. It is amazing how quickly you decide on who you can approach and who you can't. Let the scientist in you work it out when you get back.

Try combining two or more of these activities. Great scenes could develop between anglers and cleaners who require the same drain, or Film Noir spies who think the cleaners are up to something!

you a clearer idea about what it is actually like to do theatre in the street. Try them out, or invent your own along the same lines.

When you perform in the street, you immediately turn a public space into a theatre. People will automatically move aside and allow you the space to perform. You are 'taking the stage' in the most literal sense. There are, of course, many kinds of street theatre, the most common being buskers and street entertainers. But they do not surprise us. We are used to what they do and unless they are exceptionally good, we will often walk by without giving them a second thought. Their performance is largely to legitimise asking for money.

The street theatre outlined here is very different. It still seeks to be entertaining, but it also wants to make people look and think again, to give ordinary everyday activities a new meaning; the normal and the everyday are transformed into the bizarre and the funny. Street

theatre also works in the opposite way, by taking the bizarre and treating it as if it were normal. The cleaners vacuuming the pavement

> ### ⭐ *hot tips*
>
> Don't try to *do* too much: you won't have to. Just arouse the curiosity of your audience and they will immediately start trying to read ideas into the piece, ideas that you would never have thought of in a million years. Go back and raid the tool box again! A video camera would be excellent to record your audience in action. If you cannot get hold of one, at least try and take a few photographs. Keep your ears open for any choice comments from the public and make a mental note so that you can share them with the group later. People in Britain are not used to street theatre of this kind and may feel slightly intimidated. If you think you are not welcome in a particular place, just move on.

Figure 1.2   *Spying on the High Street*

should treat it as an everyday activity. If they did not it would not work as theatre.

How does it work? Simply put, it is the combination of two ordinary objects or elements that would not normally be found together, in a way which seems unnatural and throws each object into sharp relief, while simultaneously creating a new whole. Take a look at Figure 1.4, page 13: it shows some of the acts used by the Natural Theatre Company of Bath. Look at the man with a flowerpot for his head; two apparently everyday objects are colliding in a striking and unusual way. This makes the observer not only look *again*, but also see each object in a different light. Take another glance at Figure 1.2 on page 9. Two objects not normally associated with one another (spies and the high street) are placed together in an absurd way. The picture startles its observers, makes them look again and *jolts* them out of the way they usually see the world and the objects in it.

TASK

Time to invent your own piece.

Brainstorm ideas again. What are you going to do and how? There are many possible activities, but they will all have subtly different meanings. Decide what effect you want to achieve and why. However funny it is, good comedy often has a deeper meaning.

Example: If you have 20 people walking in a line like robots, all listening to personal stereos and called The Walk-Men, what are you saying about the way we respond to technology, other members of the public, our own public and private world?

THEATRE AS THE PORTRAYAL OF SOMEONE'S PRIVATE WORLD IN A PUBLIC SPACE

The following activity consists of a set of workshop exercises which you can carry out to help get the creative juices flowing, and to give an idea of the physical ingredients you are going to need for the show. Feel free to follow the workshop below exactly as it is laid out; add your own exercises as you see fit.

See Chapter 2 for a whole range of warm-ups you might use here. These exercises will help you to find a focus, develop trust in the group and discover a sense of being in your own world.

Exercises
Figure-of-eight

Two people stand still about 12 feet apart. Take turns at trying to walk a figure-of-eight around them without touching. You must wear a blindfold. Silence is needed here.

Sound circle

All stand in a circle. In turn step forward, make a silly shape and an appropriate sound. Step back. Everyone copies. Keep going until everyone has been the focus.

Machine

All stand in a circle. First person begins a mechanical rhythm with sound effect. One by one, people join on to create an enormous human machine. Stop it. Start it. Speed it up . . .

Ritual

Invent your own ritual, which you must perform in front of the group with *complete* seriousness (e.g. watch the way a golfer prepares for a putt). Your own ritual must be much more absurd. Feel free to add a noise in.

Walks

Invent a strange and rhythmic way of walking. On the command 'meet' from the leader (you may need to appoint someone), you pair up and *keep walking*. The person on the left is A and the person on the right is B. Observe your partner's walk closely. The leader then calls out 'Change to A'. Both partners instantly perform A's rhythm. When both are used to it, the leader calls out 'Change to B'. As soon as both people can do B's rhythm, the leader calls out 'Back to A and B'. You both do your original walk. On the command 'Merge', A and B join their two rhythms into one instantly and without discussion. Show each other your new walks. Do they have a character already? How would you costume them?

You can now take it a stage further if you're feeling brave. The leader calls out 'Find another pair' and the exercise is repeated, but this time in groups of four, with one pair becoming A and one pair becoming B. How far can you go?

Now brainstorm again, pooling all of the information you have gathered on rhythm, character and ritual. What kind of performance do you actually want to do out there? What kind of performance can you make by developing material from the exercises listed above? Have you seen any street theatre which you might like to try yourselves? Go for it!

A legal note

Most borough councils require street performers to have a licence. Although you will often see buskers in public spaces, they could

---

★ *hot tips*

Remember that your costumes can be as simple as you like, but they must make you look real. If you fail to appear as a professional, you will not be treated as one by the public (see Chapter 5, page 180, for more information on costume).

Some members of the public may feel intimidated by your performance. Avoid causing anyone upset or aggravation. Sometimes, the fact that you stand out can make you an automatic target for anyone who is looking for trouble. Usually, this will take the form of mockery at worst. Occasionally it can turn nasty. It is up to you to read the signs and avoid doing anything to antagonise. *Avoid confrontation at all times.* Back down and walk away, or simply ignore the interruption if you can.

---

be moved on by the police. To avoid such embarrassment and make sure you have the law on your side: *ask for a one-day performer's licence from the local council.*

Such licences are not difficult to obtain and will spare you any problems, should the police inquire if you have obtained permission to disturb the high street! Figure 1.3 shows a sample letter which you could follow.

Prearranged outdoor performances are actively encouraged and may well be paid for by local authorities. All over Europe, many festivals are organised exclusively for street theatre and most international cultural events have their street theatre contingent. There is an ever-increasing demand for outdoor theatre and gradually its contribution to the arts is becoming recognised. Newspapers have even begun to review outdoor theatre in the same way as they do indoor theatre.

Figure 1.3   *Applying for a street performance licence – a sample letter*

From: J.S. Tudent
       College of Art
       College Road
       Town and Postcode

To: J.C. Lerk
     In Charge of Public Events
     Town Council Offices
     Town and Postcode

Date:

Dear Sir/Madam

I am writing to you on behalf of my performing arts class at the College of Arts. We would like to ask permission to produce a street theatre performance of approximately one hour's duration on the following dates: 5/ /96, 6/ /96 and 7/ /96. The performance will take place between 12pm and 1pm, and consists of a group of office workers rolling down the High Street in a giant hamster's wheel. Would you be willing to grant a Performer's Licence for the show? We have painstakingly developed this piece over the course of a number of weeks and are very keen to try the piece out. We hope that the piece will be highly entertaining and also thought-provoking for the intended audience.

Please contact me at the above address at your earliest convenience.

Yours faithfully

J.S. Tudent

Interview with Ralph Oswick of the *Natural Theatre Company* (based in Bath, Avon)

How has the NTC managed to survive over the last 25 years, when so many other companies which also started in the 1960s have gone to the wall? A friend in the Arts Council or simply successful artistic policy?
Our main aim has always been to create a solid, 'straight' organisation which backs up the 'zany antics' of our performers. This organisation is entrepreneurial, efficient and makes plans for the future. In addition, because we have been present for such a long time compared to other companies, providing reliable and hard-working performers, we have an excellent and well-established reputation, which is attractive to festival organisers and promoters all over the world. In terms of artistic policy, we have a

recognisable style, but one which takes into account new ideas and uses them (if they are good). Our performers and staff are loyal and dedicated because we strive to provide the best working conditions that we can, and make sure that everyone has a good time.

What changes has the company undergone over the years:
a) regarding personnel management?
The company has evolved a great deal since the 1960s, and various structures have evolved with it. When we first started, we were all paid the same amount each (i.e. not much at all). We now have a three-tiered wages system, which means that we pay

performers differently, according to the length of time that they have been with us, and according to their experience. This system begins at the Equity minimum rate. Also we now hire performers on a short-term basis or per gig. Previously, there used to be a core team of full-time (and lazy) actors.

We have also created a Board of Management, the post of Artistic Director (me!) and a team leader system (over the summer we divide our actors into four or five teams, and allocate organisational and financial duties to a 'team leader'). The Natural Theatre Company grew from a community basis, but our day-to-day involvement with the community is now greatly reduced.

b) Regarding artistic policy?
None.

Can the company survive for another 25 glorious years, and if so, do you still want to be at the helm?
The company can definitely survive and succeed for another 25 years. We have just received millions of pounds from the National Lottery for the development of new premises in Bath, and that alone is seen as a ten-year project. Whether I will still be Artistic Director or not is a different matter. I always said that I would carry on doing it until I was 60, but I'll be a little past that in 25 years' time.

What about film or television?
Direct contact with the audience is still, and I suspect will always continue to be, the main element of our work. Natural Theatre does not translate particularly well onto the screen in any case.

What advice would you give to students who are thinking about becoming professional performers?
Decide clearly between art and show biz before starting out – but stick to your guns no matter what criticism you receive. If you go for the art side of theatre, then learn as many techniques and short-cuts as you can. Never perform in a vacuum – observe real life and be aware of real things as there is no point in a performance that is not related to everyday life. There is nothing worse than an actor who only knows the world of the theatre. Avoid theatre gurus. Take every opportunity that is offered. Acting is not special, it's just a job.

What kinds of performance do you prefer to go to, and why?
I don't go very often. I prefer way-out weirdo stuff or things with lots of scenery and nice costumes. The weirdo stuff makes you re-think things and get ideas, and the lush, conventional stuff makes you realise what you could do with a nice big budget. But at the end of the day, I have to say that I don't like plays much.

Figure 1.4   *The Natural Theatre Company of Bath*

Intervention theatre on the street
Sue Auty of *The Whalley Range All Stars*

Street Theatre: you come across it while doing your shopping, while taking the bus to work, while taking an aperitif on the terrace. You are in the same scene as the actors, you can cross the image, the image can install itself around you. This image has little chance of being the same as yesterday, because it takes place in scenery which is in perpetual motion – the street.

(Tom Roos of the Belgian company, Wurre Wurre)

WHAT IS INTERVENTION THEATRE?

This label covers many different forms and styles – everything from stilt-walkers in fantastic costumes parading through shoppers (as in the work of the Australian theatre company *Stalker*) to actors using themselves and everyday costumes to create surrealistic, humorous images inspired by stereotypes (the *Natural Theatre* company). This type of theatre is not just about 'showing' but about creating a stir. The *Desperate Men and Women* perform as groups of actors actively playing a film crew on a shoot, using the public as extras; or more abstractly, as a group of ants bent on investigating people and environment,

cataloguing samples of hair, clothing and rubbish. *The Whalley Range All Stars*' hallmark is to use masks and mechanised objects to create images which are simultaneously cartoon-like and grotesque.

Our work originates in the drawings and cartoons of Edward Taylor. Then Edward and myself realise the ideas with construction help from Greville White, a marvellously inventive maker. During the 'making' period, the original ideas are developed and extra effects added. The performance itself develops when we improvise with all the kit out on the street.

The working methods used by *The Whalley Range All Stars* are in some ways quite specific and sophisticated, but you can produce a street show using less-elaborate constructions (and with a much smaller budget). This work will give you a good introduction to our working method and also to the exhilarating performance arena of the outdoors.

HOST OF ANGELS

Begin by devising a costume with moving wings: make it simple and use cheap materials. Figure 1.5 shows the costume we designed for our host of angels in Bury.

Figure 1.5   *Use the diagrams below to create your angel costumes*

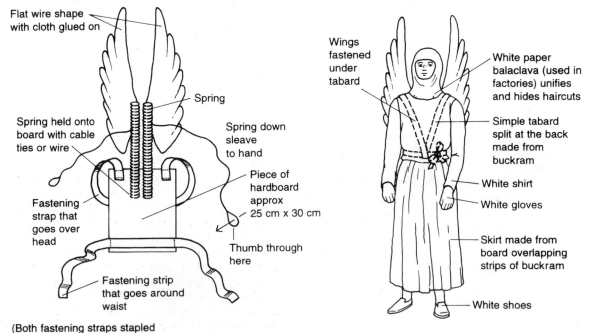

Flat wire shape with cloth glued on

Spring

Spring held onto board with cable ties or wire

Spring down sleeve to hand

Fastening strap that goes over head

Piece of hardboard approx 25 cm x 30 cm

Thumb through here

Fastening strip that goes around waist

(Both fastening straps stapled onto hardboard)

Wings fastened under tabard

White paper balaclava (used in factories) unifies and hides haircuts

Simple tabard split at the back made from buckram

White shirt

White gloves

Skirt made from board overlapping strips of buckram

White shoes

We chose to have a completely white outfit, with a unisex skirt to wear over ordinary dark trousers. Feel free to redesign the costume to suit your own circumstances, but try to avoid anything too cute or clichéd. Don't forget to include coverings for your head, hands and feet. Each person should attempt to make their own costume (with help from others, of course), as gaining experience of 'making' is an important part of the whole process.

If you have time, individuals can customise their costume, but you should aim for a certain uniformity of appearance if the angels are to have a strong visual impact.

★ *hot tip*

When you make something, it should also do something. This may sound obvious, but it is the 'doing' part that makes theatre. It may be something very small and simple, e.g. wings built onto springs attached by strings to your thumb. Such a device will repay your effort many times. It will look funny as you pump your arms to move your wings, and from certain angles it will look as though the wings are working by magic. People's expectations are at once fulfilled, as wings should flap, and so the image is complete. This device also gives you two extra and unusual limbs to play with and so entertain your audience.

DEVELOPING AN ANGELIC APPROACH TO THE TERRESTRIAL WORLD

- The angels have a mission, and that is to overturn three major aspects of conventional theatre: miming, conventional narrative and the use of words or speech.
- Angels think visually, physically and spatially.
- The aim is to produce a performance which exists in the moment, flexible enough to improvise in the street situation with people and events and also visually strong enough to create a good image in any given space.
- To create such a performance, you will need to do some physical improvisation work and some group movement work.

GAMES AND EXERCISES

Task 1
- It may be a good idea to start from very simple

★ *hot tip*

Field trips will also be invaluable: go out into the street to see what actually exists out there in terms of architecture and street furniture. It is surprising how much more you notice in the street when you have your theatrical thinking-hat on. Try making a map of your target performance area, in terms of both its physical shapes and the ideas, sensations and feelings it arouses in you. Compare maps with each other.

movement exercises, even if you already have some experience of performing street theatre. A whole mass of almost uniformed angels can have a very striking effect in a street, and the development of movement patterns can help you to put this visual impact to its full effect. Begin with general warm-up — some brisk walking or jogging in a circle, interspersed with other vigorous variations, e.g. hopping, sprinting, going backwards, turning in circles.
- Stop and rest for a moment.
- Now make large circles with your arms, forwards and backwards until you have your breath back.
- Continue the warm-up by walking in lines across the room using stretches and variations in walking styles: leaning backwards, jutting your chin forwards, holding your knees together, etc.
- Work on breathing and body awareness with gentle stretching. Concentrate on isolating different areas of the body: eyes, face, head, neck, shoulders, arms, hands, torso, hips, legs, knees, ankles and feet.
- By now everyone is warm, oxygen is flowing, your senses are awakened. Next we need to engage in some mental processes.

Task 2
Begin by walking randomly around the room. When someone decides to stop, everyone else must stop. As soon as any other person decides to start walking again, so does everyone else. Once you are comfortable with this, and have established a relationship between yourselves, try to introduce some variations. Change speeds, direction, height, how you use your arms, large steps, small steps. Work hard to achieve precision in the stopping and starting. You should find that you are using your peripheral vision now rather than straining to look around the room; a kind of a sixth sense should be developing between you all.

The transition from movement to stillness and from stillness to movement again should seem almost magical. If an outsider were to walk into the room, s/he should not be able to tell who started or stopped the movement.

Task 3

The following exercise also encourages the use of your peripheral vision as well as movement improvisation.

- Working in groups of four, stand in a diamond formation, all facing the same direction.
- The person at the front begins a slow action, and after a while they slowly begin to turn around. As everyone else follows, a new person becomes the leader.
- It is important that the people imitating the leader are as strong in their actions as the leader. Don't be hesitant even if your actions are slightly different from those of the person that is leading.

Task 4

Another important area to cover in preparation for an angelic manifestation is that of choosing a good place to stand in relation to each other, and to the surrounding architecture. Investigate this on a field trip into your target performance space.

★ *hot tip*

While it can be by far the most exhilarating place to perform, the street can also be nerve-wracking. You will almost certainly encounter every kind of response: indifference, guffaws of laughter, gawping, smiles, embarrassment, open contempt, verbal insults, and some people will actively try to join in the performance itself.

Task 5

Now work in the studio on creating group statues. Begin with one person choosing a space in the room, then allow a second person to put themselves in relation to the first, and so on, gradually building up an image which includes the whole of the group.

Task 6

You can also work in smaller groups of four or five encountering each other in the room. Discover some of the many possibilities of group behaviour: cluster-ing, forming a circle, working with distance. How can you communicate with each other. Not using speech of course, but maybe vocal sounds. Don't forget the use of gestures and of course emotions: surprise, fear, curiosity and amiability. Use your hands, eyes and shallow, readily-identifiable emotional responses. Remember you are angels, not robots. Gestures give more scope for humour and unpredictability in your responses.

Task 7: Performance

When going onto the street for the first time, keep the performance very simple and disciplined, even to the point of walking in slow motion. Find those ideal places you chose earlier on your field trip in which to make statues, and freeze. In this way you will be more able to judge the reactions of the public and the mood of the street in general.

The most difficult thing is to go out there and just exist. The temptation is to overdo the performance and this can shatter a good atmosphere. Less is more.

Task 8

Come back to the workshop or studio and spend a few more days building props which you now think you might be able to use, or developing your activities and movements.

Go out again and gradually build up the complexity of the piece. One way to do this is to divide the group and brainstorm to come up with different types of people who may be on the street. Take elements of behaviour from a particular group or type, isolate them and build them into a more complex form of behaviour. Remember that you are not trying to tell a story – the audience will invent their own explanation for what you are doing.

Another alternative for performance development is to take a very basic action and create a curious cyclical ritual out of it. For example, you could take the ritual of eating a meal, break it down into its individual components: making the food, serving it, the fanfare of the trumpets, eating the food, clearing away etc. This is, however, an advanced level of performance, and will require some detailed exploration and experience to know what to do in an outdoor situation.

THE STREET AS STAGE

> The street doesn't lie, it gives direct responses. It says, 'Yes, I like that' or it says nothing at all. Sometimes it says 'That's rubbish!' It's not an easy school.
>
> *(Tom Roos, Wurre Wurre)*

As mentioned above, the street can be an exhilarating but also nerve-wracking place to perform. The important thing to remember is that you have provoked people, and that their responses (especially if not of the most favourable kind) arise from the atmosphere and attention you have created. Don't rise to the insults; it's bad for your performance and bad for you on a personal level. You are an angel (i.e. a character) and you have the possibility of just walking away in the opposite direction.

If this is your first experience in street theatre, you would be advised to choose any day other than a Saturday afternoon to do your first shows. Saturdays bring out huge numbers of people, especially in town and city centres, which can be difficult to manoeuvre through.

The Whalley Range All Stars undertake residencies and workshops based on practical aspects of their work. This can range from devising, making and performing a piece of street theatre from scratch with BTEC students, to creating an exhibition of curious objects with primary school children.
Contact:

Whalley Range All Stars
Flat 2
35 Demesne Road
Whalley Range
Manchester
M16 8HJ
Tel: (0161) 273 5175
Fax: (0161) 272 6621

Figure 1.6   *The Whalley Range All Stars*

Character devising

Character devising is basically like writing a play, but the pen and paper are replaced by a director and the actors. The actors simply try out all of the situations in the director's mind, or ones which develop as the process grows; finally, the director or the group decides which ones will go into the final piece. You may then choose to script the piece, but this is not always necessary or very easy. Be warned: this is a very challenging form of devising. Improvisations may often seem to be leading nowhere. As a group, you will spend hours 'being real', and as with reality, this is hardly ever interesting to anyone else but the individuals concerned. But rest assured that as long as you keep working and putting the effort in, situations, tension, conflicts and humour will develop. All of these dramatic elements are likely to be much more powerful and intense than anything you have

★ *hot tip*

A great start to your project would be to watch a film directed by Mike Leigh. He is the leading practitioner in this field and has made many entertaining films using this method. Perhaps the most appropriate are: *Abigail's Party*, *Life is Sweet* and *Nuts in May*.

experienced before. You will be rewarded well for your patience.

TASK: ASSIGNING ROLES

Mike Leigh, as director, makes all of the decisions regarding content and improvisations during his process, but you may wish to take a more collective approach and make these decisions as a group. Undoubtedly the process will take longer as a collective, and there will certainly be some very heated discussions. It is also very useful to have an outside eye on the piece as it develops, because the actors participating in the devising are submerged in the action itself, and may not be the best people to judge whether a particular scene works or whether it should be cut. If you do decide to appoint a director, you must all be capable of accepting his or her decisions without ill-feeling.

TASK: FIND AND CLOSELY OBSERVE A CHARACTER

This person may be someone you know well or simply someone that you see regularly. You must have access to this character and be able to follow what they are doing without causing them or yourself any discomfort or embarrassment. Write notes on your target personalities, listing both external and internal attributes, i.e. examine not only the way that they move and talk but try to discover or imagine what exactly makes these people 'tick'.

The actors and the director might decide upon a series of questions which the characters have to answer; for example:

- What are your character's ten favourite records? books? animals?
- What are your character's ten least favourite people? television programmes? rock groups?

This is a preliminary task, a warm-up into your character's personality. Now you will want to develop an entire life story which, much like your own, will be full of moments of great achievement and corresponding times of failure. Some of your character's wildest dreams may at some point have been fulfilled, and a few of their most cherished hopes dashed. What impact have these moments had upon the way your character looks at the world? Do they feel positive or negative about themselves and the people around them?

You should try to cover every area in your investigation: employment, education, family, relationships, religion, politics – all of those factors which contribute toward making human beings such complex social animals.

Make your notes in a journal and keep it with you as you go about your day-to-day tasks – relevant thoughts will strike you at the most unexpected moments and you will want to be able to write them down as soon as possible.

TASK: DECIDE WHETHER YOU WANT A WRITER

At this stage you have to decide whether or not you want to write a script. It is possible for this kind of devised production to have no script: because the actors know their characters so well and have rehearsed the scenes so often, they are quite able to perform a continuous improvisation without the need for learning a script by rote. Using a script also means that the director/writer has more control over the actors and the shape of the piece itself.

WRITER'S NOTES

The dialogue which your characters are going to produce will be very realistic; you must be able to record this realism accurately and transform it into entertaining drama. This is no simple task and you will need to spend some time preparing your skills.

Listen to a real conversation that is taking place. Try to record it as accurately as you can with pen and paper. There will be many pauses, and the people you are listening to will probably mention the same thing many times, or refer to subjects which seem to have no relevance at all within the bounds of their conversation.

This kind of dialogue might appear very uninteresting and confusing for an outsider (yourself/the audience). It will be your job as a writer to transform this kind of speech into comprehensible dialogue, without losing the sense of truth behind it. Cut the tedious parts by all means, but be careful that you do not lose the sense of reality that the actors have painstakingly developed, by only including the funny parts. Suspense and delayed expectation create excellent drama when used effectively with humour and conflict.

TASK: PRACTICAL WORKSHOP

By now, the actors should know their character's details as well as their own, and be able to make correct responses if questioned on any topic. The director will now individually 'hot-seat' characters. This means that while the actors are in their chosen roles, the director asks them a range of questions.

- Seat the target actor opposite the director/writer and fire away with some penetrating questions.
- Begin with basic inquiries on the likes/dislikes of the character and build toward more penetrating questions on the deeper emotions. What does the chosen character fear, hope for, expect out of life? Who do they love, respect, despise?
- If the director asks a question which the character is unable to answer, the actor and the director should fill in the gaps together.

By the end of this stage, both actor and director should know the character inside-out, and the actor will have already begun to adopt the target-characteristics: voice, posture and idiosyncratic gestures (movements particular to that person).

hot tip

Cross-refer to Stanislavski and The System on page 73, Chapter 2; you may find some useful exercises to incorporate into the character-building process.

TASK: GROUP IMPROVISATIONS

You are now ready to begin group improvisations. The director/group should create a series of improvisations, each with a different scenario and combination of the characters present. Exactly what situations the director places the actors in, will depend greatly on the characters that have been chosen. Try simple situations to begin with: a doctor's waiting room, bus stop, parent's evening.

Remember that the importance of these sessions is not to create amusing scenes, as the characters will be entertaining in themselves if they are played truthfully. Try to forget that anyone is watching: lose yourself in the real time of the character's worlds.

Your characters may begin to develop relationships. The director and the actors should decide whether these relationships are worth exploring. If they are, then you will need to re-work your characters in the terms of that relationship; i.e. if you decide that two characters who were previously single are now in fact married, you will have to re-create their past histories and hot-seat them together.

TASK: MEETING UP

Develop the complexity of your devising sessions. This may happen very naturally in any case, as relationships (whether positive or negative) are created.

- Enter your characters' place of work, their home lives, the places they might socialise in, working up to the point where all of your actors are present together.
- Remember to be truthful. All of the characters must have a reason for being where they are, and for doing what they are doing; reasons which stem from their backgrounds and the characteristics you have all so carefully created.
- How do these characters meet in the play, and what happens when they do? This is essentially the stuff of your play.

By now you should have created a wealth of material, certainly sufficient for a writer to pen a script from or for a director/collective to make a play with. The narrative will come naturally from the characters themselves, or with a bit of help from an outside eye.

TASK: PERFORMANCE

You now have the choice of whether to ask the director/writer to produce the script based on the improvisations you have created, or simply to carry on improvising up until the point of performance. In the latter case, the director should work continually as the outside eye, pin-pointing conflicts, relationships and situations that are working.

Before the performance, you should have a very clear idea of what the play is going to be and the actions that are going to take place, in much the same way as a scripted piece of drama – but you should have the confidence to improvise and develop the work while performance is in progress. This may sound like a tall order, but once you have taken on the characters and completed many hours of work with them, you will be surprised at the high level of work you can achieve without it being obvious that you are, in fact, improvising.

Issue-based/community theatre

Going to the theatre has been considered an important social activity in the history of the world's civilisations since the time of the ancient Greeks. Why? Theatre is an event: it draws people together in a living arena to confirm or question our basic assumptions about life and the society in which we live. Issue-based drama and community theatre interprets these properties of theatre in a very different way from the core of the mainstream theatre available in Britain today.

During the 1960s and 70s, a number of political theatre companies operated, which directly addressed current social and political issues. Events such as strikes and demonstrations about perceived social injustices were often the subject of plays by these companies, and theatre was used as a political tool to inform and educate people about the issues surrounding these events. A great deal of this drama was formed using various devising techniques for two main reasons:

- the form of the theatre itself
- the political beliefs of the theatre companies who were performing this kind of theatre.

Forms such as Agit-prop and Newspaper theatre used contemporary, happening events in order to draw out a message for the audience. Although the performers need to possess competent acting skills in order to keep the audience's attention, there is very little time or need to make an elegant dramatic construction. Improvisation, therefore, is an excellent and accessible way of preparing a straightforward and immediate form of theatre.

TASK

- Buy a range of newspapers. Pick out one story containing socially-relevant issues which affect you now, or which may affect you in the future, e.g. an alert at a power-plant, Government policy on unmarried mothers, a strike at a factory, cuts in student grants.
- Discuss the issue: why is it important to you, and how might it be made into a short play which will inform (and still entertain) an audience?
- Improvise around the various issues and/or characters that occur in the newspaper story, and produce a startling and informative piece of theatre. (Traditionally Agit-prop and Newspaper theatre use broad character-types, extremely basic costume and tunes or catchphrases which the audience will remember and take away with them.)

Many of these companies were also left-wing, socialist theatre companies, and devising seemed to offer a way in which making theatre could be more democratic. If a piece is devised, then in theory, everyone in the theatre company could have an equal part in the play's construction and in the performance.

Although Mike Leigh's process is not a democratic one, because he makes all of the decisions regarding the selection of the final material, you can see how actors are afforded a new way of being involved in the creation of a piece of drama. The ideas and the information are coming from the actors' observations and their improvisations, and not from a single writer. Socialist devising companies used this and other similar methods and combined them with democratic decision-making procedures. This kind of structure meant that everybody in

the company had an equal right to make decisions on all matters (both artistic and economic) concerning the theatre company; these decisions were not left solely to the director or the administration staff.

Such companies as these are relatively rare in 1990's Britain. Arts Council grants to these kinds of alternative theatre companies were slashed during the late 1970s and the 1980s, so many professional companies which relied upon funding for their existence were forced to close. During this period, only a few of the largest and best established English political theatre companies managed to maintain their premises and audiences, and none survived without making radical changes either to their material or the way in which they worked.

The following sections describe the work and

methods of Augusto Boal, who uses issues drawn from personal experience to create drama and a number of contemporary community theatre companies working in different areas and sections of the British population. These methods and companies are examples of the way in which devised theatre is still used in the community today, but this is by no means an exhaustive account, and if you would like to do more work into this fascinating area, see page 38 for some ideas about further research.

FORUM THEATRE

Augusto Boal, the practitioner who has led the development of forum theatre since the 1960s, has questioned what, for thousands of years, has been understood to be the most basic principle behind theatrical performance: the audience watch and the actors perform.

> In the beginning the theatre was dithyrambic song: free people singing in the open air. The carnival. The feast.
> Later the ruling class took possession of the theatre, and built their dividing walls. First they divided the people, separating actors from spectators. People who act and people who watch – the party is over.
>
> *(Augusto Boal,* Theatre Of The Oppressed*, Pluto Press, p. 119)*

During the performance of a piece of forum theatre, the spectator and the actor merge into one and become, in Boal's words, the spectator. The intention is that a person watching the performance can actually come up on to the stage, and make a contribution which will change the course of the play itself.

Forum is such an important development in the history of theatre, because it offers every single member of the audience the opportunity to take power over the theatrical process. This form of theatre is not simply a spectacle, a passing and pleasing entertainment which the audience pays to watch and then discusses later with friends (like a television programme). Forum encourages everyone to participate in the creation of the piece of drama; it is a hands-on experience, both unpredictable and extremely challenging.

When a spectator takes the stage during a piece of forum theatre, s/he is saying, 'I want to change the way that this play is going. I have a personal experience/opinion which I want to share with all the other people here today, which will make a difference to the story.'

★ *hot tip*

Now would be a good time to read *The Story Of The False Lover*, in Augusto Boal's book, *The Rainbow Of Desires* (available in all good bookshops). This story will help to explain the development of forum theatre, in an interesting and accessible way.

Boal also sees the performance of forum as a rehearsal for life. In other words, if during the performance we can change a situation where someone is being forced to take decisions against their will, then perhaps in reality we can also do the same. The forum is a place where, in theatrical terms, we can explore all of the different alternatives that are available, and see what may happen if we take steps during the play to change that situation. Then, after the performance is over, when we return to our real lives, we might be in a better position to take the action necessary to improve our situation.

How to devise your own piece of forum theatre

Game-playing is an important part of Boal's technique for devising forum theatre. The following programme contains many such games which, as well as being great fun, will develop your understanding of each other, the way that your group works, and the idea of forum itself. All of these games and exercises can be found (along with many others) in the excellent books he has written (see page 29). Many of these games already exist in one form or another, but I have added a few variations which you might find useful. The programme is divided into sections, each section containing preparatory exercises leading into the devising of the forum itself.

Section I

Mirror and hands: the ancient game of following someone's palm all round the room. Swap over from partner to partner without a second's hesitation.

One variation is to add other pairs into your formation, or just individuals by raising the other hand and asking the leader of another pair to follow that palm, as well as lead someone else. Arrange different groupings in the same room and take feedback. The additional people can be as far away or as near as you like.

Handshake: interpret the faces of two people shaking hands. What is going on in their minds? Invent some stories, possible relationships etc.

Figure 1.7   *Moulding statues: mirroring*

- Take one person out and add a new one in, still shaking hands. Repeat questions.
- Take one person out and add a new one in, but this time they do not have to be shaking hands. Make a new shape/action.
- Then do this as a group but in pairs: one person makes a stance/shape and the other half adds in. The first person then exits and re-enters, creating a new shape/scenario. There must be no talking, and each pair should attempt to achieve a constant fluid movement.
- If there is a facilitator (the person convening the workshop session) s/he can shout out 'Freeze!', and then go round the group, turning on the sound buttons. The pairs must improvise the scenario that they have been caught in. Do the pairs ever arrive at the same thought?

Section II

The imitation game: as a group, place yourselves in a circle. Everyone watches someone else, without letting that person know that they are watching them. The movements are firstly exaggerated, and then underplayed.

Short-circuit images: group together in a circle. One person goes into the middle and throws out a word, e.g. love, hate, anger, the millennium, London, and then counts down from ten to one. At the end of the short circuit (on the number one) each individual produces a physical image on that theme. You can do this with everyone facing into the circle, or with all facing out and then turning into the circle. The game might also be played in this fashion without the use of the countdown; individuals simply turn in when they are ready.

Venetian blinds: group in pairs, then fours, then with the whole group performing an image.

- In pairs – one person makes an image, while the other closes their eyes. One person in the middle of the room shouts the commands 'Open' and 'Shut' with only a few seconds gap between them. In this short time, the person with their eyes closed gathers an impression of the statue being presented to him or her. They must then try to replicate this image with their eyes still closed. When they think they have done this, they open their eyes and compare themselves with the image of the person opposite to them, and the original image.
- Swap over and repeat the exercise.
- Do the same exercise in two pairs, then two fours, then two eights and then as a split group. In the group image, it is important that each person on each side has a partner on the other and concentrates on them.

Group images of oppression: in groups of five or six, each person within the group makes an image of a particular oppression that they have suffered. It might be a realistic or a symbolic representation. The participants will on no account have to talk about their experience, and they should not be asked about it.

The groups must also work in complete silence, using only the techniques of mirroring and moulding to form the statues; i.e. the person whose oppression it is puts people into the shape that s/he wants, or shows them what s/he wants them to do by making the shape him/herself. There should be no talking.

The person moulding the statues places him/herself in the image as the oppressed person. Each person in the group makes an image, and in a rota system they repeat the images several times, memorising the different positions they will take (see figure 1.7).

These images are then shown to the group in the rota. What can the audience say about each image? Try to stick to the shapes and positions of people, and connections you might make, rather than guessing the real scenario behind the image itself. What thoughts does the piece provoke?

Figure 1.8 *The Rashomon technique – audience suggesting alternative*

The question, 'Which image do you identify with most?' might be asked, and a vote taken.

Section III

Group images II: return to images created in the last exercise. This time the oppressed person is given three wishes to try to resolve their oppression. They do this using the same techniques of mirroring and moulding that were used before. Keep on giving the oppressed person more and more wishes until s/he finally arrives at an 'ideal' resolution. Discuss, then replay, but with the statues actively resisting (without words) the best efforts of the oppressed to realise the ideal solution. Interventions are also taken from the audience if they feel that they might be able to effect a change.

Rashomon technique: (fully covered in *Rainbow of Desires*) play a naturalistic scene, then tackle it from different participants' points of view.

One of the characters leaves the scene, and physically reshapes the other characters in the way that their character perceived them to be during the short scene. So Jane who has come out of the play, will portray Fred the father in a scrunched-up position, with a grimacing face because that is the way that Jane the character saw him, as mean and narrow-minded.

When all of the characters have been reshaped according to that one person's point of view, the scene is replayed, with as near the original text as possible, but with the actors playing through their new masks. The results are hilarious and illuminating. The process is repeated until all of the characters have reviewed the scene from their point of view.

Note: Try to avoid placing the statues in sitting-down positions as this makes for a very static replay. This is a useful technique for groups with problems working together.

Figure 1.9   *The Rashomon technique – statues in motion*

Rhythm and sound trios: each person in the trio invents a sound and a rhythmic action to go with it. The group moves forward, all completing each other's sound and movement in turn for about two minutes at a time. At the end of this process, each trio is asked to try and merge their sounds and movements.

The group continues to move forward. Individuals are then allowed to join other groups if they wish to, and try out their sounds and rhythms. Once larger groups have formed, they are asked to merge their sounds with another large group and this process continues until there is only one group in the room.

Oppression discussion: gather a list of things which people consider to be issues of oppression – race, gender, disability. Whittle the number down by giving everyone three votes each in the first round, and then one in the second round. Choose the oppressions (one per group) which get the most votes. Don't forget

that in a forum, both the personal and social aspects have to be brought into play. There must also be a struggle, a person fighting against an oppression, but always losing (remember Boal's *Story of the False Lover*), and not just the victim facing the firing squad.

Section IV

Cat and mouse: group in pairs with arms linked, but leaving one 'mouse' and one 'cat' on the loose. The mouse attempts to save itself by linking arms with a pair, and the person on the end of this pair then becomes the mouse.

● A variation on this is to have *cats and dogs*. When the mouse links arms with a pair, the person on the end who would normally flee becoming a mouse, becomes a dog. The cat then flees, joins onto another pair, and the person on the end of this pair becomes an even bigger dog and sets on the dog. This can continue *ad infinitum*.

Vowels and phrases: go through the vowels, saying them in turn, in as many different ways as possible. The group stands in a circle and a person with a contribution steps into the middle to display their expression. The group then repeats this expression and intonation three times. Then pick common phrases 'Good grief' and do the same.

Forum pieces in mime and different styles: now create your forum scenes. Typical issues are: gender, workplace oppression, sexual orientation, bullying. The scene tells the story of the oppression, very much like the *Story of the False Lover*. Now run the scenes, first in mime and then with words.

Is the story clear? Who is the protagonist/the oppressed person (there should only be one to keep things simple). Do we care about her/him? Can we see places where it might be possible to intervene? Criticise and make things difficult for the devisers in an effort to improve your pieces.

A few notes on the content of the pieces:

- make introductions in one form or another to the characters
- include language and jargon of people's professions
- refer to external economic factors/micro to macro
- include a potential ally/allies in the story
- make the pieces physical – avoid creating radio forums.

Section V

Clapping movement: complicated hand-claps combined with physical movements passed around the circle.

Flowing people: one person stands in the middle of a group of seven or eight, and whichever way the person wishes to move, the rest of the class supports them. The idea is that the protagonist is allowed to turn in any direction without fear.

Forum rehearsal techniques

1 *Stop and think!* Stop the character in midflow, and ask them to voice their inner thoughts.
2 *Emotions*: replay the scene, but with emphasis on any one of the emotions present in the scene, exaggerated several times.
3 *Interrogation*: the audience are allowed to question the performers on what exactly their motivations and actions are, at any point during the play (very similar to the well-known hot-seating technique).
4 *Any style*: replay the scene in any style that you can think of: opera, farce, melodrama, *Neighbours*, etc.

Forum practice

Now try your pieces out on each other. One person in the company acts as an intermediary, someone who stands between the audience and the action of the play. This person is known as the Joker.

Play your scene(s) out once. The Joker steps forward and asks the *audience* to step forward at any point if they see an appropriate moment to make an intervention. The Joker might ask the audience if they saw a point at which they might have behaved differently if they had been the oppressed person in that situation.

When they see the scene played for the second time, the audience-members who have something to say shout out 'Stop!' and the action is halted straight away. The Joker (who needs to have a lot of charm and personality) convinces this person to take the place of the actor playing the oppressed person). The Joker asks the spectator where they would like the scene replayed from, and the action recommences.

The audience will be hanging on every word to see how the situation changes, and whether the intervention will successfully combat the oppressors. Continue until you all believe you have made all the interventions possible.

- Beware of magic! Incredible solutions such

as rich people arriving with piles of loot to save the oppressed person, or the oppressors suddenly dying in a car crash, should not be taken seriously. The forum is a rehearsal for reality. What could you do in this situation if it were in real life?

Section VI – Performance

Now you are probably ready to take your pieces to the public. Here are some pre-performance warm-ups. Enjoy yourselves, and remember that this is the theatre of the oppressed, not the theatre of the depressed. In other words, try and find a workable solution to your problem before finishing.

Duels: one hand behind the back, palm open, in pairs. Each person must try and touch each other's palm three times.

Variations:

● In pairs, both hands on knees, try to tap the other person's knee.
● In pairs, try to tread on each other's toes.

Fluid movement: two lines of people opposite each other. One person goes into the middle; as soon as they stop another person follows. If two people enter at the same time, then they must come to a rest at the same time in the middle. Once everybody is in, they leave one by one.

Variations:

● Do the same but with all people running.
● Do the same but go in with a phrase, stick with it, and greet everybody in the middle with this same phrase. The people in the middle can respond in any way that they see fit. Also the improvisations can go on for as long as they are working well. When everyone is in the middle, people leave one by one, again improvising but this time greeting people with a new phrase.

Fantasy characters: act out your forum character's wildest fantasies.

Forum theatre audience warm-up: the Joker explains to the audience how forum works and asks the audience to store up the moments in which they might intervene throughout the play. The Joker might ask them to think of forum as a game that the performers want the audience to win. As it is a game, the Joker continues, everyone should do a little bit of a warm-up (while sitting on their chairs). The Joker can ask the audience to:

● raise one hand, make a circle, raise the other hand, make a cross then try and do both together
● do a bit of leg work: circle legs in the air from the ankle, sign your name in the air with your legs and then do both at the same time.

Have a great time!

Useful publications

Boal, A. (1979) *The Theatre of the Oppressed*, Pluto Press.
Boal, A. (1992) *Games for Actors and Non-actors*, Routledge.
Boal, A. (1995) *Rainbow of Desires*, Routledge.

Note: Adrian Jackson, the editor of Boal's books in Britain, works at the London Bubble Theatre in London, and should be contacted for any information regarding workshops and current Boal events here in Britain:

London Bubble Theatre
5 Elephant Lane
Rotherhithe
London
SE16 4JD
Tel: 0171 237 4434

OTHER KINDS OF ISSUE-BASED/COMMUNITY THEATRE

Forum theatre offers one model of how to devise a play based upon an issue within a community context. The *London Bubble Theatre* led by Adrian Jackson has worked with homeless people in this way, creating several pieces which have toured London and the regions.

There are many other forms of devised theatre in the community. *Age Exchange* works with senior citizens in London. This company gathers information from the elderly regarding a specific period in their history, e.g. the Second World War, and then, in conjunction with the elderly people themselves, writes a full-length play. This play is shown in the locality and is also taken out on tour. The pieces include songs and incidents which are part of a shared background for the audience.

In a sense this is the strength of devising work: the form allows the company and the audience to pool their collective knowledge and to create an experience which the audience can easily identify with and share. In this way, Age Exchange helps to confirm the shared identity of this particular section of the population, and because of the depth of the research gleaned from a wide variety of sources, provides a strength of expression which would be hard to match in the conventional theatre.

An issue-based piece of forum theatre structured around teenage pregnancy would have the same effect in another section of the community, but would enable its audience not only to identify directly with the issue, but also to question the causes and effects of decisions taken in the play and consequently in the world outside of the play.

★ *hot tip*

If you are interested in this particular working method, Alison Oddey offers an interesting account of the work of Age Exchange in her book, *Devising Theatre* (1994) Routledge.

Interview with Andy O'Hanlon of *Cross Border Arts*

Can you define what community arts or arts in the community are?
It's very broad. The terms describe work across a range of art forms used within different communities. For example, it might be work with members of a housing association, with recovering drug-users, or with social services at residential or day centres. Usually, but not always, it is issue-based work in a specific community setting. The word *issues* makes it all sound very worthy, but in fact community arts, sometimes known as arts in the community, are about celebrating the best things within a community. These can range in scale from the smallest kind of exhibition in the foyer of a community centre, right through to major high-profile art-works by big companies, such as The Royal Opera House. At the same time we, as a company, cater for everybody's particular needs, and within that big project there will be lots of small things going on. It's all-encompassing, really.

Can you explain more fully exactly what your company, Cross Border Arts, is?
Yes. We started out as a touring theatre company in London in 1985, with the aim of getting as much participation in our shows as possible. In 1996, we function on a number of levels in Cambridgeshire. We operate the arts and disabilities service in Cambridgeshire, employing artists in all fields to fulfil specific commissions or briefs that have been put together with hospitals or community centres or special needs groups; that is an area of ongoing work.

As an individual artist working for the company, I also respond to enquiries for other areas of work. For example, I am co-ordinating an opera project, which is a big thing and is backed up by lots of other organisations, both locally and from London. I'm also doing a school arts project in Peterborough, which is about health and food and the importance of healthy food to healthy living. I use techniques picked up over the years. A lot of them are Forum Theatre techniques that go right back to when we started as a small-scale touring outfit.

There is a third area of work that is to do with longer term aims, which is to start a county agency to bring environmental and conservation groups together with artists for specific projects. There is a small pot of development money which allows us to think about ideas and how we can move them forward strategically to benefit the issue and the artists, and to enable more artists to work in the field.

In general, do you wait for companies, groups or agencies to approach you?
Half and half, really. We always wanted to be pro-active, to be able to say 'This is our menu, this is what we do, and we'd like to invite you, as partners, to buy into this menu.' But it does not work without development money, because you can't sustain it; you cannot do the necessary research and preparation without the funding to back it up. We had never had that capital until we received revenue support for the arts and disabilities work. But through the goodwill of artists, and being tenacious, we were able to offer specific programmes of work, ways of working and organisation (a guarantee to people we work for of the smooth running of events). These are unique resources, really, that only a company like *Cross Border Arts* can offer. Otherwise it's a question of buying in freelancers who may not know each other: with us the team comes ready-made. You're buying in expertise: people who already work together and have done the research.

All that comes, however, at a premium. Sometimes that premium doesn't get paid, in which case we respond to mad requests like, for example, one from a bank in Basingstoke which we did just before Christmas. We called it our *Bank Job*. They wanted us to celebrate their opening, so we made them a giant puppet, went down there with a couple of puppeteers and had a really good time. They got a taste of our work, they liked it, we did what they asked us to do and we got paid for it!

Finance is very important. We always have to consider how the company is going to pay for itself. We have to ask 'Is it going to make a bit of a profit?' We need to aim to have a slight surplus instead of a debt each year.

What is your annual turnover?
This year it's about £100,000 (a quarter of it comes from funding, and the rest is what we actually earn). *[Out of that comes salaries, artists' fees, office-space, workshop space, administrative costs and vehicle running costs.]*

How many people does that support altogether?
We have three full-time employees. An Administrator, an Arts and Disabilities Co-ordinator and an Artistic Director, plus around 20 freelance artists employed throughout the year on different projects.

What aspect of the work gives you the most satisfaction?
I enjoy being in the thick of it. I enjoy all aspects of the work. I particularly enjoy leading a successful workshop and bringing things to fruition. For example, the thing that's uppermost in my mind right now is this food and health project which, incidentally, is funded by the Dairy Council through the Health Trust. It is hands-on, drama-based work. It's theatre; watching people begin, in a very immediate way, to lose their inhibitions about performance; saying things about themselves, learning things about themselves, and the revelation that they can in fact do things differently. They may choose not to do things differently, but they become aware of what they are doing, what they're saying, how they're behaving. It's very simple. That's what I like.

What qualities do you think someone needs to have to work in community arts?
A good sense of humour. That's essential. A high level of, well … a high *pain* threshold! They must be very tolerant and prepared to listen. Those are all very fundamental things. The basics of being human, really.

It helps if they can organise themselves and respect the backgrounds of the people they are working with. They need to understand the context in which they are working and what the demands and expectations are. They must try not to impose too much, but rather to find out the best of what is already there, the resources that already exist. They must act as glue, I suppose, to things that are there already and might need sticking together.

So you see your role as helping to bring out things that are already there in the communities that you work with?
Definitely. It's really looking at what is latent. Sometimes it's screamingly obvious, but hasn't been achieved *because* it's so obvious. For example, artists often live quite close to each other in a community, working in parallel and yet never meeting with each other. So we ran a seminar in Ely called *Art Without Walls* for care-workers, artists and teachers. Seventy-five people came to that. We had three artists run-

ning sessions throughout the day. There was a Mexican artist, a blind arts and disability worker leading a workshop in painting, and a disabled musician leading a dance workshop. It was challenging, informative and it brought people together who hadn't met each other before, who began having ideas and sparking off each other. Now that isn't really a very difficult or complicated thing to organise, but it is essential. That has led to new ideas and, of course, has been developed into more sophisticated plans for further arts work in that community.

What crossover would you say there is between the traditional theatre and performance-based community arts?
That question might have been answered very differently 10 or 15 years ago. The impact of the media, information technology and video has meant that people intuitively understand and respect cross artform work now. We hope to be at the front of the queue in terms of our ideas, particularly where young people are concerned. Multi-media doesn't mean a print workshop and clowning any more: it's a synthesis. The problem with community arts is that it is not a single discipline but a multiplicity of disciplines. The people who work in it tend to be specialists of multi-form as opposed to individual forms.

You are asking me about the importance of theatre and performance. It's very important for the person who is working in that field to understand the rest of the work and what else is going on. And it's important for other people – sculptors, artists, musicians – to understand what's happening in theatre. There will be projects where theatre and performance take the lead and those where they won't, but there will be a *consciousness* of the relevance of the various forms.

Would you say that someone whose primary interest is theatrical needs to develop an interest in other art forms?
I think it's very useful. The traditional community arts groups were established in the 1960s and 70s. Sometimes they were performance-based, but they were all, without exception, interested in experimentation from the very beginning. Some of them looked specifically at what the community wanted from them, while others felt that the art form is the most important thing: 'We'll use members of the community and we'll show them how we do it.'

There is still a tension between these two ways of working, but the important thing for anyone from theatre coming into community arts to be aware of, is the centrality of trying new things out; not being afraid to have a go, to be brave, to take risks. Innovation and experimentation is something that the Arts Council is always talking about. With us it is often about those very experimental and innovative

things happening for people who would never normally go to a dedicated arts venue.

The point that I'm making is that there's a gap in perception. A lot of people think that community arts is the cuddly toy of the arts world, that it's not real, it's just one of those things that ex-teachers do. In some circles there isn't a lot of respect for it, to be honest. I'm hoping to do my bit to correct that, because it is about *quality* and *excellence*.

So to you there is no distinction between community arts and real art?
Absolutely not, no. It's very unfortunate that community arts has got this record.

Why do you think that is?
I think it is because the work often makes a virtue out of being low cost. It has always wanted things to be free, because it works with under-resourced groups and sometimes with disadvantaged groups. I've only ever known that particular world of work on its knees – since I started in 1982 there has been one cut after another, and what I've seen are very fine people working, constantly battling against the odds and making virtues out of necessity. That sometimes means that you have to take short cuts, which all adds to the negative record, and then there are the people who say 'Oh, they will do it because they love it. They'll do it because they're there, because they're not going anywhere else and they really believe in their work, so why do we need to fund it?'

If you want to develop your career, think very hard before going into community arts. You have to be motivated by things other than career and money. It *is* very exciting and wonderful to be involved in. I'm looking for ways of developing it as an industry, hoping that we'll be able to build enough partnerships to make that realistic, not a dream. I certainly get a buzz out of it.

There is a wide range of courses that claim to train people in community arts. Would you recommend them as the appropriate route into work in the industry?
The honest answer is, I don't know. I'm aware of the existence of a number of such courses, but quality and the perception of the worth of the work is paramount, and at the moment there isn't enough understanding of the worth of the work in such places for me to advocate going there. It is very much a trade, and building it up is a bit like saying 'If you really want to be a jobbing community artist you have to get to know your business.' As long as the course you're looking at provides good after-sales service; if they give you a useful model for earning a living through using your skills, then, yes, I think it would be worth

it. Any course that does has obviously worked it out. If they're not doing that you should ask why not; what sort of a deal are they giving you for when you leave? I went to art school and they didn't do anything for me at all. It took me years to work out what I was doing wrong. There may be better ways of going about it. Part of your training should be planning your career, planning your business.

Can you give me an example of a particular project, how it came about and how you tackled it?
Let me talk about the food project that I'm in the middle of right now.

I received a phone-call from a community dietician, asking if we could discuss doing a drama project in schools she had worked in. She had been to an arts in health conference where she had seen some forum theatre and she wanted to know more about it. We met and talked about possibilities, and then met up with a teacher to discuss the ideas. Together we drew up a schedule of school-time workshops which used drama to look at young people's eating habits and food issues. At the same time I did a bit of research which involved eating a lot of school dinners, listening and watching lunchtime activity at school, and looking at surveys compiled by the health care trust on the subject of eating habits.

After this stage I started work with the school drama club. Our work on food issues was fast and furious, isolating behaviour patterns revealed during the lunchhour, and we also did some elaborate work on characterisation. I then wrote up the various scenarios devised and the characters developed and wove them into a 20-minute piece of theatre. The group then read the script and began an intensive rehearsal period.

The piece is now touring schools. It's a piece of forum theatre: they show the play once, and then show it again, allowing opportunities for the audience to stop it, to intervene, to change things by taking the place of the actors and showing how they would do it (see page 23).

There will be an evaluation at the end of the project, asking whether the project met the targets that we set, whether it worked, whether there are any possibilities of continuing the work and broadening the project out, should we put it away or show it at a health conference? That process involves one artist, a teacher and the original dietician.

Cross Border Arts has recently changed its name from Puppetworks. Can you say why?
We originally called the company *Puppetworks* because it was a synthesis of all the art forms, just as puppetry itself is. We changed the name in July 1995 because people kept phoning us up and asking us if we did children's parties.

We thought it was time for a change. The final straw was when the Eastern Arts Board wanted to cut our grant to nil last year because we were a puppet company, despite having written to us to say that they understood the cross-arts nature of our work. *Cross Border Arts* now seems to capture something of the age. Every time I hear the news it seems to be about people in Bosnia and elsewhere marking out their borders, saying this far and no further, this is who I am. We want to investigate all the issues of boundaries in a constructive way, recognising that we need them, but making them matter less because we know more about them.

Experimental devising companies

The final section of this chapter describes the work of two companies: *IOU* and *Forced Entertainment*. Both of these companies, in very different ways, present challenging and exciting new ways of looking at the theatre experience, and use devising as their means of achieving this aim. It is very difficult to describe the experience of seeing shows by these companies. The photographs on pages 35 and 37 will give you an idea of the work both companies carry out.

IOU THEATRE COMPANY

This award-winning theatre company is probably the longest-running devising theatre company in the UK. They are based in Halifax, and have been touring their form of devised work since 1976. They operate with a core membership, which consists of designers, actors, artists and musicians, and hire in other members for specific work.

What do IOU do?

They devise shows probably unlike anything you have ever seen before; they combine with equal weight, music, dance, text, strange instruments and designs into enchanting, ironic and often disturbing pieces. They tour their shows around the UK and Europe, or create shows for one place (these are called site-specific pieces) for a particular point in time.

> The starting points for shows can often be paintings, book illustrations, cartoons, newspaper clippings, dreams, films, bible stories, fairy tales and myths. A photograph or an object might form the basis for a small detail of costume or the whole concept of a show. It is always the case that IOU visualises first and then makes stories around those images which ring out, persist or disturb. Buildings and landscapes can also be the inspiration for a show, shaping and generating ideas. Disused houses, market-halls, canal basins and railway sidings have provided the settings for special commissions. IOU has performed on beaches and mudflats, in castles, catacombs and courtyards.
>
> *(IOU company information)*

How do IOU devise?

The company principally uses a method called 'mapping' which is ingenious and highly-useful for any deviser. 'Mapping' is basically a way of organising and selecting (through a variety of media) the thoughts, emotions and the stimuli that are thrown up during the devising process. If you want more information about this method, you could book an IOU workshop or contact the company at the address below. The results are free from the usual limitations of narrative structure and veer off into completely unexpected directions, which nevertheless seem to have an internal logic. It is hard to appreciate the method or the rationale unless you do one of the workshops, and before you do one of these, you should try to go and see one of the shows. They can be contacted at:

IOU Theatre
Dean Clough
Halifax
West Yorkshire
HX3 5AX
Tel: 01422 369217
Fax: (01422) 330203

IOU Theatre's Musical Director, David Humpage, writes about the origins and development of the company's award-winning show, *Distance No Object*

The basic idea for *Distance No Object* arose from an 'atmosphere' concerning railways and life/death journeys. We had been particularly interested in the railway photographs of O. Winston Link. Ostensibly documenting the last days of steam locomotives in parts of America, these pictures almost always involved trains as ghostly presences (frequently by night), or glimpsed as strange intruders on scenes where they had no business (through a lounge window, heading down a small-town street in the dark etc.). They have something in common with Edward Hopper's paintings (same use of windows/atmospheres) and also certain earlier pictures of Georgio de Chirico (empty streets and deserted arches, often with train in the distance).

A set model (white arches, somewhat de Chirico) was constructed. David Wheeler (IOU's Artistic Director) then made a 'scrapbook video' to illustrate the intended atmosphere of the show. This video used simple tracking across a number of Hopper/Link/de Chirico pictures, interspersed with short clips from relevant films (e.g. David Lean's *Brief Encounter*) and sequences involving projection of various slides/films on to the set model. At this stage, we were interested in a white set as a possible ground for projection. I added a sound track featuring a lot of haunting distant train sounds, footsteps from invisible characters, and a slow desolate static piano waltz. This video helped describe the atmosphere of the show to performers and to the commissioners, Warwick Arts Centre.

As I had envisaged the atmosphere of the final show as quiet and distant, the principal musical problem was how to work-in some higher energy points for contrast. Then the possibility arose of working with the Creative Jazz Orchestra, a highly flexible and exciting group known for working closely with contemporary composers. The problem now became: how

to make space (in a dream-like piece) for musicians accustomed to playing their hearts out energetically without tight time-limits! I decided on a basic structure, generating contrast of off-stage (dream-like) and on-stage (energetic band) musics.

Several years ago, we had made a short film (*Windfall*) as part of a BBC documentary on IOU, involving a character summoned on a mysterious train journey. This became the thread of the new show. Things now became rather more music-led. We divided our proposed show length (75 minutes) into five roughly equal acts or 'symphonic' movements (to be heavily musically contrasted) as follows:

1 Dream sequence; premonitions of journey; delivery of 'message'.
2 Awakening; setting out on journey; passengers on station.
3 In the train.
4 Arrival at the seaside.
5 Desolation on the beach; arrival back in bed.

The 'hero' was to be a passive, victimised figure. Meanwhile, ideas for the set had changed radically. In order to avoid having to place the band between stage and audience, we decided to put them on a platform in the air, above most of the action. David

Figure 1.10   *IOU Theatre Company,* Distance No Object – *'Time is short and the platform is long'*

Wheeler then invented an all-steel viaduct-style set, a cross between a Victorian station roof and a pier, strong enough to support the musicians and gear. Props were constructed: half-section carriages (reversible to view interior/exterior), a mobile Punch and Judy booth that could pursue its observer, a 'cinema' in which the protagonist whiles away time at the seaside (missing the main action) etc. The five parts spawned their own developments and characters; a mini-opera in the train (pt. 3), the awful end-of-the-pier band and the cinema/usherettes/goldfish sequence (pt. 4), the Purcellian echo-chorus of donkeys (pt. 5). Parallel with all this, Lou Glandfield wrote song words, and I completed the bulk of the music (a few pieces were added late in the rehearsal stage). Then the final sequences of action detail were worked out in rehearsal.

The important stages of the evolution of an IOU show are:

- atmospheres/general subject matter
- bone-structure (music/action)
- detailed music/props, plus list of 'possible' events
- final working-out plus adjustments.

This 'plot last' approach allows for musical or visual items to generate action, and is in complete contrast to normal theatrical methods of 'illustrating' a plot through props and music.

Forced Entertainment

ARTISTIC POLICY

Developing ideas and strategies from one project to the next, *Forced Entertainment* is concerned with urban experiences, with ideas about identity in the media-saturated world, with the collision of cultures, languages and texts that make-up and mark-out our lives. The group's longevity and commitment has lead to a theatrical language, process and set of skills which are more or less without parallel in the UK. Ideas about structure and form have been developed over ten full-scale shows and three commissioned works. In recent years *Forced Entertainment*'s activities have become increasingly diverse – projects in unusual sites, in galleries, in publishing and in electronic media now augment and inform their theatre practice.

Through articles, essays, public talks and lectures, members of the company seek to place their work, and that of other experimental practitioners, in an informed context, highlighting their concerns and ambitions.

EDUCATIONAL ACTIVITIES

The company are actively involved in teaching at a number of levels. An initial programme of one-day workshops, presentations and discussions to accompany performances has grown into a flourishing independent programme of work with such diverse groups as BA and postgraduate students, Adult Education, BTEC, sixth form colleges and young practitioners. The company runs a regular programme of residential workshops in Sheffield.

These activities serve as a way of sharing information and ideas about performance, aiming to act as a catalyst for new work and to provide non-practitioners with new ways of thinking about the theatre and themselves.

BACKGROUND INFORMATION

Forced Entertainment was set up in 1984 and comprises a core group of six with a growing network of artistic collaborators both short and long term. Based in Sheffield, the company receives regular funding from the Arts Council England, Yorkshire and Humberside Arts and Sheffield City Council to create and tour work in the UK and overseas. Since Summer 1993 the group has been based at Unit 102, a purpose built office and rehearsal space which also serves as a resource for other artists and a focus for performance activity in the region.

FUNDING THE COMPANY

We do not have much secure funding. We receive annual programme money from Yorkshire and Humberside Arts and from Sheffield City Council, but for the rest, we exist in the unpredictable world of project grants. We submit a separate application for every project we wish to make – usually to the Drama department at the Arts Council of England – and then wait.

Surviving on drama projects is very hard, because of the uncertainty, and for other reasons too. The 8–12 weeks we spend devising a major project from scratch are perceived as luxurious compared to companies who can rehearse a play in one month. It's impossible to plan ahead, which makes life very hard if you want to talk seriously to festivals and international venues. Worst of all perhaps, projects

Figure 1.11   *Forced Entertainment,* Hidden J

cannot provide money for core costs – management, administration and project development outside of actual rehearsal periods. Given the scale, longevity and reputation of what we do – perhaps a major touring show, a site specific, a revival of an old piece, a gallery installation, some film development work, a couple of small publications and eight or more weeks of foreign touring in a year – this kind of ad hoc funding is ludicrous.

In the last few years, drama seems to have become more conservative – less innovative work is funded. In particular, projects – home for most of the radical stuff they do support – has been chosen by the drama department to bear the brunt of repeated government cuts imposed on the department and on the Arts Council as a whole. This makes the fund very pressurised and over-subscribed. There was a battle over the funding for our project *Speak bitterness* (refused and then later given money by ACE Drama), which highlighted a difficulty the department has in dealing with work outside of particular theatrical aesthetics. It is a difficulty that needs to be addressed.

Alongside our drama projects, a growing strand of our work takes place outside of theatres: in sites, galleries, publications, making installation, live art durational performances, photographic collaborations and even films. Funding for these projects comes from separate sources; via direct commissions from festivals or gallery curators, from other funders like Combined Arts at the Arts Council, Sheffield Media Development Fund, etc.

We have had a reasonable amount of success in raising money for capital needs, due for the most part to the efforts of Deborah Chadbourn, our administrator who is a founder member of the company. We now have our own small rehearsal studio and office which we are also able to develop as a resource for other artists – a space for workshops and training, and in which new work can be developed and presented to the public. Funding for this space has come from Yorkshire and Humberside Arts, the European Regional Development Fund and The Foundation For Sports and the Arts as well as, more recently, from the National Lottery.

How is devised theatre used today?

There is a relatively strong tradition of devised theatre in modern Britain, which can be traced back to the work of Joan Littlewood and Ewan McColl and the Theatre Union in the 1930s, and then forward to the work of the Belgrade Theatre in the 1960s, numerous theatre companies in the 1970s and 1980s including Joint Stock, Red Ladder, Women's Theatre Group and Gay Sweatshop, Lumière and Son, the Natural Theatre Company, Shared Experience and of course the work of Mike Leigh and Ann Jellicoe. Into the 1990s we find groups such as: Forced Entertainment, Théâtre De Complicité, DV8, IOU, Welfare State, David Glass Mime Ensemble, leading practitioners such as Augusto Boal and writers such as Caryl Churchill. The work ranges from the directly political to the innovative and artistic (although these two characteristics are not mutually exclusive), and all are well worth investigating.

TASK

Research one of the above-named companies/practitioners/writers. What kind of plays have they produced, and what devising methods did they use? Important factors to consider are: the time-scale, size of the company, the company's/writer's aims in creating the piece, the starting point of the devising process, the venue, and the target-audience. Write at least 500 words.

Interview with Elyse Dodgson

Elyse is an Associate Director of the Royal Court Theatre, responsible for international and cross-cultural work at London's premier new writing theatre. We asked her questions about herself as a theatre and educational practitioner and the nature of theatre education work outside schools and colleges.

What is your current title and how did you find your way into this kind of work?
I am an Associate Director, and my responsibility has been for education. The title of director is important because it links me firmly with the creative and artistic side of the Royal Court and gives equal status to education work. Education posts are too often seen as primarily administrative.

I started out as an actress. I came over from the States 30 years ago to go to drama school after doing a theatre degree. I stayed and worked in early fringe theatre in this country in the 1960s at the Brighton Combination. I was one of the first members of the company. Howard Brenton was the writer in residence, and David Hare used to visit with his *Portable Theatre Company*. Even there I became involved with working with young people, doing Saturday classes. When I had my own children I realised that this was an area of work that I loved and that was very new. I felt there was a great affinity between some of the drama-in-education work and those early fringe theatre companies, which had a different political outlook and were much more experimental than the mainstream companies of that time; so it wasn't very difficult to shift from one to the other.

I also did a teacher's training course and started teaching drama in London. I worked for about five years as a classroom teacher at Vauxhall Manor School. I was lucky enough to get a grant from the old Greater London Council (GLC) to do a two-year research project which combined theatre and community.

We produced a piece called *Motherland*, based on the migration of Caribbean women to Britain who were the mothers of the girls of Vauxhall Manor School. The first year of the project used oral testimony to develop the play, which then took off. With this technique, girls would interview their own mothers about their lives, in particular why they came to Britain and what their early experiences were, and we translated that oral testimony into a play. At the same time, the whole school focused on this theme. Over 80 per cent of the girls in the school had an Afro-Caribbean background. The history classes were teaching it, and so were the social science classes. It wasn't just a drama project, the whole staff were involved in it for a whole year from 1981–82. For me it was the culmination of five years' work at the school.

Motherland became a video project and I published it as a book in 1984, which told the story of the project. It also reproduced the script, and had photographs and exercises for lessons in the classroom. The copyright of the play's text still belongs to the company, many of whom are mothers themselves now. Instead of using our script, they wanted other people to create their own, similar projects. Using personal testimony, sometimes known as *verbatim theatre*, is something that has been a very important part of my work as a result of that project. It was actually as a result of *Motherland* that I got the job here, because I went on to become an advisory teacher on drama for ILEA (Inner London Education Authority, now defunct) Equal Opportunities Inspectorate. Max Stafford Clark, the director at the Royal Court at the time, had seen *Motherland* and that helped me when the job of director of the *Young People's Theatre* came up here.

Did you write the script for Motherland?
I co-ordinated the script, but it was very important to me that I did not write it myself. We developed a way of working that involved people taking responsibility for writing different bits. Much of it was based on improvisation, but there were songs in it that individuals wrote, and various scenes that were written by different people. Marcia Smith (my chief researcher on the project) and I then put the thing together. It would be hard to say who wrote this bit or that bit; it really was a collective effort.

Companies who devise work often do still have that special role for an individual writer.
Yes, and I've gone on to do that at the Royal Court, using what is called *The Joint Stock Method*. This is named after the *Joint Stock Theatre Company* and the way they devised with writers like Caryl Churchill and David Hare. It is similar to the process we used with *Motherland*, but in this case the writer is ultimately responsible for the piece.

So that brought you in here as Director of the Young People's Theatre?

Yes. It was a very interesting time for the *Young People's Theatre*. We were still in a small office in The Royal Court itself, on Sloane Square, but they had just purchased a building on the Portobello Road, which would offer much greater access to young people. There was a purpose built studio that took years of funding. I was appointed three months before we moved into the new space, so it was a very creative time.

What kind of productions did you put on there?
In the beginning I brought a lot of what I'd already been doing. The first project I did there was called *Women and Sisters* (a response to some of the criticisms of *Motherland*) which was about the role of black men. Some people felt that the testimony was too critical of black men, and this new project looked at a time in the nineteenth century in the States when there was a movement to abolish slavery and, at the same time, the suffrage movement to give women the vote (led by black activists, such as Frederick Douglass). There were many parallels between this and the tensions between gender and race in England in the 1980s. It was scripted by three writers, one of them being Marcia Smith who worked on *Motherland*, so I brought a lot of that work with me.

The last production I did at the Young People's Theatre was written by Winsome Pinnock, who is now a very established writer with a new play coming up at The Royal Court. She had been in the writers' group of the *Young People's Theatre* and we did a project on the life of Claudia Jones, a black activist deported from the States in 1950 during the Macarthy era, who came to Britain and started the black press in this country. Very little was known about her, so we did a lot of research and interviews. This was different for me because this was the first time I got to work with a single writer. The final play, *A Rock in Water*, was Winsome's work.

A consistent theme seems to be the black experience in Britain?
That was ten years ago and derived directly from my experience at Vauxhall Manor and from the kind of people coming into the *Young People's Theatre*. There was a strong feeling at the Royal Court that the black experience in Britain was not being represented enough; there is such a powerful voice out there to be heard that it remained a constant theme for me. But I think that my focus has changed in that I am not directing anymore. I became much more interested in new writing and the potential of developing the work of young writers, as opposed to directing myself and working on productions.

Can you say more about the writers' group at the Young People's Theatre?

In the mid-80s it was run by Hanif Kureishi, who hadn't become a star yet. *My Beautiful Launderette* had just been released and Hanif and I went to all the local schools and showed it before it went on general release. He was a very inspiring writing tutor. Winsome Pinnock was in the writers' group at the time. Working with writing has always been a very important part of the *Young People's Theatre* philosophy. The Royal Court is a new writing theatre, and that was the emphasis of the *Young People's Theatre* as well.

How did the Young People's Theatre *begin?*

The *Young People's Theatre* at The Royal Court is one of the oldest youth, education and community departments attached to a main theatre in this country. It started in 1965, and was the brainchild of George Devine, who founded The Royal Court in 1956. He said even then that 'it all starts in school'. That was extraordinary for a leading theatre professional to say at that time.

Were you a founder member of the education department of the theatre?

Yes. Initially, the *Young People's Theatre* stood for the education department, but, in some ways, I believe, it needed to be the other way around, because everything comes under the heading of education. At the time there wasn't a consistent programme for schools and colleges, and from the Portobello Road it was even harder to concentrate on the work that was going on in the actual theatre. There was always a tension between the two spaces. The work of the *Young People's Theatre* very much concentrated on the youth theatre side. It was also in the Portabello Road and the North Kensington community, and as much as I wanted to shift the focus into more work in schools and colleges, I had to concentrate on being established in that community. Eventually, I moved back to the main theatre building and began building the department here.

How did the department begin to function?

The YPT was a very small, underfunded department, always fighting for its life in those early years. It took a long time to establish a system for the work, particularly to get the funding to have an education programme attached to every play we put on. But we did get funding from Sir John Cass's foundation and from British Gas (North Thames division). That was quite significant because Sir John Cass funded all the work that was done in ILEA London Boroughs, and British Gas funded any work done in schools north of the river. Between the two we managed to cover all of London. I always felt a bit frustrated for schools out-side of London because we couldn't offer the discounts, but we were offering £4 a ticket for a schools matinee and a whole pre-performance workshop which was only £1.

The whole idea was to teach young audiences to appreciate new writing. We would go into schools with members of the production team of the piece they were going to see and do a workshop that was actually based on the rehearsal methods used in creating that play, really giving an insight into the work. This gave the young people ownership of the working methods. It was no longer a secret, special knowledge. This work has been going on for about four or five years now in a very consistent way, and it is so rewarding to see students that have come over a number of years, who are so articulate about what they see. Often you say 'schools matinee' to actors and they groan — they think there will be a load of screaming kids, but they have often been the most rewarding experiences I've had here: to go to a schools matinee and to see actors being so excited by the response they're getting from these young audiences, who are so knowledgeable about what they're seeing, and so appreciative. Sometimes a play is performed that hasn't been fully realised, but because the workshops are about creating that piece, they are always a really important learning experience.

This aspect of the work is complemented by a programme we run for teachers called *Rehearsing New Writing*, which is an ongoing course for teachers to look at the work of the Royal Court, and to explore with writers and directors how they go about creating their work. It is aimed at teachers at their own level; it is for them to apply what they get out of it in the classroom in their own way. I believe you need to have the skills of a playwright and a director combined, to be a good drama teacher. Some teachers find the approach quite refreshing, because we don't say you *must* do this with your 14-year-olds.

We also have a system for reaching a younger audience by running playwriting workshops in schools — most of our plays are only suitable for 14 years or older, so we don't normally reach the lower ends of the secondary school or primary school children. In the playwriting workshops, however, we work with eight and nine-year-olds as well, and that has been fantastic. We bring in a practising playwright, who does a workshop about the different elements of writing a play and how it differs from other kinds of writing. It's a very practical, basic workshop. Then we ask them to write a first draft of something, we come back with a director from the theatre and some professional actors, and we workshop what they've created. They can actually see what works and what doesn't. When that process works it's quite thrilling, because, although most young people do wonderful creative writing in schools, few teachers have the skills to teach playwriting. I think you do need to be a practising playwright or at least a theatre practitioner to see what works.

Our most successful recent innovation is to offer playwright residencies. April de Angeles recently did two weeks of a residency with a particular group of students at City and Islington College. In the end they created a piece. It was a devised piece, but it was based on their own writing as a result of working with April. This was very exciting because I worked with this group for a long time and I thought they were incredibly talented, but what I noticed was that their devised material was not as strong as they were as performers. The material was lifted beyond comparison when they had this time with a professional writer.

Do you find that many of the artists find it difficult to make the transition from their own working practice to teaching it in a workshop format?
I think that's where my job comes in, because I have a foot in both camps. There are some playwrights and directors who are natural teachers and are brilliant at it, and who love doing it, there are others who need a little encouragement. I usually bring in people whom I know and trust, so I can say to them 'That won't work with nine-year-olds.' Max Stafford-Clark, who has been into a lot of schools with me, was the first person to say how hard it was, so much harder than directing a play; actors can be as bored as they like but they have to pay attention, whereas in school you have to *keep* their attention.

Schools work has been a revelation to many playwrights and directors. Some of them find it rather thrilling and others don't; they know it's not their thing so I don't ask them and they don't volunteer. The meeting of these two worlds, the worlds of education and professional new writing, is really important to both of them. It enriches and uplifts them, but, unfortunately, they don't meet enough.

How many schools and colleges regularly use your work in the London area?
Quite a few. There is a core of about 20 that will use us more than once a term, and several hundred who will use us once a year. Our most successful work recently has been doing one-day workshops. We recently had a day with Athol Fugard [– *a South African playwright whose highly articulate voice criticised the Apartheid regime through theatre. He developed his work with the Market Theatre of Johannesburg, and his*

most recent play, Valleysong, *in which he also acts, was performed at The Royal Court early in 1996*], which inspired a new generation of young people. He really wanted to share his skills and art. It was just a beautiful meeting of imaginations. Teachers have said that students were transformed by this day with him, through seeing him perform and hearing him talk about his work. I could sell that workshop every day of the week.

I use teachers from our regular schools to help me plan. I have a teachers' advisory group, which meets twice a term. At those meetings, teachers talk about the programme and also what they think their needs are. Many of the things we do here have been as a result of these meetings. Recently this produced a design day with Stephen Daldry and Ian McNeil. This developed from teachers feeling they didn't have the skills to teach design for the 'A' level syllabus, so we looked at a play that was on at the Royal Court. Everyone from the sound person to the lighting person, right through to Ian and Stephen, the director and designer, worked and demonstrated every aspect of what they do. Those days are very special.

Has the attitude to education work changed over recent years?
Very much so. What's really exciting is that education work is acquiring a much higher profile. I was talking with Jenny Harris, head of education at the National Theatre, a couple of weeks ago and we were both saying it's an easier time for education; people have more respect for it and are putting more value on education within theatres. We have been fighting for this for a long time and finally there's getting to be more focus on it.

Why do you think that is?
It's a gradual shift. The Arts Council saw the value very early on and they have pushed it, in some cases not funding theatres that didn't have education departments. But the world of theatre has realised that unless you can bring in young audiences, unless you can make them literate about theatre, and unless you can also bring them in as theatre practitioners, the theatre will die. It's all about developing the potential of many and the excellence of a few.

Do you see much conflict between teaching theatre skills and using drama as a learning tool?
I've never joined either side of the debate. I think if you separate them it's a disaster. There are some teachers, perhaps fewer now, who have no theatre skills, who teach drama without ever going to the theatre, who don't take their students to the theatre and who teach them that 'actor' is a dirty word, that

everything should be role-play. I think that's suspicious, just as I think anybody who would try only to look at the performance side of theatre and teach only those skills without looking at the whole purpose, the whole meaning, the whole subject matter, is at a loss as well. The debate has died down a lot, but it rears its head from time to time.

I think that the demise of theatre-in-education (TIE) is interesting and sad, but I've always felt that the best theatre for young people is the *best* theatre, and I don't think you have to create a separate theatre for young people as long as you make that work accessible in some way.

Isn't that partly what TIE was doing?
Sometimes I think it was saying 'We're going to create this play that's just for young people, it's not suitable for adults.' One of the criticisms I have had of TIE in the past is that it's been so heavy on what it has to teach that it's been a less good play, which is why I value the work that happens here. But, of course, not all work here is appropriate for all young people and some of the work produced by the TIE movement has been fantastic.

But many companies have gone to the wall in the last ten years …
Yes, they have and it's interesting to see that at the same time the education departments of theatres have flourished. Young people are getting directly involved in the theatrical product itself, In real theatres. The process is, of course, hugely important. You can't have a good product without a fantastically rich process. But the thing that I value when I bring my young people to perform in the Royal Court theatre, is that they then have access to the most fantastic technical skills available, and can show their work in such a wonderful light. I'm not saying that's the be-all and end-all, but working with skilled technicians who are willing to share their knowledge can also be a very important experience.

You've seen a number of young people pass through and become successful. Do you have any particular advice for

those studying now? Is drama school the best way forward?
I think the problem with drama school training is that not enough people have access to it, and, with the grant situation, it's getting worse. Soon only people with money will be able to enter the profession. I've seen lots of students that I've put forward to drama school struggling because they can't get grants and they're trying to work at the same time and it's impossible, so we've got to find alternatives. I think that some of the work that FE is doing is fantastic, so imaginative and experimental. We ran a big conference for FE teachers called Beyond Naturalism, it's connected with our experimental theatre festival here, Barclay's New Stages, and what emerged from many teachers working on BTEC and other FE courses is that when their students finally get into drama school, they don't find it as creative as they had done at college level. Sometimes youth theatre is the way in, sometimes work experience is, I would never give one kind of advice. People have to find the way in for themselves.

Are there any particular highlights for you of your work at the Royal Court?
I used to produce the Writers' Festival, focusing on different areas of the country, and a young 19-year-old from Hull came along, Jonathon Harvey [*now recognised as one of Britain's foremost young writers*]. After ten years of working with young writers I've seen many 'babies' reaching maturity, not just the overtly successful ones. An administrator in the office next door was in the *Young People's Theatre* and the *Writers' Group*. So for me the highlights are the young people whom you see over a number of years and the effect that theatre has had on their lives. With all the frustrations that young people have now, I don't envy their trying to enter the theatre profession, but somehow some of them seem to have the stamina and the imagination to try a whole range of possibilities. Seeing them succeed and the world of theatre and new writing becoming enriched – that is the best thing.

Useful publications

Boal, Augusto (1992) *Games for Actors and Non-actors*, Routledge.

Clements, Paul (1983) *The Improvised Play*, a Methuen Theatre File. This covers the work of Mike Leigh.

McGilvray, D. (ed) (1991) *British Alternative Theatre Directory*, Rebecca Books. This will give you most of the names and addresses you need if you wish to make a written/telephone inquiry.

Ritchie, Rob (ed) (1987) *The Joint Stock Book*, a Methuen Theatre File.

Wardor, Michelene (1980) *Strike While the Iron is Hot*, Journeyman Press.

chapter two
ACTING TECHNIQUES

This chapter will guide you in both your physical and psychological development as a performer. The overall aim is to identify the basic tools an actor needs to begin work, and to suggest a whole range of exercises for you to borrow from and develop.

There are many theories about the conscious and unconscious processes that contribute to the art of acting. The Western, naturalistic tradition seeks the actor's *belief* in the character's motivations. The comic tradition, however, relies less on belief and more on quick external characterisation and timing. In addition to these there are the demonstrative techniques of Epic theatre and highly physical phenomena such as the Biomechanics of the director Meyerhold. It is also true to say that much Western theatre has been influenced, in this century, by the theatre of China and Japan, where the belief is in the gesture and the form rather than the internal psychological world of the character.

Stanislavski, Brecht and Artaud, the three most influential European theatre practitioners, borrowed from the East (see Chapter 6 for analyses of their individual theory and practice). Stanislavski was fascinated by the internal preparation and commitment produced by the yoga techniques of the Madras school in India, Brecht made great use of Chinese folklore and performance style, and Artaud took his inspiration from the trance-dancers of Bali. In other words, what we call modern Western theatre is thoroughly eclectic, dipping into and borrowing from other cultures and traditions at will.

It is no accident that one of the most successful and admired British theatre directors, Peter Brook, has created a multi-cultural, international company where he quite deliberately makes use of the differing theatrical skills and traditions of the individual performers. Throughout his career he has quite openly borrowed from many cultures and from all three major practitioners.

When you go to the theatre, particularly if you see the work of innovative companies who are developing new styles and new material, there will be many influences at play. The essence of them all, whether psychologically motivated or not, is that actors must *believe* in what they are doing and give a committed performance. It is for this reason that we shall concentrate in this chapter on the structure of actor training developed by Stanislavski at The Moscow Art Theatre. This became known as The System (see pages 73–75), and these exercises now form the basis of most professional actor training in Europe and America.

The System itself falls into three main sections:

- the internal preparation of the actor
- the external preparation of the actor, i.e. of body and voice
- the actor's work on the text.

Our chapter follows this structure, starting with the detailed preparation needed for both rehearsal and performance. The games and exercises suggested here are no different to those being practised in the nation's universities and drama schools. You will often have to repeat them. Try thinking of them in the same way you would of playing a sport or keeping fit – the rules and equipment don't change, *you* simply get better!

In each of the following sections, 'Preparing for work: energisers and line games', and 'The actor's imagination', we have provided instructions detailing the games and exercises that we find the most fun and useful to make any workshop session happen, to improve performance skills and develop scenarios. Many you will already know, but may find them here in adapted form. There are many excellent resource books to which we owe much of our rehearsal practice and which we list on page 72.

In the second half of the chapter we focus on character-building exercises, and explore text by looking at a scene from *A Night Out* by Harold Pinter. The tasks suggested can be related to that text or to any other you happen to be working on.

Preparing for work: energisers and line games

We play games to prepare for drama because they are fun, create energy and change the way we behave with each other. They give us the opportunity to overcome our basic inhibitions. We all have inhibitions and in everyday life they serve a useful purpose, but for acting we must break them down. As we get older we become more afraid of letting go, particularly in front of others. As children, however, we used to run around the playground, screaming and shouting. To recapture that feeling, we start with the sort of games we used to play as children. You will no doubt know many of your own, but here are a few old favourites.

ENERGISERS

Stuck in the mud

One person is 'It'. If they tag you, stand still with your legs and arms spread. You can be rescued by someone crawling under your legs. The It tries to get everyone stuck and the rest try to keep everyone moving. In a big group you may need more than one It. Change them over before they pass out with exhaustion!

Chain tig

One person is 'It'. When they tag someone, they join hands and are both It and so the chain grows. Only the end people can tag others, and then only if the chain is unbroken.

Variation:

* When a chain gets to four it splits into two new chains.

Hug tig

One person is 'It'. If you are tagged, you become It and the other person stops. You can

---

★ *key point*

In games we accept that there are rules and that we must *play a part* to make the game happen. It's the most basic form of acting.

---

avoid being caught either by running away or by hugging another player until danger has passed. As soon as danger has passed, set off and help rescue others. The group is working well when the It cannot tag anyone because they are all rescuing each other. Only hugging in pairs is allowed.

Below the knee

Use a sponge ball to avoid damage to people or equipment. One person is the thrower and tries to hit the others below the knee with the ball. As soon as another person is hit they also become a thrower. From this moment on, no one can run with the ball. Each new victim becomes a thrower. You will soon find that the more the players pass the ball to each other, marking their potential victims, the more successful they will be. Just slinging the ball wildly makes for a dull game. As usual, good team work is necessary.

LINE GAMES

Safety first *These games all involve two lines meeting in the middle of the space. One line then turns and runs while the other chases. Make sure each team knows where 'home' is and that it is a clear wall or marker with no obstructions or bits sticking out. In the heat of the chase people can easily get hurt.*

Crows and Cranes

Two lines of roughly equal size face each other in the middle of the room one pace apart. The umpire names one team 'Crows' and the other 'Cranes'. If the umpire calls the name of your team, you turn and run. If the umpire calls the other team you chase them. If you get caught you simply join the other team, remembering also to change from Crow to Crane or vice versa. Great mayhem and confusion.

Wizards, Pixies and Giants

This is a version of the old Scissors, Paper, Stone game but on a much larger scale with some very basic acting! Two lines face each other in the middle. All take three large paces back. This is the starting point. Each team decides which creature to be. Each creature has a sound and a gesture and everyone in a given team must be the same:

- *Wizards* stand on one leg, point both forefingers, arms stretched and shout 'Shazzam!'. Wizards defeat Giants by casting spells on them (i.e. Giants run).
- *Giants* stretch up and stamp while shouting 'Fee Fie Fo Fum!'. Giants defeat Pixies by stamping on them (i.e. Pixies run).
- *Pixies* crouch down, use their forefingers as pointy ears and squeak 'Wee wee wee wee!'. Pixies defeat Wizards by shinning up the inside of their robes and stealing their wands (i.e. Wizards run).

The routine: both teams have ten seconds to agree on their creature. They face each other, take three paces together, reach for the sky and touch the floor twice shouting 'One, two, three, up, down, up, down . . .' and then perform their action. The winning team chases. Victims join the other team. If both teams choose the same creature, all turn and say 'mutter, mutter, mutter', all the way back to their line. A little complex but great fun.

Lemonade

The quintessential acting line game. Each team decides on a trade and a place where they are from. These need not be connected, e.g. car mechanics from Alaska. Both teams start three large paces back from the centre. Team A is challenged first. Teams speak the following lines, stepping forward together each time:

A: Here we are!

B: Where are you from?

A: Alaska.

B: What's your trade?

A: *Lemonade*!

B: Show us your trade if you're not afraid.

Each member of Team A then individually mimes their trade and members of team B shout out what they think it is. As soon as the correct answer is heard, A runs and B chases.

Anyone caught joins team B, has the new trade and place whispered to them if it has already been decided and off you go again with B being challenged. After each set, stop and let the groups decide on new trades and places of origin.

Good mime is crucial here. Do not use sound effects, or it will be too easy. Make your gestures really clear. The idea is to enable the other team to guess your trade.

TASK

As a group, invent your own unique chase game. Play it until you have refined the rules and ironed out any teething problems. Give your game a name. Who knows, perhaps your game will end up being played in drama sessions around the world in years to come . . .

The actor's imagination

RELAXATION

The key to relaxation is good breathing. Good breathing can enable you to take control of your body. It can help you conquer fear and pain. It allows you to clear your mind of all distractions and concentrate on the task in hand. Much of what we know about breathing comes from Eastern traditions of meditation, particularly in disciplines such as yoga, now widely practised in the West.

★ key point

Stanislavski was introduced to yogic breathing and the concept of Prana (the essential life-force in all things, which he associated with the Creative State of Mind) by Leopold Sulerzhitski in 1906.

Exercise 1

Lie on your back with your arms down by your sides. Close your eyes and breathe slowly and deeply, in through the nose and out through the mouth. Control your breathing by using the following rhythm:

- breathe in for a count of four
- hold the breath for four
- breathe out slowly over four
- hold for a count of four
- repeat.

A leader can help at the start by counting out loud for you. Once you've got the hang of it you can use it by yourself anywhere, any time. Practise at home, walking, on the bus; it'll give you a great sense of control and freedom from stress and anxiety.

Variation: build the number of counts as you breathe, e.g:

Figure 2.1   *Group relaxation*

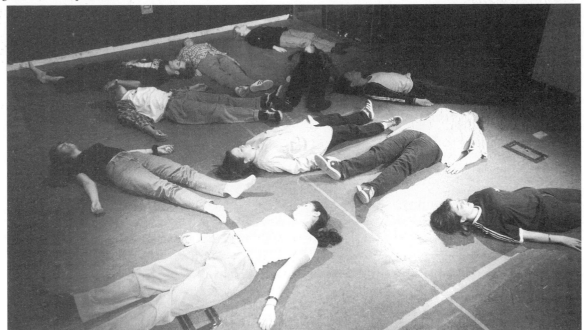

- breathe in for four and out for four
- in for five and out for five
- in for six and out for six etc.

Stop if there is any strain. Make sure you breathe all the way through the count and don't just take a quick breath and hold it for longer. It is the control over the intake and exhalation of air that matters.

Exercise 2

Lie down as for exercise 1. Feel the weight of your body sinking into the floor. Starting with your toes work your way up the body tensing each set of muscles on the in-breath, holding for a count of four and relaxing on the out-breath. Do this as a group with someone talking you through, or do it on your own with your own timing. Once a set of muscles has been relaxed, try not to move them again. It is as if they are not there any more. Work through the body in this order:

1 Toes, feet, ankles, calves, knee, thighs, pelvis/buttocks: *when you relax here, feel the lower half of your body drifting away.*

2 Fingers, hands, forearms, upper arms, head/neck/face, shoulders: *when you relax here, feel the upper half of your body drifting away.*

3 Upper back/chest, lower back/belly: *when you relax here, feel your belly crumbling into a pile of dust and gently blowing away.*

You will now have achieved a state of total relaxation. Your breathing is slow and deep. Your muscles have lost all their tension. Just check your neck and shoulders. The head is very heavy and is constantly being supported, so that is often where the greatest tension is. Lastly, check your tongue. Make sure it is fully relaxed on the floor of your mouth.

This exercise is precisely what happens when you yawn or stretch. Breathe in, tense and relax on the out-breath: this should just make you aware of the natural rhythms of the body.

Exercise 3

Now that you're in a state of complete relaxation, you can begin to explore the imagination further. We do this by way of guided visualisation. Eventually you will be able to do this for yourself; initially, however, it helps to have someone talk you through. As the guide you need to use a clear, strong voice and see the visualisation yourself in order to describe it. You must go at the same pace as the group, giving them enough time to develop each image. Here is an example of a visualisation:

You are lying on your back on the grass
On a hillside
In the middle of the country
It is a warm summer's day
Feel the warmth of the sun on your face
    and on your body
Turn your face towards the sun
Sense its brightness through your eyelids
Listen to the breeze and the occasional
    lazy insect buzzing
Smell the freshness of the air
And of the grass warmed by the sun
Feel the grass tickling your skin
Through your light summer clothes
Feel the roughness of the earth under
    your back
Now turn your face away from the sun
And open your eyes
See the green hills and trees
And the blue sky flecked with small
    white clouds
You get up and stretch
You are barefoot
Begin walking now
Feeling the grassy earth beneath your feet
Be conscious of the heat of the sun
And which part of you it is warming
Walk towards the gnarled oak tree you
    can see ahead
Watch it grow bigger as you approach
Walk under its canopy of leaves and
    sense the cool of the air
Approach the trunk and study its thick
    bark
Reach out your hand and touch it with
    your fingertips

Then with the palm of your hand
    explore the tree
As you move around it you notice a hole
    in its side
Just large enough for you to crawl
    through
Climb inside
It's dark and musty
Feel the cool earth under your feet
Reach out your hands and touch the
    sides
They are cold to the touch and are not
    wood but rock
As you follow them with your hands you
    realise you are travelling straight on
The ground slopes steadily down
It gets colder and is so dark you can see
    nothing at all
Feel your way with your hands and feet
The walls and floor of the tunnel are
    becoming damp now
They are wet to the touch
Soon icy water is pouring down around
    you
You sense you are in a vast underground
    cavern
Feel the space around you
Listen to the sound of the water
Feel it on your feet as it slowly rises
Up over your ankles and on up your
    calves to your knees
You wade further and further into the
    freezing water
Until it reaches your shoulders
Suddenly your hand finds metal sticking
    out from the wall
Look up and see a bright dot of daylight
    up above
What you are holding is a ladder built
    into the wall
Begin to climb
The round metal rungs hurt your feet
    but all the time the light above gets
Nearer and brighter
You are frozen and tired and cold
And your feet and hands hurt

But you keep climbing up
At last you reach the top and you climb
    back out into brilliant sunshine
Dazzling you
Drying you
Warming you
Lie down on your back in the grass and
    enjoy the heat of the sun

Notice how your imagination adapts to each new demand; how quickly one mental image is replaced by another. What matters is not so much the logical sequence, or story, but the intensity with which you imagine each individual moment.

TASK

Take it in turns at different sessions to take each other through a guided visualisation. Write it out beforehand and try it out on your own. Take your time: it should last a good three to four minutes. If you are worried about getting it wrong under pressure, make a good quality recording of it.

CONCENTRATION

The next task is to ensure that the actor is fully concentrated at all times on both the internal world of their character and the external world of the stage or rehearsal. Stanislavski said, 'an actor must have an object of attention every moment that s/he is on stage'. To do this we will concentrate individually, in pairs and in a group.

Individual concentration

1 Keep your eyes shut. Count the change in your pocket/purse.
2 With your eyes shut, think about your hands. Imagine every hair, mark, crease.
3 Without looking, describe in every detail the room you are in.

4 Hold a lemon in your hand. Smell the lemon. Taste it in your mouth.
5 Calculate 107×4. Then 12×59. Then 344 divided by 8. Then the year of your birth divided by your age.
6 Listen to all the sounds in the room. Isolate just one and block out all the others.
7 Think about one of your fellow actors and describe in detail what they are wearing.
8 Try to beam a thought to another actor.
9 Look at a bit of wall or floor. Detect the patterns and find them beautiful.
10 In your mind draw a map of how to get to where you live. Include street names and as much detail as possible.

TASK

Invent your own list of ten. Write them down and try them on the group.

Below is a list that the German writer and director Peter Handke suggested should be given to his actors in the preface to his experimental work, *Offending the Audience*.

    Rules for the actors

Listen to the litanies in the Catholic churches.

Listen to football teams being cheered on
    and booed.
Listen to the rhythmic chanting at
    demonstrations.
Listen to the wheels of a bicycle
    upturned on its seat spinning until the
    spokes have come to rest and watch

the spokes until they have reached their resting point.

Listen to the gradually increasing noise a concrete mixer makes after the motor has been started.

Listen to debaters cutting each other off.

Listen to *Tell Me* by the Rolling Stones.

Listen to the simultaneous arrival and departure of trains.

Listen to the hit parade on Radio Luxembourg.

Listen in on the simultaneous interpreters at the United Nations.

Listen to the dialogue between the gangster (Lee J. Cobb) and the pretty girl in *The Trap*, when the girl asks the gangster how many more people he intends to kill; whereupon the gangster asks, as he leans back, 'How many are left?' and watch the gangster as he says it.

See the Beatles' movies.

In *A Hard Day's Night*, watch Ringo's smile at the moment when, after having been teased by the others, he sits down at his drums and begins to play.

Watch Gary Cooper's face in *The Man from the West*. In the same movie watch the death of the mute as he runs down the deserted street of the lifeless town with a bullet in him, hopping and jumping and emitting those shrill screams.

Watch monkeys aping people and llamas spitting in the zoo.

Watch the behaviour of tramps and idlers as they amble on the street and play the machines in the penny arcades.

(Peter Handke, Offending the Audience, *1971, Methuen)*

TASK

- Discuss the list of 'rules'. Is Handke entirely serious?
- Suggest a reason why each instruction should be given to an actor.
- Notice the way in which Handke's language does the work of the thing he is describing. You don't actually have to have seen the film *The Trap* to get the meaning, your imagination does the work. The description of the bicycle wheel imitates the slowing down of the wheel itself.
- Now invent your own *Rules for the Actor*, based on your own experience and imagination. Suggest at least ten. Use language to capture the feel of the thing you are describing.

Concentration work in pairs

The mirror

One of the classic concentration exercises.

Two actors face each other about three feet apart. A leads and B mirrors exactly each movement. It is important that A moves slowly enough for B to keep pace. The object is not to catch each other out. Someone watching should not be able to tell who is leading. When the leader calls 'change', B starts leading. It is important that B continues whatever move was already underway. Don't stop and take up a new position. Again, an observer should not be able to see the leader role changing (Figure 2.2).

Variations:

- The leader keeps on calling 'change' until eventually they call 'no leader'. A and B must then copy each other simultaneously.

Figure 2.2   *The Mirror*

Generally, both have a sense of who is leading at any one moment, but it shifts fluidly. Sometimes, there are extraordinary moments where a particular pair genuinely do not know who is leading and are simply working in perfect harmony.

- A goes through a series of movements. B repeats them. A then repeats them again, making clear B's mistakes. B performs again. Swap roles.
- Do all of these but vastly increase the distance between the actors.

Tracker Dog

B holds palm of hand six inches in front of A's face. A follows, maintaining distance, as B moves the hand around, up and down, stops, etc. Again, you are helping your partner to move and not trying to catch them out. Maintain close concentration at all times; see Figure 2.3.

Lift and hold

Two of you lie on your backs with the soles of your feet together. Together you lift your heads, look each other in the eye and say 'hello'; see Figure 2.4. Rest. Then sit up together, look each other in the eye and say 'hello'. Rest. Next time you will both come all the way up, lifting your feet off the floor and balancing on your buttocks. Look the other person in the eye at all times. Use their energy and give yours to them. It is not a competition. Try to know when you can both take it no longer, without giving any overt signals. Finish

Figure 2.3   *Tracker Dog*

Figure 2.4   *Lift and hold*

strongly by clapping your right hand on your left arm, left hand on right arm and then slapping your hands on the floor as you collapse. Shout 'Hah!' with each gesture. Try to do this together, but it will take a bit of practice.

Group concentration work

For this kind of work, the best possible formation is invariably a circle, because:

- everyone is equal
- we can all see each other
- anyone can instantly become the focus
- the group energy is contained
- the circle has power.

Stand in the middle of the circle to feel its power. Each person in the circle is contributing to the energy and can take from it. It becomes a living organism and it is up to us as actors to learn to use it; see Figure 2.5.

Energy is to do with science so let's get scientific: you are going to conduct a series of experiments into pure energy. Remember you are scientists so be prepared to observe as well as participate.

Bouncing electrons

Everyone in the circle is an electron. The circle itself is a giant mirror. An electron A in the cir-

Figure 2.5 *Energy circle*

cle sets off towards another electron B, almost opposite them. They make eye-contact immediately. As soon as B senses the eye-contact they set off towards someone else. The direction of B is determined by the angle at which A approaches: B goes where A would have gone had it bounced off the wall of a pure circular mirror. B moves towards C who sets off towards D and so on.

Figure 2.6   *Bouncing electrons*

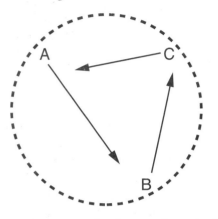

Once you have got the hang of it, the leader can increase the speed. Remember: you are not a character now, you are pure energy – you must maintain the energy of the incoming electron and pass it on to the next.

Mexican wave

Groups of electrons moving together function as a wave. The human version is the Mexican wave and involves large numbers of people passing on the same energy, allowing it to move through them without stopping. As soon as one person slacks, the wave loses power and begins to die.

- First, try to get a perfect Mexican wave in your circle. Keep it going round and round, checking energy levels with scientific precision.
- When you are satisfied, move on to creating new movements and sounds. A makes a sound and a gesture which is immediately copied by B, then by C and so on.

When it has gone all the way round, A repeats it and B introduces a new sound and gesture. Make sure the energy does not slack, and that the new gestures move around just as fast as the wave did. Introduce speech and this becomes a great exercise for cue-biting (starting to speak almost before your cue-line is finished, so that there are no unintentional pauses between lines)!

Alphabets

Everyone sits in a circle. Speaking one at a time, in random order, try to get through the alphabet. As soon as two people begin speaking at the same time, the whole groups starts again. You will need to listen intently to each other. Don't give any sneaky signals, just concentrate. Any concentrated group can get to the letter Z. The key is to relax, take your time and wait for your moment to speak. Persevere – it's a great feeling when you get it right.

Variation:

- Try it with the lights out or all eyes shut.

Zip Zap Boing

A concentrator's classic; see figure 2.7.

- All stand in a circle. A zip is sent by clasping your hands together, pointing them

> ## ★ *key point*
>
> It is crucially important that the leader uses tactics to ensure that energy and concentration games achieve *genuine* energy and concentration. Individuals or groups who are new to this work often try to sabotage it because they simply cannot see its value. Unfortunately, you cannot communicate its value by talking about it; you have to show it. Be tough. Make yourself and your group succeed. When a group completes these exercises well it grows in confidence, as do the individuals in it.

Figure 2.7   *Zip Zap Boing*

quickly at your neighbour and saying 'Zip!' The neighbour immediately passes it on, Mexican wave style. Practice sending zips both clockwise and anti-clockwise as fast as you can around the circle.

- Now introduce the Boing! This reverses the direction of the zip by rebounding it. Instead of passing the zip on, lift the appropriate arm and say 'Boing!' This means that the person who just zipped you must now zip the other way. Practice this for a while.
- Sometimes people use the boings to keep the zip trapped in one bit of the circle. This can become a trifle tedious for other players.

- Time to introduce the zap. This involves firing across the circle with a two-handed pistol action. The zap is immediately zipped one way or the other. Some versions of the game allow for a zap to be boinged as well. Introduce this to sophisticated and unselfish players only.

Note: It can be a good idea to restrict players to one zap each in any particular round of the game. If people are being sluggish, make them play it solidly and well for at least a minute before moving on.

TRUST

The key to successful work on stage is the trust between actors and the individual performer's trust in themselves. This is essential for the Creative State of Mind (CSM). Take great care during these exercises to ensure that participants feel safe and secure at all times; avoid any behaviour that might destroy trust or make a given individual feel uncomfortable.

TASK

As a group, draw up a list of basic guidelines for trust-work. Reach a consensus and stick to it. Be strict with yourselves and each other. Nothing is easier to destroy than the quiet concentration required for positive trust-work.

Safety note: make sure that there are no objects around that could hurt anyone if they should happen to fall. Clear chairs, bags, etc. out of the way. Ask people to remove all buckled belts and jewellery, particularly rings, dangly earrings and watches. Soft shoes only should be worn, or bare feet. Never start an exercise unless you are absolutely sure that everyone involved is ready. People very rarely fall doing these exercises but, if genuine relaxation is involved, even if they do they won't hurt themselves. People who faint or fall when very drunk rarely hurt themselves for the same reason: they are too relaxed.

Trust circle

Groups of between five and eight stand shoulder to shoulder in a circle. One person stands in the middle, relaxed but straight, with their eyes shut and their arms folded across their chest, their hands clasping their shoulders. Each person in the circle spreads their feet and lifts their hands to support the person at chest height. A leader should keep a hand on the person at all times to start with. As a group, gently guide the person around and across the circle, taking them lower only as you feel comfortable. *Lift* them back to the middle, but do not push them. Let them fall only.

Pair-work

Try the same sort of work in pairs. It helps if partners are roughly the same size and shape, particularly when starting out. Experienced trust-workers can deal with anyone. Below is a list of the basic positions and routines:

Leaning arches

Stand facing your partner, about three feet apart. Place the palms of your hands together and then move your feet back so that you are supporting each other with your own body-weight. Your bodies should be perfectly straight. Keep your arms straight also. Any strain is then borne by your shoulders and not just your arm muscles. Look at Figure 2.8 and notice the differences.

Now gently move your hands around, without bending your elbows. This will bring your bodies together and then further away. You must give each other your weight. Only if you both lean in together with straight arms and bodies will you avoid strain.

Back-to-back

Stand back-to-back with your partner, making sure that your spines are in maximum contact all the way up. Move your feet out a little. Count to three and sit down together, comfortably and smoothly. Keep your position, because now you're going to count and stand up again. Practise this until you get it smooth, then work with another partner; see Figure 2.9.

Falling

As with the trust circle, but this time in pairs. Stand your partner in front of you with their eyes closed. Take your braced position, place your hand on their shoulder to let them know you are ready for them to fall. Let them fall only a short distance at first until you get used to their weight and they feel safe; see Figure 2.10(a). Take it gently. Don't treat it as a competition or you defeat the purpose of the work. Repeat, letting them fall a little further each time.

Variation:

- Try falling forwards, arms crossed or uncrossed as feels comfortable. Then fall sideways.

Falling all the way to the floor

This involves the faller having their arms uncrossed and relaxed. You are going to take their weight on your chest with your elbows hooked under their arms. As they fall, step back and guide them down to the floor; see Figure 2.10(b). If your stance is good, you should be able to take them down and lift them back up again in one smooth move. This, of course, can be a very practical skill to have in any play that involves people falling or fainting.

Figure 2.8 *Leaning arches*

Figure 2.9 *Back-to-back*

Figure 2.10(a) and (b)   *Pair-work (a) falling back (b) falling all the way to the floor*

Guiding

Partners can guide each other, blindfolded or just with eyes shut, in a number of different ways. One of the simplest is where you guide your partner by holding their hand and elbow very lightly and walk alongside them. Start slowly, gradually picking up speed as you feel their trust in you grow. If a whole group is going at once, there will be many changes of pace and direction, so make sure they are light, poised and responding to your every signal.

Waltzing

Here partners place their hands on each other's shoulders. One shuts their eyes and is guided around the room, forwards and backwards. Again, increase the speed when you feel ready. With even a small number of couples, the effect is like a bizarre ballroom.

Obstacles

Create an obstacle course and guide your sightless partner through it, first with touch, then at a distance with only your voice.

Group exercises

Jump and catch

You need a minimum of eight people catching to make this safe; see Figure 2.11. Again, check your area and make sure it is clear of obstacles. There are numerous ways of approaching this exercise; this is the one we are most familiar with. Catchers stand in pairs facing their partner. They reach across and clasp each other by the wrist. The four or more pairs then shuffle together to provide a bed of arms for others to leap onto. Those jumping must run straight, dive with their arms forward and keep their

Figure 2.11   *Group exercises – jump and catch*

bodies relaxed. Don't panic. It looks frightening but is in fact very safe. Have a go: it's great fun!

Variation:

- Have people fall from a chair or something higher. They can go forwards or backwards. Again, they must keep *straight*. Someone falling backwards who bends in the middle, risks going right through!

IMPROVISATION

Improvisation can serve a variety of different purposes. We improvise to:

- generate ideas

Sitting circle

You need at least ten people for this one, but twenty is better. Everybody stands in a circle and turns to the right. Then they all shuffle in towards the middle until they are as tightly packed as they can be. On the count of three, everyone sits back onto the lap of the person behind. If the timing is right and the circle pure everyone will be sitting comfortably. Now try and get out of it.

- create scenes and characters
- test out situations
- explore issues
- find out about ourselves.

The results may be comic, tragic or both, but if they are done well, the audience will be entertained and we will have increased our understanding of the structures of drama.

> ## ★ hot tip
>
> This section owes a great debt to Keith Johnstone and his seminal work *Impro*, based on his years of teaching and exploration at RADA and The Royal Court. Many others have used and explored improvisation, but no one else has written up their findings in such a comprehensive and directly useful manner: you are well advised to read and absorb his work.

It is difficult to write about performance of any kind; it is even more difficult with improvisation. The results are so fleeting and the changes in mood that produce the audience reaction or liberate the improviser to be free to create are so subtle that you can only understand the work properly by doing it. What follows is a basic menu derived from many years of improvising, and adapting Johnstone's ideas and others for use in schools, colleges and youth theatres. Take the exercises and adapt them to suit yourselves.

We are now very familiar with improvisation in the form of Clive Anderson's hit television show, *Whose Line is it Anyway?* Few fans of the programme realise that it is based on practical stage work developed over the last 30 years in specific drama schools and theatre groups. One of these was *Theatre Machine*, whose whole performance consisted of taking suggestions from a live audience and acting them out.

When we watch good improvisations we are amazed by the complex sequences the performers come up with. It is difficult to believe that it is not scripted and rehearsed. This is because, although the actual actions and words on stage are unplanned, each improvisation is underpinned by basic principles.

In brief, these principles are:

1 Adopting clear status.
2 Being spontaneous rather than 'original'.
3 Accepting what other performers are doing, and building on it (i.e., no blocking).

Here is a brief menu for the improviser:

> ## ★ hot tip
>
> Be willing to make a fool of yourself. The audience want you to do on stage what they dare not do in real life. If you are only on stage to look cool, you are in the wrong business.

Warm-ups

Gibberish insults

Everyone moves around the room uttering foul insults at each other in gibberish. This generates huge energy without anyone feeling they are under personal attack.

Word association

Everybody stands in a circle (you can sit down, provided energy and concentration are maintained – if energy flags then stand, run around, get the energy back). Each person says an associated word in turn. Go as fast as you can to beat the 'cop in the head'. This game derives from early experiments in psychoanalysis and is designed to produce spontaneity. Don't worry about what you say. All sorts of things will come out. Just make sure that, as a group, you keep going.

Variations:

- Play it tough: any hesitation and you're out! Keep going until only a handful of players are left.
- Play it in pairs to increase the demands on each player.

Note: any hesitation is a sign that the player is censoring themselves.

Anti-word association

The same game only this time each word must *not* be connected to the previous one. This is actually much more difficult than associating. The natural tendency is to make associations, to connect. This game deliberately goes against that tendency. Trying not to associate makes your head want to explode!

Some people will say they cannot think of a word when asked to associate. By playing this game, they will become conscious of all the words they are *rejecting* in order not to associate.

It seems easy to think of a word and trust that it will be disconnected to the one said by your neighbour. Sometimes this is true, but if you are thinking of 'window' and someone says 'door', you will not have time to change your mind. Practise leaving your mind blank: it's scary, but the results are much richer in the end.

Variation:

- Play it with each person pointing at the next person to speak; this makes it more difficult for anyone to prepare.

Originality

One of the reasons why we panic when asked to improvise, is because we have a firm belief that to be creative we have to be original; what we say must be being said for the very first time. If that were true, Shakespeare would never have written a single line! Almost all of his storylines were borrowed from somewhere else and yet, more often than not, we regard Shakespeare's version as the definitive one, because of what he *did* with the idea. Perhaps the first lines or moves in an improvisation *have* been used before, but the dynamic between good improvisers will lead them somewhere else. These next exercises relieve the individual from the burden of responsibility for creation.

The collective mind can take stories to a place where the individual often cannot.

One-word stories

Sit in a circle. Each person says one word only, fitting it into the growing sentence. You will know automatically when each story has ended. It may take a few attempts to get it working right. What happens in the story doesn't matter at all, so long as the story keeps going. Difficulties arise when sentences become too long. Be conscious of when there is a full-stop and you have to start a new sentence.

Interviewing the group expert

This is a version of the one-word story, played out in an interview situation. One person is an interviewer, and four or five people play the expert. The interviewer's job is to keep the improvisation moving by feeding questions to the resident expert and maintaining the style and format of the television interview: i.e. being polite and deferential to the expert at all times. A typical interview might go like this:

Interviewer: Good evening, ladies and gentlemen and welcome to Factfinder. This evening I'll be talking to Professor Helge von Schwartzbottom, a world expert in making kites out of refridgerators. Good evening professor.
A: Good
B: Evening.

Interviewer: It must be very difficult to make a kite out of a refridgerator?
C: Yes
D: It
A: Is
B: Hard
C: But
D: I
A: Have
B: Found
C: Ways
D: Of

A: Making
B: It
C: Work.

Interviewer: Could you tell our studio audience some of the methods you use?

D: Yes
A: Of
B: Course
C: First
D: Of
A: All
B: I
C: Find
D: A
A: Refridgerator
B: And
C: Tie
D: It
A: To
B: Some
C: String
D: And
A: Wait
B: For
C: The
D: Wind

Interviewer: I see. Do you use ribbons?

It is hysterical to watch the various professors trying to keep their story together. It is essential that the experts maintain their expert status at all times, and take their skill very seriously.

Variation:

● Play the game with just one expert.

A–Z conversations

A real brain-teaser, but highly satisfying. Two actors meet and converse: each sentence begins with the next letter of the alphabet. For example:

A: Ah, Jenny
B: Bella, how are you?
A: Can't complain
B: Dreadful weather, isn't it?
A: Fog

B: Grime
A: Hail
B: Is it ever going to end?
A: Jeremy says we'll never see the sun again . . .

Try it out in pairs, developing a situation as you go. Then give yourselves a situation before you start, e.g. at the doctor's:

A: Alright Mr Jones, please come in
B: Boy am I glad to see you doctor
A: Clothes off please
B: Doctor, it's about my chest
A: Every reason to give you a thorough examination, Mr Jones
B: Flies are stuck!
A: [*offers to help*] Good Lord, so they are
B: Have you got any pliers
A: I'll have a look
B: Just try wriggling a bit
A: [*with pliers*] Keep still, Mr Jones [*pulls*]
B: Look what you've done
A: My word it's a big one
B: No-one told me you were a madman!
A: Oh, nothing to worry about, we'll soon have your erm . . .
B: Penis
A: Quite. We'll sew it back on in no time
B: Really [*advancing*]. You'll just sew it back on, will you?
A: Something like that
B: Trained to sew willies on, are you?
A: Under normal circumstances, no, but . . .
B: Very well, hurry up!
A: Where's the needle and thread? I'm always losing it
B: X-ray eyes. I've got X-ray eyes. I'll help you look.
A: Yes, please. Though I think I may have left it at the erm . . .
B: Zoo?

Notice how the actors here help each other out, particularly the way A helps B find answers for the difficult letters X and Z.

If you cannot go all the way through the letters, it is sometimes worth agreeing to stop at W. You can always go back to A and allow the scene to continue. Try adding more characters.

Key-words

Another fun warm-up is *key-words*. Set up a situation where people come and go, e.g. a restaurant. Two diners, a waiter/waitress and restaurant manager. Each actor has a key-word. If they are on-stage when they hear the key-word, they must leave, and if they are off-stage when they hear the key-word, they must re-enter. Always justify an entrance or exit. If the waitress's key-word is 'waitress' you can have the bizarre situation where one of the guests is talking to her and she leaves. They curse her for leaving and she returns, but must apologise for having left! For example:

Female diner	key-word = order
Male diner	key-word = wine
Waitress	key-word = waitress
Manager	key-word = menu

Everyone is at everyone else's mercy: anyone on-stage can use any of the key words to control the movements of the others. Some restraint must be exercised to maintain a good scene:

Waitress:	Good evening, Sir. Good evening, Madam.
Male diner:	Table for two, please.
Waitress:	Certainly. If you'd like to follow me [*she leads them to a table*].
Female diner:	Could I see a **menu** straight away please, we're in a bit of a hurry.
Waitress:	Certainly madam [*continues preparing tables*].
Manager:	[*entering*] Good evening. I hope everything is to your satisfaction.
Female diner:	Not really. I just asked for a **menu** and I'm still waiting.
Manager:	I'll fetch one for you personally, Madam [*exits*].
Female diner:	Excuse me, **waitress**, I'd like to see [*waitress exits*] a **wine**-list please.
Male diner:	Oh, this is quite ridiculous! All we want is a **menu** [*exits to toilets*].
Manager:	[*entering*] There we are, madam. I'm sorry it took so long.
Female diner:	That's alright. It's just that we're off to the theatre and don't want to be late.
Manager:	Perhaps you'd like to **order** some **wine**?
Female diner:	Excuse me. I'm afraid I need the lavatory rather urgently.
Manager:	Past the bar on the left, Madam. [*She exits, passing male diner on his way back*]. Ah there you are, Sir.
Male diner:	Well? Where's the **menu**?
Manager:	Madam must have taken it to the toilet, Sir, I'll just go and fetch it [*exits after female diner*].
Male diner:	**Waitress**!
Waitress:	[*entering*] Yes, Sir.
Male diner:	We'll have two gin and tonics while we're waiting.
Waitress:	Certainly, Sir. And can I take your **order**?

Female diner:	[*entering*] Of course you can't. We haven't seen a **menu** yet!
Manager:	[*entering*] I'm sorry, Madam, you left this in the toilet [*hands her menu*].
Female diner:	Thank you. Shall we have some **wine** first, darling?
Male diner:	I've ordered some G&Ts. Excuse me one moment . . . [*exits*]

Chaotic, hectic and hilarious! Try with three characters first and then add more. Bear in mind that the characters must cooperate to create a good scene.

Freeze tag

Two people play a scene. At any point, someone in the circle can shout 'Freeze!' Both players freeze. The one who shouted then moves in and taps one of the players who returns to the circle. The remaining player stays frozen until the incoming player starts a scene.

Try and freeze people when they are in an interesting position, and look to produce those positions when you are acting. Help each other out: the more dynamic the position, the more clues you will be giving to other actors. There is no rule of theatre that says you have to use the position exactly as it is. The main thing is that you get in there and start a scene *spontaneously*.

The other important thing is that the incoming player gives a strong signal to start the scene. If you are really unsure:

1 Copy the other person's body shape; start moving around with grunts or gibberish. It does not have to be a 'talkie'.
2 Go in and ask what they are doing. Help each other; keep the thing moving and something will emerge:

A:	What are you doing?
B:	[*in slightly huddled position*] Oh nothing.
A:	Oh yes you are. You're up to something, I can tell.
B:	Honest, Mum, I'm not.
A:	What have you got in your hands? Show me.
B:	There's nothing to show.
A:	How many times have I told you? Now put them back.
B:	Do I have to?

Good improvisers can make sense of such a scene without either of them having to determine what is being referred to. Eventually, one of them will move it on, but what matters is the relationship between them (see pages 67–72, status).

Standing, sitting, bending

A hilarious improvisation game: put three actors on stage and give them a situation (bank robbers, flight crew, etc.). At any one time, one must be standing, one sitting and one bending over. Each time one changes position the others must shift correspondingly. Never allow two people to be in any one position at the same time. As with the key-words game, players must justify their change of position.

Saying 'Yes'

The key to success in all these games is saying 'Yes'. You have no doubt experienced improvisation dominated by people determined to get their idea across or who consistently deny what others suggest. Some people cling onto their own idea in a desperate bid for originality. In fact, if they were not so afraid of being unoriginal they would not worry so much about having their idea accepted – they would trust to the fact that they'd have another one soon.

In *Impro*, Keith Johnstone develops the concept of making, accepting or blocking offers. An offer is anything an actor does or says on stage. It is most readily understood when spoken, e.g. A goes on stage and says 'Look, they're robbing that bank!' But an actor could just as well go on stage and keel over dead, or start dancing a jig. These are all offers: it is up to the other actors to accept them and build on them. If the offer is blocked the scene is destroyed:

A: Good morning, can I help you?
B: I'd like four pints of milk, please.
A: I'm afraid this is a clothes shop.
B: Then why have you got a sign saying dairy products in the window?

Both these actors are determined to set their own scene, and will not accept the other's offers. If played to its logical conclusion it can still work. The classic *Monty Python Cheese Shop* sketch works on this principle, where the expectation of any kind of cheese in a cheese shop is consistently thwarted. However, when two actors are trying to develop a scene, it can dishearten them and destroy the energy when anyone blocks.

A block does not have to be someone actually saying 'No'. It can be anything that denies the offer being made:

A: My God, you look peaky.
B: Yes, but I'm feeling much better than I was.

B said the word 'Yes', but actually blocked the offer. See what might have happened if B had accepted.

A: My God, you look peaky.
B: Do you think so? I feel dreadful.
A: Just look at the bags under your eyes.
B: I'm exhausted. I can't sleep. I can't keep my food down.
A: You should see a doctor.
B: That's where I'm off to, right now, only I feel too weak.
A: Here, I'll help you …

If, at any point, B says she's feeling better the improvisation will falter. If anything she must get sicker and sicker. There's also no rule that says 'because this is improvisation – it *must* be funny'. Skilful improvisers can touch our hearts as well as making us laugh!

Here are a few saying 'Yes' games to get you going:

Think of a situation

Each person in the group thinks of a public situation which would involve large numbers of people. In turn, players come out into the space and start their scene with a strong and clear offer. As soon as they realise what is going on, the other players rush into the scene and join in. For example: A goes into the space and says 'And do you, Jemima Anne Pinkleton take this man …', by which time we should have a bride, groom, choir and entire church congregation on stage. With practice you will be able to start these scenes with great speed and accuracy, so that you can then freeze them, question the participants' motives, find out their thoughts and set the scene moving again. Any public event will do.

Variations:

- Do this as *tableaux*, adding people in one by one.
- Add people one by one, but with full action.
- Divide a large group into smaller groups. Groups take it in turns.

Watch out for focus. The crowd have to decide very quickly which way the pulpit is facing, where exactly the fire is, who's cheering for the home team, etc. Bear in mind that in most group scenes, the majority function as a unit, e.g. audience, congregation, by-standers at an accident. You won't all be able to play hero, villain, priest, police officer, etc., but the crowd role is just as important.

The Magic Box

This is a classic Johnstone-style game. The group sits in a circle. One player has the Magic Box in front of them. They reach into the box and take out an object. Depending on the shape they make with their hands, we will know its rough size, but beyond that nothing is determined, and even that can change. Players ask them questions about the object, helping them to determine its nature. Again, the responsibility for the entire improvisation is removed from the individual and becomes a shared process. Beware of loading too many questions onto the player with the object. Give them time to respond and establish new information in mime. Each new bit of information is an offer which the group also needs to accept. For example:

Q: What kind of shape is the object?
A: It's round with little bumps all over it.
Q: Do the bumps feel rough to the touch?
A: Yes, they're quite coarse and scratchy.

Q: Is the surface soft?
A: Yes, it's really squidgy.
   Look [*starts squashing with fingers*].
Q: Does it have a taste?
A: [*tasting it*] Umm, yes, it's delicious. Strawberry flavour. Would you like to try some? [*breaks some off and hands it round*...]
Q: You're right. It tastes fantastic, though I can't seem to swallow it ...
A: Nor can I, it's gluing my teeth together ...

Q: Is the surface hard?
A: Solid. Look [*bounces it on floor*].
Q: Is there something inside it?
A: [*shaking it*] Do you know, I think there is. I can hear a rattling sound.
Q: Is there any way of opening it?
A: [*Looks*] Yes, it unscrews.
Q: What's inside?
A: Something soft ...

The answer always accepts the offer made in the question. The two possible strands show that whichever way it develops, something interesting can be made out of it. In the first case, it becomes a group activity. This takes skill to manage, but experienced groups will handle it well. You will notice that the person with the object turns the tables by asking the questioner to try some of the imaginary food; the roles become shared and fluid. In the second example, the object becomes its own secondary Magic Box with another object inside it. Like the imagination itself, the Magic Box is never-ending.

Two further points:

1 A classic block here that poses as an acceptance is to name the object. For example:

Q: Does it make a noise?
A: Yes, a ticking sound. It must be a watch.

End of improvisation! Not everything that ticks is a watch. If you say it ticks, you may be thinking 'it must be a watch', but you have not said it, so you can still answer 'Yes' when someone asks if it has ears. Suddenly, it's nothing like a watch at all. The imagination is endlessly flexible.

2 Remember to put the objects back in the box when you've finished with them!

Yes windows

Anti-blocking games can be applied very effectively to story-telling. This game is for two players who stand in front of the audience and pretend to be looking through a window. A makes an offer. B accepts it and makes one of her own. A accepts that and makes an offer back, etc. Each offer must be accepted and another offer made, as in the following exchange:

A: Look at that dog over the street. Can you see it?
B: Yes. Big, isn't it?
A: Huge. Looks more like a horse.

B: It is a horse. Look at those ears.
A: And that mane.
B: It's in mint condition. Must be a pedigree.
A: I should think so. Look at the way it runs.
B: Good God. It's going like the clappers. And there's another one.
A: And another. They're all over the place.
B: It's a stampede, and they're coming this way.
A: Good Lord, so they are. The ground's beginning to tremble ...

It is essential that both players describe what they are seeing, and do not just offer opinions or play a scene between them, as in:

A: Do you see that woman over there?
B: Yes. It's Mrs Hardcastle, isn't it?
A: That's right. I think she's really odd.
B: Yeah. She's married to that funny bloke ...

and then:

B: Look. She's heading into the bank with a gun.
A: So she is. Shall we call the police?
B: I think we'd better. Where's the phone?
A: I'm not sure.

In each case the urgency of telling the story and believing in the reality of what you are looking at begins to disappear. Try it. Not only does the energy drop, it actually becomes more difficult to think of something to say.

Suggestion: Play it as a 'gong-show'. Pairs go up in turn. As soon as one or other *blocks* the pair are 'gonged off'. See who lasts the longest.

Status

The key to all good improvisation and, indeed, all good drama, is status. Keith Johnstone's work is definitive in this area:

Imagine that two strangers are approaching each other along an empty street. It's straight, hundreds of yards long and with wide pavements. Both strangers are walking at an even pace, and at some point one of them will have to move aside in order to pass. You can see this decision being made a hundred yards or more before it actually 'needs' to be. In my view the two people scan each other for signs of status, and then the lower one moves aside. If they think they're equal, both move aside, but the position nearest the wall is actually the strongest. If each person believes himself to be dominant a very curious thing happens. They approach until they stop face to face, and do a sideways dance, while muttering confused apologies. If a little old half-blind lady wanders into your path this 'mirror' dance doesn't happen. You move out of her way. It's only when you think the other person is challenging that this dance occurs, and such incidents are likely to stick in the mind. I remember doing it in a shop doorway with a man who took me by the upper arms and moved me gently out of his path. It still rankles. Old people who don't want to give way, and who cling to the status they used to have, will walk along the street hugging the wall, and 'not noticing' anyone who approaches them. If, as an experiment, you also hug the wall very funny scenes occur when you stop face to face – but the sideways dance doesn't happen because you're conscious of what you're doing. Old people in, say, Hamburg, often collide with young Britishers in the street, because they expect the young to step aside for them. Similarly, a high-status stripper will walk stark naked into a stagehand who stands in her way. In the Russian *Hamlet* film there's a moment where Hamlet finds his way momentarily obstructed by a servant and he smashes him down. When you watch a bustling crowd from above it's amazing that they don't all bump into each other. I think it's because we're all giving status signals, and exchanging subliminal status challenges all the time. The more submissive person steps aside.

(Johnstone, Impro, *p. 61)*

TASKS

1 What does this extract say about our attitude to the elderly in Britain? Are you aware of it being different in other cultures or countries? Do you agree with Keith? Try it out: shift your status.
2 Observe status transactions in the street. Make notes on your findings and bring them back. Enact the transaction in groups and turn them into scenes.

Below are a few initial exercises in status.

Masters and servants

In this game the servant does whatever the master (or mistress!) requires, without hesitation. Commands are mimed and the servant maintains appropriate servant-like behaviour at all times. If the servant displeases the master in any way, s/he is ordered to commit suicide, which must be done instantly.

The game runs best in two main ways. Firstly, with one master and many servants. Continue until the stage is littered with dead bodies. Secondly, in pairs where the servant has any number of lives but wants to lose as few of them as possible. In our experience, servants are ordered to commit suicide for the following sorts of reason:

- running, being too slow, grinning, laughing, answering back, grovelling, getting too close, standing too far away, being rude, slouching, scratching, twitching, etc.

You will soon get a feel for what constitutes polite, efficient but unobtrusive servanting. If you have the opportunity, watch silver-service waiters at work and, in the game, watch those servants who are difficult to kill and see how they survive.

For the master, it is fine to criticise your servants for their behaviour, but *not* for aspects of the mime beyond their control; for example:

Servant: Here is your tea, Sir.
Master: [*drinks*] Ugh, it's coffee – die!

It is important that the master is high status. An uncertain or grinning master breaks the illusion and makes it harder for the servant or the audience to believe in the stage reality.

igh status is slow – low status is fast. Compare with the use of slow-motion to add weight to a moment in a film, or the use of speed in a *Keystone Cops* chase sequence. Play with the 'speed dial' as you improvise a scene.

The status party

This is a more realistic way of exploring status. All walk around the room, half making full eye-contact with everyone (*high* status) and half looking away as soon as their eyes are met (*low* status). On a command from the leader swap and try it the other way.

- Discuss this: how did it feel? Which one did you find most comfortable? We all have

a natural status and usually like to stick to it. Low status players will often find it uncomfortable playing high and vice versa. This often becomes very clear in improvisation and it is very important that you learn to play *against* your natural status.

- Now pick the one you were least comfortable with and move around again, this time developing a character and brief history. Give yourself a name. You are on your way to a party. High status players may be called Jemima and own a stable of racehorses, or be called Nick and be a sixteen-stone bouncer. In other words, you can be low or high social status, but you must be high *stage* status. The same goes for low status players. You can be a beggar or a judge, but you must be a low *stage* status beggar or judge.

- Decide who is hosting the party and let them set up. Have a doorway and a butler who lets people in, finds out their names and occupations and announces them to the rest of the gathering. Let the guests arrive gradually, one by one, giving them time to introduce and establish themselves. In groups of more than ten or twelve it may be best to go in two groups with the other group observing.

- Once the party is in full swing the leader calls out 'swap status'. Everyone immediately changes status over a few seconds without changing what they are doing, who they are talking to or what they are talking about. The character's history must remain the same; it is only the status that changes. For example, high status Jemima and low status Nick begin to swap. Jemima may own racehorses and be frightfully rich but she feels undeserving. She begins to do herself down, saying she inherited it all and has done nothing for herself. In the meantime, she raises Nick's status by saying how good it must be to have a real trade, real strength, etc. Nick accepts this rise in status and goes on about the pleasures of betting on the horses without all the trouble of breeding them. Jemima agrees, saying what a dreadful bind it is and how she wishes she could be free of it. She then further raises Nick's status by finding him terribly attractive and trying to tell him so. He lowers hers by telling her she looks a bit like one of her horses, and so on.

- If the people in the group swap status very gradually over many minutes, the party begins to look more and more real. At a real party, status games are always there but everyone tries to conceal them. Get players to play just above or just below the status of the person they are talking to.

TASK

Now hold your own status party.

★ hot tip

Hints for status:

- High: keep your head and eyes still and talk in complete sentences
- Low: keep head and eyes on the move and allow hesitation to creep into the voice.

'Dark glasses raise status because we can't see the submission of the eyes.'
(Johnstone, Impro, p. 42)

The card game

Playing very high or very low is relatively easy but it is important not to ignore the bulk of status transactions which take place nearer the middle of the range. In this game, everyone takes a card from a shuffled pack without letting anyone else see it. Ace is low. There are then two main ways of playing:

1 Stick it on your head. Do not look at the card, but hold it with a finger onto your forehead with the picture facing out. Everyone else now knows your status and will respond accordingly. Depending on their reactions, you will decide what you think your status is. In the meantime, of course, you are reading all the other cards and reacting accordingly to them. After about five minutes, line up with all the other players, putting yourself where you think you should be in the line, with Ace at one end and King at the other. Now all look at your own cards and discuss the results.

2 This time, look at your own card and conceal it. Have a couple of observers (or more) watching. Everyone mills around acting their given status to the other players and adjusting their behaviour according to the status messages they are getting in return. After a few minutes everyone stops and the observers try to put you in order. Then all reveal their actual cards. Discuss the results.

With a little practice a group can get it all right nearly every time.

TASK

Individuals tend to have a preferred status. As an actor it is important to know what your preferred status is, as it will affect your interpretation of character. Work out your own preferred status and practise playing with it and against it.

Chairs 1–10

Another way to understand the gradations in status is to play status to the space. Place a chair centre stage. Players approach the chair with different status levels, working from one up to ten. Status 1 will hardly get near the chair before scurrying off. Status 3 might gingerly sit on it. Status 5 or 6 will sit on the chair in a relaxed, neutral manner. It will look as though it genuinely is their chair. Status 8 will move it around, rock on the legs etc., and status 10 will stand on it. Watch people go in turn, but then it is fun to do it all as one group with each person having one chair and approaching it ten times, raising their status each time. You can feel the energy in the room change drastically.

★ *hot tip*

Get your status a little below or above your partner's and it works because you have to relate your behaviour directly to theirs.

Status swap

Now create scenes between two people. A starts off at status level 10, B is status level 1. You can either decide where you are before starting, or just go into it and see what happens. Gradually A and B swap status until A is 1 and B is 10. An example may help:

A: [*10 – complete control*] Yes, what do you want – can't you see I'm busy?

B: [*1 – abject humility*] Er, I'm terribly sorry, Madam, I've just been told to deliver this parcel to you.

A: [*9 – annoyed*] I don't want any parcels. Get out.

B: [*2 – scared but knows she has to stay*] It *is* marked urgent, Madam.

A: [*8 – forced to let messenger in*] Well put it over there and hurry up. I have an important client arriving any moment.

B: [*3 – allowed into space*] Yes, Madam, I'll be as quick as I can. [*rising to 4*] Shall I put it by all these dirty cups and ashtrays, Madam?

A: [*7 – humbled by acknowledgement of dirty office*] Er, yes, and take the dirties out with you.

B: [*Rising to 5*] What, and the soiled underwear down here?

A: [*Crumbling to 6*] Yes, quickly, Miss Bashum will be here any minute.

B: [*Rising to 6*] I'll do it just as soon as I can, Madam, but there is such a lot of mess and I do have to put this up [*opening parcel*].

A: [*Falling to 5*] Put what up?

B: [*Rising to 7*] This portrait. Lovely isn't it? I think it'll go really well. Can you just hold it for me?

A: [*Down to 4*] But . . . but . . . it's a picture of you!

B: [*8 – smug and confident*] Good likeness, isn't it? Pop it over there by the pot plant, would you, old girl? Come along now. Chop chop!

A: [*3 – utterly confused*] I . . . er . . . but . . . this is my office . . . isn't it?

B: [*9 – not even looking at her*] Would you be so kind as to read the name on the portrait for me?

A: [*2 – completely flustered and embarrassed*] Oh my God . . . it says . . . Miss Bashum . . . oh, I'm so sorry . . . please excuse me . . .

B: [*10 – total control*] Too late, I'm afraid. You're fired. Now get out of my office!

A: [*1 – humble, snivelling wreck*] Yes . . . right away . . . Miss er . . . yes . . . [*exit*]

Accepting each offer is essential here. The scene only works if both players conspire to allow the status shift. If either player hangs onto their preferred status, they will inevitably block and the scene will not work. Early attempts at these scenes often result in players shifting too quickly. Sudden reversals can be used to great comic and dramatic effect, but the pleasure is all the greater if they are gradual.

TASK

Repeat all status exercises in gibberish to emphasise that the status played is more important than what is being said.

Useful publications

Barker, Clive (1977) *Theatre Games*, Eyre Methuen Ltd.

Boal, Augusto (1992) *Games for Actors and Non-actors*, Routledge.

Johnstone, Keith (1981) *Impro*, Eyre Methuen Ltd.

Miles-Brown, John (1985) *Drama Studio Sourcebook*, P. Owen.

Brandes, Donna, Phillips, Howard (1990) *The Gamester's Handbook*, Stanley Thornes (Publishers) Ltd.

Building a character

In this section we look at ways of understanding character and realising it in performance. What is a character? The word is used in many ways. You will often hear people saying things like: 'I saw a really interesting character in the pub'; 'She's a real character'; 'He's a man of good character'; or, 'I love it, it's got character'. A letter of the alphabet is also a character. None of these, however, describes a *theatrical* character, because, as yet, they are not involved in an action and have no *wants*. A character is someone who wants something.

This definition of character must be distinguished from *characteristics* such as accent, mannerisms, occupation, etc. You may give your Hamlet a limp, but the key to the character is his conflicting desires and not the way he walks. As an actor, however, you must *ground* your character, to give them recognisable form. This is done by way of characteristics that you build up to make the character real for your audience.

Below we suggest ways of fleshing out character with appropriate characteristics (often determined by the playwright), and ways of examining their wants by looking at Stanislavski's System.

Begin by selecting the character you are to play. If you are unsure, you could use Albert or Mother in the quoted extract from Pinter's *A Night Out*, page 75.

The first thing to do is your research.

For your character, consider the following:

Period	Country
Social position	Mannerisms
Age	Social conditions
Sexuality	Family background
Accent	Gender
Race	Speech
Voice	Appearance
Clothing	

Invent the character's pre-history, using evidence from the play. Try to find the walk, mannerisms and voice of the character.

Do you need to add any props or costume at this stage? For example, your character may wear robes, habitually rummage in a handbag or pick their teeth. Anything that will affect the way you move should be added at the earliest possible opportunity. Even if you are not going to perform with these things, they can be useful as rehearsal tools; they may assist you in *believing* in your stage reality.

Many workshop exercises are things you will not actually do on stage, but they help you discover something about the character. Extreme examples of this are found most often in film actors who live the part as much as they can in their own lives. For example, Dustin Hoffman lived with severely autistic people for many months before making *Rain Man*, and Robert de Niro improved so much at boxing while working on *Raging Bull*, that he nearly won a title.

Some of this work is simply impossible on stage; de Niro became genuinely unhealthy, gaining much weight to make the second half of the film. The stage version of *Raging Bull* would have to find another solution. Whatever the style, however, learning about a character directly through spending time in similar circumstances adds enormous depth to initial impressions.

Knowing someone directly on whom to base your stage character is not always possible. In such cases you will have to find the nearest approximation, or refer to film or television, or just your imagination!

TASK

Find a real life model for your character. Observe them closely. Can you learn anything from them; identify any mannerisms of movement or speech?

Borrowing in this way is what Stanislavski called Image-Acting. It is something most actors do, and need to do: to observe and copy. The danger is, that however well you 'borrow', you could still end up with an empty shell, not very different from the old-style 'craft' actors with their stock gestures. Your mannerisms, however subtle, must still be informed by the 'actor of experience', living the inner life of the character to the full. To find this, we shall look at some key points of the System.

KONSTANTIN STANISLAVSKI'S SYSTEM

The super-objective

The *super-objective* of a play often provides the main thrust of the plot: e.g. Macbeth wants to be king at any price or Albert wants a single moment of power over women to rid him of his mother's domination (*A Night Out*, page 75). Everything else in the play should serve the super-objective; this should help you find the perspective of your role and relate it to the whole play. This is sometimes referred to as *the ruling idea* of a play, i.e. what it is about.

TASK

What is the super-objective of the play from which your character comes? Try to encapsulate it in one sentence.

The inner truth

Use the evidence in the text to create an imaginary life for the character before the play begins. This will help you find the *inner truth* in a part, and begin to assume the character psychologically and not just physically.

The subtext

The *subtext*, or *inner life*, of a part supplies clues to your hidden motives in the play. This is the life between the lines; everything that is unspoken and must be imagined. Just as in real life, characters on stage do not always say what they actually want. In Act 4 of Chekhov's *The Cherry Orchard*, Varya pretends to be looking for something, when in fact she wants Lopakhin to propose to her. The moment is painful because neither of them is able to say to each other what they want.

Given circumstances

What are *the given circumstances*: i.e. what has the character just been doing before they start talking to us and how will it affect them? Try a few different ones until you find something that works consistently. This will enable you to be acting at the outset. You will already be in your character's imaginary world.

The given circumstances also include and influence the setting. Imagine the setting for yourself in as much detail as possible. Demonstrate a clear sense of where you are by moving around the stage as you perform your speech. Decide what is essential for your speech (e.g. throne, sink, tree), and place them. Use objects to represent them, at least while you rehearse, so that you can imagine them. If your character is talking to someone, place a fellow actor there while you practise.

The Magic If

Ask yourself *The Magic If*: i.e. what would you do if you really were the character? If I were Miss Julie, what would I do now? The *Magic If* was Stanislavski's way of encouraging actors to play. It is the key question of the imagination: what would happen if . . .? The young Einstein once tried to imagine what someone would see if they rode on a beam of light. His theories were the end result, but could only happen because he dared to ask the question. In the same way the actor needs to ask 'If I were Macbeth, or Jocasta, or Miss Julie, what would I be thinking or doing now?'

This is not the same as believing that you actually *are* the character. It is a popular misconception of Stanislavski that he required actors to *be* the part. He only required them to live it, with the *Magic If*. Part of your *given circumstances* are also always that you are on a stage!

TASK

Unlock the imagination. Play the *Magic If* with your character.

FURTHER SPEECH WORK

Here are some exercises you can do with one or more people, to help get life, energy and variety into your character.

The hot-seat

In pairs or small groups put each character in turn in the hot-seat. When in the hot-seat, answer the questions others ask *as if you were the character*. Use whatever background information you have already built up. If you are asked something you have not already prepared for, make it up, staying as true to your character as you can. Afterwards, find out what seemed true or convincing and adjust your characterisation accordingly.

Improvisation

Devise an improvisation for one or more of the characters. Use group scenarios, such as:

- parties
- chance encounters at railway stations
- doctors' waiting rooms
- weddings
- conventions.

These are all good places to explore a group of disparate characters. All sorts of mobile *hot-seating* takes place. Characters have to respond quickly to all kinds of questions and stimuli. Working out what your character would think or do under these circumstances is difficult, so trust to your actor's instincts and let your subconscious do the work.

★ *hot tip*

Read the interviews with Mark Rylance (page 143) and Grainne Byrne (page 83) for more ideas.

Working with text

The key with any text is to read it very carefully, trying to pick up all the available clues as to character, action and setting, whether given as stage directions or in the body of the text.

Here is the opening scene from Harold Pinter's *A Night Out*:

Mother: Albert, I've been calling you. [*she watches him*] What are you doing?
Albert: Nothing.
Mother: Didn't you hear me call you, Albert? I've been calling you from upstairs.

Albert:	You seen my tie?
Mother:	Oh, I say, I'll have to put the flag out.
Albert:	What do you mean?
Mother:	Cleaning your shoes, Albert? I'll have to put the flag out, won't I?

Albert puts the brush back under the sink and begins to search the sideboard and cupboard.

	What are you looking for?
Albert:	My tie. The striped one, the blue one.
Mother:	The bulb's gone in Grandma's room.
Albert:	Has it?
Mother:	That's what I was calling you about. I went in and switched on the light and the bulb had gone.

She watches him open the kitchen cabinet and look into it.

	Aren't those your best trousers, Albert? What have you put on your best trousers for?
Albert:	Look, Mum, where's my tie? The blue one, the blue tie, where is it? You know the one I mean, the blue striped one, I gave it to you this morning.
Mother:	What do you want your tie for?
Albert:	I want to put it on. I asked you to press it for me this morning. I gave it to you this morning before I went to work, didn't I?

She goes to the gas stove, examines the vegetables, opens the oven and looks into it.

Mother:	[*gently*] Well, your dinner'll be ready soon. You can look for it afterwards. Lay the table, there's a good boy.
Albert:	Why should I look for it afterwards? You know where it is now.
Mother:	You've got five minutes. Go down to the cellar, Albert, get a bulb and put it in Grandma's room, go on.
Albert:	I can't go down to the cellar, I've got my best trousers on . . . I've got a white shirt on.
Mother:	You're dressing up tonight, aren't you? Dressing up, cleaning your shoes, anyone would think you were going to the Ritz.
Albert:	I'm not going to the Ritz.
Mother:	[*suspiciously*] What do you mean, you're not going to the Ritz?
Albert:	What do you mean?
Mother:	The way you said you're not going to the Ritz, it sounded like you were going somewhere else.
Albert:	[*wearily*] I am.
Mother:	[*shocked surprise*] You're going out?
Albert:	You know I'm going out. I told you I was going out. I told you last week. I told you this morning. Look, where's my tie? I've got to have my tie. I'm late already. Come on, Mum, where'd you put it?
Mother:	What about your dinner?

Super-objective of the play

This opening scene establishes the relationship between Albert and his mother. As actors, you will need to pick up the clues as to the location and action of each character and then look for the meaning, for the subtext.

Setting

Where are they? The stage direction after line 7 tells us that they are in the kitchen.

Action

What are they doing? She asks Albert what he is doing. He answers 'nothing'. She then tells us, six lines later, that he is cleaning his shoes. His action, then, is to clean his shoes, hers is to watch him do it. This leads us to one of the first rules of acting:

Never trust what characters say about themselves – always investigate thoroughly.

Character

Why does Albert lie? The immediate answer is because the question was unnecessary. His mother can see precisely what he is doing. She is therefore not asking for genuine information, but is challenging him. His response then is a defence. She has also been calling him and he has not responded. Our first clue to character is that she attacks and he defends.

Atmosphere

One of the keys to any staging is the establishment of atmosphere. Always look for this without speech first. Speak when the atmosphere is right, and your lines will have purpose and depth. We are beginning to understand that the atmosphere here is tense and full of unspoken thoughts.

TASKS

1 In pairs, stage Albert being called by his mum. She must call from off stage, while he tries to ignore it. Space the calls out and see how long you can keep it up while building the tension. Build it until she would *have* to enter the stage and look.

2 In pairs, say these lines with as many different tones and expressions as you can:

- What are you doing?
- Nothing.
- Didn't you hear me call?

The next offer that Albert makes is to ask if she has seen his tie. She evades the question and is sarcastic about his shoe-polishing. He continues to rummage in the kitchen cupboards. Here we have our next clue to unravelling the text. Why would anyone look for a tie in the kitchen? The answer has to be because he thinks he might find it there. In other words, someone has put it there. In this case his mother: she has *hidden* his tie. This explains why she avoids his questions.

He asks again, and again she avoids the issue, by bringing in some quite extraneous information about the bulb in Grandma's room which she wants him to replace.

TASK

Run through the opening dialogue at first in complete innocence, and then showing clearly that she knows what he is doing and he knows that she has hidden his tie.

Albert then informs us that he gave his tie to his mother that morning to be pressed. This not only confirms that she has hidden it, but gives us an insight into the degree of his domestic dependence on his mother. He is capable of cleaning his shoes, but she presses his ties. They seem to have clearly demarcated roles in the home.

Mother then challenges Albert about wearing his best trousers. He clearly does not wear them often and tonight is a special occasion. He does not reply, again, because she already knows the answer. He is going out: he has told her many times, but she spends the entire scene behaving as if he is not going out. Her manner is attacking, but it emerges that she is on the defensive. She wants to conserve the status quo. She wants him at home and he is going to go out and leave her.

She puts moral pressure on Albert. The bulb needs changing and she has cooked his dinner. She calls him a 'good boy'. We do not know from the text here how old he is, but he tells us that he works. Mother uses language designed to reduce his status. She wants to keep him as a boy and doesn't want him to grow up.

TASK

Compare this with your own experiences of wanting to go out when parents or guardians are disapproving. Are there any similarities?

Despite all these attempts to knock him off course, Albert continues to search for his tie. He knows she has hidden it and yet he never says so. He offers no direct challenge but remains assertive and calm. In other words, he accepts, and perhaps even expects, her behaviour. This can only be because he has seen it many times before. When she sounds surprised that he is going out he replies wearily. The scene now begins to look like a weird ritual where outrageous and spiteful behaviour (not answering questions, hiding things from people) appears and is accepted as normal. This is why, despite the surface appearance of Naturalism, Pinter is an absurdist writer.

★ key point

Absurd: when the weird and bizarre is made to appear normal.

To conclude: the 'wants' of the characters function on three essential levels:

	Albert	Mother
level 1	wants his tie	wants him to put a bulb in Grandma's room
level 2	wants to go out	wants him to stay in
level 3	wants to break out of her control	will use any mechanism at her disposal to keep him as he is

TASKS

1 Read the scene, bearing this information in mind.
2 Run it without words. You will invariably end up physicalising level 3 of their wants, with Mother restraining an Albert who is desperate to leave.

★ hot tip

Run any scene without words to discover the character's real wants.

Suggested character breakdown for Albert

Period	1960s
Country	England
Social conditions	Lives alone with mother in Victorian terrace in London's East End
Social position	Low-paid office worker
Mannerisms	Nervy. Wipes palms on trousers
Family background	White working class. Father dead. Clinging mother with social aspirations
Age	28
Race	Caucasian
Gender	Male
Sexuality	Inexperienced. Heterosexual but unable to deal with women or his desire for them
Voice	Slightly high-pitched
Speech	A man of few words. Speaks when spoken to
Accent	Light cockney, but trying not to be
Clothing	Best suit. Ten years out of date. Blue striped tie
Appearance	Awkward. Overgrown schoolboy

Suggested rehearsal costume and props for Albert's mother

Mrs Stokes is in her early fifties and maintains a neat and tidy house, her empire. She would wear neat, tidy clothes from the late 1950s with her hair pinned up on her head. Rehearse in a 50s skirt and 'sensible' shoes. She likes to keep everything in order and needs to have things on stage to organise. She also plays cards by herself.

Use of improvisation

- hot-seat characters
- Mrs Stokes at earlier family occasions
- Albert at parties
- run the scene, freeze and ask characters for their inner thoughts and motivations.

LINE-LEARNING

Line-learning can be a chore, but it can also be a great opportunity to explore text and to find out about character. Play around as you learn, and you will enjoy it more, and find it more satisfying.

Unfortunately, there are no real short cuts in line-learning; no mystery techniques. Different actors remember lines in different ways, and you will need to understand how best to do it for yourself. Generally, lines are remembered visually; i.e. the actor sees the word on the page in their mind's eye; or by association with moves ('when I get here I say this'); or from the cue-line in dialogue; or purely by the sense. The way you learn lines will probably involve a combination of all these. Often the process is quite conscious as you are learning the lines but, by the time you get on stage, what enables you to remember them has become as instinctive as how you know your way home from work every day. Like driving a car, all the different operations merge into one until you seem to do them *automatically* and at the same time.

Some line-learning hints

Make sure you understand exactly what the speech is about. It is almost impossible to learn what you do not understand.

- Learn the first line. Then the first and the second. Then the first, second and third, and so on. Always go back to the beginning of the speech.
- Learn in short but concentrated bursts.
- Run through what you know so far *every day*.
- Run through without looking at the text as soon as possible, however many mistakes you make. Get a friend to help prompt you.
- Record the lines and learn them while doing something requiring minimal concentration.

AUDITIONING

This is an essential skill for the actor. Auditions come in many forms; increasingly they are in the form of a workshop session, but the need to have your own well-rehearsed and varied audition programme is paramount.

Finding the right speeches

The best way to do this is to read a lot of plays. Half the stage time in a play is taken up by action, so scripts are often not very long. Many modern scripts can be read in an hour or so. Whichever speech you choose, you must read the whole play in order to understand the character and their motivation. Too many actors simply do not read plays: anyone who does stands out very clearly.

There *are* short cuts if you are in difficulty, do not have access to a good library or are short of time. There are a variety of books with collections of monologues and soliloquys that give a brief synopsis of plot and character. If you use such a book, make sure you still get hold of a copy of the play. There is *no* substitute for reading the full version.

> ★ *hot tip*
>
> **R**emember: memory is a muscle and can be trained. The more you learn the easier it becomes. Learn a speech a week, or a poem, just to keep in practice. Imagine, by the end of the year you would have a potential 52 audition speeches ...!

For dialogue:

- Learn the cues as well as your own lines *from the outset.*
- Record the cues on a tape, leaving long enough gaps in between for your responses. The possession of a dictaphone can be invaluable.

Repertory (Rep) companies will often ask you to prepare pieces for a season of plays, but often insist that they are not taken from the plays themselves. Drama schools often provide a list of pieces to choose from or, in the case of Shakespeare, may give you a list of what to avoid. This is because such pieces are often performed, which can be a disadvantage, so widen your search as much as you can. It is always exciting for a director to hear new pieces, and it will make you stand out.

Note:

- Unless otherwise stated, always assume that your audition piece should come from a published play. If other abilities are to be tested, this will usually be done in a workshop format.
- Wear appropriate clothing. You can damage your chances if you do not.
- It is often advisable to use your natural voice/accent unless specifically asked for something else.
- Play characters of your own gender and age.

The way you deliver your speech will depend on your own preferences and abilities, and the production or company for whom you are auditioning. Tastes are so varied that there can be no golden rule; a classic performance to one may appear stilted to another. You will never know exactly what your auditioner is looking for, so you should be true to yourself; try to develop your own style and interpretation for each piece. Your performance will work better if you find your own truth.

Extra work on audition speeches

For this you need to work in pairs, with A doing their speech while B listens. There are three stages to this exercise:

1 *B stands still. A moves freely around the stage. B listens.* This gives A enormous power.

Enjoy it. See what effect it has on the delivery of the speech.

2 *A stands still. B moves around. A tries to get their attention using the speech.* Very frustrating for A. B can do all sorts of distracting, irritating things. Make A work as hard as you can to get the speech across. Reward A occasionally if they are genuinely winning your attention.

3 *B moves around, but this time A can follow.* All of A's pent-up frustration is released, but B can still get away, leave the room etc. This can lead to some funny and also powerful performances.

Note how the status shifts from A in the first one to B in the second, becoming fluid in the third.

STYLISATION AND NATURALISM: A CONTINUUM

The boundaries between what is stylised and what is naturalistic are often more blurred than much critical writing implies. Good quality theatre aims for truthfulness on stage. Neither Stylisation nor Naturalism, by themselves, makes theatre any more or less real. Before all else, whatever the convention, your theatre must be good.

What do the terms mean?

There are many terms we must be wary of in art and in the theatre because they refer to the art of specific times. An example would be Contemporary Dance, Modernist Architecture, or Experimental Theatre. Each would seem to be describing something that is quite up-to-date; in fact, something contemporary, modern or experimental. The terms were coined, however, much earlier this century, at a time when each art-form was breaking new ground. We might now think that much Modernist Art is old-fashioned, since much of it was created before the First World War. Contemporary Dance developed in the 1960s

and Experimental Theatre in Germany, in the 1920s. The same is true of difficult terms like *naturalistic*, or *realistic*. We use them to mean 'it is convincing', but they also describe particular theatrical genres that we might find totally unconvincing now. (See page 230 for a detailed introduction to Naturalism's origins as a movement.)

Let us assume that when we use the term *naturalistic*, we mean 'recreating the rhythms and behaviours of everyday life'. For Stanislavski, this would have implied a life-like set with as much detail as possible. In a school, college or small theatre, however, this is often not practical, and so we *stylise* the environment. The simplest example of this is where we turn the environment into the set and focus on the acting, in what is now known as the Black Box Theatre. Interestingly, it was Stanislavski himself who pioneered it for a production of Leonid Andreyev's symbolist play *The Life of Man*:

During an early rehearsal for *The Life of*

Man, Stanislavski revealed the black velvet marquette to the performers. A black-costumed figure became lost in the stage model. Suddenly an idea occurred to the master – convert the evening into a magician's chamber of tricks and disappearing acts. The black box theatre was born. Originally, Stanislavski wanted to use black costumes to mask the natural and full movements of the actors. That way, only those areas of the body, especially the faces and hands, could be uncovered at the director's will. For the first time, Stanislavski's acting experiment worked. What looked like grotesque and stylised acting was wildly applauded for both its mise-en-scène and deep, forceful characterisations.

(Gordon, The Stanislavski Technique, *pp. 35–6)*

TASK

Stylisation helps to stage the unconscious.

In groups, tell each other of a particularly vivid dream. Recurring ones are often best. Pick one and find ways to stage it. Naturalism simply will not work here, as dreams distort time and distance and have no respect for observable fact – and yet we use them as a way of showing us a much deeper truth.

Develop a project around your dreams and their meanings.

Shakespeare's skill was such that, at an age before scientific understanding of the unconscious and the development of Naturalism, he created fully realised characters whose very language gave us access to their innermost thoughts – to the imagery of dreams. The language of the plays conveyed this, but we now have to find other ways. Television and film give many privileged viewpoints, but the theatre has its own bag of tricks for the same purpose; for example, allowing characters to deliver soliloquys i.e. talk alone on stage about their thoughts and feelings. This enables us to explore the deeper motivations, to get inside the head of the character. How do we make the character soliloquise? In a Shakespeare play they would just start talking, often directly to the audience.

In Peter Schaffer's *Equus*, the disturbed young Alan Strang is persuaded to talk by a psychiatrist's pretend hypnosis, allowing for an on-stage confession. Many writers use monologue. Stylisation can turn these monologues into soliloquys by spot-lighting the actor and freezing all other stage action. What matters is that we create a stage convention whereby we can simply allow a character to speak and the audience to accept it. The critic and thinker Raymond Williams has the following ideas on theatrical convention:

In the . . . practice of drama, the convention, in any particular case, is simply the terms upon which the author, performers and audience agree to meet, so that the performance may be carried on. Agree to meet, of course, is by no means always a formal or definitive process; much more usually, in any art, the consent is largely customary, and often indeed it is virtually unconscious.

This can be seen most readily in the conventions of our own period. In a naturalistic play, for example, the convention is that the speech and action should as closely as possible appear to be those of everyday life; but few who watch such a play realize that this is a convention; to the majority it is merely 'what a play is like', 'the sort of thing a play tries to do'. Yet it is, in fact, a very remarkable convention that actors should represent people behaving naturally, while all the time maintaining the illusion that, as characters, these persons are unaware of the audience's presence. The most desperate private confession, or the most dangerous conspiracy, can be played out on the stage, in full view and hearing of a thousand people; yet it will not occur to either actors or audience that this is in any way strange, because all, by the tacit consent of custom, have accepted this procedure as a convention.

(Raymond Williams, From Ibsen to Brecht, *1987, Hogarth Press, p. 13)*

Naturalism, therefore, is simply one of the many ways theatre has discovered to get at the truth. It can be limited by a need to access characters' inner thoughts and motivations, by showing us what they might do or say in a believable everyday situation. Stylisation can go beyond this, but risks producing narrow, unconvincing characters.

TASK

Take a story from the newspaper that grabs your interest. Work out roles and responsibilities. Some groups tackle it purely naturalistically while the other groups allow themselves a range of stylised techniques. Discuss them and list their relative advantages and disadvantages.

Interview with Grainne Byrne of *Scarlet Theatre*

Grainne Byrne has acted and directed with Scarlet Theatre since 1987. She talks about the way the company generated their two most recent devised performances, *Paper Walls* and *The fruit has turned to jam in the fields*.

Can you tell me the history of Scarlet Theatre?
The Scarlet Harlots started in 1981. They were a group of women who didn't know they were starting a theatre company, they simply put a show together for the Edinburgh festival. It was called *We Who Are The Beautiful* and was about the massacre of six million women for witchcraft during the Middle Ages. They were then given money by the Greater London Council (GLC) to put on another show. That's how it began. Every year for about five years they gathered a team to make a show. They became highly respected, producing very visual work, using masks and stilts, which was all revolutionary at the time. I joined in 1987 to do a show called *Appetite of the Heart* with Emma Barnard, who is my co-director for this show, and after that did another one with them called *La Folie*. Then there was a huge change of personnel and I kept the company going under the name of *Scarlet Theatre* from 1990 onwards, establishing it formally with the Independent Theatre Council (ITC), using Equity contracts, becoming a registered company, and later becoming a charity. That wasn't all my effort; a series of marvellous administrators sorted the company out. Elements of the *Scarlet Harlots* performance style have remained: being highly contemporary, highly physical and using humour.

Does the company have a particular policy?
Yes. We want to enthuse female performers, to give them the opportunity of working in a way that they wouldn't work in other companies. This also includes giving people opportunities beyond their normal brief. For example, the two Alices who directed *Paper Walls* are designers. I swapped hats to become a director: I wanted to give those opportunities to other people. We want to entertain, always to entertain. We have an internal politic about recruiting women, but we don't use it as a marketing tool. We make our marketing as sophisticated and glamorous as possible.

So you don't market yourselves as a women's theatre group?
We clothe it. We describe ourselves as one of the most acclaimed touring companies in the country today, and then we say that it's a collaboration of female theatre practitioners. That's an important thing to say, that our work is *collaborative*. We bring together a team of people in order to create the work, so design and music are always very important.

Not everyone who works for us is female. The music, for example, is always done by Nigel Piper, who happens to be a bloke. He's just very good and can interpret our shows very well musically. We've used him for the past five years.

But you wouldn't use a male performer?
It's funny you should say that because I will. I've got a plan for a show in which I do want to use men. The company is female driven; the management and the Board of Directors are female. We want to give women more opportunities to determine their own work; to create the sort of roles in theatre that are not only interesting and good for *them* to be in, but

also good to watch; to create the sort of roles that aren't around at the moment for women performers, because the traditional theatre is so male-dominated. But it doesn't have to exclude men where there is an artistic imperative.

With the exception of Nigel, your last two productions have been staffed entirely by women. What difference does it make working in an all-female company?
When women tell each other stories they often make tragic things very funny, and that typifies our work. We like to tell grim little tales, but using humour along the way. Humour is our main tool. And it's a gentle kind of humour, different from male humour, I think. More internalised.

Do you mean less at someone else's expense?
Maybe, yes. A woman's humour tends to be at her own expense. If a woman is telling a funny story, it's about how terribly embarrassed she was, how she's making a complete idiot of herself and then to cap it all ... and everybody's laughing. But our shows are not about women as victims – far from it. We'll take a scenario that has interested or moved us in some

Figure 2.12   *Scarlet Theatre Company,* Paper Walls

way and then try to get that across, using humour as a tool. We don't do it to wipe out the sympathy or empathy of the audience. The way in which we use humour enhances it.

Where do you start with an idea?
With *Paper Walls*, it was my idea to ask the two designers to work with people, and they decided that they would build a little shed with a little window. They thought it would be fun. Then the actors worked with going in and out of the shed, bringing out objects. And then we worked on the idea of somebody watching you. At the same time, in the devising process, people brought in stories. We knew that we wanted to work with a story, and we also knew we wanted to address the audience directly, to talk to the audience, and to use as few 'acting techniques' as possible. When we were making that show we thought, 'Isn't it a disappointment sometimes when people come on stage and just start acting?' We knew we wanted to be in character, but also to talk to the audience.

What do you mean when you say someone comes on and starts acting?
I mean, when people are on stage and *encased* in a character and they're relating to another character on stage. The curtain goes up, the set looks fantastic and people suddenly come out talking in a funny voice, conscious of the fact that they're acting, even if they're very good. We noticed that we did that and we decided we wanted to perform in a more relaxed way in *Paper Walls*. We wanted the characters to have a direct relationship with the audience, to stand there and say something, show something, being aware that the audience was there; using clowning techniques, if you like; being conscious of the audience.

Where did the story come from?
The story came out of a newspaper cutting and seemed absolutely appropriate for the set. It was a landmark case in which some women who killed an abusive man were let off. *Brookside* followed it. It was when the whole notion of cumulative provocation was first established. So we had a shed and some props and then someone brought in the story which set everything in motion: the continuous DIY, the fact that he made them wear the same coats. I wasn't in the show, originally; I produced it. I helped prepare the two Alices for working with the actors because they hadn't done it before. I also helped a little bit with the structure of the show and would come in and be an outside eye. The flavour of the piece was to do with the actresses in it. Joyce Henderson was one of them and she trained at Lecoq school in Paris

as a clown, so that informed the work. I then took over her role for the Edinburgh Festival and the subsequent tour.

Was it difficult slotting into someone else's role?
No, it was easy actually, because all the decisions had been made. I made it quite different, but I kept the same rhythm and timing and relationship with the others. The two other characters were also not original actresses, they were replacements for the tour. So a lot of different performers can work on a piece who aren't necessarily involved in the devising process. It was a great show. An Arts Council report said they had never seen a set which was so organically part of the action.

In your latest piece, The fruit has turned to jam in the fields, *you started with a script. What kind of brief did you give the scriptwriter?*
I had worked with Jill Bradley before. She came to me with a text she had written (dense and elaborate like a labyrinth), and three of us staged it for her. We then performed it at the Institute of Contemporary Arts (ICA) where it was very well received and I decided to commission an original piece from her. I wanted something about the Second World War, because of the fiftieth anniversary in 1995. I had also been reading *Birdsong* (by Sebastian Faulk), about men going 'over the top', and the dreadful things that people witnessed that they could never talk about, so they would go to the pub at night and tell jokes. They'd seen brains spattered all over the place, and when they dug down for another trench they came across so many arms and legs. We'd all read that book and were very affected by it. At the same time I was doing reminiscence workshops at the Old Bull Arts Centre with elderly ladies who told us some hilarious stories about their wartime experiences. Then Jill wrote the text, which was an extraordinary piece involving three women playing *Dad's Army* characters. We did a development workshop on it and decided to give it the context of a blown-up library. We decided that there had been an apocalypse, they'd been blown up and they'd militarised themselves in an absurd way, because our only knowledge of the war has been handed down through *Dad's Army*. We decided that it would be limbo-land, purgatory, but it was like ten green bottles – the rest were already dead and they would be next.

And where did Mr Sloanes as a psychopathic butcher come in?
It doesn't greatly matter whether the audience follow this or not, but the cast all have two characters: library women and member of army. But there's another pair, Mrs Hedges and Sloanes, who are no

longer there. They all have to play Sloanes now because the other woman who used to play him is in the cupboard, dead, because they've eaten her. She was dead anyway. This was something that did occur in prisoner of war camps. Nobody in the audience really gets that, but it's a secret that the performers have, it gives a certain tension, a hiccup when they mention Mrs Hedges. It's not there in the text, it's all coded. We decided they'd taken shelter in these characters and in this mad world, and that words had become their currency; they're walking on books as if the words on the books are coming up through them and that's why they are able to speak as they do. We made these decisions through a lot of work, and it gradually evolved as we worked on it.

What kind of work do you do in rehearsal for a piece like this?

Because the text didn't easily fit the narrative we were developing, we worked with the actors on their through-line. On the wall we had three journeys. We would say, 'right, we need to show that they've been there a long time' and then create the opening sequence, marking the walls with chalk, counting the days. Before that opening sequence you've got cityscape, lonely music, to show a devastated landscape, shining lights across the books to look like rubble and so on. Then we needed to map out each character's journey through that landscape. So we decided to have a sequence of actions, of events on the wall, written on a different coloured paper for each character. That helped us to see the piece of text, to start to shape it as a play, depicting what was in the text and the story we placed around it. We had to write it down and map it out, otherwise we would have lost our way. Then we used a technique called *instant acting*, whereby the actors would read the text onto a tape without acting it at all. The instant acting technique is where you have several impulses: you are either *compelled, impelled* or *repelled*. If you say a line

it may impel you to move towards a person, it may repel you from that person or it may compel you to stay where you are. Those were the rules and the actors had to stay in character. We spent a week with them simply running around the set with all the words on the tape. We never used the same recording twice. After we had finished running through a scene, we would tape it again immediately, and that would inform the way in which they said the text and where they were moving. They would sit down and read the text with different nuances. And then we would do it again. They had to stay in character and to follow compelled, impelled, repelled. Then the piece evolved very quickly. We decided the characters were playing a game and the words were part of that game, which they were using for their own purposes.

So you had a text and had to invent another play to go underneath it?

That's right. When they first did it, we were very conscious of the scenario, of trying to make the narrative work, but as the show has developed in performance the text works better and better. The actors have really responded, and grown along with the ears and eyes of numerous audiences. It's a very funny text, which the actors have to allow to bounce along; they mustn't overplay the emotions, particularly with the death – it would be wrong to become over-emotional; it would lose the delicate balance of the piece.

One last question. What was it like working with a co-director?

Great. A really enjoyable process. But you have to be several steps ahead of the actors all the time to move things along. Emma and I would always meet one hour before the actors arrived and stay to discuss and plan one hour after they had gone.

chapter three
MOVEMENT AND VOICE

In order to express a most delicate and largely subconscious life it is necessary to have control of an unusually responsive, excellently prepared vocal and physical apparatus.

(*K. Stanislavski*, An Actor Prepares, *p. 16*)

Whatever the acting style, it is important to move well and fluidly. This is more a question of understanding and working with the natural rhythms of your body and removing any blocks than it is of learning complex physical techniques. The following exercises are designed to make you aware of the messages you unconsciously send and help you find your neutral body.

You should always wear loose comfortable clothing for movement work. If you do not, there will always be things in a movement session that you simply will not try because of what you are wearing; you will already be censoring yourself. By wearing everyday clothing, we can cling on to our everyday behaviour; this makes us feel safe, but it will not encourage us to learn new things either about ourselves or performance. This is particularly relevant for footwear. You need to be able to feel the floor, so wear extra-light, gripping shoes. You would not wear jeans to a serious football practice or to a dance class. Take yourself and your movement seriously – wear the right gear.

Physical warm-up

First complete the physical work of 'bouncing electrons and waves' in Chapter 2, pages 53–5, then move onto the physical warm-up. You should allow at least ten minutes for this, and ideally half an hour. Throughout these exercises, stay relaxed through the body and breathe with the movement.

Head rolls

Stand with your feet slightly apart. Drop your head onto your chest and roll it gently round to your right shoulder. Then back round to your left. Repeat. Do four sets and leave your head down.

Curls

Now let the weight of your head pull the upper half of your torso down. Gradually let your shoulders sink and your arms hang. Keep the legs as straight as you can, but bend the knees as necessary to allow yourself to flop from the waist. Have a bounce around, ensuring that your head and neck are completely relaxed. Now uncurl very slowly, straightening the legs first. Imagine a cord is attached to your pelvis and is pulling your hips forward. You will feel your back slowly uncurling, vertebra by vertebra. Try to avoid getting nearly to the top and then lifting your head up; keep going right up through the neck. Repeat.

Arm stretches

Feet slightly apart. Stretch up with each arm in turn, reaching directly up and feeling the full stretch down the side of your body. Do eight on each side; then four each side twice; two on each side four times, and one on each side eight times. Each set makes 16 stretches. It helps if someone counts.

Side stretches

Repeat the arm stretches. This time, the arm goes sideways over the head. Keep your shoulders straight and avoid twisting the body, or the stretch will not go down your side.

Pelvis

Spread your feet and bend a little with the knees. The more you sit into the position, the greater freedom you have to move. Push forwards from the hips, feeling the tightness across your pelvis. Now push back with the hips, feeling it tighten across the small of your back. Repeat. Do four sets.

Now repeat this exercise, but pushing the pelvis from side to side, keeping the upper half of your body still. Imagine your hips are on a skewer and you are sliding them along it from side to side. Do four sets.

Leg stretches

Stretch each leg out to the side in turn, supporting yourself on your hands and keeping your back straight. Use the out-breath to relax into the stretch. Imagine your breath moving inside you to the stretched part. Do this with your toes pointing forwards, and then your toes pointing up to the ceiling. Each exercise stretches different tendons along the inside and the back of your thigh.

Squats

Squatting is a great stretch. Spread the feet. Keep the back straight. Take your weight on your hands and ease yourself into a squatting position. This is an ability we have as children (watch toddlers squat without difficulty as they play) but lose as we grow older. Practice will improve the length of time you can comfortably remain in a squat.

Balance

Stand straight but relaxed. Fix your eyes on a point at eye-level (choose something stationary). Lift your right leg and take it in both hands, keeping your back straight. Pull the knee up to your chest. Reach behind and take the foot in your right hand. Pull it up behind you, feeling the stretch on the front of your thigh, keeping your eyes fixed on your 'point' to maintain balance. Now stretch the foot out behind you with your right hand, and reach forward with the left hand, bending the supporting leg. Hold this balance for a count of ten. Repeat sequence with left leg. See if the whole group can perform this together, gracefully, without stumbling. Use each other's energy and work together.

TASK

There are many exercises in common use that are not included here. Use the exercises above and ones you have learned elsewhere to devise your own perfect physical warm-up. Write it down. At an agreed session, take the warm-up for your group. Take yourself seriously and make sure everyone is doing the exercises properly. Don't rush; enjoy.

Exercises

Below are a list of games and exercises, each in their own right a trust, energising or concentration game, with some combining several functions. These are now grouped according to the way in which they develop the mover.

ENERGY AND CONTACT

Funny walks tig

Usual tig rules, only this time the person who is It moves in a strange and weird way making bizarre noises. Everyone copies. When someone is It they produce their own movement and sound. Ensure a regular change of It. Releases inhibitions and gets people moving.

Hand-fencing

In pairs. Each person keeps their left hand behind their back with the palm facing out. Try to touch the other person's hidden palm with your right hand. You score each time. A variation is to hold the concealed hand palm up and place a small coin in it. Try to get each other's coins. Swap hands and or partners from time to time. Encourages agility and speed, extending the fluidity of the body.

Rolling logs

Everyone lies on their backs side by side, shoulder to shoulder. The person at the end starts rolling over all the other logs, then the next person goes, and so on. This generates great energy and hilarity. Keep the body straight, arms and legs straight and roll from the hips. Keep relaxed and you won't hurt anyone, however heavy you think you are!

Knots

All close eyes and squash together. Reach out and find one hand with each of yours. Now open your eyes and try to untangle without breaking the chain.

Body to body

A leader calls out 'Body to body'. Everyone attaches themselves to one other person. Whichever two body parts the leader calls out, each pair must make meet, e.g. elbow to knee. Build up speed and complexity. Each time leader calls 'Body to body', you find a new partner.

Walking and stopping

An exercise in maintaining energy on stage even when not moving. Do an uncurling up the spine as preparation for this, so that you are properly straightened and stretched. Everyone move around the space in a balanced and alert way. When the leader says 'Stop!' everyone pauses instantly. When the leader says 'Go', you start again, but without any extraneous movement. Normally, when we stop we relax slightly; there is a slight slump in the body. Here there should be none of that. Keep on stopping and starting at the leader's word. Be ready to go at all times without telegraphing your intentions.

Imagine a cord is pulling you along. It is the cord that stops and starts. This will help you maintain the energy.

Variations:

- Leader keeps giving instructions, but gradually increases the pace until players are sprinting round the room. The balance must still be perfect and you must be able to stop instantly and start again without slumping.

- Back to walking pace until the instruction is given, 'On your own'. Now the group stops and starts together without any external signal. It will seem uncertain at first, with some people obviously moving first, but soon the group will do it without an observer being able to tell if anyone was leading. Sometimes the group genuinely does not know itself.
- As for the second variation, but this time with eyes shut. This sounds scary, but if you walk gently, keeping light on your feet, you can stop at the slightest touch. You will also sense when people are near even without seeing them. You may have the odd collision, but if you are relaxed, you won't hurt yourself. Keep your arms down by your sides, relax, concentrate and go for it. This really develops all those other senses!

Group rush

The whole group squashes into one corner of the room. Squeeze as close as you can without hurting anybody; breathe to the centre of your being and feel the energy build. Be conscious of the energy building in the whole group. Eventually, without anybody having moved, the energy is so great that everyone simultaneously rushes to the opposite corner. Try it. It will soon become clear when a group is functioning together and when it is not. You must wait until the energy is there.

Body parts leading

Look at how each member of the group moves. The aim of this exercise is to find out where you naturally walk from so that you can either exaggerate it or deliberately lead from somewhere else. This is not to say that your walk is wrong or needs changing, but rather to make you more aware of, and therefore more in control of, your own body. We all have physical idiosyncrasies and often know about them, but our particular twitches and walking rhythms

are something we rarely see. Here, we have an audience who will show us what we do. It may be a rolling gait, a head that lolls to one side, an arm that swings up, or feet that sweep round from the side and then flick. Whatever it is, we must learn to use it to our own advantage. So, let's put our actor's body into:

The Body-Lab!

If you have time and space, let each member of the group show their walk to everyone else. In a large group this may be a luxury you cannot afford, so people should work in pairs or small groups, watching each other and making supportive observations.

Where do you walk from?

Each person in turn walks up and down in as relaxed a manner as possible. As they walk, observe them carefully. You are trying to determine where they walk from. It helps if you imagine a cord is attached to one particular part of them and is pulling them along. With some people it is obvious: you will immediately be able to say 'she walks from the knees', or 'he walks from the forehead'. Imagine the cord at different points of the body: forehead, nose, shoulders, chest, hips, thighs, knees and feet are the most common leading points. Sometimes there are two or more cords that seem equally strong. This often happens with people whose posture has been trained in some way, such as dancers. They have already had the peculiarities of their walk removed, which has advantages for formal movement, but is less interesting for character work.

Wobbles and twitches

When you have determined where people walk from, look at the other peculiarities of their walk. This is easiest to identify when walking very fast or even jogging. When walking you may be able to glide along, disguising your wobbles and twitches, but when you jog you have much less control. Relax and go for it; find out about yourself. Unless you learn about, understand and love the peculiarities of your body and the way it moves, you will find it difficult to persuade an audience to love them. If you are self-conscious, you will spend all your time on stage denying basic things about yourself. It is the actor's ability to be open about all the things that we normally expect our clothes to conceal, that enables an audience to identify with them.

Movement for character

Michael Chekhov was a pupil of Stanislavski who developed his exercises further. He suggested inhabiting a character's *imaginary body*.

To create characters with different physical features an actor must first visualise an Imaginary Body. This Imaginary Body belongs to the character, but the actor can learn to inhabit it. Through constant practice the performer can change the length and shape of the body and physically transform themselves into the character.

(Mel Gordon, The Stanislavski Technique *1987, Applause Theatre Books)*

Voice

What is a good voice, and how do you get one? In real life, as on stage, your voice conveys what you are: it tells us about your background, what you think of yourself and how you wish to be perceived by others. We know this from the 'timbre' (quality) of your voice, from your accent and from your use of vocabulary. The 'timbre' of vocal sound is something most people do not change without special help. Accents also tend to remain, although some people pick up new accents wherever they go, if they have a musical ear.

Vocabulary, however, is something over which we all have a fair degree of control. We all shift 'register' for different occasions: you will express yourself differently with family, friends, teachers or at a job interview. In some people this change is so extreme it is almost as if they have more than one personality.

Our voices can let us down at crucial moments, however; for example, confronted by someone we find really attractive, or when speaking in public, we often suddenly no longer know 'how to sound'. All our insecuri-

ties about our voices come to the surface, resulting in high-pitched squeaks, low croaks, talking drivel or not being able to speak at all. At times like these it is easy to hate your voice. We all hate our voices sometimes. We must all have had the experience of hearing ourselves recorded and disliking the sound, but some dislike them so much they work hard to change them permanently: Margaret Thatcher had voice training to lower the pitch of her voice, which helped her political career considerably.

So what is a good voice? Any voice can be a good voice if it is used well. When a voice does not sound good, it is restricted in some way. Sometimes this is caused by nervousness and other times it is because the voice is trapped in the throat or nasal area. Often it is a combination of the two. Voice exercises are designed to free up your natural voice, to use all your own vocal qualities and not to 'give you a new voice'.

TASK

1 Record three different actors whose voices you like. Give reasons for your choice.
2 Record three people you know from everyday life whose voices you like. Give reasons.
3 Write down three things you like about your own voice and three things you dislike. Give reasons.

RELAXATION AND BREATHING

They key to good voice-work is relaxation. Relaxing the whole body as well as the neck, throat and tongue, ensures that all of the body's resonators are able to do their work. You should begin your voice-work after the tense-and-relax exercise on page 46, or some other total body relaxation.

Voice exercises can be carried out in a number of positions, each with their own advantages.

Lying on your back

Lying on your back after relaxation enables you to maintain the relaxed feeling. Working with your eyes shut in this position also minimises embarrassment in groups with little or no experience in this kind of work. The danger is that energy levels will be low, so be prepared to run around afterwards.

Sitting on a chair

This requires more energy than lying down, but allows resonators to work with an upright body. It is more relaxing for extended voice-work than standing. Again, closing the eyes helps concentration.

Standing

This is the best position: good for full release of voice, directing the sound around the room and generating energy. There is a clear relation between the exercises and the function of voice when acting, but it can be tiring for long periods.

Resonance

Your body is a giant resonator. Think of yourself as a guitar – your vocal cords are the strings, but they are of little use on their own; they need to be amplified by the sound-box. Your chest is your primary sound-box, although, as we shall discover, most of the body acts as a resonator if used correctly.

After your relaxation exercises, check that no tension has crept into your shoulders, neck or throat. Take a deep breath in and hum a comfortable middle-range note. Feel the vibration in your lips. If you cannot feel it, then you need to relax your lips some more. Now place the palm of one hand directly on top of your head and the palm of the other hand on your chest. Feel the vibrations. Start with a low note and crescendo up, always checking the resonance in the lips, head and chest. Feel the note rise up from your belly, pass through your chest, up your neck and finally come out of the top of your head. Try to keep the transition smooth all the way, particularly as the sound shifts from a chest-note into a head-note. Now start at the high note and bring it all the way down.

Finding the diaphragm

The diaphragm is the muscle that controls your breathing by pushing up under your lungs to get the air out. Only by locating it and learning to work with it will you have real control over your voice as an actor and avoid unnecessary strain on your neck and throat.

Lie on your back with your feet flat on the floor and your knees raised up to take the strain off the lower back. Breathe in through the nose and out through the mouth. Concentrate on the rise and fall of your stomach and allow your back to relax into the floor. Place the backs of your hands against your lower ribs and feel the ribs opening as you breathe. Breathe in over a count of five and then out over a count of five.

Now place one hand on your belly just below the ribs. Let the breath out as a gentle pant making a soft 'Huh' sound. The pulsing movement beneath your hand is your diaphragm at work. Panting, sobbing and laughing make great use of the diaphragm which is why it hurts our stomachs sometimes when we laugh: it is just the diaphragm working hard. Now extend it to 'Huh Huh', then to 'Huh Huh Huh'. Keep each 'Huh' as strong as the others, building up the number of pushes to each breath. Increase to 15 or more, ensuring that there is no strain or tension, and that you finish before you run completely out of breath.

Feather exercise

This exercise is about pushing the voice out and extending control of the diaphragm. Lie on your back with your knees up. Relax your breathing. Take a deep breath in and sing out a quiet middle-range note, starting with the lips together and then opening the mouth. Like this:

Mmmmaaaaaaaaaaaaaaaaaaah . . .

Imagine a feather hovering just a few inches above your lips, held there by the force of the sound. Use your diaphragm to control the sound and keep it constant. Relax, breathe deeply and begin another note. This time, push the feather two feet above your open mouth, then four, then eight, until you are pushing it against the ceiling with the force of your breath. Push it beyond the ceiling if you can, just as long as you are not straining.

Variations:

- Imagine the ceiling itself is just above your lips. Push it up and down with the sound.
- Do the exercises standing, facing each of the four walls. This is particularly useful when in a performance space, allowing you to feel the space with your voice and discover what you have to do to fill it with your sound. Visualise your sound and push it into each area of the space you are in. Imagine it reaching out behind you, to the sides, up above, etc.

Golden towers

This is a wonderful meditation that releases the voice through the whole body. It needs someone to talk the group through an initial guided visualisation. After practice, however, a group can do it on their own.

Everyone takes their shoes off, and sits on the floor in a circle with backs straight (on heels or cross-legged). Close your eyes: relax into the position and find a deep breathing rhythm ('4 in / hold for 4 / 4 out / hold for 4'). Then begin:

You are sitting on the ground
The sky is blue and the sun is shining
You are on a circular platform made of
  pure gold
The platform is the top of a solid tower
  made of gold
The golden tower slowly pushes you up
  from the earth
See the ground disappearing beneath you
And feel the sun becoming brighter
Sense its golden rays of light all around
  you filling the air
Breathe the light in
Let it fill your entire body
Breathe it out through every pore
Send it streaming out in all directions
Listen to the sounds the sun-rays make
Hear them filling the air
Breathe them in with the light

Breathe them out with your own sound
Send pure sounds out from every pore in
  your body
Listen to the sounds play

The Greeks had a concept called the 'Harmony of the Spheres' and this is what it feels like you are creating. You are alone in the sky at the top of your tower, yet surrounded by sound. Let your voice out to join it. Each person must strive to believe in the tower and the light. If, for a moment, you allow yourself to think that it is just a group of people sitting on the floor singing notes, you will probably lose concentration altogether. Should this happen, just sit quietly and watch the concentration on the other faces. Do not move around or distract anyone.

You know your group has reached a high level of concentration and vocal freedom when they can release themselves into this exercise, letting out sound and light, harmonising with each other, without breaking concentration. Often, the exercise comes to a natural end, the sound tailing off. It is good if the voice talks everyone back down, letting the tower move back down toward earth until everyone is sitting back down on the ground. Everyone opens their eyes. When you do such an exercise for the first time, it is a good idea if everyone has the chance to say how they felt during it. Let each person speak in turn around the circle. Can the group make it work better next time?

Swinging alphabets

Use this as a good diaphragm loosener:

Choose a nursery rhyme. Stand straight and speak the rhyme, without pushing it.

Now bend from the waist, your feet about three feet apart and swing from side to side, bending your knees and letting your fingers brush the floor. Make it all very relaxed.

As you swing down, the breath is forced out of you and as you swing up the diaphragm forces breath back in. Keep swinging, letting the sound out as a pant: 'Huh'. Build the volume without pushing. Now go through the pure vowels on each swing, prefacing them with a 'H ...' to ensure use of the diaphragm, like this:

Hah – as in *a*ntlers
Heh – as in t*e*rrible
Hih – as in l*i*ttle
Hoh – as in b*o*ttle
Huh – as in tr*u*th

Now stand up and speak your nursery rhyme again. Feel the difference. The voice is opened up. The diaphragm pushes the sound out effortlessly. The upper body resonates easily. People have been known to produce twice the sound without even realising it!

Glottal sound

The pulsing sound you create when a word begins with a vowel (as in 'owl', 'under', 'after' etc.) is *glottal*. Run through the vowels again, this time removing the 'H' at the beginning of each one. Be conscious of pushing the sound out from the diaphragm. Place a hand on your stomach under your ribs and feel the diaphragm pulse as it did before:

Ah
Eh
Ih
Oh
Uh

This will help greatly with spoken clarity on stage. An audience often misses the sense because the beginning of a line, or word is not delivered with enough definition.

Some suggested speeches and poems are:

● Faustus' final speech in *Doctor Faustus* (Christopher Marlowe): *Christopher Marlowe, The Complete Plays*, J. B. Sloane (ed), 1986, Penguin.

- *Sailing to Byzantium* (W. B. Yeats): *Yeats Selected Poetry*, 1974, Pan Books.
- *The Wasteland* (T. S. Eliot): 1980, Faber & Faber.
- *The Jabberwocky* (Edward Lear): 1995, Barefoot Books.
- The Prologue to *Romeo and Juliet* (Shakespeare): 1988, Routledge.

TASK

Find a good, rhythmic poem and learn it. Repeat the exercise with the poem. Swing while repeating the poem, letting the sound be forced out of you. Repeat standing comfortably. Formal poetry with heightened language usually works the best. It encourages you to explore the power of your voice. Perform your poem to the group, once cold and once after a full voice warm-up. Discuss the difference.

TONGUES AND TEETH

Now the voice and its resonators are all working, it is time to concentrate on the tongues and teeth, to ensure clarity of diction. This is not about getting you to talk 'properly': it is about making sure that what you say on stage can be clearly heard, whatever your accent or linguistic register. The primary purpose of the voice is to communicate, and too much is lost on stage because actors mumble, talk too fast, or swallow the sounds they make. Here are a few exercises to get it all working. Ideally, you would run through a sequence such as this each day. Do each one of these for ten to twenty seconds:

- massage your face all over
- chew imaginary food (chew hard, really work the jaw)
- with the lips together, run your tongue all the way around your teeth
- blow kisses at everyone: long slow ones, quick fast ones
- blow raspberries
- snort like a horse
- trill your tongue
- poke your tongue out: try to lick your nose and chin ten times; move it from side to side ten times.

In her books *Voice and the Actor* and *Your Voice and How to Use it Successfully*, the voice-trainer Cicely Berry divides the consonants into categories and suggests exercises for each one. We summarise the information here, but recommend you obtain a copy of either book for your personal library. No aspiring actor should be without them!

Consonant sounds are made by interrupting the flow of air with part of the mouth. The plosives are made by the lips and teeth; read aloud the following:

De de de de de de dah	× 5
Te te te te te te tah	× 5
Be be be be be be bah	× 5
Pe pe pe pe pe pe pah	× 5
Ge ge ge ge ge ge gah	× 5
Ke ke ke ke ke ke kah	× 5
Moo Moh Mah May Mee	× 5

Tongue-twisters

'The lips the teeth the tip of the tongue'

'There'll be a tattoo at twenty to two
A ratata-tatata-tatata-too
A dragon will come and beat his drum
At a minute or two to two today
At a minute or two to two'

'Red leather yellow leather red leather
yellow leather'

'She sells sea-shells on the sea shore'

Now go back to your poem, or choose another.

Chor. O for a muse of fire, that would ascend
The brightest heaven of invention
A kingdom for a stage, princess to act,
And monarchs to behold the swelling scene!
Then should the warlike Harry, like himself,
Assume the port of Mars; and at his heels,
Leash'd in like hounds, should famine, sword and fire,
Crouch for employment. But pardon, gentles all,
The flat, unraisèd spirits that hath dar'd
On this unworthy scaffold to bring forth
So great an object. Can this cockpit hold
The vasty fields of France? Or may we cram
Within this wooden O the very casques
That did affright the air at Agincourt?
O, pardon! Since a crooked figure may
Attest in little place a million:
And let us, ciphers to this great account,
On your imaginary forces work.
Suppose within the girdle of these walls
Are now confin'd two mighty monarchies,
Whose high uprearèd and abutting fronts
The perilous narrow ocean parts asunder.
Pierce out our imperfections with your thoughts:
Into a thousand parts divide one man,
And make imaginary puissance;
Think, when we talk of horses, that you see them
Printing their proud hoofs i'th'receiving earth;
For 'tis your thoughts that now must deck our kings,
Carry them here and there, jumping o'er times,
Turning th' accomplishment of many years
Into an hour-glass; for the which supply,
Admit me Chorus to this history;
Who, prologue-like, your humble patience pray
Gently to hear, kindly to judge, our play.

Be sensitive to the texture of the language, its rhythms and meanings.

Dealing with heightened language

Shakespeare's language is rich, varied and notoriously difficult to get to grips with. Once you become familiar with some of the more archaic Elizabethan constructions, however, it seems far less daunting. Here is the opening Chorus from *Henry V*:

The speech is written in *Iambic Pentameters*: in each line there are five feet (penta–metre), each foot consisting of two beats, one short (ˇ) and one long (–). This two-beat sequence is called Iambic, and is the natural rhythm of the English language. Five feet of two beats each, makes each line ten beats long:

Suppōse withĭn thĕ girdlĕ ōf thĕse wālls

Arĕ nōw cŏnfin'd twŏ mīghtў mōnărchīes

Read through the speech, maintaining this iambic rhythm. Each line does not always fit perfectly, but it is pretty close. Some of the peculiarities of Shakespearean spelling and language are explained by this verse-structure, since things sometimes need to be changed to fit the rhythm. For example, in line 27:

> Printing their proud hooves *i'th' receiving* earth;

This is a contraction of *in the*, to make it last one beat. Or in line 28:

> For *'tis* your thoughts that now must deck our kings,

'Tis is a contraction of *it is*. We do much the same in modern English, but in slightly different ways: *it is* becomes *it's*, *do not* becomes *don't* etc. Most directors today, however, prefer clarity and comprehensibility to accurate verse rhythms so, if you cannot manage to say *i'th'* say *in the* instead.

TASK

Learn and recite this speech together, as a group.

- Enjoy its power.
- Try it outdoors.

RELAXATION, CONCENTRATION AND VOCAL IMPROVISATION

There follows a series of games and exercises designed to explore, stretch and enjoy the voice to the full. Different things work for different groups. Go with what works for you.

Finding rhythm

From speech to music and from bird-song to road-drills, all sound has rhythm. Try these exercises to develop group rhythm:

Clapping

Everyone stands in a circle. The leader then asks certain people, roughly half the group but dotted around, to sit down. You are going to clap hands in rhythm together, focusing on each group member in turn. One clap for a standing person and two for someone sitting. It is important that the group all focus on the same person at the same time or it will not work, so decide who you are starting with and go clockwise. To ensure an even rhythm, it is also best if everyone keeps a 4/4 beat in their head. Count it quietly to yourself, clapping on 1, or 1 and 2; for example:

(Leader counts four in:)

	one	two	three	four
Standing	clap	two	three	four
Standing	clap	two	three	four
Sitting	clap	clap	three	four
Standing	clap	two	three	four
Sitting	clap	clap	three	four
Standing	clap	two	three	four
(and so on …)				

Now add a complication. Whether sitting or standing, all people with black hair have three claps. Try this out. Then add in four claps for anyone wearing white. Your selection will vary according to the group and what the group is wearing. You could go with gender, shoe-colour, jeans, joggers. You can vary it each time. Keep the pauses, and some very interesting rhythms will develop.

Variations:

- Half the group clap clockwise, and the other half anti-clockwise.
- Half clap their count on the off-beat and not the on-beat, i.e.:

  1 and 2 and 3 and 4 and   becomes
  1 clap 2 clap 3 and 4 and

- Learn the entire rhythm and move to it. Turn it into vocal sound.

Into voice and back

All stand in a circle. Someone counts or gives a 4/4 beat, leaving time for the off-beat. In turn, each person introduces their own rhythm and sticks to it. When everyone is clapping, the leader gives a command: each in turn produces their rhythm vocally and stops clapping. Break the circle and start moving round the space, maintaining your rhythm. Feel how it makes you want to move. What kind of a creature is it? Find the movement that goes with the sound. Stretch it as far as you can, stamping, crawling etc. Meet other creatures, keeping your rhythm. Eventually, make your way back to the circle.

★ *hot tip*

It helps with all these things if the leader uses his/her hand as a volume control. Flat hand at knee height is quiet, chest height is normal and full stretch up is loud.

Variation:

- Meet someone else and, on a cue from the leader, take on their vocal rhythm while they take on yours. Make your way back to the circle, turn your new vocal rhythm back into a clap and finish.

Note: If your group is new to rhythm-work, practise clapping the off-beat against the on-beat. Half the group clap:

  one and *two* and *three* and *four*

while the other half clap:

  one *and* two *and* three *and* four *and*

Sound environment

This is a great exercise to discover the power of the voice. Get into groups of four or five. Decide on an environment, e.g. a zoo. Recreate it, using only voices, and perform it in the dark: keep your eyes shut. If you reproduce human voices they must not become intelligible speech, not even gibberish. Try just to give the tone and rhythm in a muffled way as if an alien had landed and was hearing all these sounds for the first time. Give yourself 15 minutes for rehearsal. Imagine the alien is moving through the environment: what would it hear at different points? Perhaps a story will develop, but don't worry about specifically creating one; it is the quality of your sound that we are interested in.

Playing with poetry

Remind yourself of the words of one of the poems you learned. Recite it to your group in the dark. Discover how much more you can create through voice alone.

- Take your poem and speak it in as relaxed a manner as you can while carrying out a number of physical tasks: climbing on chairs, crawling under tables, lifting someone up, lying down and trying to get up without using your hands etc. Use the diaphragm and try to keep your speech as fluent and as smooth as you can. Now let the positions really affect the voice. Use the rhythm of lifting boxes or climbing a ladder to affect the way you speak. It's good to do this with verse (e.g. Shakespeare) so that you are not too precious about making it sound beautiful.

- Try some choral speaking. Start with one voice and gradually add more. Can the group speak as expressively as one individual? Set off at a good pace, speaking clearly. Avoid a dull slow rhythm. Deliver the poem while playing tag: obtain a beanbag; only the person with the beanbag can speak. Throw it to people at odd moments and let them continue. Do this while running around the room.
- Take a line of verse and say it round the circle, *one word* per person: make it flow.
- Pick up on the inflection of the speaker before you. Find your own line, or try it with:

To be or not to be, that is the question.

PROJECTION

Stretching telephones

The group divides into pairs. Stand in two lines, facing your partner about three feet away. Start by improvising a telephone conversation (remember to accept offers). Gradually, you both move back. There are a lot of other conversations going on, so you have to project to keep the conversation going. Don't strain but do push the voice, enunciating clearly, making the shapes with your mouth as wide as possible to help your partner work out what you are saying.

Pushing

Face your partner in the middle of the room. Place your hands on their shoulders. They place their hands on your shoulders. Keep thumbs out of necks and lean in, taking the strain. You are going to push them across the room. They let you push, but give you resistance. Now use your voice. Reach for the far wall with your voice as you push. Make sure the sound is centred and is coming from the diaphragm. Feel the strength of your voice. Now let your partner push you.

Outdoor poetry

Go outside with your group and recite your poems to each other over increasing distances. Always check that you are pushing with the diaphragm and be conscious of any constriction in the neck or throat.

TASK

Invent your own projection exercise and try it out. (Be careful not to strain.)

SONGS IN THE ROUND

These are not only popular around campfires, they are great for voice-work, building the confidence of people as singers, and for ensemble work. As on stage, you have your part to sing, but it has to fit in with all the others. If you do your own thing, the round will not work. There are many examples; it is possible to get the music for them, but just asking people to sing them to you is usually the quickest way. Here are a few examples:

Rose Rose Rose
Shall I ever see thee wed?
Ay, marry, that thou wilt
An' thou'lt but stay

By the waters, the waters of Babylon

We lay down and wept, and wept
For thee Zion
We remember, we remember,
We remember thee Zion

London's burning, London's burning
Fetch the engines, fetch the engines
Fire fire! Fire fire!
Pour on water, pour on water

Try these in two, three and then four groupings. Once you are all singing confidently, break up and move around the room still keeping in time and, hopefully, in tune. Come back to the circle. Try taking the volume up and down.

African chants and songs are also wonderful for group work. Like the *rounds*, they are an oral tradition. If you do not know any, listen carefully at workshops. If you have difficulty remembering the tunes, take a tape-recorder.

WORD ASSOCIATION

An example of word association can be found in a play called *The Skriker*, which Caryl Churchill wrote for the National Theatre in 1994. She uses a technique of word and idea association to create a language for supernatural beings. The fact that the skriker (a vicious fairy who suffers because no one believes in her any more) freely associates, suggests that she is not inhibited like humans. It also suggests that the supernatural and our unconscious are closely linked.

Heard her boast a roast beef eater, daughter could spin span spick and spun the lowest form of wheat straw into gold, raw into roar, golden lion and lyonesse under the sea, dungeonesse under the castle for bad mad sad adders and takers away. Never marry a king size well beloved. Chip chip pan chap finger chirrup chirrup cheer up off with you're making no headway. Weeps seeps deeps her pretty puffy cream cake hole in the heart operation. Sees a little blackjack thingalingo with a long long tale awinding. May day, she cries, may pole axed me to help her. So I spin the sheaves shoves shivers into golden guild and geld and if she can't guessing game and safety match my name then I'll take her no mistake no mister no missed her no mist no mist no me no. Is it William Gylliam Guillaume? Is it John Jack the ladder in your stocking is it Joke? Is it Alexander Sandro Andrew Drewsteignton? Mephistopheles Toffeenose Tiffany's Timpany Timothy Mossycoat? No 't ain't, says I, no tainted meat me after the show me what you've got. Then pointing her finger says Tom tit tot! Tomtom tiny tot blue tit tit! Out of her

---

TASK

Read the passage through carefully, giving each word equal measure. Enjoy the internal rhymes and the play of the language. It clearly means something and yet that meaning is constantly slipping away.

- Read it round the circle one word at a time.
- Go back over the same sentence finding different rhythms.
- Take sections in groups and work out a staging, giving emotional quality to the piece.
- The emotions and tone change sharply, often several times in a line. Plot these changes and enjoy them.

pinkle lippety loppety, out of her mouth-trap, out came my secreted garden flower of my youth and beauty and the beast is six six six o'clock in the morning becomes electric stormy petrel bomb. Shriek! shrink! shuck off to a shack, sick, soak, seek a sleep slope slap of the dark to shelter skelter away, a wail a whirl a world away.

You'll notice that the text primarily tells the story of Tom Tit Tot, who is an English version of the German Rumpelstiltskin. The story is almost exactly the same. A miller boasts his daughter can spin straw into gold so that the Prince will marry her. She is then put in a dungeon with a spindle and some straw. Tom Tit

Tot offers to help if she'll give him her first born child. She agrees and he spins the straw. She marries the prince and has a child. The mischievous Tom Tit Tot turns up to claim his prize. He offers to let her keep the child if she can guess his name. A blackbird overhears him sing his name in the forest and says it to the girl who then says it to Tom Tit Tot who runs screaming into the forest. Have another look at the passage with the story in mind.

Further reading

Berry, C. (1973) *Voice and the Actor*, Harrap.
Berry, C. (1975) *Your Voice and How to Use it Successfully*, Harrap.

chapter four
DIRECTING TECHNIQUES

The role of the director is to provide a realistic framework for the actors to work within when rehearsing the play. In practice, this means that the director must furnish an understandable interpretation of the text and provide ideas about how to realise the text in production. This chapter guides the student through the vital preparation work prior to rehearsal, and helps you build your own approach. It also contains exercises to be used during rehearsal, and notes on how to reconstitute the various elements into a recognisable whole.

The role of the director

CREATE THE FEELING OF A TEAM

Use games and exercises to forge your actors into a conscious and supportive team. Cross-refer to Chapters 1 and 2 on acting and devising techniques, for detailed exercises. Work on group concentration, energy and trust is particularly important.

Play these games for their own merits initially, but you will want to develop them in tune with the specific text/production you are working on. Often it is the game that will give the structure for a scene or stage routine; e.g. a game of tag can develop into a movement sequence, or a trust exercise into a procession.

GIVE INFORMATION ABOUT TEXT/ERA/STYLE

You have chosen the play and will have some sense of what you think it is about and why you want to do it. In order to give your cast a sense of purpose and involvement, you will need to give them as much information as you can. Sell the piece, even to your cast. Be positive about it at all times. Do not assume that they will feel involved just because they want to act. Even if they are, they will work harder if they are enthused about the ideas and the style of the production.

KNOW THE PLAY

If you are working with a published play-script, read it *ten times*. Read around the story/issues, find pictures, listen to appropriate music, talk to everybody and anybody about it. As director you will eat, sleep and breathe this play, at least until the opening night.

Research tasks can and should be shared out (you cannot and should not do it all), but you must maintain an overview and look over *all* the material produced. You will, after all, have the job of structuring the final piece.

BE PREPARED

It is not a good idea just to arrive at the re-hearsal room, saying 'Right, what shall we do today?' Some directors are better at thinking on their feet than others, but you should always have some idea of what you are looking for from any particular rehearsal. If you change direction because a scene or set of characters produce the unexpected, this is good – you know something is working – but at least you have something to fall back on. Above all, your cast need to feel secure; to feel that you, at least, have a sense of where you are going and how you are going to get there. It will not always feel that way, but like a general leading an expedition, it's not always a good idea to tell your weary soldiers you think you've lost the compass.

Rehearsal structure

- rclaxation
- concentration
- physical and vocal warm-up
- reminder of work at last rehearsal – set the scene for this session's work
- improvise/rehearse
- run through what you have done
- ask questions
- make notes and give any tasks so everyone is ready for the next session.

READ-THROUGH

At some point you will need a complete read-through of the play. The whole cast should sit in a circle with note-pad, pen and copy of script. Experienced actors know not to act too much during a read-through; you are looking for an efficient reading that gives a sense of the rhythms of the piece and an initial idea of how the voices and characters might begin to work together. Less experienced performers some-times feel they need to prove themselves or jus-tify their casting, even at the read-through. While this is understandable, virtuoso readings at this stage will not enable you to get the bal-ance of the piece. Stating this at the outset will release the cast from the pressure to perform by relaxing them and enabling them also to listen to the whole play.

OTHER PRODUCTIONS

One question that always seems to crop up is whether you should watch other productions of the play you are doing. Often there are film or television versions on video readily avail-able. This is particularly true of Shakespeare, but you can also get Pinter, Chekhov, Ionesco, Mamet and many more. The fear is that the style and individual performances will have such an influence on the cast and company that you will not create your own, original production.

Provided you are not watching *in order to* copy, other productions are just another re-source for you and your cast to make use of. They can provide you with an excellent refer-ence point for your own production, begging the question, 'That's how they did it, how are we going to do it differently?' We often use a film version of a play as a short-cut to getting the story across. Usually film versions are suffi-ciently different from what is created on stage, that there is little danger of just copying them.

For example, watching Roman Polanski's *Macbeth* or Derek Jarman's *The Tempest* is unlikely to alter greatly how you would tackle the plays on stage. Recently, however, a group of students were working on a scene from *Oleanna* by David Mamet, an intense two-hander in which characterisation greatly influences where the audience's sympathies lie. In this case, it was good that the cast did not see the film version until well into their rehearsal process. In the end they actually preferred their home-grown version!

Ultimately, you will make your choice according to what is available and the style of production you are working on. Often you cannot stop intrepid actors doing their own research, so you might as well watch things together and discuss their relative merits. It is important to know what your actors have seen, otherwise strange impersonations creep in and you have no idea where they are coming from!

DURING REHEARSALS

Low concentration, restlessness and messing about are all signs that the cast are confused or have lost direction. Look for the signs and be prepared to stop for a short break, change the activity or stop and chat to find out if there are unacknowledged problems with scene, character or overall production.

If a cast is unhappy, it will turn on the director. Should this happen, be aware that there is no one else they can turn on, so don't take it personally; it's a necessary part of the process. They are often looking for reassurance.

REGULAR FEEDBACK

It's best to build in some method for getting regular feedback from the cast and company. We suggest a free feedback circle. This involves everyone meeting in a circle and having the opportunity to say something about the day/ session *without interruption or comeback*. Take it in turns, going in one direction round the circle. Each person is entitled to a brief statement or to 'pass'. This will often need some practice, as it involves each member of the group finding the self-discipline to keep quiet even when they are desperate to give an opinion. Discuss the principles of the exercise, avoid making things personal and do not be drawn into personal defence: you must lead by

example. Reflect quietly on what has been said and consider how it might affect the way you proceed. Often these sessions involve huge amounts of praise and enthusiasm, so don't panic! A circle should ideally be held at the end of each rehearsal day/session. Depending on the size of the company and the time available, decide how often you can afford to have one and block it into the rehearsal schedule.

Feedback sessions are particularly important in a large cast. When rehearsing individual scenes, actors can easily lose a sense of being part of a bigger company, and sight of the direction of the production.

YOUR PERSONALITY AS DIRECTOR

How you present yourself will make a huge difference to your effectiveness as a director. You have to play a number of different roles at

different times (sometimes the director has to be the best actor of all!) and you will need to include these possibilities in the personality you present. If you are too stern, too soft, too jokey, too distant, some of them will not work. Here is a rough list of some of the titles on your job description:

- chairman/woman
- personnel manager
- guide
- friend
- counsellor
- parent
- academic
- mediator
- slave-driver
- disciplinarian
- coach
- expert
- energiser
- resource
- interpreter
- communicator
- publicist
- trainer
- facilitator
- scapegoat
- chef.

TASK

Put the job-titles above in order of priority, and give reasons for your choice. Do you agree with them all? Or are there some things here that are not the director's responsibility? Either way, you can see from this that there is much more to directing than just saying where people should move on stage!

Choosing the play

We have talked at great length about the process of devising elsewhere in this book. For the purposes of this chapter, therefore, we will assume that we are going to work with a published play-text. Your first task is to decide which play you are going to do. Subsidised theatres will often have their own script departments (The Royal Court, The Traverse, The National Theatre, etc.) which read and advise on new scripts; but often, in both education and the professional theatre, it is the director who decides which text will be worked on.

This involves reading a huge number of plays. In order to help the director, many amateur theatre groups operate reading committees. Recommended scripts are then brought to a play-reading session to help the group choose. Within a school/college you will often seek a recommendation from a tutor, particularly as the restrictions of time mean you may be directing only a section of a full play.

TASK

Get a complete list of play-texts available from your school/college library.

- Is it broad enough?
- Are there plays from all different eras and cultures?
- Are female playwrights represented as well as male?
- Are playwrights from non-western traditions well represented?

If the answer to any of these questions is 'no', talk to your tutors or teachers, and see if you can draw up a purchase list. What kind of budget does your library have? If it is small or non-existent, think of an appropriate sponsored event to raise the money.

In educational theatre the reasons for choosing a play range from giving your cast performing opportunities, to exploring a particular play or writer. Ideally, you can combine these two reasons, but this means you are looking for a play with a set number of characters (often quite large), and with a particular balance of male and female parts. This can become a nightmare even for the most experienced director.

NEEDS ASSESSMENT

It is a good idea to do a quick *needs assessment* on you and your group. Writing down what people need in order to explore and develop will help you make your decision with maximum information. This can be done in discussion, but bear in mind that quieter people often do not have their say in such a forum. A brief, written questionnaire will often elicit a more honest response from everyone: see Figures 4.1 and 4.2 below.

The group's needs

Figure 4.1   *The group's needs – a questionnaire*

1   What types of play have you already explored?
----

2   What kind of play would you like to explore?
----

3   Which skill are you interested in exploring/required to explore?

Acting   Dance/movement   Song/music   Technical

Design   Administration/marketing   Other

4   Please give a brief statement of what you are looking for from the next production.

You may not have the luxury of time for such a democratic process, but if you do, it will often guide your choice and make it easier for you to sell the idea of the production to the cast, because *you have already considered all the options*. Often you will have an initial idea, and this process will just serve to confirm that you have made the right choice. Nothing makes for an unhappier cast than forcing them into the wrong production for the wrong reasons. It will make your job as director so much more difficult.

Now use the results of your survey to analyse your own needs and the constraints and opportunities they present.

The director's needs

Figure 4.2   *The director's needs – a questionnaire*

---

1   What types of play have *you* already explored?
----

2   What kind would *you* like to explore?
----

3   What are the demands of the course/assignment?
----

4   What facilities do you have access to:

    for rehearsal
----

    for performance
----

    lighting
----

    sound
----

    other?
----

5   How long do you have for this production?
----

6   How large is the cast?
----

7   What is the balance of male/female?
----

8   What particular skills are available from your company?

    Production   Technical   Movement   Music   Acting

On this basis, draw up a shortlist of plays and/or scenes from plays, and then ask yourself the following questions:

- Do you need copyright permission. If so is it available and how much will it cost?
- Can you sell the play to the company?
- Is there an audience for the play and does it suit you?
- Can you direct comedy, tragedy, social realism, epic etc.?

Before the detailed 'diary of a production' (page 112), we have included an interview with Ewan Marshall of the *The Graeae Theatre Company*, in which he describes the nature of their casting process and discusses his role as director.

Interview with Ewan Marshall: discussion on *Fleshfly*, the *Graeae*'s version of *Volpone* by Ben Jonson

The Graeae are a theatre company of disabled actors. They are renowned for their difficult and challenging work. We discussed their recent adaptation of Volpone, featuring Nabil Shaban, one of the company's founder members.

SYNOPSIS OF THE PLAY

A wealthy man, Volpone, pretends to be terminally ill. He has no heirs and all his wealth will be bequeathed to whoever he likes most when he writes his will. A variety of greedy men and women heap gifts on him, in the hope that they will inherit his wealth.

His manservant, Mosca, facilitates the deception, by telling his master that one would-be heir, Corvino, has a very beautiful wife, Celia. Volpone desires her, and attempts to rape her. To avoid punishment, he pretends that he is dead and that Mosca is his heir. Mosca takes possession of his master's money and keys, but they are both exposed and punished by the court.

One significant structural change made for *Fleshfly* was that Celia was Corvino's virgin bride-to-be, and was played by a man.

You have just produced an adaptation of Volpone *with a cast with varying disabilities and degrees of disability. How did you cast the production?*
What we always do on our productions is to have a practical development workshop. I don't cast when I go into the workshops, and there are no guarantees for the actors that it will go any further. It works both ways as well; they are not guaranteeing that they will be in it if I offer them a part. It's pure development. Everybody's employed, everybody's working on it and I'm trying to find the team that will do the play. Obviously, I have some notion of casting when I do that, so it was perhaps always clear that Nabil was going to be Volpone, but that wasn't confirmed until after the workshop.

The most important thing at these workshops is exploring the play to see whether it is a good play for us to do, particularly when it is an existing classic and essentially grotesque theatre; *Volpone* is full of negative characters. The central message of this play, after all, is that moral imperfection leads to physical imperfection: Volpone's original family, his bastard offspring, the hermaphrodite, the eunuch, the dwarf, fulfil the classic role of literature. They are the warning, they are the bizarre. Some of the actors were rather hesitant, asking 'Is this a big own goal?' To solve this I wanted to bring the family forward, and actually work from the premise that the family are presenting the show. How far that would go we didn't really know. We actually ended up staying quite faithful to the original, and just doing a condensed version, although everything was rewritten to accommodate certain actors. Such practicalities exist for any theatre group. We had to bring it down to six actors and an interpreter, and we needed to check if that would work.

The writer, Trevor Lloyd, was at the development workshop, and we worked together beforehand setting up the framework for exploration. The central factor in deciding whether or not it is a good piece for us, is *satire*; whether it is an ironic thing to do, to play Volpone when the man feigning illness is actually a severely disabled man in a wheelchair. For *Volpone* we had a very good workshop period and those who were uncertain ended up saying 'No, this isn't an own goal for disabled people, this is really empowering.'

The next stage is to work on the condensing, working out who will be best playing whom and improvising around scenes. We were rewriting it to make it accessible, not only so that disabled performers could manage it, but also for the audience, because it's a classical play and needs updating. If you sit down and read the original *Volpone*, even with a classical dictionary, you will spend a long, long time and still not achieve what was originally intended; it just goes past an audience. I don't think that's worth doing really. I was much more interested in Trevor taking the intention and making it more obvious, more accessible, so that it is relevant to a wider audience and not just a museum piece.

Essentially, we played around; I think we spent six days on this by the end of which we had cast and decided on the structure after testing the original idea. We also workshopped some of the most difficult things like the big courtroom scenes, some of which were done better after two hours in a workshop than we perhaps managed in the actual show. Sometimes, in a workshop, people are quite bold and will just go with something, whereas when you have more time, self-doubt creeps in and some of the courage goes. We did some quite absurd things, such as the whole court scene dissolving into chickens, improvisational moments which were quite rich but never fully recaptured.

The main thing is that the development workshop feeds the writer who can then go away knowing what to write, what about and for whom, which is particularly important in a company of disabled actors. As a result, Trevor's first draft was very good and written very much with our actors in mind. It's very important to have as many of the creative team working on the project as early as possible: writer, designer and movement specialist.

What kind of work would you ask a movement specialist to do?
Uri Roodner works from impulses and ideas that are not physically prescriptive. He works with freedom, with possibilities. I am bored by a lot of choreography, however technically excellent, because it seems so contained. In rehearsal Uri would often lead the session. I might say 'This is what I want for this scene', particularly the court scene, and ask him to be really bold; he would take it away and work on it. What is particularly interesting for us with Uri is his Bouffon work. It has been very valuable for us; our company has been very much a company of outsiders.

What is Bouffon?
It evolved in medieval France. Outside the walls of the city would be the undesirables who had been kicked out of town. These would include all the riff-raff and certainly the disabled. Once a year they would come back in to perform to the lords and masters. It was that one gracious act where you were allowed back in, you were entertained, you were fed, and you would perform. Parodies would go down well, and the performers clearly performed from an enormous level of hate, but should they ever display that in the slightest way, then they would be killed. They had no status or power. There was a level of cheek and satire allowed in the performance, but it must always be hidden, contained, held back.

If we're doing satire and black comedy, it is a very valuable thing for us to explore. It's also a very interesting approach to movement. Certainly one of the great strengths of Bouffon is learning to achieve a lot by doing very little, virtually nothing on stage. For a company of disabled people, Bouffon articulates theatrically what our lives off stage are like.

An example of this is when we were working on our last show, *Ubu* (see Text Focus in Chapter 5, page 155–56), which is also grotesque theatre like *Volpone*, though also wildly different (one terribly made schoolboy play contrasted with a recognised well-made play). We were working with students at Lancaster University, exploring Jarry's sense of anarchy and shared sense of humour; but we were bored with the campus, so we set off for Morecombe, a rather run-down seaside resort. The whole programme was being videoed: we tried to guess how long it would take after we got out of the mini-bus before someone asked us 'Are you happy?' and patted one of the company on the head. Nobody got it right, it was so quick, it took ten seconds and it was the traffic warden; literally, it took *ten seconds.*

We were quite a sensation in Morecombe. There are lots of disabled people in Morecombe, but they were all being led by someone. We were really confusing because we were a group of disabled people that had no leader, no able-bodied person with a white coat on saying 'This way'. Jamie, who played Ubu, got on the go-carts; the organisers patted him on the head and then watched in shock as he sped around the track. He was very polite. That is the essence of Bouffon: you are always polite, but you're constantly sending people up.

Back at the university, there was a porter, who we used for a character in one of our plays. He once said 'Alright, one of you in this group is disabled. Which one of you is having the disabled room?' We said, 'Have a browse, *you* decide.' He replied, 'No, one of you must have the disabled room ...' Finally one of us said, 'Oh alright then, I'll be disabled,' and shouted 'I am!' That is where Bouffon takes our off-stage life onto the stage. There is a level of aggression and contempt for your audience, but it actually becomes a rather warm thing. In the theatre itself, of course, it risks being very alienating.

In *Ubu* and *Volpone* there isn't a redeeming character in sight. Every vice is on display. And I think you reach another level when you play it with a whole group of disabled people. Sometimes, there is a low expectation about our work. Not always, of course, but people come with all kinds of attitudes and some are really quite shocked to see that there are genuinely good actors, that there's actually a great deal of wit, intelligence and thought about what you're doing. Although neither of these plays are about disability as such, they can be and were about *being disabled*, because we are doing them, and because of the angle that we are taking on them.

Isn't it also because the expectation of disabled people is that they will be cute, they will be nice, and you're putting them in roles where they have to be grotesque and offensive?
Very much so. Some of our deaf actors are just so pleased to be able to swear in sign language on stage. Part of our workshop is to make up new swearwords, to explore sign language a little bit further,

give your worst ones and make some compound ones. Particularly with sign language, people have this patronising idea, the *Children of a Lesser God* thing, that 'it's great, it's really nice', so to use it in a violent, aggressive, dirty, offensive way is massively liberating. When that extends to playing nasty people it's sometimes a great joy. You easily end up clinging to a narrow definition of what a positive role model is; for disability that is limiting and inaccurate and untrue.

Your last few productions have been adaptations of classics, albeit in a grotesque style. Do you create original work as well?

Yes. Our next play is a co-production with a theatre company called *Basic Theatre*, a black-led, deaf theatre company. It will be a new piece essentially attacking white liberalism in the disability sector, although it's also much wider than that. The writer, Ray, went to a workshop in the States entitled *Very Special Arts*. There was a bit of a warning in the title there, and, needless to say, within five minutes he found himself holding a balloon watching the American National Anthem in sign language. I think this whole piece is his revenge on how reduced he felt by that experience.

It also explores the way in which religion is responsible for the bad experience that disabled black people have. He's calling it *Sympathy for the Devil*. We're also going to do an adaptation of Rabelais' *Gargantua* and possibly Gogol's *The Government Inspector*. In addition Nabil Shaban is writing a new piece for us, so there will be a mixed programme.

Do you find it more difficult to sell the original work?

Originally, the company did all its own work and used to be perceived in a certain way. Probably the most destructive perception was that it was just 'worthy'. In fact, there really is good and bad theatre, and it was very liberating when we decided to work on a classic. Suddenly people started saying, 'oh, actually, they're not just worthy, this is a very good company'. Doing classic plays does bring in a different audience. It will be interesting to see, after two classics, who comes to see this production. It's certainly booking well.

You renamed Volpone *and called it* Fleshfly. *Was that to signal that you were doing an adaptation or to conceal the fact that you were doing a classic?*

To show it was an adaptation. We didn't know how far it would adapt, but we always publicised it as coming from *Volpone*.

Who makes the decision as to the next production?

I do.

How long have you worked with the company?

Four and a half years.

Prior to that, did you work as a director?

Yes, in various community theatres and freelance jobs. I have been associate director at the London Bubble and Theatre Venture.

Did you train as a director?

I did a drama degree and you have to direct something as part of your degree, which got me interested. There's not much actual training for directors about, you learn it as you go along. In *The Graeae* we have an associate director and we're planning to start a traineeship for a disabled director. The Arts Council are interested, and we've already created a traineeship for administrators.

Do you think about Brecht, Stanislavski or Artaud in your directing work?

Not very consciously, but I couldn't possibly not assimilate. I'm familiar with all those people and I've read a lot of their work. Everywhere in the theatre you are assimilating, and you will be taking on aspects of the work of all those people. They've had a profound impact on theatre. I'm not aware of following one doctrine or person as such, although the person I admire most is Peter Brooke. His way of distilling complex theatre to what appears simple is fantastic. The best theatrical experience I've ever had was watching the *Mahabharata* over three nights. I had thought, 'No interval, over three hours each night, a hard bench', and at the end of the third night I couldn't bear for it to end. It was seamless, wonderful theatre. I find all his writing on theatre to be inspiring – it always makes you want to do something. Antonin Artaud really inspired me as well; barmy, yes, but makes you want to do things. Theatre of Cruelty is very interesting.

To what extent do you consciously aim to change people's perceptions through your theatre (both of disabled people and of disabled theatre)?

We always think about audience to some extent. We think about the effect the work is having, and that is affected by who we play to. For us that is both a disabled and non-disabled audience, so we are working on a number of different levels. With some things we do there'll be an instant shorthand, and 90 per cent of the disabled people out there will know what we mean immediately; they will be way ahead of the non-disabled members of the audience, because it's not their experience.

We try to be inclusive: you want to attract people, to bring people into your world. If you just attacked an audience or hectored them, then you genuinely would alienate them. In Berlin, one magazine reviewed *Ubu* and said 'this company achieve an alienation other companies can only dream of'. In the home of Bertolt Brecht we were chuffed with that, as a warm and inclusive comment! If your audience understand what you are doing, you can take them with you and keep needling them, challenging and prodding them, in a positive way. The key is to challenge people and push their thinking a bit further.

There is an interesting example in *Fleshfly* when Volpone comes to the court, feigning severe illness. Nabil came on as Volpone and exaggerated his disability, took on a different impairment (something akin to severe cerebral palsy) and then added enormous dribbling. That punched a hole in certain delicacies straight away, and played all kinds of games for both disabled and non-disabled audiences. He was actually doing a skit on Daniel Day Lewis! On top of that you have the added irony of an all-disabled cast accusing him of malingering.

Another aspect is Volpone's sexual attack on Celia. The all-disabled cast are looking at him and saying 'Could this man do anything sexual?' This goes back to what I was saying about disabled people and casting. Nabil doesn't normally get cast as someone who could be capable of rape, or is sexually wicked or attractive. But here as Volpone he does all those things and people are not ready for it. He's a very robust, physical actor and the audience see him about to rape someone, and then you increase the disability and he comes back on looking even more impaired; we ask, could this person do something like that?

Yes. I found that moment very disturbing, and also the attempted rape when Volpone used his fingers on Celia, whom you altered to be a virgin, so his fingers were covered in blood. That challenged two things: a disabled person's supposed lack of sexual interest and the brutal violence of the act.
Yes. That was the only bit that we received complaints about. Some people found it offensive. I feel that pretending it's just a normal 'ha-ha, chase-me-round-the-bed' routine is offensive. I wouldn't accept the complaint. I just felt 'that's your problem'. When something is turned into a saucy seaside postcard in a dark play like *Volpone* then you're ignoring something, you're hiding and trivialising it.

The extraordinary thing was that those who complained accepted the fact that the scene was played between two men, one in a wheelchair and the other a deaf man in a two-dimensional dress; for them that wasn't the issue. It was good that the theatricality was accepted.

It's also interesting when you get that degree of gen-

uine shock. If you haven't done it *just* to shock, then it's usually achieved something. We certainly didn't do it just to shock. We thought long and hard about it. Some of the cast were uncertain. I felt that you cannot pretend the play itself is liberal; it isn't, it's a deeply male, misogynistic (woman-hating) play. You can use that, you can comment on it, but the worst thing you can do is ignore it.

What differences are there between a disabled and a non-disabled theatre group?
There are differences, but I would want to emphasise the similarities. We are trying to be a good theatre company like every theatre company in the land, and our artistic influences are largely the same. The differences are there, of course, and are largely practical. For example, on our last two or three shows, we worked in two languages right through rehearsal and into production – British Sign Language (BSL) and English. My feeling is to put people where they are strongest. Disabled people are usually put where they are weakest, but if somebody's first language is BSL, then they will work better in that language than in English. We play to people's strengths.

There are, of course, extra requirements. You need interpreters in rehearsal; the writer needs to take the grammatical differences between those languages into account; everything has to be translated, which is the biggest difference. Instead of having an interpreter's platform at the side, we have been trying to make it much more inclusive, integrating it more into the performance.

Another factor is that disabled actors are denied access to training, so you're always working with people who are new to theatre, without a frame of reference, often without an arts background. Take Jamie, for example: *Ubu* was his first show – he was brilliant and received fantastic reviews. He was working alongside others with a wealth of training and previous experience and they all have to be rehearsed together. You cannot just assume common ground, unlike a non-disabled company where everyone has been to drama school and done a number of shows. We don't have a company like that so we work in different ways.

Accommodation, transport and building access are clearly also issues, but they're the easiest to overcome. Our physicality as a company influences how we make work, but it is far more positive and creative than negative.

Who funds you?
The Arts Council of Great Britain, London Arts

Board, Camden Council, London Boroughs Grants Scheme and a variety of Trusts and Foundations. Our biggest funder is the Arts Council.

How conscious are you of your funders in your programming?
The more I do, the more I am convinced that the best thing you can do is please yourself. Obviously, you do take your funders into consideration and you will have agreed to produce a certain amount of work, but there must be flexibility.

Are there comparable companies abroad?
No. I've not found a single disabled-led company outside Britain.

Diary of a production

In order to make the processes of directing as clear as possible, we are going to look at a particular production from start to finish. We have chosen a production by a group of second year students on a BTEC National Diploma in Performing Arts. Their assignment is to stage an adaptation of *Oedipus The King* and *Antigone*, both by Sophocles.

Note: The exercises and activities developed during the process and outlined below can be adapted to fit almost any production. They are not exclusive to these plays or to Greek drama alone.

TASK

As you read the following descriptions, bear in mind a recent or current production of your own. At each point cross-refer to your own experience. Could any of these exercises and activities have been adapted to suit your production? Did you have a totally different approach? Could you have used some of your ideas here? Our list is by no means exhaustive; it is simply composed of things we find have been effective and successful.

Oedipus the King and Antigone

WHY CHOOSE THESE PLAYS?

1 The plays have been chosen because of their grand themes, powerful language and the opportunity they provide for creativity in all areas of production, in particular, movement and music.
2 Being classic verse texts, they are suitable for radical adaptation – it is often much easier to try different staging ideas out with a classic (Greek, Roman, Elizabethan/Jacobean, medieval etc.) than a modern play. We want to squeeze both plays into one two-hour performance, so some drastic cutting and adapting is necessary!
3 It is a requirement of the course of study that students explore movement, voice and music-making as part of the performance. No-one knows exactly what form the singing and dancing of the Chorus in a Greek tragedy took, but we do know that they sang and danced. A fantastic opportunity to create our own material around a flawless dramatic structure.
4 We have a group of 29 students. Doing both plays will give more opportunity for individuals to explore different roles and aspects of the production process.
5 *Oedipus The King* is an 'A' level set text. A production will benefit 'A' level students and hopefully attract an audience from other schools/colleges.

> ## TASK
>
> Choose a target group and select a play (or section of a play) for them. Justify your choice. Try to give at least four or five comprehensive reasons.

The first thing you have to do is know the play(s). Here is our programme note to the audience about Sophocles and his trilogy of plays:

Sophocles

Sophocles (c.497–406 BC) wrote 123 plays and won 24 victories in Athens' annual dramatic contests. Of these, only 7 tragedies are preserved in full.

Sophocles introduced certain technical innovations to the Greek stage which made the drama more realistic. According to Aristotle, Sophocles added a third actor, introduced scene painting, and increased the chorus from 12 to 15 members. The third actor allowed for more complex characterisations and a wider range of personal encounters. Aristotle praises Sophocles for his close integration of the chorus into the action.

The Theban Legend

Many writers of the classic Greek period (500–300 BC) borrowed from this well-known legend for their drama. Sophocles' trilogy of plays is the best known example and certainly represents the pinnacle of his achievement.

OEDIPUS

According to legend, Oedipus is fated by Apollo to kill his father and marry his mother. To avoid this, his parents, Laius and Jocasta, plot his murder as a baby. Chance intervenes, however, and the baby is adopted and grows up in Corinth. As a young man Oedipus hears of the prophecy and runs away to avoid fulfilling it. Unwittingly, however, he does so: he meets and kills his real father on the road.

He arrives in Thebes, not knowing it is his birthplace, and finds it in the grip of a plague sent by The Sphynx, a mythical beast made up of lion, woman and bird, who will not release the city until someone solves her riddle. Oedipus solves it and saves the city. He marries Jocasta and becomes King. They have four children together and all is well for 15 years until plague strikes again: this is where the play begins. Sophocles starts here because he wants to show us the moment when Oedipus *discovers* the truth. He is warned off the search many times, but somehow he is compelled to know; that drive is the source of his tragedy.

OEDIPUS AT COLONUS

This second play was written last, when Sophocles was an old man. It is the most static and least dramatic of the three, although containing some beautiful passages. The essence of the story is that Oedipus, blind and exiled, seeks sanctuary at Colonus, outside Athens. Creon, now king of Thebes, tries to bring him back to appease the gods. Oedipus refuses and goes off to die. His two sons (and brothers) fight for control of Thebes. Both are killed. Creon orders that Eteocles, defender of Thebes, should be buried with full military honours, and that Polynices, attacker of Thebes, should be left to rot in the field – a dishonourable fate for any soldier.

ANTIGONE

Although the last in the trilogy, *Antigone* was written first, some 25–30 years before *Oedipus the King*. It is a conflict of ideals, embodied in the characters of Creon and Antigone. Antigone breaks the law and buries the body of her dead brother, Polynices; she is punished for it. Creon is the ruler, advocating that a state needs strong leadership in order to survive. Antigone represents the individual, presenting Creon with a dilemma he is unable to resolve. His inability to acknowledge his mistakes leads to tragedy.

A NOTE ON THE CHORUS

In ancient Athens the Chorus were all men who sang

and danced on stage. Their function was to observe and comment on the action – a sort of 'on-stage audience' interpreting and reflecting on the information for the real audience. Successive Greek writers relied on the chorus less and less, but when Sophocles was writing, the Chorus was at its height. They spoke or sang in heightened, poetic language designed to accentuate the feelings of the audience.

TASK

What have you found out about the play you are directing? Present it in a clear format, using words and terms that your cast will understand. Let your enthusiasm come across.

Remember: you have to sell the production to the cast and take them with you at all times.

GROUP TASK

All present your research, in turn. The group then assess how well the directors have done in convincing them that the proposed play is:

- exciting
- challenging
- possible with institutional constraints
- saleable
- appropriate for the group, its interests and abilities.

Casting

First of all, you need a comprehensive knowledge of the play and its characters, so that you know what you are looking for. Make notes and keep them near you during audition. Make detailed notes on each person that you see – if you are seeing a number of people you will quickly forget.

At audition you are looking for several things:

- physical type
- vocal quality and range
- movement quality
- ability to improvise
- ability to work creatively with others
- ability to take direction
- emotional range
- specialist skills – dancing, singing etc.

You may prioritise these differently depending on the production. Often the ability to improvise, work with a group or respond well to direction is as important, if not more so, than the physical appearance of an actor.

Try to avoid an *us and them* approach. Auditions are very stressful things for actors, so you should do all you can to put them at their ease. Explain what you are looking for from the audition and why you are setting the exercises suggested. You will get more out of them in the end.

While it is a perfectly reasonable idea to ask people to learn a particular speech from the play and audition for a particular part, you would do well to avoid anything that encourages 'star' mentality.

key point

All the great formative directors of the twentieth century (including Stanislavski, Brecht, Grotowski, and Brook) have opposed the star system. All have sought to create ensemble companies. With the exception of the RSC, the National Theatre and a host of struggling small-scale companies, the majority of British casts are put together for one season or show – often with only two or three weeks' rehearsal.

Audition methods

You will find out most if you give your actors a short extract to learn and give them a series of tasks appropriate to the production and characters in hand.

Always foster the notion of *ensemble* in your cast. This is the French word for 'together', and was originally coined to describe the togetherness of musicians in an orchestra. The word was later adopted by practitioners in the theatre keen to encourage the same approach to acting. Having 'stars' works directly against good group-work on stage. It is, however, useful to know that a performer can learn and develop a part, so hear a prepared piece that is relevant to the play, as well as doing some workshop material.

Workshop Casting for *Oedipus The King* and *Antigone* by Sophocles

Ask all the women auditioning to learn the following lines from Antigone:

> This is a mockery!
> My dying is no joke!
> I am no figure of fun, no child
> To be humiliated and insulted
> As I leave you forever
> Victimised as I am
> By an unjust law.

– and all the men these from Oedipus:

> Is there any man on earth
> More miserable than I am?
> Every god will hate me.
> No-one will speak to me.
> I cursed the murderer.
> And the weight of that curse
> Now falls on me.

These lines are now your resource. You can ask people to say them separately, together, whisper them, shout them and speak them with as many different tones as you wish. See people in twos or fours; this will enable you to see how they improvise, work with each other and work with text. Men and women create different dynamics on stage, so try to see mixed groups if you can, to get as much variety as possible.

If you do not know the group in question, play a few warm-up games to put them at their ease, and then move onto the more challenging material.

The key to these exercises is helping people find and use their own energy and explore their emotional range. Here are a few ways of working with our selected lines (but they could be used with almost any text).

The gateway

You need a minimum of four people for this exercise (see Figure 4.3). Create a gateway with chairs, stage-blocks or a pool of light. This should face the front of the stage. Ask your small group of auditioneers to move around the stage mumbling or whispering the lines. In turns *but in no particular order*, they approach the gateway and say some or all of their section of text, and then move through the gateway, round and back onto the stage.

Figure 4.3   *The gateway*

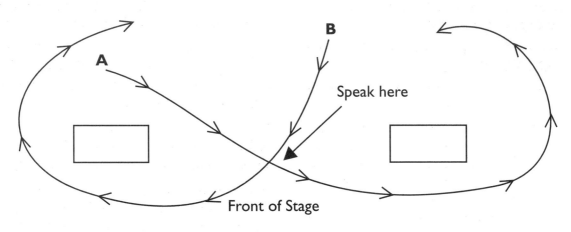

As a group, ask them to try out different emotions and tones, and gradually to build the intensity and frequency of their visits to the gateway until they are literally shunting each other aside in their urgency to tell their story. Insist that they function as a group and lift the energy *together*. Anyone clearly trying to show themselves at the expense of others could be difficult to work with in rehearsal.

You will soon get a sense of who searches well for new expression and tone, and who times their arrival well; i.e. is aware also of the other people on stage who may be heading for the gateway.

Note: if two or more people arrive at the gateway at the same time, it is important that they are not put off but still say their lines. If they are clever they will say their lines together, using each other's energy.

Once the group has reached a crescendo, or you realise they simply cannot produce any more, thank them and offer them each the chance to say the lines on their own, either just once or repeating them two or three times so that they can build the energy and emotion. By the end of this simple exercise, you should have a clear idea of people's ability to work both alone and collectively.

Conversations

Next, ask your actors to work in pairs and use the same piece of text to have a conversation. Use the text as a loop so that the scene keeps going: i.e. as soon as one actor has said the last line they both go back to the beginning. Get them to explore as many different emotions as they can, co-operating with each other at all times, allowing their bodies and voices to respond to the demands they make on each other.

Note:

- If actors are having difficulty, prompt them by suggesting different *emotions* or *situations*.

⭐ *hot tip*

If you are unsure of how well the exercises will work, try them out with a few people prior to the audition, to get an idea of what you might be looking for.

The solo piece

You might only have time to hear a prepared solo piece, or it may be your preferred audition method. A typical audition instruction in both amateur and professional theatre is to prepare two pieces, which should be:

- fully learned (provide a copy of the script)
- from a published play
- of between one and two minutes in length
- contrasting in style.

As you listen to the pieces and jot down some questions to ask about the characters' backgrounds and motivations, in order to check understanding of the pieces. If you have time, give the actors a task to perform with one or more of the speeches. For example, if it was a classical speech, ask them to do it as if they were chatting in a pub; if it was a comic monologue, ask for it as a funeral oration. You want to see if they can respond to improvisation tasks. They will have rehearsed their pieces and may well have received direction on it elsewhere. You want to know how flexible and creative they are going to be in your rehearsals.

If possible, give time for a sight-reading from the play for which you are auditioning. This is also an excellent test of an actor's speed at picking things up from a text.

When they have finished, be positive. If you feel someone has not done well, try not to show it; they will feel bad enough already.

Put a cast list up as soon as you possibly can to relieve unnecessary anxiety. There will always be some dashed hopes and bruised egos, but everyone will generally accept your decisions if they can see that you have gone through a thorough and fair process.

CASTING WITHOUT AN AUDITION

When you know a group well, you certainly can cast without an audition; in the professional theatre, known actors rarely audition. But in our experience, particularly within education, groups get a great deal out of the audition process. First of all, it is always good experience and requires actors to get their pieces together. Secondly, groups who are used to each other function very differently under audition conditions and it is valuable for you as director to witness that transition. Thirdly, it is an ideal opportunity to establish yourself in your directorial role, to introduce the play and the production methods. Finally, it will not seem a waste of time if you introduce workshop exercises that are geared towards the production; simply treat it as the first rehearsal.

★ *hot tip*

There are no small parts. Only small actors.
(Konstantin Stanislavski)

The brainstorming session

Sometimes it can help to generate a whole body of ideas with a company by brainstorming. This works well in small groups, but you can also do it with large numbers. Use the technique at any point in the production process, for a whole show or perhaps just for one scene or character.

You need a board or large sheet of paper (flip-chart or bigger), someone selected to write suggestions up (the scribe) and a marker pen. As director it will be your job to introduce the session and deal with the information as it emerges. Decide what you are looking for from the session; this will depend on the point you have reached in the process.

- If you want to gather information on a particular character, write down the name of the character on the page, and ask for immediate responses to, and first impressions of, the character. All responses should be noted and grouped after further discussion.

- Imagine that you have just read *Macbeth*, and you want a modern understanding of the operations of fate/witches/magic etc. Use this method to ask the company for as many suggestions as possible.

Brainstorm on *Oedipus/Antigone*

In a brainstorming session, we came up with the following ideas:

power sickness prophecy justice sex death
birth doing right bunker fallout dictatorship punk
futuristic desert blindness dance ritual discovery
finding the truth song pain suffering arrogance
mutation incest taboo Freud storytelling militarism
aggression rubbish trash TV surveillance plague
rations geiger counters rebellion hanging scared

These could then be grouped together:

Set/props	Costume	Character	Image	
trash	punk	dictatorship	sex	ritual
rubbish	mutation	aggression	death	blindness
rations	militarism	rebellion	birth	prophecy
bunker	ritual	discovery	dance	plague
futuristic	sickness	finding the truth	song	
desert		power	pain	
TV surveillance		justice	suffering	
geiger counters		doing right	taboo	
fallout		arrogance	incest	
		scared	rebellion	

As a result of our brainstorming, we decided that, for *Oedipus*, we were looking to create a post-nuclear world, immediately after the apocalypse, as people try to establish a new society from the wreck of the old. The Sophocles play begins with Thebes in the grip of a plague. This plague, we decided, would be radiation sickness. For *Antigone*, society had moved on. Creon had established control and was absolute ruler, but had no faith in his own power. He had become a tyrant, addressing people from video monitors around the stage in a futuristic techno-world. We needed, then, to create these worlds on stage and to find appropriate movement and performance styles.

TASK

Run a brainstorming session for *your* production.

SHOULD THE DIRECTOR PROVIDE ALL THE IDEAS?

It is much more rewarding if you can involve the whole group in the process. This doesn't mean the director cannot or should not have ideas of their own; it means acknowledging that sometimes two, five or twenty heads can be better than one. Ultimately, yes, the director must choose, and has the final say as to what actually happens on stage, but why not increase the pool of ideas you have to choose from?

By having regular discussions, brainstormings and feedback sessions, you are also democratising the process, i.e. allowing everyone the opportunity to have input. It is then easier to pick the best ideas without people getting upset that their ideas are being rejected. People can become very possessive about their ideas, and you need to find tactful ways of discarding the ones that are inappropriate to the production.

Be wary of having an idea in your head and expecting the group to come up with it. You will be disappointed if they don't and you will want to keep hold of your idea anyway. Be honest when you have a fixed idea in your head, and find ways of letting the group try it out.

Note: you cannot incorporate everyone's ideas, so it is advisable not to try.

> ★ *hot tip*
>
> You never know where the good 'idea' will come from. It is often from the most unexpected source.

Forming the production team

The basic roles of the production team can be found in Chapter 5, pages 149–53.

It is your job, as director, to liaise with all of these people on a regular basis. You need regular production meetings for the whole team, but creative work should be done individually. In particular, give yourself plenty of time to discuss things with your designer(s).

Theban production meetings

The whole group met on a Tuesday evening and all day Friday. In a school/college setting, you never have this much time, so organisation is all the more important. Half an hour before our Tuesday evening rehearsal and over the lunch-break on Fridays, we held a production meeting. At this meeting the production manager presented the minutes and recorded decisions of the last meeting, with an action column of who was doing what.

We could then check through and see what had been done and what had not. Regular items on the agenda were:

● minutes and decisions of last meeting
● rehearsal reports from Assistant Stage Manager (ASM)
● report from publicity group
● report from set and lighting group
● report from costume/make-up group
● Any other business (AOB).

LAYING THE GROUND-RULES

Depending on the nature of your group, its size and your working relationship with the members, you may want to devise some production and rehearsal ground-rules. This is never a waste of time: a theatre group must respect itself and take itself seriously. Each group member must respect *themselves* and take *themselves* seriously. This does not mean you cannot have fun. Laughter is one of the most important things in any performance group and rehearsal process, but you must know when it is appropriate and when it is damaging to the work in hand. Performers need maximum trust and security during the workshop process if they are to develop challenging and meaningful performances. It is largely your responsibility as director to ensure that the group supports its members when they are improvising, performing, discussing ideas, feeding back etc.

TASK

In small groups make a list of the basic DOs and DON'Ts of the rehearsal process. Be as positive as you can. Expect the best of yourself and each other. It is all too easy to accept that 'we're not good enough to do that ...'. You *are* good enough. Determine to prove as a group that you are disciplined, determined, supportive, respectful; you are much more likely to be creative. Refer back to the list from time to time as seems appropriate.

Publicity

We wanted to distribute posters three weeks at least before the production. Six weeks before that date, we had a poster brainstorm. In small groups, the cast talked about posters they had seen that had worked well and the kind of effect they wanted to create. Each group then sent a representative to write their idea on a white-board; they suggested:

- a tree with character items and image-words hanging off it
- the words 'Oedipus' and 'Antigone' separated by a bolt of lightning
- a face emerging from a brick wall
- a body shape with a body in it, with another body in it, getting smaller and smaller.

The group liked the face and the separated words, in particular. The general feeling was that, in the absence of any brilliant artist, we should work with photography. We had also recently seen the opening clips of the film of Stravinsky's opera, *Oedipus*, in which a giant puppet baby is suspended by a red umbilical cord. The ideas were then combined into one photographic image:

- Against a brick wall background Oedipus is curled up in a foetal position, suspended by a rope which looks like his umbilical cord; Antigone is looking dangerous with the other end of the rope near or around her neck.

We then booked a local photographer, Rick Fiore, and arranged our shoot. It was too early, at this stage, to use a rehearsal photograph. We were looking for a resonant image that derived from our understanding of the plays so far. We did an initial shoot ourselves to find out what image would work best.

We certainly discovered that suspending someone from a wall in jockey shorts in a draughty hall in the middle of winter while someone else takes photos, can be a frustrating experience! In the end, the most successful shots were from above and not against a wall at all. The rope survived into the final image, however, as did the underwear, giving an enigmatic balance of strength and vulnerability. The rope emerges from Oedipus' belly and Antigone's end of the rope is around her neck. The image consisted of complementary opposites: birth and death, white and

Figure 4.4   *Poster for* Oedipus *and* Antigone

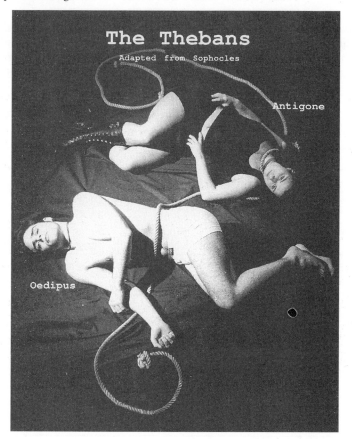

black, Yin and Yang, umbilical cord and rope around neck. These vulnerable and yet challenging expressions are infinitely resonant.

You have cast your production, allocated production roles, provided the cast with copies of the script, arranged copyright, had a read-through and an initial brainstorming session. Now you need to organise the rehearsal schedule.

Rehearsal schedule

To set the schedule, you will liaise with the production manager, who will have compiled a list of everyone's availability, and broken the play down into scenes. Create a rehearsal plan enabling you to have at least two sessions in each scene in detail, before you start running the play from start to finish.

Ensure that all rehearsals start and finish on time. The director *must* take the lead here and set by example. If you do not, then discipline will fall off and so will cast confidence. In big productions, particularly those involving a number of skills, make sure you schedule rehearsal times for *routines*, e.g. dance sections, singing, fight scenes.

Rehearsal schedule for *Oedipus*

When rehearsing *Oedipus*, we worked first of all on the chorus routine, then the scenes, then the routines and scenes together – each time adding new layers of detail. The danger of this method is that the beginning of the play is well-rehearsed, but the ending is not. The advantage is that the organic development of the early scenes gradually informs the developing style; the first few scenes took many hours, but the last few were put together in a fraction of the time.

Figure 4.5   *The rehearsal schedule for* Oedipus, *ensuring two rehearsals of each scene*

	wk 6	wk 5	wk 4	wk 3	wk 2	wk 1
Mon	1.i	3.i	5.i	2.i+ii	5.iii+iv	Full run on set
Tues	1.ii	3.ii	5.ii	2.iii+3.i	1+2	Set & costume
Weds	2.i	3.iii	5.iii	3.ii+iii	3+4	Full run & repairs
Thurs	2.ii	4.i	5.iv	4.i+ii	5	Tech & Dress
Fri	2.iii	4.ii	1.i+ii	5.i+ii	Stagger through*	Opening night

* Stage manager and lightning designer will need to see the first stagger through as early as possible, to give them a chance to put the technical requirements together.

It is the DSM's responsibility to post the rehearsal call and arrange the space.

Figure 4.6   *An evening's rehearsal schedule*

Day	Time	Venue	Scene	Cast required
Thurs	6–7	Room 12a	1	Steven, Liam, Chorus
Thurs	7–8	Room 12a	4	Louisa, Steven
Thurs	7–8	Church Hall	dance	Chorus
Thurs	8–8.30	Room 12a	4 + dance	Loulsa, Steven, Chorus

THE FIRST REHEARSAL

We made a list of appropriate warm-up exercises for each rehearsal. These would inevitably vary to a certain extent, according to the demands of each session. The following are for full cast rehearsals; see Chapter 2 for a description of these games.

Energy	Chain tig	
	Bombs and shields	
	The Theban game	3 mins
Relaxation	Talk through body	5 mins
Physical	Stretches	5 mins
Concentration	Bouncing electrons/ Mexican waves/ Blinding walking	5 mins
Trust	The aggression game	5 mins
Voice	Solo-work	5 mins
	Group chant/song	2 mins
Total time		30 mins

THE EXPERIMENTAL PHASE – PLAYING AND RESEARCH

We invented *The Theban game*, which is based on a game called *Ship to shore*. We wrote out the four place-names from the plays: Thebes, Corinth, Delphi, Athens, and placed them on each of the four walls. People take it in turns to be Apollo. Everyone gathers in the middle of the room and goes wherever Apollo says, or performs the task Apollo asks them to. Examples are:

- have the plague
- hang yourself
- poke your eyes out
- find someone to bury
- walk through all the ways of thought
- pour libations
- go to Corinth
- oops it's Oedipus
- get to Delphi
- be a Sphynx.

People can be excluded from the game for being the last one to get there or perform the activity, or on the grounds of poor performance quality. As Apollo, you are a god after all, and if some mere mortal is giving a paltry performance, you do not have to justify why you punish them. Just do it. A particularly nasty Apollo might leave a miscreant in the game and have them punished by the other humans. Ultimately, what you are looking for is energy and committed acting!

The game is also an excellent short cut to understanding the story and getting familiar with the manners.

FINDING A STYLE – THE CHORUS

Now we had to find a style for the production; in particular, ways in which the Chorus would move and use their voices. We have no clear idea of what the original Greek Chorus would have done. We know that they would have sung and danced, but that's all we know. For the Chorus in our production, then, we had a blank slate.

In one rehearsal we extended a voice exercise into a technique for the Chorus to use. All lay on the floor on their backs, relaxed, breathing deeply. All took a deep breath in and sang out at the bottom of their range, rising up to the top of their range *with the rest of the group* reaching a crescendo together. Next, we started at the top and worked down, still keeping together. When both could be done successfully, the group went up and down in one breath. Then we added movement, rising up to standing on the way up and collapsing back down again. They were asked to be led by the voice; pulled up by the voice, as if it were an external force. To create the idea of post-nuclear mutation we then asked them to use the rising note to find a stretched, distorted position and hold it. It had a very powerful effect, like a phoenix rising from the ashes. This led onto the idea of distortion. To avoid caricature, we needed to find out how each Chorus member naturally moved.

Body parts leading

We looked at where each member of the cast moved from.

We ran through the exercises listed on pages 89–91 with the Chorus and then asked them to move around, extending from their own leading point into a stretched and distorted way of moving. Next we asked them to find a voice that emerged from that way of moving, and to try moving at different levels.

The next step was to give groups of four a series of tasks on stage to see how they worked as an *ensemble*. For example:

- it's dawn and you all emerge from your shelters
- you are feeling particularly ill and in pain
- you're all hungry. One person finds a crust
- Oedipus is coming – he'll save you – plead to him
- he can't help – show your anger
- the queen is dead – how do you react?
- someone cracks a really funny joke
- using sounds but not words – show the audience how you feel about Oedipus' fate.

Much of this exercise was quite funny. We discussed why this was so, and whether it was a problem. Through moving in a distorted way and producing distorted sound, the Chorus exhibited aspects common to many physical and mental disabilities. This produced laughter and uncertainty. It was funny, but should we be laughing? Suddenly, in the middle of a simple movement exercise, we had hit a taboo: disability was not to be laughed at. If this was so, why did we want to laugh? It was time to introduce the cast to Aristotle's concept of Pathos.

Pathos

The original Greek word *pathos* meant suffering, and is the noun from which we derive the adjective 'pathetic'. The Oxford English Dictionary defines pathos as:

> 'That quality in speech, writing, music, or artistic representation which excites a feeling of pity or sadness.'

Nowadays, 'pathetic' has a very negative meaning, suggesting something inexcusably weak and *self-pitying*. In Greek tragedy, however, the suffering hero had to be strong and noble in order for the pathos to have its desired effect on the audience: to produce a catharsis, or emotional cleansing. Fate strikes a blow to bring the tragic figure down, which must be perceived as essentially unmerited. Oedipus may be arrogant, but he was cursed from birth: what could he possibly have done to deserve his fate? The sense of unmerited punishment is all very true of those people with disabilities. Those afflicted from birth with some crippling disease, or struck down by accident later in life, have done nothing to merit punishment, or if they have their crime is no worse than those committed by many others who continue unimpaired. The chance that paralyses one and leaves another untouched seems without motive. In order to explain it, the Greeks created a pantheon of jealous, spiteful gods who bickered and fought, using humanity as pawns in some Olympian game of chess.

When confronted by someone with disabilities, the non-disabled person often experiences pity and fear. Pity, because they are genuinely affected by someone else's plight, and fear, because they realise that such a fate could just as easily afflict them; in other words, they are confronted with the possibility of their own suffering. As such, it seemed highly appropriate that the Chorus itself should confront the audience with its own modern, twentieth-century sense of pathos, while the structure of the whole piece and the fate of Oedipus himself confronted the audience with the much older, Aristotelian sense of pathos.

THE FUNCTION OF THE CHORUS

1 The Chorus would function as citizens of Thebes, suffering from the plague:

> Our agonies are beyond telling
> A whole city slowly dying
> From an enemy no man can fight

2 They are observers and commentators on the action:

> Was there ever a reversal of fortune
> More terrible than this?

3 They have a religious role, singing and praying:

> Great father Zeus, you who punish with fire
> Incinerate the god of war
> Before we all lie dead

4 They question the motives of the protagonists:

> Teiresias has spread fear and confusion
> Should we believe him or not?

5 Occasionally, they try to influence the action:

> Great king, be prepared to change your mind.

They are an audience on stage, which mediates the experiences of the real audience. In other words, the Chorus serves to clarify how the audience *might* be feeling, in much the same way as members of a congregation in church are assumed to be thinking and feeling the same thoughts as they respond to the priest.

Note: a protagonist is the principal character in the plot or story.

THE OEDIPUS COMPLEX

We were also interested in the nature of Freud's understanding of the sexual development of children, and his unearthing of what he called the Oedipus Complex. Like most of us, Oedipus engages in the active expression of his desires (killing his father and sleeping with his mother) without conscious recognition of what he is doing. In Freudian terms, he is

acting out repressed desires, which are buried so deep in his unconsciousness that he genuinely knows nothing about them. As such, the Chorus is also in Oedipus' unconscious. Like dream figures, they enact the slowly emerging story; the nightmare from which he cannot wake up. Here is what Sigmund Freud claimed:

> Like Oedipus, we live in ignorance of these wishes, repugnant to morality, which have been forced upon us by Nature, and after their revelation we may all of us seek to close our eyes to the scenes of our childhood.

> There is an unmistakable indication in the text of the Sophocles' tragedy itself that the legend of Oedipus sprang from some primaeval dream-material which had as its content the distressing disturbance of a child's relation to his parents owing to the first stirrings of sexuality. At a point when Oedipus, though he is not yet enlightened, has begun to feel troubled by his recollection of the oracle, Jocasta consoles him by referring to a dream which many people dream, though, as she thinks, it has no meaning:

> > As for marrying your mother, you're not the first
> > To have dreamed that dream; every son
> > Is his mother's lover in imagination
> > Or in day-dreams. It's commonplace.
> > (*trans. D. Taylor*)

> Today, just as then, many men dream of having sexual relations with their mothers, and speak of the fact with indignation and astonishment. It is clearly the key to the tragedy and the complement of another dream, in which the dreamer's father dies. The story of Oedipus is the reaction of the imagination to these two typical dreams. And just as these dreams, when dreamt by adults, are accompanied by feelings of repulsion, so too the legend must include horror and self-punishment.
> (The Interpretation of Dreams, pp. 365–6)

If all drama is about bringing the truth to light, what better example than Oedipus?

In *Antigone* the Chorus are, initially, simple servants of the state, but there is also a sense that they are the repressed desire for truth and freedom embodied in the figure of Antigone herself. Towards the end of our production, when Creon's power has collapsed, we wanted the Chorus to come back on stage, beating out rhythms in the set, taking over again, producing a threat of just the kind of anarchy Creon wished to suppress.

Essentially, then, the Chorus would function as:

- narrators/storytellers
- observers/commentators
- people of Thebes/victims of nuclear plague.

Research/resources

For the post-nuclear world of Oedipus we looked at:

- photos of Chernobyl
- *Beyond Thunderdome*
- the Japanese staging of the Stravinsky opera, *Oedipus*
- Freud's model of the unconscious and the Oedipus Complex

For the repressive techno-world of Antigone, we watched two films:

- *Brazil* – Terry Gilliam
- *1984* – George Orwell

THE EMERGING VISION

After watching *Beyond Thunderdome*, we decided that our world was very much like that of Bartertown, and the Chorus was like the lost tribe of children creating their own mythology and retelling its story: 'It's time to do the telling.'

Cast members gathered bits of costume appropriate to our emerging picture. Oedipus and Creon were both clad all in leather, and covered themselves in weapons. Teiresias, the fortune-teller, wore leather and flowing robes; Jocasta had a leather-punky look. This immediately affected the acting of the characters, and the kind of exercises we would put them through.

We started creating the set out of junk. All the action of the play takes place in front of the palace in Thebes. Junk doors gradually gave way to a simple dais made of industrial pallets, leaving the rest of the stage clear as an 'orchestra' for the Chorus: see Figure 4.7.

For *Antigone*, the growing picture was one of distant technological power, divorced from the reality of people's lives. The old, pre-war routines were being re-established. We knew we wanted Creon to appear on screen, at least for the first half of the play;

Figure 4.7   *The set for* Oedipus

so we needed to find enough video monitors to do this. In the end, we used one central screen, with Creon performing live on camera from a dressing room. The screen was his symbol of power: see Figure 4.8.

Figure 4.8   *The set for* Antigone

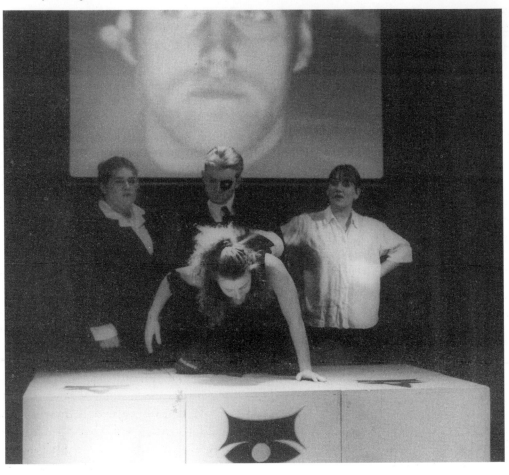

ACTORS MUST UNDERSTAND THE TEXTS

It is your job to ensure that the actors know the meaning of their lines. You don't have to have all the answers, but it is fair to say that actors will expect you to have most of them. Think deeply about the words in the play. Test your understanding against the cast's and share the problem where uncertainty exists. If there seem to be several possibilities for a certain line (there often are), you must decide on *one* which fits your characterisation and interpretation. Check the understanding of lines in each scene straight away.

★ *hot tip*

Discussion and textual analysis are essential, but they can drag energy down which diminishes a group's thinking capacity. Solve as many problems *on your feet* as you can.

Blocking

The word *blocking* is used to refer to the positioning of actors in the stage space throughout the piece. Some directors allow actors to develop their own blocking through rehearsal, while others prefer to decide it all. George Bernard Shaw favoured working all the moves out in advance, using a chess-board and pieces. Other directors never fix the moves at all; you will find your own balance. Have some idea of the moves you want, but allow some improvisation as you shape the scene.

★ *hot tip*

Ensure that your Stage Manager records all the moves as they are blocked. These should be noted in pencil, as they may alter somewhat at future rehearsals. These notes will be placed at the beginning of the prompt copy, from which a stage manager will run the show.

The director needs to develop a keen visual sense, so that moves made by actors:

- make sense in terms of character
- make sense in terms of given circumstances and objectives
- create a good stage picture
- do not block the audience's view of anything they *need* to see.

This last factor is most important. In a film, you can only point the camera one way at each moment; the skill is in the sequencing of shots. In theatre, everything on stage is in full view for almost all of the time. As director, you will establish the audience's *point of focus*: you must decide what they should be looking at, at any one time, and block and pace the scene appropriately. This becomes increasingly important when there are many people on stage. Here are some tips you may find useful:

- Find the focus. Produce a tableau of a scene or moment from a scene making the *point* or *focus* clear. Bear this in mind as a marker when you run the scene.
- Freeze the action. As you run scenes, freeze the action from time to time and then ask: does the picture you see make sense of story/character?
- Each new actor takes the focus. When an actor enters the stage-space, a new dynamic is introduced, and everyone already on stage needs to alter their behaviour or movement, however slightly, to compensate. In other words, each character focuses on the incoming character and decides how to respond.
- Actors should use their lines to move. It is much easier to find motivation when speaking text. This does not mean that no one who is not speaking should move. Every action produces a reaction, and this is how it should be on stage.
- It is correspondingly difficult to act when you are not the focus. Have your actors practise, continuing with their own character and motivations while being aware of the focus elsewhere and their contribution. This is known as *off-cue* acting. Be careful however, as inexperienced actors can easily overdo off-cue acting and upstage those speaking.

There are some sound ground-rules for the positioning of actors which will help keep your blocking lively and the interaction between characters dynamic:

- Avoid extraneous movement. An actor must have a reason for moving. If an actor moves and you are unclear why, ask them. Often there is a very good reason; they have understood something intuitively about the character's needs or wants at that moment. Sometimes, however, actors panic and move because it 'makes it more interesting', or they 'haven't moved for a while'. Moving without good reason will make a performance look stilted.

- Avoid actors standing in flat lines. Spread them out forwards and backwards on the stage. This will help create depth to the stage-picture, and free the actors up to move.
- Avoid symmetry, certainly in a naturalist production. People do not naturally form symmetrical shapes.

- Centre stage is such a powerful position that it is difficult to give the focus to anywhere else on stage, and actors can be stuck there: avoid this if possible.
- Beware of 'polite social distance' where actors perform dialogue standing about three feet apart. This is where we stand when we bump into someone in the street and is often the least interesting position actors can be in. Stretch or contract the space between actors where possible.

TASKS

- Explore the 'Zoom lens'. In pairs, produce a scene in which two characters meet briefly and exchange a few words, or just a look, and then part. It lasts for mere seconds. Choose the key second and expand it *in slow motion*, showing the full facial expression and body language. Click back into normal time before finishing. Both performers must click in and out of slow motion at the same time.
- Pick one zoom-in you like and gradually add in more and more extraneous characters, who have their own activities, but focus on the main moment, also in slow motion.
- Now try the same, but at full speed. Aim for this precision with *each moment* on stage.

Take a piece of dialogue from a play you are working on (a handful of lines will do). Try it three feet apart. Now try it twenty feet apart. Now try it three inches apart. Does it require a different delivery to make sense of the lines? Note the changes in dynamic and experiment with further positioning.

Tips on blocking can usefully be reduced to:

- be wary of anything which leaves an actor rooted

- use all the stage space
- create variety.

TASK

Read Stanislavski's *An Actor Prepares*, Chapter 3, pp. 33–37, where he describes actors learning to sit. Try this exercise yourselves. When watching someone do this exercise, imagine the stage space flowing around the actor.

Directing the actor

Each actor must research their character. Whatever the play, ask them to prepare a character study. Mike Alfreds, founder director of *Shared Experience*, suggests looking for four elements:

1 concrete facts about the character
2 what the character says about themselves
3 what other people say about the character
4 what the character says about other people.

This will give you a detailed knowledge of all the available information on that character from within the play: brainstorming can help here.

- Find the super-objective of the play. What is the play about? Try to do this yourself by writing one sentence that encapsulates the essence of the play
- Test this out using your actors by asking them to do the same thing in theatrical terms by producing a *tableau* (or *image*) that encapsulates the essence of the play.

Neither should be a particular moment from the play, but rather a composite image that shows the play's main concerns. For example:

- The essence of *Oedipus* can be summarised as: 'a proud man insists on *investigating* his own past to uncover the horrific truth of his birth'. The image might show Oedipus heading forwards to the full knowledge of his own destruction, being held back by a terrified Jocasta, his hand pushing a rejected Creon aside while Teiresias points a warning finger.
- *Antigone* can be summarised as: 'the blind exercise of state power destroys everything the state was created to protect'. The image might show what should have been (a happy Creon at the wedding of his son and daughter-in-law), contrasted with the reality (Creon weeping over their dead bodies). A wedding becomes a funeral.

There are many possibilities. For any play, you should find an objective that makes sense in terms of the evidence in the play, and also captures your own interest. You cannot direct a play well unless you find it interesting. Despite the need to find the objective, bear in mind that you do not have to understand a play fully before you start work. The process of directing is itself one of exploration and discovery.

★hot tip

Different directors and companies will select different objectives for different productions at different times. Great plays contain many themes and are capable of numerous interpretations.

THE INDIVIDUAL SCENE

We are going to look at a scene between Oedipus and Jocasta. His super-objective is to unlock the secret of his birth; hers is to stop him. The structure of the play is so simple and pure that the individual objectives in each scene do not diverge from the super-objective. Another, simpler way of phrasing this is to ask in each case, 'what does my character want now?' A character's wants will change from moment to moment, breaking the objective down into *units* or *beats*. The director should help the actors find these units and justify their moves and delivery accordingly (see also Chapter 2, pages 75–79, *A Night Out*).

Jocasta:	Please tell me. What harm Can Creon have done to provoke such fury So suddenly? I am worthy of your trust.
Oedipus:	I am sickened with disgust At the scope of his conspiracy.
Jocasta:	What conspiracy? And why do you accuse my brother?
Oedipus:	He says I'm responsible for Laius' murder.
Jocasta:	Has he any evidence? Or is it hearsay?
Oedipus:	He says nothing himself. That corrupt fortune-teller Speaks for him.
Jocasta:	And is that all? Set your mind at rest. No-one can forecast the future. I know What I'm talking about, from personal experience. I have proof! When Laius was alive An oracle told him – that he would be killed By his own son – our own child. But it didn't happen. Laius was killed By persons unknown, foreign robbers – According to the story – at a place Where three roads meet. As for the child, It was abandoned on a deserted mountain Before it was three days old, by a servant. To make doubly sure, its ankles were pierced And strapped together with leather thongs. So that prediction didn't come true, In spite of Apollo. Laius was murdered, But not, as he feared, by his own son. So why take notice Of these fortune-tellers and astrologers? The gods always get their own way, Without anyone's help, when they are ready.
Oedipus:	Something you said Jocasta . . . I remember . . . My brain's a turmoil . . . feelings, memories . . .
Jocasta:	Why do you look at me so strangely? What's the matter?
Oedipus:	You said, didn't you, that Laius was butchered At a place where three roads meet?
Jocasta:	It's the common story.
Oedipus:	Where? What country?
Jocasta:	At a place in Phocis, Where the road from Thebes forks to Delphi.
Oedipus:	And how long ago did all this happen?
Jocasta:	You hadn't arrived. The news became public. A short while before you became king.
Oedipus:	Oh, Zeus, what will you do to me?
Jocasta:	Oedipus . . . you look terrified. What have I said?
Oedipus:	Not yet. Don't ask me yet. How old

	Was Laius? What kind of man was he?
Jocasta:	A big man.
	Hair greying. About your build.
Oedipus:	Maybe Teiresias could see after all:
	Tell me one more thing.
Jocasta:	Why are you frightening me? I'll tell you everything.
Oedipus:	Who was with the king? A few attendants,
	Or was he travelling in state, with servants and armed men?
Jocasta:	Five men, all told. One of them a herald.
	Laius himself rode in a carriage.
Oedipus:	Ahh . . . .
	Nothing could be clearer than that. Every detail.
	Where did you get this information?
Jocasta:	There was one survivor, a servant.
Oedipus:	Is he here now?
Jocasta:	No, he begged me on his knees to let him go
	Away to the country to be a shepherd.
	He said he wanted to be done with Thebes,
	Out of sight, out of mind. So I let him go.
Oedipus:	I want him here at once, today.
	Can we find him?
Jocasta:	Of course we can.
	Why are you so anxious?
Oedipus:	My dear wife, I'm frightened,
	Of what I've done. Of what I'm doing.
	I've already said far too much.
	I must see this shepherd.
Jocasta:	You will see him. We'll send for him
	But why are you so worried? You must tell me.
	I do have a right to know.
Oedipus:	Yes, yes.
	You have a right to know. If the truth
	Of this is what I think it is,
	No one has a better right to know
	Than you. I'll tell you the whole story.

★ key point

Notice the constant references to proof and evidence. The play's super-objective is an investigation into a man's origins. It is right, then, that each character is like a witness whose evidence must be examined. This will affect the staging as we shall discuss later.

Analysis

A great deal has clearly happened in the past that is only just coming to light. For the purposes of the drama, Sophocles has all the relevant facts of the back-story delivered at this point in the play. It is difficult to believe that a real-life Oedipus and Jocasta would never have discussed the death of her first husband, the previous king. Especially as his death took place just before Oedipus arrived. The excuse is made elsewhere in the text that everyone was distracted at that time by the arrival of the Sphynx.

There is a fairy-tale, mythic quality to the story; a 'once upon a time' feel that argues against psychological realism. And yet we must make these characters live, and, as such, meet them in our imaginations, making sense of them to ourselves and then re-presenting them on stage.

Look at the *given circumstances* for Jocasta. An embarrassing and unexplained row has just flared up between the king and her brother. She has to care for her status and for the status of her family and so she has diffused the situation. Creon has sworn his innocence and left. Jocasta is divided between loyalty to her husband and loyalty to her brother. Her first want, then, is to find out what is going on in order to:

- reassure herself
- calm her husband
- defend her brother's honour.

She cross-examines Oedipus briefly and finds out that Teiresias is involved. She immediately belittles Oedipus' interest in the fortune-teller by telling him how she thwarted the oracle's dreadful prophecy about her own son. She does so, ostensibly, to set Oedipus' mind at rest. Ironically, she delivers information that disturbs him even more. She is forced to give this information as it is her only evidence for the ineffectiveness of prophecy. What she is actually doing is confessing to the deliberate murder of her own baby son. We know now that any such action would have huge repercussions for the mother. Is this the first time she has spoken of it? How does she feel making such a confession? If she has borne the burden of guilt all these years, how would it make her respond now?

Her wants here are twofold:

- to reassure her husband
- to unburden herself by telling her story.

She can afford to do the latter, because she perceives in Oedipus someone who is equally terrified by prophecy. Little does she know that it was exactly the same prophecy that she tried to avoid all those years ago. But is there perhaps a third want? If she paid the heavy price of losing a son in order to thwart a prophecy, she needs to believe that the price was worth paying. She needs to know that prophecies do not have to come true. She is seeking to reassure herself that she did the right thing in killing her son.

To give her a wistful, confessional quality, while playing the overriding objective of comforting Oedipus, Jocasta sat behind him on the dais and cradled his head, stroking his hair as he spoke. This maternal behaviour was designed to point with subtle irony to the fact that she is indeed his mother. (In our production, we gave Jocasta a bundle of baby clothes that she carried like holy relics, most notably when she came to pray.)

Oedipus has to listen and gradually register his dismay. He may have just cursed himself. He breaks the comforting maternal embrace and looks her straight in the face. His language becomes disjoined, in a turmoil, just as he says his mind is. His look of terror terrifies Jocasta. He now cross-examines her in turn, but all gentleness is gone. His overriding want now, is to find out all he can about the murder of Laius. Look at the staccato questions he keeps firing at Jocasta. The actor here must not let her off the hook for a second.

We practised with Oedipus pushing Jocasta across the room. She would try and get away, but he wouldn't let her. This helped him find the driving energy of the questioning and her find the fear and panic it engendered. They were then asked to perform it while staying still, but to maintain the same energy and intensity.

TASK

Try this yourselves, both in your own words and with the text. Notice the way it is difficult to maintain the momentum through the non-questioning lines, such as 'Oh Zeus, what will you do to me?' Here the frustration is inwards or upwards towards the god himself. The actor must not lose the main thrust of the questioning, and so must deliver these almost as quick asides.

Shaping the production

Oedipus is about investigation. If this is the super-objective, then each scene must bear this out. Try to find the setting, image or shape of a scene with this in mind. At times, in our production, the chorus were used as an on-stage jury. Evidence was presented to them. At others, they themselves were in the dock 'if any man here…' with Oedipus patrolling round them like a headmaster with some naughty schoolchildren.

At other times the Chorus were used to set, or frame, other characters, e.g. Creon and Teiresias. We have said elsewhere that each new actor should take the focus. This was particularly important here where the characters are high status, but are being presented in a small studio theatre. We needed to give them a real entrance. Creon's return from the Oracle could not just involve the actor walking onto the stage. The Priest says 'There is the signal'. We had a conga beat given on beer kegs, while the Chorus produced a short dance of welcome based on African dance moves. This broke up the stage pattern, introduced thrilling sound and movement, and elevated Creon's status. To the continuing beat, Oedipus and Creon performed their own male-bonding ritual. This served to establish that there was trust between them, but their status was sufficiently equal to imply that Creon would indeed pose the only realistic threat to Oedipus.

The Chorus also welcomed Teiresias, who was played as a woman. The Chorus were all female, and seemed immediately in solidarity with her, demonstrating the respect accorded to her in this society. They welcomed her by whooping and ululating, trilling their tongues and drumming on the ground. We then chose to show her prophetic powers on stage. Oedipus asked for help and said 'We are in your hands'. She stretched out her hand and moved in a slow circle; the Chorus were all kneeling or crouching and spread round her. They began to breathe heavily, raising and lowering their backs as if all in the pangs of childbirth. Teiresias began to shake, entering swiftly into a trance state. The rhythm built and built until the whole group lunged at Oedipus.

The investigation through trance had led to him. When Teiresias uttered the next lines 'mine is a terrifying gift', we believed her.

In the absence of stage directions, we were inventing our own routines and rituals, breaking up the play into sections and making sense of each separate one. This was done in a variety of different styles, but all with a ritual/tribal/religious theme, so that when they were put together, they seemed part of the same style. We had created our own world on the stage with its own logic; a space where tribal dance, gospel, shot-guns and leather could all meet.

SET

Both sets underwent radical revision after their initial conception. As the action on stage became more complex, so the debris on stage had to be minimised. In *Oedipus*, the junk gradually disappeared, including the cabinet that had been the entrance to the palace. It proved unstable and risked blocking sightlines for a number of the audience. Three simple industrial pallets suggested the steps of the palace. When inside, Oedipus and Jocasta leaned against the wall or the dance-ramp. The dance-ramp was initially constructed by two members of the group who were given the task of portraying the battle between Oedipus' two sons, Polinyces and Eteocles, in which both die. This was to be the only on-stage representation of the middle play of the trilogy, *Oedipus at Colonus*. The sequence involved jumping from a ramp, up onto a wall (about 8 feet high). The construction of pallets and board was hinged and bolted for safety. It would clearly take too long to construct at the end of *Oedipus the King* and certainly could not be left on stage during *Antigone*, so we used it as part of the *Oedipus* set. The battle ended the first half.

In *Antigone*, a complicated scaffolding tower construction was replaced by a simpler mini-stage of blocks, embellished with an invented Creon logo and surmounted by the projector screen from which Creon, and later Teiresias, would speak.

COSTUMES

These were finalised when everyone was requested to bring in proposed items. They dressed and the costume team checked who still needed what. The costumes for *Oedipus* were, by now, relatively easy. The Chorus were to wear dark and dirty leggings, ripped shorts and T-shirts, while the high-status characters all wore leather. In other words, those with power had protective clothing and those without did not. *Antigone* was a little more difficult. Here the world was technological, but power was still vested in king and court. The designers chose tight black lycra leggings tucked into knee-high boots with military-style tunics on top. Soldiers were to wear standard combat greens, and the Chorus were to have silver make-up and black shawls.

LINES AND MOVES

The cast need to commit lines and moves to memory as soon as possible. Actors will find the best way for themselves, but your job is to get scenes up and running smoothly, helping actors embed moves and lines in their memory. It often helps just to run the lines of a particular scene, before working on the moves; see Mark Rylance's interview on page 143 for 'reading in' technique. This is called a *line run*. Once you have added in the moves, these also need to be drummed into the head. A very useful technique for this is the *speed run*.

Speed run

This entails running through the script as fast as possible, without gabbling, and putting in all the moves. You need to decide in advance of a speed run whether you are going to miss out routines or include them; for example, an instruction might be 'let's speed run Act 1, missing out the fight'.

Speed-running is a technique which has to be learned before it proves useful. Actors need a high concentration level because the opportunities for distraction are also high. It is important to make sure that actors do not go so fast that they trip up over the words, or start forgetting moves and business. If it is clear that actors are not concentrating enough to learn from a speed run, it is a waste of time.

Actors failing to learn lines and moves can be a frustrating business. Sometimes individuals need the pressure of line and speed runs to help them learn. Be realistic about how useful they will be.

Giving notes

Make notes during the rehearsal, recording whom the note is for, which section or lines it refers to and the nature of the note. It might look something like Figure 4.9:

Figure 4.9 *Notes from a run-through*

Joc	On entrance – don't pre-empt, we could see you getting into position
Oed	When Joc throws you down, you got straight up again
Cre	Problems with costume? Kept hitching trousers
LX	Chorus light late for Oedipus backstory
*Chor	Rehearse second half of backstory
Oed	Talk directly to Chorus. They *are* the body of Laius.
LX	Fade up at end backstory. Change to snap.

Putting an asterisk in the margin tells you what you must rehearse again. Listing notes like this makes it easy to skim down and find the relevant note for the relevant person, whether cast or stage crew. There are no rules about it, and you will doubtless discover your own shorthand.

Important advice: do not give notes at the end of a heavy run-through unless it is something that *must* be worked on before the next rehearsal. It will be much more effective if you give notes immediately before the next run-through. Allow yourself a clear and peaceful half hour, all your cast being armed with scripts and pencils. Don't be made to feel guilty about having everyone there even if only one or two notes affect them. It is the only efficient way of delivering notes. Actors also often have important notes for each other about things you haven't spotted. Note-giving is a *whole cast responsibility*.

The Get-in

A schedule was issued to the company; see Figure 4.10.

Figure 4.10   *A Get-in schedule*

The Thebans
Schedule for *Get-in*, *Performance* and *Get-out*

Thursday 14th March

Time	Location	Action
9am	College	Lez + van with: Gareth, Emma, Leigh, Liam, Caroline + Darren J for sound fit-up
9am	Room 1	Full call for remainder of company
1.45pm	Studio	Full Company. Into costume
2.15pm	„	Tech/Dress rehearsal

Remember: Tech and Dress rehearsals can be long. Bring some refreshments, a book and some patience.

Time	Location	Action
7pm	Venue	Company warm-up on stage (basic costume)
8pm	Venue	Performance

Note: All costumes, props etc. to be neatly stored, dressing room and green room cleared. No-one is to leave the Dixon until permission is given by Lez.

Friday 15th March

Time	Location	Action
9–12am	College	Contingency Time
12noon	Venue	Full Company
2.30pm	„	Performance
4.45pm	„	Clear and set for evening show
6pm	„	Full Company
8.15pm	„	Clear and set for next show

Saturday 16th March

Time	Location	Action
6pm	Venue	Full Company
8pm	„	Performance
10.15pm	„	Strike

Note: the strike and get-out are a whole company responsibility. No one leaves until cleared by Stage Manager.

THE TECHNICAL REHEARSAL

This is where you hand over to the Stage Manager, all your careful production planning comes to fruition and, hopefully, all the ingredients are simmering nicely. It never feels that way, of course, and the overriding feeling will probably be one of panic.

It is rarely useful to have the entire cast present when plotting the lights. One or two people standing in appropriate places is all you need. It will be your responsibility to make sure the cast get plenty of rest and reassurance. They will be hyped up and nervous; it is important to keep them and yourself calm.

Once the lights are plotted, you should then call the cast in for a *cue-to-cue*, with all the technicals in place, and the Stage Manager calling the cues.

This familiarises everyone with the technicals, allows the cast a practice of entrances and exits etc. Now you are ready for the dress rehearsal.

THE DRESS REHEARSAL

This should be run exactly as a full performance, with everything in place. Every now and then an actor can be heard to say 'Is it all right if I don't wear this for the dress run?' or 'Do I need full make-up?' The answers are 'No, it is not all right' and 'Yes, you do'. The next time you are on the stage, there will be an audience, and you will all want to give them your best. Don't scrimp on your dress run and never, ever stop it unless absolute disaster has occurred.

For *The Thebans*, shortage of time meant that we only had a tech/dress, which meant that the lights were being plotted as the dress rehearsal went along. This is not ideal, because the actors don't get used to the right lights coming on at the right time, and have to trust that it will happen correctly later. This is sometimes inevitable, however, because of shortage of venue time.

THE FIRST NIGHT

Go for it! Adrenalin will see you through: first nights may be rough and ready, but they usually have an energy about them, a sheer freshness, that works. They can often be better in many ways than later, smoother performances that have lost their raw edge.

SECOND NIGHT DOWN

You may have heard this phrase, and, yes, it often happens. The build-up to the first night is often so intense, with all efforts geared to one performance, that afterwards everybody relaxes. It is not a conscious process, but you are exhausted. Consequently, concentration is a little lower on the second night, energy levels are down and mistakes are made. Technically, second nights are usually better than firsts, but the acting is weaker. This is particularly noticeable with comedy; a second night audience never finds it quite so funny, because, without realising it, the cast are not giving as much.

You cannot avoid the energy slump totally, but you can take steps to minimise its impact.

Instead of staying, 'They did well last night, we'll call them in an hour before the show', call them in at least *two* hours before. Get everyone on stage in workshop gear and take them through some relaxation exercises. Play some games: now is a time for the cast to enjoy playing together again. This is probably more useful than notes on a second night. Give them a good hour's work, with a thorough voice warm-up, then give them private time to change and prepare.

DURING THE RUN

Casts find it useful to continue receiving notes during a run, however short. If you don't keep tackling a performance and analysing its subtle changes night by night, you will find that crisply acted scenes become soggy very quickly. Each performance must be freshly created, with the lines spoken and moves made as if for the very first time. This requires constant vigilance, particularly once the excitement of the first night is over.

In *Antigone*, Creon's row with Haemon had a real second night down. All the moves looked choreographed and unmotivated, so we analysed it in detail during the note session before the third performance, and from this, the scene worked better than ever before.

THE SHOW REPORT

It is the Stage Manager's responsibility to give a show report to the director after each performance, giving an account of how things ran and any errors that need addressing. This can be a very useful document, as the Stage Manager is in the best position to observe all backstage and technical goings-on. In format, it will be similar to the Director's notes.

SOME FINAL THOUGHTS

- Remember to give praise to your cast wherever possible.
- Try to observe other directors at work. You will constantly be seeing how things could be done differently and thinking about how you would tackle the same problem.
- Always share a problem with cast and company. The director does not have to provide all the ideas. In fact, if you do, the likelihood is that the cast will not feel involved in the creative process. Persuade them to pool their ideas and pick the ones that fit the picture growing in your head.

This is what Eugenio Barba, the director of *Odin Teatret*, says about finding your way on a production:

'It is not certain that the idea to be discovered will be there waiting for us, willing to be pursued. It is pure potentiality. We do not know what it's about, nor what it might be used for. Sometimes, it all comes to nothing. Other times, something new presents itself, like a surprise which obliges us to become involved in an unexpected area. Some scientists change their field of research; some writers give up the story they have been working on and follow the new peripeteias of characters who have practically imposed themselves; in the midst of work on a production one becomes aware that in reality *another production* is leading us by the hand, without yet knowing where it is leading us.'

(*Eugenio Barba,* New Theatre Quarterly*)*

Any theatre group is made up of a wide range of talents and personalities. People also have very different creative rhythms. The experimental, ensemble approach we were taking was difficult for some members of the company, as they were not used to it. Some wanted to be told where to stand and how to say their lines. We do not believe it is the director's job to tell actors how to say lines, but to provide a framework within which the actor can discover how to say the lines. A director who tries to show an actor how to do it, is saying 'you can't act, but I can', and disempowers the actor.

This is not to say that demonstration is not occasionally appropriate, if it helps clarify something, but if the actor is just copying and not producing, then the acting will inevitably be shallow. It must come from within them if it is to be true.

Influential directors

Within education, there will be many different directing styles in operation among both teachers and students. Most of the ideas and styles will have their origins in the work of the most influential directors and practitioners of the modern age; the great scientists of the theatre. The following is a brief list of some of the most influential directors, and a few designers, of the twentieth century.

APPIA, ADOLPHE (1862–1928)

Swiss designer who helped lay the foundations of modern staging. He originally studied music and began to write about the staging of opera, particularly Wagner. He rejected traditional methods of scenery painting and developed stagings with pure form and light. Appia formed a close partnership with Emile Dalcroze and wrote two books: *La Mise en Scène du drame Wagnerien* (1895) and *The Work of Living Art* (1921).

Further reading

Beacham, R. C. (1987) *Adolphe Appia,* Cambridge University Press.

ARTAUD, ANTONIN (1896–1948)

French director who saw all theatre as having its origins in ritual; see Chapter 6, pages 237–40. He expounded his notion of a Theatre of Cruelty in his book *The Theatre and its Double* (*Le Theatre et son Double*), which has greatly influenced many theatre practitioners since (notably Jean-Louis Barrault and Peter Brook). Artaud attempted to create total theatre by barraging the audience with sound and image, which he privileged over text. He wanted the audience to be caught up in the theatre the way worshippers are caught up in a ceremony (viz. the trance-dancers of Bali) and to connect with its primitive self, which he saw as being impeded by the rationalism of Western society.

Artaud wrote poetry, plays, essays and manifestos. He only wrote and directed one play, in accordance with his own theories, *The Cenci* (1935) which was not well received. Artaud suffered mental illness throughout his life and, after a spell in Mexico, was confined to the sanatorium at Rodez for the last ten years of his life.

Further reading

Artaud, Antonin (1970) *The Theatre and Its Double*, Calder & Boyars.

Esslin, Martin (1976) *Antonin Artaud*, Fontana.

Knapp, Bettina (1980) *Antonin Artaud: Man of Vision*, Swallow Press.

BERKOFF, STEPHEN

Modern British writer, director and performer who trained in Paris with Jacques Lecoq and developed an exaggerated physical and vocal style. Attempted in his own plays to create a modern state idiom as rich as the language of Shakespeare, while full of the raw energy of his native East End. He is best known for writing *Greek, East, West, Decadence, Kvetch*. In 1994 he performed three of his own monologues, in an evening simply called *One Man*. His work is typically featured by large-scale mime and satirical characterisation; the complete absence of props, with everything being created by the actors' bodies and voices; and his use of verse that is blunt, poetic and full of raw energy.

BRECHT, BERTOLT (1898–1956)

German director and playwright working in an era of revolution; see Chapter 6, pages 240–50. He regarded audiences passively watching plays as a middle-class phenomenon and wanted to create an active, working-class theatre; a place for thought and discussion as well as entertainment. He saw theatre primarily as story-telling and the actor as narrator, never quite *becoming* the part. To do this he developed the technique of the 'alienation effect' (*Verfremdungseffekt*), requiring objectivity from the audience by breaking up the action with songs and poems, and deliberately breaking stage illusion by using bright white light and exposing the mechanics of the theatre to view (something we now take for granted in our black box studios with scaffold sets). For the actors this meant *distancing* themselves from the characters they were playing, by showing that they were only representing them. This involved developing 'gestic' acting, for which actors would train by narrating their character in the third person. It emphasises stylised gesture and facial expression rather than the empathy so sought after by Stanislavski.

His first success was *Drums in the Night* (1922), but he is most famous for his music-theatre piece *The Threepenny Opera* (1928), for which he collaborated with composer Kurt Weill. Other notable plays include *Mother Courage and her Children* (1939), *The Life of Galileo* (1939), *The Good Person of Setzuan* (1940) and *The Resistable Rise of Arturo Ui* (1941). His last great play *The Caucasian Chalk Circle* (1945) was written while in exile from the Nazis in California. After being hounded in America as a Communist he went to East Berlin and founded the Berliner Ensemble. He remained there until his death.

Further reading

Esslin, Martin (1984) *Brecht: A Choice of Evils,* Methuen.

Willett, John (1964) (trans.) *Brecht on Theatre,* Methuen.

Willett, John (1968) *The Theatre of Bertolt Brecht,* Methuen.

BROOK, PETER (1925–)

British director now working from Paris at the Bouffe du Nord with an international company of actors he has collected from around the world. Brook achieved prominence with his interpretation of Peter Weiss' radical play *The Marat/Sade* and his daring circus staging of *A Midsummer Night's Dream* for the Royal Shakespeare Company in 1970. He moved abroad and collected a band of international performers with whom he has staged many Shakespeare plays and the entire Mahabharata, an ancient Indian myth cycle.

Further reading

Brook, Peter (1972) *The Empty Space,* Methuen.

Brook, Peter (1987) *The Shifting Point,* Methuen.

CRAIG, GORDON (1872–1966)

An English designer but highly influential with many directors. Established his reputation with productions of Purcell's *Dido and Aeneas* (1900), Handel's *Acis and Galatea* (1902) and Ibsen's *The Vikings in Helgoland* (1903). His work was highly acclaimed and featured vast structures and atmospheric lighting. In the end, however, his designs were deemed too impractical. Craig was a prolific writer about the theatre, his most influential work being *The Art of the Theatre* (1904). He also published journals and founded his own School for the Arts of the Theatre.

Further reading

Bablet, Dennis (1966) *Edward Gordon Craig,* Heinemann.

Innes, Christopher (1983) *Edward Gordon Craig,* Cambridge University Press.

Walton, J. M. (1983) *Craig on Theatre,* Methuen Drama.

GROTOWSKI, JERZY (1933–)

Polish-born director who established the Theatre Laboratory in 1959. Greatly influenced by Artaud. Achieved notoriety in Britain after a visit to the Edinburgh Festival in 1968. Confined to a small group of actors he experimented with a return to myth as a spiritual search; he got rid of all representative scenery, make-up and any other illusion. He wanted only the raw energies of the actor and the audience: precisely that which cannot be achieved by film. He explores his own practice in the influential book *Towards a Poor Theatre,* first published in 1968.

> The Theatre is an act engendered by human reactions and impulses, by contact between people. This is both a biological and a spiritual act.
>
> *(Jerzy Grotowski)*

Further reading

Grotowski, Jerzy (1975) *Towards a Poor Theatre*, Methuen.

JARRY, ALFRED (1873–1907)

French director and playwright; see Chapter 5, pages 155–57. Famous for the *Ubu* plays based on a mixture of Shakespeare's *Macbeth*, *Hamlet* and his old teacher at school. He wanted actors to function as marionettes on stage and created appropriately grotesque characters: a kind of *anti*-theatre of sophisticated, full-size Punch and Judy. There was a riot in the theatre on the night of the first performance of *Ubu Roi*.

Further reading

Beaumont, K. (1984) *Alfred Jarry*, Leicester University Press.
Esslin, Martin (1982) *The Theatre of the Absurd*, Harmondsworth.

MAROWITZ, CHARLES

A New Yorker who first came to London in 1956, and was Artistic Director of the Open Space Theatre in London from 1968–80. Before that, he was one of the artistic triumvirate of the Travers Theatre, and in the mid-1960s was co-director, with Peter Brook, of the Royal Shakespeare Experimental Group. As playwright, he has had his plays performed throughout Europe and the USA – including Broadway where *Sherlock's Last Case* was premièred in 1987. Marowitz has over a dozen books to his credit, including his own 'collage' versions of some of Shakespeare's plays. As a drama critic his reviews have appeared in *The Times*, the *Guardian* and the *New York Times*.

Further reading

Marowitz, Charles (1990) *Burnt Bridge*, Hodder & Stoughton.

MEYERHOLD, VSEVOLOD (1874–1940)

Influential Russian actor and director famous for his invention of the movement system known as Biomechanics. He played Konstantin Treplev in the historical first production of Chekhov's *The Seagull*, performed under Stanislavski at the Moscow Art Theatre. His angular acting style led him to explore symbolism, Oriental theatre methods and other non-naturalistic stagings. He experimented with the relationship with the audience, creating theatre-in-the-round and developing the single three-dimensional set. He directed for the Imperial Theatre as well as creating experimental work that used clowning and acrobatics. Biomechanics suggests that the actor represents a character, and does not become it. His fierce artistic independence was to cost him his life, however, and he was imprisoned by the Stalinist regime in 1939. He died in custody.

Further reading

Braun, Edward (1988) *The Theatre of Meyerhold*, Methuen Drama.
Symons, James M. (1973) *Meyerhold's Theatre of the Grotesque*, Cambridge Rivers Press.

PISCATOR, ERWIN (1893–1966)

A German communist who developed a style which became known as Epic Theatre. The technique used captions, slide projections and 'alienation'. He worked with Bertolt Brecht and was influential in the political theatre of 1920s Berlin. He worked in Russia in the 1930s and then later worked in New York running the Dramatic Workshop. In 1951 he returned to West Germany. He took over the *Freie Volksbühne* in 1962.

Further reading

Innes, Christopher (1972) *Piscator's Political Theatre*, Cambridge University Press.

Ley-Piscator, Maria (1970) *The Piscator Experiment*, Southern Illinois University Press.

Willett, John (1978) *The Theatre of Erwin Piscator*, Methuen.

STANISLAVSKI, KONSTANTIN (1863–1938)

The most influential figure in the training and development of the actor in the West. Stanislavski was an actor in Russia who spent his early years observing the great actors of the day and figuring out what enabled them to produce such powerful and convincing performances. In 1897, together with Vladimir Nemirovich-Danchenko, he founded the Moscow Art Theatre (MAT) and began developing his system of actor training to enable all actors to reach the height of their ability (*The System*). Stanislavski and the MAT achieved success with the first productions of plays by Anton Chekhov: *The Seagull* (1898), *Uncle Vanya* (1899), *The Three Sisters* (1901) and *The Cherry Orchard* (1904). To enable actors to be natural in these discursive, philosophical plays, Stanislavski encouraged them not merely to represent but *to experience* the inner emotions of the characters (*Method Acting*).

Further reading

Gordon, Mel (1986) *The Stanislavski Tradition*, Applause Theatre Books.

Gordon, Mel (1987) *The Stanislavski Technique: Russia*, Applause Theatre Books.

Stanislavski, Konstantin (1980) *An Actor Prepares*, Methuen.

— (1980) *My life in Art*, Methuen.

STRASBERG, LEE (1901–1982)

Born Budanov, in Austria, he moved to America and changed his name. He formed the Group Theatre in 1931 and furthered Stanislavski's methods in training film actors. In 1947 he joined the Actor's Studio and trained such greats as Marlon Brando, Julie Harris and Paul Newman. He wrote about his methods in *Strasberg at the Actor's Studio* (1965).

DIRECTING TODAY

The modern director will often pick and mix from the above in order to suit their tastes and the demands of the production in hand. Sometimes someone will deliberately attempt a production in the style of a given director, and other times the influences will come through at both a conscious and unconscious level.

Interview with Mark Rylance

Mark trained at RADA, has worked extensively as an actor with the *Royal Shakespeare Company*, directs his own independent projects with his company *Phoebus' Cart* and is currently director of the Globe Theatre in Southwark, which is gradually being refurbished and is planning to put on its first production, *Two Gentlemen of Verona* in the summer of 1996.

Here we discuss Mark's recent production of *Macbeth*, which was set in a religious sect. Many of the cast had shaved heads, and wore orange and yellow robes. The set included a functioning car, and the witches were played as young girls in a rave club. (See Chapter 6, page 222 for a synopsis of the play.)

How did you first become involved in the theatre?
Play-acting was something I liked to do as a kid. At 12 and 13 years, I began to find an outlet for it in school in various drama classes. Then I became very involved in building the scenery and doing the lighting. My first attempts at acting were pretty bad but I was desperate to be part of the theatre group, so I did whatever was needed. Gradually, I became more and more involved in acting. This was in Milwaukee, Wisconsin, and then I auditioned for RADA and came over to Britain. I was there from 1978–80.

And did you then go straight into the profession as an actor?
Yes, I did. My first job was at the Citizen's Theatre in Glasgow (producer of the recent film, *Trainspotting*). They used to have an open audition: I went along and did a bit of *Hamlet* and something I'd written about a mortician who falls in love with the dead bodies. They hired me for a 60-week season with a Brecht play, a Goldoni play, a modern version of *Don Juan*, a modern play about Redcar in Yorkshire, and *Massacre at Paris* by Marlowe. It was a great first season; I was very lucky. I started out before those kind of opportunities were closed for a young actor.

You've worked with Shakespeare a great deal. Where did your fascination begin?
I don't remember ever being taught Shakespeare. My first recollection is having to act Shakespeare at high school, at about 15 to 16 years. And then my parents used to take us to plays – they were teachers and took school trips over to England. I saw Stonehenge, the Royal Tournament; I remember we used to have a talk from someone about a particular play before we went in to see it, to tell us what the story was about or what the interesting questions in it were. I used to love that – it was a real occasion.

But I think that it was the playing of Shakespeare that made the difference to me. I found things expressed there that were not expressed elsewhere, in the playful language of human encounter. There was so much mystery in it that you could bury yourself in it for ages. It was like a drug, a release. That was where I released things – behind a mask.

Your productions of Shakespeare are not traditional. Why did you start to experiment?
I'm really not sure about this word 'traditional', particularly now I'm working at The Globe. We have a particular idea of tradition but, take costume for example. 'Traditional' costumes are hopeless today. It's equivalent to someone going to a big bank where everyone is wearing lovely Italian silk suits, and cutting them to the same size, sewing the shirts and the jackets all into one, and then making them out of curtain material, all heavy and cumbersome. A lot of nonsense is spoken about what 'traditional' performance is, even if you do have supposedly authentic costumes.

Since working with Mike Alfreds of *Shared Experience*, I've known what I was hunting after, which is the *human* aspect of it, the interrelations between people; that's what I get from the plays, and is the most interesting thing. I love a good design, lighting etc., but it is the playing of the people that draws me in. I look back now to discover what the original *vitality* might have been, the kind of relationship Shakespeare had with his audience, and the kind of relationship he had with his players. I see him taking an archetypal story from Ovid or from Virgil; I see him taking a historical narrative, from Holinshed as in *Macbeth*'s case, and altering it, one one level for the same reasons that *Spitting Image* takes an archetype and alters it, to look

Figure 4.11   *Mark Rylance, director of the Globe Theatre*

at something that's happening right now. Shakespeare was looking at the 'now' of his time. And also, because he was using an archetype, he was saying there is something larger going on, that repeats itself.

I became more and more wary of setting the plays in a distant future or past, of not grounding them, because what Shakespeare seems to do is to take those stories and archetypes and ground them in real people. Beatrice in *Much Ado About Nothing* is very like Dante's Beatrice, and yet Shakespeare has rounded her, made her real, and heightened certain qualities of judgement and perception. You can trace this in his development as a writer. In our first play here at The Globe, *The Two Gentlemen of Verona*, it is not yet real, it is still boldly archetypal, with Proteus and Valentine as two different kinds of love, and with a very faithful, emotional love in Julia and a bright, intelligent love in Sylvia, with this incredible forgiveness in the end. It is linked to medieval literature, which isn't fully naturalistic; it is allegorical and symbolic, talking about the transpersonal qualities within each of us. But Shakespeare took this, and made it much more real, which is what I find outstanding. With good acting, the characters sound just like a normal person, perhaps a little more poetic and more empassioned, with many more colours in their vocabulary. But they are grounded in the 'here and now' and

so my 'traditional' response is to ground them in the present time, to find a world for the characters.

I am always looking for a world in which the characters can play. That approach risks being reductionist and simplistic. That's why, in doing *Macbeth*, we resisted the obvious grounding of setting it in an army corps, the RAF or some kind of modern military faction. The warriors in the time of the play and also in the Elizabethan time, had a sense of their actions displaying their spirit; there was a certain spiritual warriorship, a collective ethic which I no longer sense among soldiers in contemporary wars; the same sense that Crazy Horse, the American Indian, or someone like that, had of being a warrior. There's a sense of magic to their warriorship. It's not just for gain or for money: they dedicated themselves to the greater good of the whole. That sense of selflessness was difficult to find in the modern concept of a warrior.

So you chose to set it in a cult?
Yes, eventually we did, but only after quite a journey. We first thought of doing *Macbeth* as a commercial option, to raise money for another production, but I couldn't find a way in. If I don't love the thing I'm doing, I'm not going to do it very well, or put enough time into it. And then the Nick Leeson affair happened [*he caused Barings bank, the oldest and most*

prestigious *merchant bank, to become bankrupt*]. The interesting thing there was the sense of these big corporations being the new modern nations, and that their warriors are these young brave men. Leeson was able, on that floor, to persuade others to follow him: he had bravura, and was an economic warrior in a world where money matters.

I thought we should do a production without much preparation, comment very immediately on the Barings issue and see what the archetypal story of *Macbeth* said about it. Initially, it seemed very promising. Leeson was dealing in the futures market which carried a whole sense of prophecy and being able to discern the future (all modern echoes of the prophecy in *Macbeth*).

As we looked at it more closely, however, it seemed to fit less well, particularly spiritually. I found in the banking world the necessary qualities of family connections, of a close-knit community serving one principle, the possibility of murder and of violence, albeit in the shadier aspects of the city; but it didn't have the collective spiritual belief I needed. I discovered in the play the powerful sense the characters had of being able to call upon a power of grace or good. Macduff and Malcolm call to God in the most profound way; Macbeth had the sense of a golden warrior, of someone blessed with fearlessness. We went and looked at a large city bank. (Outside of it was a tiny little bell and on it was written 'The Porter'!) We watched some economic news being delivered to the trading floor – it really was like a John Wayne movie in the Second World War, the way everyone was shouting and calling and the sheer urgency of it! With all the telephones and information being brought in, it was like a command centre or some incredible battlefield, and all they were doing was selling money. There was no spirit, and yet the play has this great collective spiritual belief. Where could we find that now? A tragedy has to involve somebody falling from something very pure.

Then we stumbled upon the whole movement of uplifting consciousness that *is* very similar now, with new religions and new spiritual beliefs being born as the established church falls apart. It's full of people changing consciousness, people leaving family, homes, jobs, things that were traditionally of value to them and joining a group or a cult. We read a book called *Spying in Guru Land* which interviewed cult members. This was great source material for *Macbeth*; suddenly brotherly friendship became real, we could call each other 'brother' in the play with full meaning, and other words like 'milk' came to have great meaning (in a Shiva/Hindu based cult). We began to examine

the ways in which people seek enlightenment, the way they avoid temptations and repress their senses, like fasting yourself to give you visions, or cutting all your hair away.

Macbeth is believed to have been written for King James I, who claimed descent from Banquo. The more we looked at King James, too, the more we realised what a puritan he was, what a patriarchal thinker, moving these dark witches aside, or torturing them and killing them, trying to clean everything and yet being full of very dubious qualities himself as a leader. Look at the Gowrie conspiracy, where he killed two brothers in the same house and then had them tried; had them sat up in court after they were dead to prove their treason. There were specific things he had done and the play related very directly to them; I felt that of all the plays, *Macbeth* would be particularly relevant to a modern audience in this respect.

So many of the paths towards enlightenment, now and in the Elizabethan period, had to do with gnostic self-repression; usually that included the repression of women because they 'tempted one away' from illumination, as in *Love's Labours Lost*. Most of these societies are very benevolent, you know, and are bowed towards charitable actions or charitable prayer, but occasionally you get something like the WACO disaster (David Koresh and his followers burned to death), where someone is tested by fate or by fortune in an area of vulnerability.

We worked in this world; we tried to retain a platform of the heavens and earth in the staging. I was trying to put real people on an Elizabethan three-level structure of a ground, a soulful level and a heaven.

Did you have any reaction from people who are involved in cults?
I had a great reaction from the man who wrote the book, but no negative reactions. I expect the fundamentalist movements in America would have been horrified.

I found the contrast between the gentle Duncan and the bloodthirsty Macbeth very convincing in this reading.
That is the traditional Holinshead reading, that Duncan *was* very gentle. In fact he was too gentle; he has been too lenient, which is why the war at the beginning of the play is happening – there would have been no rebels. In our world we imagined the rebels were more to do with the drug-related fringes of a cult, which is sometimes where the cult's money is made, and so you come into conflict with the law and other violent elements.

What qualities would you look for in an actor?
I look for a playfulness; I want someone who will play rather than perform, in the sense that theatre is about discovery – each night you're going to go out and you're going to play it, find a solution. You're going to be open and play with the other people, like someone in a sports team, not just doing their one thing but playing together; or like musicians in an orchestra, that you listen as well as play. I look for someone who has a particular need, who is at a point where they have a need to try something new.

How do you find those qualities? Do you have a standard audition procedure?
I talk to people to see where they are now. I audition people with a sonnet: I ask them to learn a sonnet of their choice, and we work on it like a little play. I ask them to speak it to me or to someone else, but not to treat it as a bit of poetry. From that I get a sense of their use of the words, whether they're using the words too formally, or to express something that is beyond words; I'm looking for the connection between heart and mind to body or speech. You might see someone who's just got a mental connection to their speech, and you want to see if they can dig deeper into the heart; or someone who is very emotional and modern, but without an appreciation of the form of their speech.

Another quality is an openness to being still; how comfortable they are with being still. People are rarely shown being still; it takes great confidence just to do nothing.

I explain to the actors that I will not block the play unless I have to, that it's going to be open and playful, that we'll work with the inner needs of the characters as much as on the outer form of how they express those needs. I will be able to see if they are interested in that kind of work or not.

So you work on it in quite a modern, psychological way?
Yes, I'm interested in the psyche. I'm looking for actors who are committed to revealing themselves; people who are not just jobbing, but are using the theatre to express something they know to be true because they have experienced it, or something so secret that you could only share it by pretending to be someone other than who you are. The basic need to act is something to do with a kind of sickness or block; you cannot express something with the tools given to you as an identity, so you take on other identities to express these other qualities in yourself or the people around you.

Is that a view of acting/theatre not widely shared in the modern climate? Do you feel isolated in that view?

No, not really, I find that most actors enjoy the work. They have come into theatre for something like this. Many actors have some kind of debilitation, like shyness or family difficulties, or perhaps just greater awareness that people are playing roles; this gives them more flexibility in the game of identity. It's not an easy profession, and the flexibility does get worn out of you. I feel that I have been very fortunate in keeping that as the guiding principle of what I do. A lot of people are forced to give in, unfortunately, and take any work, to pay for a house or just to make ends meet, because there is so little work. But I think your only real chance of success is to share something boldly from yourself.

I remember first being asked to play Hamlet and panicking, thinking I would have to read all the records up at Stratford about the great performances of *Hamlet*, and add my little twig to the great oak-tree of *Hamlet* performances. An old friend said to me, 'You're a fool, *you*'re the one who's been asked to play this, you're the one who lives in the world now; the only reason for doing the play is for what it relates to *now*; there'll be another *Hamlet* in five or six years; all you have to do is understand it as well as you can and commit yourself to it nakedly and fearlessly.'

How do you structure a day's rehearsal?
I learned most of my rehearsal techniques from Mike Alfreds of *Shared Experience*, who now works for a company called *Method and Madness*.

I spend about three hours on each character in a *character session*, where the actor is asked to write down everything the character says about themselves, everything they say about other people and everything other people say about themselves; also to write down any facts they know about the character, and any feelings of intuitions they have as they do this homework. They also write down the basic plot of what the character does, and we read the information together; the whole company takes part in these character sessions. We talk about people we know who are similar to this character; what animal this character might be like; if someone knows about Laban movement training, we do that.

Eventually we all play the character for 20 minutes or so in a free improvisation in the room, not interrelating with each other, just being the character. The actor who will play the character watches this and sees what other people with just three hours' work and no responsibility can do. Then if we have time, we will have some interviews. We might ask the actor to come in as the character, and we'll just pop questions to them which they don't answer in a prepared way – they answer just in a moment – and then afterwards we'll say 'That's interesting, it's not what you said in your facts but may actually be true.' So we try and involve intuition as well. But it is building up the player so that the whole group knows what task the player has to perform.

At the same time, we do scene work. From the start I don't like people holding books, so we use a technique called 'reading in' where you have neutral readers feeding lines to the actors. So, in this case if I had a line to say, someone would just have said to me 'in this case, if I were saying that ...' and I can choose, I can just hang there, having been given the ball in a sense, and play it in whatever way I want to. From the start you are saying 'This is a ball-game – I want something from you, you want something from me, what is stopping us from getting those things?' It's a good technique. The readers have to be very neutral. They have to feed enough so that someone has enough to play with, but they have to feed it neutrally, they mustn't give any intonation themselves. I always use the image of the ball-boys at Wimbledon, the way they throw the ball in with just one bounce so the tennis player knows exactly where it's coming.

Do actors get used to it quickly as a technique?
Yes, they do. It slows everything down a bit and it takes quite a bit of concentration, but it keeps the ball in play and makes you find the wants, or objectives, of the character. That's the value of playing with objectives for me, you're not attaching yourself to an outer form which will eventually die. Even the most brilliant outer form, production or character eventually has no life, but if you attach yourself to a profound and true need of the character then you have enough to play with; you can go out and the whole set can fall down and you'll still have enough to hold the audience with your belief and your need (unless your need is to hold the set up!). I work on that a lot and then try to layer the scenes by doing points of concentration, so you might take a scene between Macbeth and Lady Macbeth and have right in the front of our mind the question 'What happened to our child?'

I also break the scene up into units or beats, saying 'this question is driving this beat', now someone's brought another question or another need in and that's driving that next one; and so you start to identify shapes and corners in the conversation, much like a skier has to go around certain bends. And you have to make decisions. When Macduff flees to England and Ross turns up, you know that up until the point where he says 'your children have been killed', something is going on that must change. But what is it?

That's a huge corner for Macduff, but is it a verification of something he's feeling intuitively, or is it a complete surprise?

Digging out those surprises is a good thing for Shakespeare plays because they are so well known, yet the detail of most of the stories is overlooked. It's important to have a sense of where a scene is going, how much characters are surprised and how much the story goes off on unexpected paths. If you truly feel this as an actor, the audience will also be surprised, and even though they may know the play very well, they'll hear it for the very first time; as an actor you will steal the show. Children do this very naturally, which is why people don't like to act with them, as they are so fresh to the situation. But our training is too much based towards a performance, and not towards the re-creation of life and the surprise that life has moment to moment.

I'm not so interested in the push towards form and proper verse speaking. I'd learn more from watching a group of kids play at being firemen in a playground than from an actor speaking verse properly, if it doesn't live up to the discipline of Shakespeare, in terms of reflecting life. He never wrote any philosophical tracts, but his plays are full of philosophy; always in the mouths of characters, in this playful mode, through the recreation of human settings and emotions.

We found this in the scene between Malcolm and Macduff [*Act IV, Scene III*]. Out on tour it was very fiery, but beforehand it was very uncertain. I hadn't cut the scene at all – it's a massive scene in which Malcolm has a huge proposition which he tests by pretending to be something he's not, and proves his intuition that Macduff is a good man. This is the complete opposite of someone like Macbeth who just acts on intuition and prophecy, but doesn't prove it, doesn't test it.

The actors were quite nervous and restrained, but when they were out on tour the scene took off, and they were getting applause at the end of the scene. They were really burning up things inside of themselves, but then it started to go dead for them. We had to sit down and say 'Well, you've got to let it go, you've got to calm down', and that's one of the hardest things for an actor. You can't always be firing on all cylinders; there are times when you will go through a fallow period, when things retreat as well as go forward.

That sense of your performance being dull or confused, is hard for actors to embrace, and yet it's only by going through that, that you find new things. I don't know if that is taught, but you certainly learn that in the profession. It's very frustrating when you come into the profession with such high ideals, and then you have to embrace the fact that you can't do it brilliantly every night; some nights it will be a duller colour.

Until you start acting professionally, you never have to do more than a handful of performances, do you?
That's right. I met a guy recently doing an eight-month run of a Tennessee Williams play, his first job out of drama school. He'd only ever done plays for five days before that. I remember finding it very tricky myself. It's not unlike what they're saying about football; they have to play too many games, the players are too tired and the games suffer because of it.

Did you find yourself working hard as an actor to make a performance fresh?
It is hard work. Hopefully, the work done in the re-hearsal room is sufficient and it's a question of letting it be, of not holding on. The real traps are when you do something good, when you make the audience laugh or it feels good, and you want to hold onto that. But you must hold on with a loving embrace only, and when it wants to go, let it. If you hold it, it dies or turns malicious on you and forces you into contor-tions of voice or speech because you're straining at something that had life a few days ago, but doesn't have life now.

My particular thing is to remind myself to look out at the other people and find what I'm doing with them and not on my own. If I have a weakness it is that I have been given certain gifts of facility in this particu-lar area of work and I can do things on my own too much, and so I have to keep looking out to the audi-ence and to the other players particularly.

Do you continue rehearsing when you're out on tour?
Yes. Not as much as a company like *Théâtre de Complicité*, who are very rigorous. I find that parties and playfulness are useful; doing things together as a company in a playful mode. Sometimes you need to work, of course, but often I find that playing together loosens people up and you learn a kind of language for talking about what's happening on the stage.

How much have you been influenced by the practitioners, such as Stanislavski?
I never read or studied Stanislavski, but his methods were passed down to me orally. I used to read Meyerhold and Brecht. Nowadays I read about things I want to explore through theatre, rather than about theatre itself.

chapter five

PRODUCTION TECHNIQUES

The main aim of this chapter is to provide an overview of the processes involved in mounting a stage production, and also the functions of the personnel who work in this area of the theatre. The most fundamental techniques of lighting, sound and stage management are discussed in some detail, but you will certainly need to refer to other books (see reference section at the end of this chapter) to conduct more in-depth work. Several professionals working in the various roles of these areas have made contributions to the writing of this chapter. The information they have provided is relevant, practical and up-to-date, and should therefore be of great use to anyone seeking an introduction to the techniques of mounting a theatre production.

The most common problem with any production the authors have been associated with in an educational setting, has been a lack of money and the absence of the right equipment. Those involved in production have to improvise with the resources available. Creativity and a certain amount of 'front' are as vital as a knowledge of the 'correct' techniques in these circumstances. Lighting, sound, costume-making and set-building all require some basic equipment which you must possess, or have some way of borrowing, before you can being on a production. You also need a knowledge of the possibilities which the space and the equipment can offer; you can then exploit these possibilities with your own creativity.

In addition to a description of the most basic techniques and theory, we have also included tasks allied to a text focus of *Ubu Roi*, by Alfred Jarry. The idea behind the tasks is that you can immediately put into practice the theory and techniques which have been explained.

At the end of the chapter you will also find a section which is designed to help you understand theatrical terminology and a list of books you should consult for further information.

Before moving onto the specific techniques, we provide a brief run-down of the roles you might be expected to take up in the professional theatre. Even if you do not create all of these roles during your own productions, after reading the following breakdown of roles, you will know who might be asked to complete each production task in the professional theatre.

Overview of roles

THE ARTISTIC DIRECTOR

The Artistic Director may once have been an actor, or may have learned his/her craft in university, an Arts Council Directing Course, drama school, a director's/writer's course, fringe theatre, on secondment to a director, or as a Deputy Stage Manager (DSM). The director needs to have a sound knowledge of administration. He or she is responsible for directing productions and choosing the acting company, the season of the plays, those actors s/he wishes to direct, the director for other departments and the design team (usually an acquaintance of the director who understand his/her way of visualising.

THE DESIGNER

The designer is the head of the design team, which may comprise of: assistant designer, painters and prop makers. The designer will have trained at university or college (the Wimbledon Art School is one of the most well reputed for producing theatre designers of a high calibre), or perhaps through an appren- ticeship. The design will have been created out of the director's vision and a combination of the designer's pragmatism and artistic flare. More recently, the designer has had to embrace mechanics and engineering to keep up with technological advances.

THE ADMINISTRATOR

The Administrator may once have been an accountant, and is solely responsible for the theatre's gross budget. S/he is in charge of the employees' contracts (from the actors to the cleaners), the administration, publicity, sponsorship, grants and seat prices.

THE THEATRE MANAGER

The Theatre Manager is the assistant to the administrator, and is responsible for the day-to-day running of the theatre in all Front of House areas, including the cleaning, the box office and the bar. S/he may double as the House Manager.

THE PUBLICITY OFFICER

This member of staff is responsible for public relations, press releases, star-billing, local television and radio advertisements, and the design of posters and programmes.

THE PRODUCTION MANAGER

This is the head of the production, construction and stage management teams, responsible for all of their backstage departments and for overseeing the maintenance of all technical areas. S/he will hire and fire the stage management, flying, lighting, sound, carpentry, wardrobe teams and the casual staff. The Production Manager (PM) is in charge of the production budgets (a ball-park figure of £3,500–£5,000 in a major production venue). From this budget, the costs of all the other areas will be drawn, including design, construction/hire of the set, furniture and prop hires/buys or makes, hardware and stock for sound, stage flys, lighting and wardrobe departments, lighting designs, special effects hires and rehearsal spaces.

The PM will create the production flow-chart, arrange deadlines, organise and run production meetings, sort out transport of props etc., run the fit-ups around during the technical and dress rehearsals to overcome any problems that may arise with the respective heads of departments. S/he needs to be aware of any calls/overtime accrued by the actors or technical teams.

The PM will also arrange licences for child actors, hire chaperones, pay any script/music royalties. On the opening night the PM will hand over to the Stage Manager.

THE MASTER CARPENTER

S/he works with a multitude of materials; from timber and canvas to create stage flattage, to steel, polystyrene and latex to sculpture or form variously-shaped rostra or stage scenery such as trees. The carpenter will take the designs and also working plans produced by the designer and turn them into a reality.

THE COMPANY AND STAGE MANAGER

S/he works directly under the PM. (In some repertory theatres there may be both a Company Stage Manager and Stage Manager, but in many there is only a Stage Manager. In theatres with both posts there may be no Production Manager, in which case the Company and Stage Manager will have to divide the PM's duties between them.) The Company and Stage Manager(s) will meet with the director, designer, lighting designer and PM during the pre-production period to discuss the designs, style and period of the piece.

The Stage Manager (SM) will organise the rehearsal schedule, and rooms, and will sort out the furniture, props, heating and refreshments. If the rehearsal rooms are not within the theatre complex, maps of the stage area will be distributed, indicating the action/priority props/furniture. The SM also keeps a day-to-day running account of the finances and will receive a float from the PM. The SM also attends the rehearsals to see how (and if) the props and furniture are due, and subtracts or adds to these as the rehearsal process continues.

During the week of the production, the Stage Manager will organise the pick-ups/buys with the PM, and the insurance of valuable items. The SM will, in conference with the PM and Chief Electrician, organise the hire/buys of special effects equipment, e.g. dry ice, live sound, telephone bells, etc.

The Stage Manager also assists during the fit-up, runs the scene changes and the crew from the start of the technical rehearsal, and delegates tasks to the Acting Stage Manager (ASM). SM also liaises with the Front of House (FOH) Manager for clearance, makes sure that everybody is standing by, and tells the Deputy Stage Manager when to start the show. In the unlikely event of a fire/bomb threat, or if the show or an actor cannot continue for technical reasons, it is the SM's responsibility to make the announcement. If an actor drops in the middle of the show and there is no understudy, then the Stage Manager will have to read in the part.

THE DEPUTY STAGE MANAGER

The Deputy Stage Manager (DSM) runs the rehearsal on a day-to-day basis in conjunction with the director. At the start of each rehearsal the DSM will set up the rehearsal props and the furniture, and will do so for each subsequent scene. S/he sends daily reports to the head of each department to keep them informed of any changes to the script, props, furniture, sound requirements, special lighting, costume additions or special effects, that are decided in the rehearsal.

The DSM will make notes 'in the book' (the document which contains the lighting and sound cues written alongside the script) during rehearsal of obvious lighting cues. S/he blocks the actors' moves and prepares a props/furniture/set-running list.

During the plotting session, the DSM will mark up in the book the lighting cues, the sound cues and any set change or entrance that s/he will be required to call during the show. This duty includes the courtesy calls to let the actor know that they are due on stage.

During the technical rehearsal ('tech') the DSM will call the show (the DSM relays the lighting and sound cues one by one to the sound and lighting operators, in addition to all other cues such as special effects) to see if any cues/standbys need to be moved, then, the dress rehearsal is called as if a show. Once in performance, the DSM will be in rehearsals during the day for the next show while calling the one in progress.

THE ASSISTANT STAGE MANAGER

The ASM's job is to assist the SM and DSM. In rehearsals the ASM will help in setting props and furniture. S/he will make notes as to where and when an actor is going to need these props, and where to get rid of them. S/he will also note which props will become personal to a specific actor, and which will need to be handed to, or received from, another actor.

It may be necessary for the ASM to run a rehearsal, if for example, a dance and singing rehearsal takes place simultaneously. The ASM may also be required to make simple props, and to help the SM in finding priority props and furniture. The ASM will help the SM with the get-in, and will be delegated to run certain sections of the scene changes during the show, as well as setting props.

THE CHIEF ELECTRICIAN

The chief electrician (Lx) is responsible for all aspects of lighting, from rigging and maintenance to operation during the show. The chief Lx will often design the lights for most of the season's plays, and will be required to assist and explain the system to an outside designer, either for a show that has been farmed out for

special attention, or for the occasional show that may be brought in during a 'dark' period (when there are no shows going on in the theatre).

It is the chief Lx's job to train the followspot/line operators.

THE HEAD FLYMAN

The head flyman will assist during the fit-up with the construction of the set, but otherwise

is responsible for the safe rigging and operation of all scenery, cloths and lights overhead.

THE WARDROBE MISTRESS

The wardrobe mistress looks after and maintains the wardrobe where all the costumes are stored. S/he is responsible for outfitting the cast for the play, which may mean making costumes from the designer's plans, revamping and repairing existing costumes, or arranging to hire them.

THE SCENIC ARTIST

This job may be filled by an assistant/trainee designer or freelancer, and will often have graduated from art school. S/he may paint the set in such a way as to create an illusion of depth, or an image of a forest, city, etc.

Figure 5.1 shows a flow-chart, which clearly delineates the structure of the roles in the theatre industry.

Figure 5.1   *Roles in theatre industry*

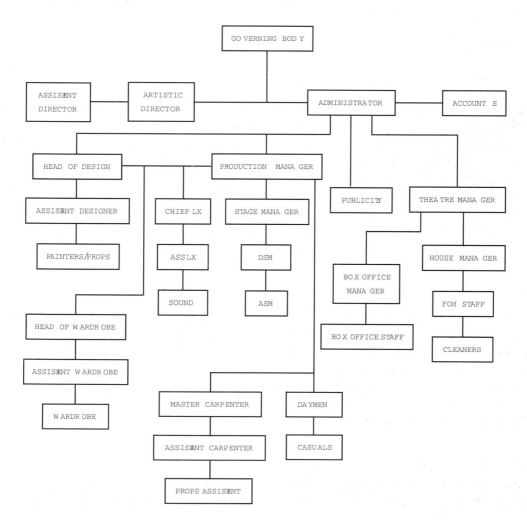

Text work and research

The use of the various techniques will be demonstrated throughout the section by reference to an imaginary production of *Ubu Roi* (written by Alfred Jarry). Tasks relating to this text, which you can carry out in your own space and with your own equipment, will also be set at the end of each section. The text is readily available from all major booksellers. (In terms of text, the Methuen edition of the Ubu trilogy is recommended, providing some interesting source material such as letters written by the author, and also a good, readable introduction. The translation by Cyril Connolly is excellent.)

Before beginning work, the director needs to understand the play and exactly what will be needed in order to mount a production of it. With any production, the director has to form an opinion about what s/he thinks the play is about and what kind of production s/he intends for the company. The best way to do this is to read the play a number of times and find some historical information or other source material such as reviews of the text, the writer or the various productions. Obviously, you will find more reviews and general information when researching classic, older texts. The added advantage of producing a play whose author has been dead for over 70 years, is that you will not have to pay for copyright, and you will also be able to adapt the play freely, without hurting the writer's feelings.

Text focus – *Ubu Roi*

BIOGRAPHY OF PLAY AND WRITER

Alfred Jarry was born in France in 1873 and died in 1907. In 1888, Jarry wrote a play which satirised his physics teacher, Monsieur Hebert (aka Père Ebe, and to become Pa Ubu in the play) with a couple of classmates, Henri and Charles Morin. The play was called *The Polish*, and it was first performed as a piece for puppets. Jarry re-wrote the play in 1891, and called it *Ubu Roi*. The play was published in 1896, when Jarry met the famous Lugne Poe, director of the Théâtre de l'Oeuvre, in Paris. The first public performance of the play caused a riot, mainly because of the 'bad language'. Of course, Jarry became a celebrity overnight and a reference point for those who wished to revolt against conventional theatre forms in the future of European Theatre: the Dadaists, Surrealists and Absurdists. Jarry was also to become a critic, novelist and publisher in his own right. Like many other dramatists, Jarry became an alcoholic and died a pauper.

STYLISTIC AND HISTORICAL CONTEXT

In terms of style, the play is a forerunner to the later Dadaism, Surrealism and Absurdism (see Chapter 6, the History of Theatre). The play is also burlesque in nature, because of its wild and ludicrous caricaturisation of historical drama.

Naturalism was the dominant culture at the time of Jarry's writing, and the theatres mainly produced well-made plays for the middle-classes. Costumes, sets and dialogue were as true to life as an illusionistic form of entertainment could be.

Jarry was reviled by supporters of the dominant convention as an anarchist.

PLOT

The play centres around the character of Pa Ubu, who is both malicious and despicable. His wife, Ma Ubu, persuades him to kill the King of Poland, and in this way the play is a satirical version of Shakespeare's *Macbeth*. Pa Ubu goes completely mad, and kills his own noblemen for money.

THE SET

> The action, which is about to start, takes place in Poland, that is to say nowhere.
>
> *(Jarry)*

The set should represent the qualities of timelessness and lack of specific location. Arthur Symon, a British critic, described the original production:

> The scenery was painted to represent, by a child's conventions, indoors and out of doors, and even the torrid, temperature and arctic zones all at once. Opposite to you, at the back

of the stage, you saw apple trees in bloom. Under a blue sky and against the sky, a small closed window and fireplace through the very midst of which trouped in and out these clamorous sanguinary persons of the drama. On the left was painted a bed, and at the foot of the bed a bare tree, and snow falling. On the right, palm trees, about one of which coiled a boa constrictor; a door opened against the sky, and beside the door a skeleton dangled from the gallows.

COSTUME

Jarry asked for costumes which were 'lacking in local colour and historical detail'. The original Pa Ubu (Firmin Gemier) was fat and wore a pear shaped mask with a bowler hat on top. A false stomach was made out of cardboard, and M. Gemier used a lavatory brush as a huge sceptre. Jarry made the masks himself.

Most of the actors wore everyday dress in the original production, and in the Peter Brook production in the Bouffes du Nord, Paris, in 1977, the actors wore no costume at all, just their own clothes and without masks.

ACTING STYLE

The actors performed as if they were huge puppets, in a mechanical manner and wearing masks.

This is just a sample of historical research you might wish to carry out. Studies of visual materials, such as photographs or drawings of sets and costumes, will help enormously if you are still short of inspiration after reading the text.

For more information about surrealism and the theatre of the absurd, see Chapter 6.

Below are a few pages of the play, which will be used throughout the rest of this chapter as the basis for some staging exercises.

Ubu Roi TEXT EXTRACT

Act 1, Scene 1

Pa Ubu:	Pschitt!
Ma Ubu:	Ooh! what a nasty word. Pa Ubu, you're a dirty old man.
Pa Ubu:	Watch out I don't bash yer nut in, Ma Ubu!
Ma Ubu:	It's not me you should want to do in, old Ubu. Oh, no! There's someone else for the high jump.
Pa Ubu:	By my green candle, I'm not with you.
Ma Ubu:	How come, old Ubu, you're not content with your lot?
Pa Ubu:	By my green candle, pschitt, madam. Yes, by God, I'm perfectly satisfied. Who wouldn't be? Captain of the Dragoons, aide de camp to King Wenceslas, decorated with the order of the Red Eagle of Poland, and ex-king of Aragon. You can't go higher than that!
Ma Ubu:	So what! After having been King of Aragon, you're content to ride in reviews at the head of fifty bumpkins armed with billhooks when you could get your loaf measured for the crown of Poland?
Pa Ubu:	Huh? I don't understand a word you're saying, Mother.
Ma Ubu:	How stupid can you get!
Pa Ubu:	By my green candle, King Wenceslas is still alive, isn't he? And even if he does kick the bucket, hasn't he masses of children?
Ma Ubu:	Why shouldn't you finish off the whole bunch and put yourself in their place?
Pa Ubu:	Ha! Madam, now you have gone too far, and you shall very shortly be beaten up good and proper.

Ma Ubu: You poor slob, if I get beaten up who'll patch the seat of your pants?

Pa Ubu: So what! Haven't you got a bum like everyone else?

Ma Ubu: If I were you, I'd try to get that bum sitting on a throne. You could become enormously rich, eat as many bangers as you liked, and roll through the streets in a fine carriage.

Pa Ubu: If I were king, I'd get them to make me a great bonnet like the one I used to wear in Aragon, which those Spaniards had the nerve to pinch off me.

Ma Ubu: And you could get yourself an umbrella and a guards officer's greatcoat that would come down to your feet.

Pa Ubu: It is more than I can resist! Pschittabugger and buggerapschitt, if ever I come across him alone on a dark night, he's for it.

Ma Ubu: Well done, Pa Ubu, now you're talking like a man.

Pa Ubu: Oh no! Me – a captain of dragoons – brutally murder the King of Poland! I would rather die!

Ma Ubu: [*aside*] Oh, pschitt! [*aloud*] So you want to stay poor as a church mouse, Mister Ubu?

Pa Ubu: God's bones, yes, by my green candle, I'd rather be poor as the skinniest mouse than rich as the cruellest cat.

Ma Ubu: And your bonnet? And your umbrella? And your Greatcoat?

Pa Ubu: And then what, you old cow?

[*He leaves, banging the door behind him.*]

Ma Ubu: [*alone*] Pfartt, pschitt, I think I've got him shifting all the same. Thanks be to God and myself, in a week, perhaps, I may be Queen of Poland.

[*A room in Pa Ubu's house, where a magnificent collation is set out.*]

Ma Ubu: Well, our guests are pretty late.

Pa Ubu: Yes, by my green candle, I'm dying of hunger. You're looking exceptionally ugly tonight, Madam, is it because we have company?

Ma Ubu: [*shrugging her shoulders*] Pschitt.

Pa Ubu: [*seizing a roast chicken*] I'm quite hungry. I think I'll get my teeth into this bird. Hm, a chicken, I reckon, and not bad at all.

Ma Ubu: Stop it, you wretch! What are our guests going to eat?

Pa Ubu: There'll still be plenty for them. I shan't touch another thing. Go and look out of the window, Ma Ubu, and see if our guests are arriving.

Ma Ubu: [*going over*] I don't see a soul.

[*Meanwhile, Pa Ubu gets his hands on a fillet of veal.*]

Ma Ubu: Ah, here comes Captain M'Nure and his merry men. Hey, Old Ubu, what are you eating?

Pa Ubu: Nothing, nothing. Just a spot of veal.

Ma Ubu: Oh, my veal, my veal! The lout! He's eaten the veal! Help! Help!

Pa Ubu: By my green candle, I'll gouge your eyes out.

[*The door opens*]

(Jarry, Alfred The Ubu Plays/Ubu Roi, *Methuen; translated by Cyril Connolly and Simon Watson Taylor)*

Set design

Decisions regarding the set design will be made in conjunction with the director, relatively early in terms of the whole production process. The Artistic Director should have an overall idea of the way in which s/he wants the audience to see the production in terms of its style; s/he will then feed this information to the set designer.

The designer must fulfil the following basic criteria to do the job properly (the order of these criteria is not fixed in terms of their importance):

1 Design a set which can be built within the terms of the budget and resources at the disposal of the company.
2 Design a set which, in terms of entrances and exits, answers the needs of the actors.
3 Design a set which helps to interpret the director's concept of the themes and the meaning of the piece.

As designer, you will need to hold all of these criteria in your mind when you are creating your plan. Taking stock of your production room and finding out what the budget is, will help you to draw up a plan which is workable and resourceful. Reading the play several times will help you to become aware of the performers' needs, in terms of getting on and off the stage. The director should make the designer aware right from the start, exactly what s/he requires in terms of concept and theme. The basic design, answering the above criteria, must be completed within or preferably before the first few days of rehearsal, so the actors know exactly what they are doing

STAGE SHAPES

Regardless of the quality or quantity of your resources, or the size and shape of your space, you have an enormous range of possibilities to choose from in your design. The first options you will have to consider are those relating to the shape of your performance space, and

Figure 5.2 *Different types of stage (depicted by the shaded areas)*

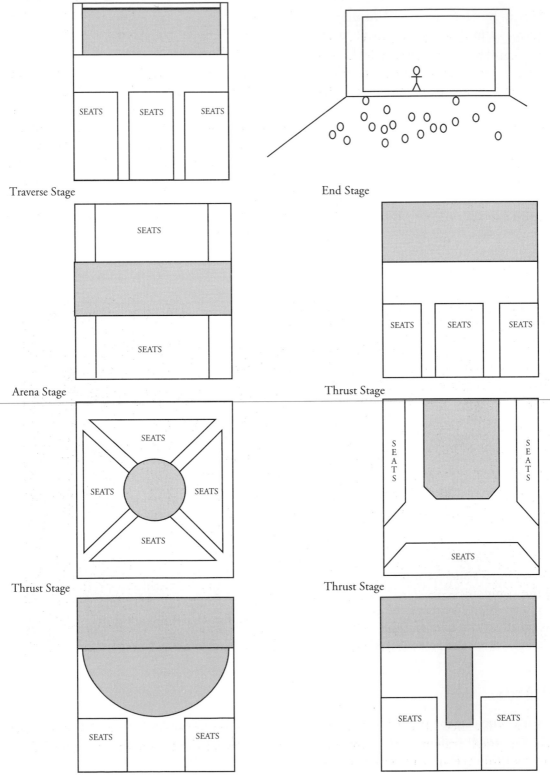

consequently where you are going to put the audience. There are five shapes you should consider (see Figure 5.2):

- Proscenium arch: this is the shape you will be most familiar with, although as the older stages are being replaced, more adaptable spaces are being used and designed
- Traverse stage
- End stage
- Arena stage
- Thrust stage.

In addition to spatial arrangements, you might consider using different levels to their best effect. Most spaces are equipped with rostra (wooden blocks), which can be invaluable for indicating changes of location and setting, especially in a studio. Other equipment you might consider using include cycloramas, projectors, flats or scaffolding.

In Figure 5.3, you will see a set which was made for a Gothic production. Camouflage nets were borrowed from a local army camp, and draped all over the seats and also beneath the lights. This transformed the whole (small) space into a dark forest. The chairs, tables, and different levels all signified different locations. The difference in location was emphasised with the use of different coloured lights and different levels.

Figure 5.3 *The set for* Vampirella

GROUND PLAN

Once you have considered all of these possibilities, you can start drawing up a ground plan, which is a birds-eye view of how you intend your set to look. Figure 5.4 shows the ground plan of the set shown in Figure 5.3.

Figure 5.4   *The ground plan for* Vampirella

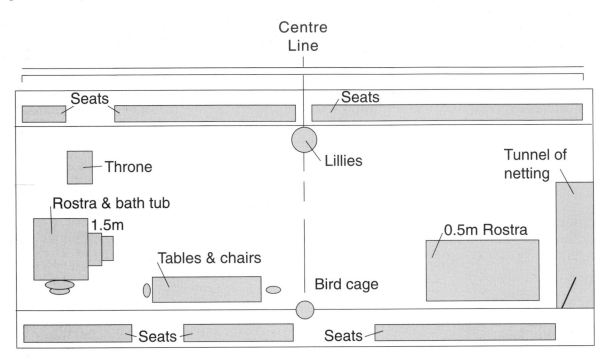

TASK

- Realistic sets require the accurate representation of life; *Ubu Roi* calls for the exact opposite. You need to create a set which defies belief in the eyes of the audience while at the same time serving the purpose of the play, which is to ludicrously imitate historical-romantic dramas.
- Fictionalise a budget, draw up a resource list of exactly what is available in your studio, and what you think you can obtain from willing donors. Then draw up a ground plan for the first two scenes of *Ubu Roi*, working within these limitations. Think in terms of the concept of a 'bonkers' form of theatre (re-read the descriptions of the original form on pages 154–55), and also the actors' entrances and exits.

MAKING A SET MODEL

After you have drawn up your ground plan, and it has been approved by the director and the rest of the production team, you need to make up a model. This will help you to work out the size and type of materials you are going to be using, and will help the rest of the company to see exactly what you have visualised for them. This model will also be used by both the sound and lighting designers. It is usual to build models on a 1:25 scale (1cm on the model equals 25cm on the real sets). You can buy a special ruler which will convert your measurements from a local art shop. Ask the assistants for advice on the right materials to help you build your set.

Tools and materials you will need for this purpose include:

- various thicknesses of card
- paint
- balsa wood
- a set square
- a metal edge
- a ruler
- a scalpel
- compasses
- glue

- fimo.

First of all, you need to build the space in which your production is going to be set, and then fill it with the props and furniture indicated in your ground plan. Using fimo, build Ma and Pa Ubu and put them on the set so that you can see if everything works to scale.

In the professional theatre, you would now need to make a line drawing, accurate to the nearest millimetre, from which all of the technicians and construction staff could work. Consult one of the resource books listed at the end of this chapter to help you do this if such a technical drawing is required, and for information about set-up building techniques.

Lighting

This is one of the most time-consuming and demanding components of the production process. The lighting process itself can be split into two distinct areas:

- the planning/design stage
- the production stage.

DESIGN

The lighting design will always be affected by the limitations of time and/or money, but must strive to support the overall artistic design and direct the audience's attention to the actor(s) at the appropriate moments. These aims are achievable with proper planning and organisation. The first stage in the design process is to meet with the director and/or artistic designer so that you can find out exactly what they want. Each play has a distinctive style, and your job as lighting designer is to support the style decided upon by director and artistic director – not to completely re-interpret the piece in your own style. By the time that the lighting designer becomes involved in the process, a set model should be

prepared. This set model will be of great help to you in the initial stages of planning and experimentation; see Figure 5.5.

Manufacturers of lighting equipment produce filters and swatch books which act as a directory to all the different colours of filter available. The filters are placed in front of the lights to create different effects; armed with a swatch book (or larger examples of the filter you are thinking about using), a torch or angle-poise lamp, you can explore the different possibilities on your set design. With this minimum of equipment you can experiment with the angles and colours of your potential design, and build an idea of the cues that will be needed. You can

Figure 5.5   *You can experiment with lights, using a 3-D set design*

also see an approximation of the way the light will behave on the stage.

In both cases, with or without a set model, you should visit the theatre in which the design is going to be carried through. This will afford a more accurate picture of what is or is not possible. What lights do they have available in the theatre for your use? How much will it cost to hire the difference? If you use three profiles on

a lighting tree USL (Up Stage Left), will their beams shine into the audience's eyes?

Once you have been through these initial steps you can start to plan. Divide the set into a grid, and allocate the effects you will need to achieve in each section of the set.

On an open stage with little or no set, the lighting design will aim to cover the stage equally, in each of the grid boxes or modules. Many sets, however, are much more complicated than this, and require the introduction of 'specials' or effects which are used for one character and in one scene only. From this preparatory grid, you will be able to see the number of lights you are going to need, their colours and an idea of the angle at which they are going to be set, in order to provide the required cover. Look at the 'Cheat Sheet' in Figure 5.6: this kind of grid will allow you to make a rough plan of each state.

★ *hot tip*

Of course, you will not always be able to gain access to a 3-D set design. There may not be the time or the expertise to build one, in which case, you need to get a ground plan and use your imagination.

Figure 5.6   *A cheat sheet*

1	2	3
4	5	6
7	8	9

TASK

The quality of the effect achieved greatly depends upon where exactly the actor or piece of scenery is lit from.

- Are you going to light from the front, from the floor, from behind, directly above or from the side? Grab an actor or piece of scenery and try lighting the subject from all of these different angles with just one light to begin with.
- Do the different angles suggest different moods to you, or different times of day? A floor lighting, pointing straight into an actor's face, for example, achieves quite a chilling atmosphere. A back light above the actor or piece of scenery can suggest night or suspense.

After you have tried these positions with just one light, introduce one and then two more lights. Combine lights pointing at different angles, e.g. two lighting the subject from the side and one from the front; experiment again with mood and style.

COLOUR

The maximum amount of colours you are likely to have at your disposal will probably never exceed 20. The colours you choose will depend on the style of the piece and the colour and material of the stage set. Pale filters are more suitable for straight drama, and darker colours for heavily stylised pieces. Again, it is only by experimentation that you will see the quality of the effects that you can achieve with these filters.

TASK

Repeat the above exercise but this time use different combinations of filters. In addition, experiment with the strength of the light, as this radically affects the colour of the beam on stage.

TYPES OF LIGHT

There are two types of light: flood and spots. All lights can be *tilted* (moved up or down), or *panned* (moved from side-to-side). If you have carried out the task above, you will already be familiar with these actions, which can be carried out by altering the screws on the pivoting devices attached to the box containing the light.

- Floods are used mainly to light scenery. Their beams are fixed and cannot be altered, so they are unsuitable for lighting the stage floor or the actors; see Figure 5.7.
- You may be familiar with the term 'footlights'. This is a bank of floodlights set out in a long box called a batten, and placed on the floor. The batten can also be placed on a bar and used to light scenery from above.
- Fresnels produce a beam which has a soft edge when it hits the floor. They may be used with barn doors which create shadows and can block out parts of the beam. The beam is both wide and controllable; see Figure 5.8.
- The pebble convex or PC is basically the

same as a fresnel, but with a tighter edge. It can also be fitted with barn doors; see Figure 5.9.

- The Parcan is similar to a car headlamp, producing a light across the stage. The only control available is the angle of the elliptical beam, which can be turned at different angles; see Figure 5.10.
- Variable Beam Profiles create a hard edge (profile) on the floor. The shape of this profile can be moved and altered. There are two lenses inside the barrel which can soften/harden and widen/narrow the beam. The distribution of light within the beam can also be altered, so the light pinpoints or washes; see Figure 5.11.
- Gobos (metal masks with shapes cut in) can also be added onto lights. The beam acts as on a projector, throwing the shape cut in the metal onto the stage; see Figure 5.12.

Lights can also be softened with diffusion sheets, available from the manufacturers, placed in front of the lens like a colour filter.

Figure 5.7   *A floodlight*

Figure 5.8   *A fresnel with barn doors*

Figure 5.9   *A PC (pebble convex)*

Figure 5.10   *A Parcan*

Figure 5.11   *A Variable Beam Profile*

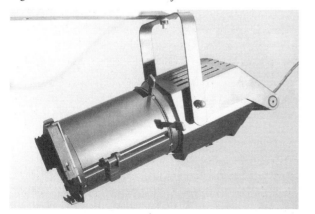

Figure 5.12   *A Gobo*

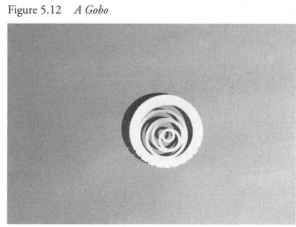

LIGHTING PLAN

By the time you have experimented with the lights themselves and the various filters on the stage, you will be ready to create a rough lighting plan. For this you will need a stencil (available from lighting equipment manufacturers), a ground plan and tracing paper. Using the tracing paper, build up your plan, layer by layer, module by module. The plan and the stencil are usually created on a scale of 1:25. Scale symbols are cut out on the stencil; each shape symbolises the individual kind of light. Inside the shape of the light drawn on the plan,

is the number of the colour filter (these numbers are also the industry standard). The focal point of the light on the stage is written next to the shape of the light, and in a small circle the number of the dimmer channel is noted; see Figure 5.13.

This rough plan will be taken along to the rehearsal and altered accordingly if the director makes a modification to his original concept, or the actors have thought of an idea not included in the original design.

Figure 5.13   *A section of a lighting plan*

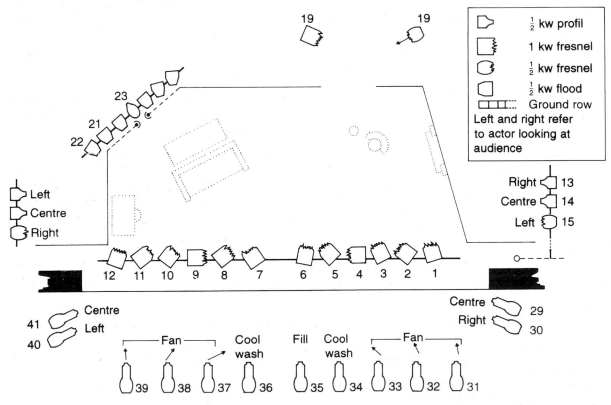

PRODUCTION OF LIGHTS

Rigging

The operation of putting the lights onto the bars is best carried out on ground level, with

the bars being hoisted after the initial procedures have been carried out. Of course, this is not practicable in a studio or theatre where the rig is fixed, so the rigger will have to work hard, balancing on a ladder and dealing with awkward angles. In this case, a talloscope is your best friend, both in terms of comfort and safety. If you are using a ladder, always make sure that someone is holding it at the bottom.

Lighting rigs will support different amounts of current, and, in addition to time and expense, this limits the amount of lights that you can use in any circuit or on the rig as a whole. The stage electrician will inform you as to what is an acceptable load for the particular rig/circuit.

If you have planned the lights according to the procedure laid out above, look at the lighting plan, and fix the lights onto the bars according to the drawing. If the lights are on the floor, then you can position them, open barn doors and shutters, and add the filters as required before they are lifted. This will save a great deal of fiddling about and time-wasting at the next stage.

Focusing

Focusing is varying the angle and direction of each individual light, and is part of the rigging process. As with all of the other techniques, you will only really learn how to rig, by getting onto a stage and doing it. Here are a few helpful tips to aid you. You will need a minimum of two people, but preferably at least three: one standing on the stage, one in the audience and one on the ladder. The person on the stage

may stand in for an actor. The designer should be on stage or in the audience, issuing the focusing person with the necessary instructions, achieving the required effect by asking for barn door angles, lenses and the tilt and pan of the lights to be adjusted.

Cueing

The designer, lighting operator and SM have to agree on the cueing of the lighting design. The cue tells the lighting operator and the SM the exact point in the script at which a particular arrangement of lights are to be brought into action, and also when to take them down. The level, or strength of the light depends upon the precise effect the designer wants to achieve. When this has been agreed, the level will be written into the cue, alongside the time over which the designer requires the cue to be brought in. The agreed level will depend upon the type of board being used.

Memory boards are common in all but studio theatres and will enable the designer to choose from a range of levels between 1–100 (the manual board has only a range of 1–10). How much light is actually delivered onto the stage, depends upon the light you are using. Bear in mind that the largest visible difference in light output is between 30–40 per cent, and between 60–70 per cent.

In Figure 5.14, you will see an example of a script with the LX (lighting effects) number

Figure 5.14 *A lighting effects cueing sheet*

LX	Channel	Time	Level	Act I Scene I
Standby	Q.1			
Q1:	5&6 up over 20 s		60%	Pa Ubu: Pschitt!* Ma Ubu: Ooh! what a nasty word
Standby	Q.2			
Q2:	Xfade 1 up over	5&6 down 20 s	0% 80%	Pa Ubu, you're a dirty old man Pa Ubu: Watch out I don't bash yer nut in, Ma Ubu!

written down. These numbers must be the same on all the separate cueing sheets. Every technician and designer has a different version of the cue sheet, but so long as they contain the vital information of level, cue number, time and the point at which the cue is made, you can lay them out as you like. Figure 5.14 shows one version, which is quite simple to make. Paste the pages of the play onto the right hand pages of an A4 pad, and use the left hand page

---

★ hot tip

A useful technique is cross-fading: bring one lighting state down, and at the same time, bring another cue up.

---

to write in the cues, with arrows leading to the appropriate point in the script.

TASK

Take a piece of text and your set design; light the design in your studio. Bear in mind that your first job as lighting designer is to illuminate the actors. Set up a cue sheet like the one above, and while the actors run through their lines, cue in the lighting states. It will take you more than a few attempts to get it right.

Sound

The creative use of recorded effects during a production, and the effective amplification of live or recorded effects are crucial parts of the production process. In this section, we aim to provide a basic description of the techniques and equipment associated with the various sound processes.

WHAT IS SOUND?

Sound is produced when an oscillating object causes the air around it to move. The result creates a wave motion which can be heard if it is within the human hearing range of 20Hz–20kHz. Frequency is measured in *Hertz* and is defined as the number of waves that pass a specific point in one second. As we get older, the hearing range decreases. A 20-year-old person will probably have a range of 20Hz–18kHz.

Sound travels through the air in the same way that a ripple moves away from an object that has been dropped in a pool of water. As the wave moves away from the source, it becomes weaker. The human ear is better at distinguishing the source-direction of high-frequency sound and notes than the source-direction of low-frequency sounds and notes. This information may be useful to you when you are trying to work out where to place the loudspeakers in your auditorium. High-frequency notes are termed as directional, and low notes as non-directional.

In order for sound to be recorded or amplified, it has to be turned into electronic pulses (an amplifier simply enlarges the size of these pulses) before it is passed on.

THE MICROPHONE

A transducer can convert an acoustic source, such as the human voice, into an electrical signal. This conversion of movement into electricity is a property that is common to microphones. The electrical signal increases in proportion to movement and sound increases.

Microphones pick up sounds in different ways, so it is important for the producer to choose the correct microphone to match the task in hand. Microphones have different sensitivity patterns, e.g. figure of eight, cardoid, omnidirectional. Omnidirectional microphones are widely used in recording audio. They pick up sounds in a single direction and are useful for recording vocals and eliminating sound sources from other directions. The most practical microphone for the theatre is the 'moving coil' type, which is durable and of good quality.

Radio microphones are also extremely useful, allowing the performer freedom of movement. Miking-up bands can be a tricky process, especially if you have a limited number of microphones at your disposal. The quieter instruments will need dedicated mikes if they are to be heard. Remember that a bass note is omnidirectional and will find its way to the mike as long as it is near enough, whereas the higher-frequency, more directional notes will need a mike pointing at them in order for them to be picked up. It is also better if the performers speak or sing over the top of the microphone, as this will reduce the sound of the performers breathing.

LOUDSPEAKERS

The two different types of sound we have mentioned so far, the low-frequency and the high-frequency notes, need different kinds of loudspeaker to produce their sound effectively:

- a *Woofer* produces the low notes
- a *Tweeter* produces the high notes.

Both of these kinds of speaker are usually found in the same box/cabinet, the Woofer being the larger one. A third speaker is commonly utilised for the pulses in the mid-range. The *crossover* device ensures that each speaker receives the correct pulse. The kind of speaker you might have at home will probably be

Figure 5.15   *The effect of loudspeakers*

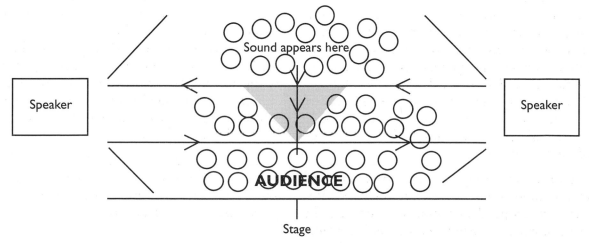

around 30 Watts in power; to fill an auditorium, a speaker will be up to 100 Watts.

The location of your sound equipment is extremely important, whatever kind of space you are working in. If the speakers are hidden on stage, placing them behind cloth or gauze will not affect the speakers' performance if the weave of the cloth is open at least 50 per cent. Solid objects concealing the speaker should have holes drilled in, to let the sound through. Experiment carefully with the position of the speakers in your space before assigning them a final position. Speakers placed on a horizontal axis opposite each other, producing an equal volume, will create the illusion that the sound is appearing from a point on the centre of this axis, and thus from centre stage.

Of course, your stage design will present difficulties for this kind of location arrangement, if it is anything other than the completely conventional one represented in Figure 5.15. Speakers placed directly above the staging area will produce the impression that the sound is coming from the performer(s) centre stage, but will be less effective for the audience who are sitting further back. Stage designs such as *in-the-round* and *promenade* will present their own problems, which the sound designer will have to overcome.

Feedback is a nuisance, and occurs when the microphone picks up the amplified sound from the speakers. To avoid this, ensure that the speakers are facing away from the microphone(s).

RECORDING AND EDITING EFFECTS

The only machine to use for this purpose is the reel-to-reel tape recorder (commonly known as a Revox, after the company which made a great deal of sound equipment for use in the theatre). If you do not have access to a reel-to-reel, you will be tempted to use an ordinary tape cassette; this is completely impractical for use in the theatre because it is impossible to cue up precisely and will make the operators' task a living nightmare during the production. *Cartridge* tape recorders are different instruments, and are used in the theatre, because the continuous loop of tape makes this piece of equipment ideal for long repetitive effects. Compact discs, minidiscs and record players are also impractical because they are too delicate and impossible to cue-up with the required precision.

The reel-to-reel machine uses two spools of magnetic tape (see Figure 5.16). The tape has to pass over either the *playback, recording* or *erase* head to complete one or any of those

Figure 5.16   *A reel-to-reel tape machine*

functions. In order to edit a sound effects tape for a play on one of these machines, you will need to learn how to record and mix your target effects, and then how to splice the effects together.

The machine in Figure 5.16 can record directly from other devices such as record players, microphones or tape cassettes, by means of a connecting sound cable. All of the equipment has to be compatible, however, and you may face interference problems. Consult an electrician about how to deal with these problems.

Mixing

Mixing is the operation whereby the effects are altered and modified in one way or another before being laid down on the final track. Reel-to-reel tape players like the one shown in Figure 5.16 are usually capable of supporting stereo sound. In this instance the magnetic tape is divided into two. These machines are capable of supporting a maximum of four channels; therefore the tape decreases in quality. Multi-track recorders, much more commonly found in a recording studio than in the theatre, may have up to 64 tracks, and use wider tape than the standard 5mm seen on the Revox.

If you are serious about mixing and using a modern studio with multi-track and digital facilities, then read the following information about the recording studio. If you are happy with the basic reel-to-reel then skip onto the splicing section (page 174), which shows you how to put a tape together.

PRODUCTION AND THE RECORDING STUDIO

The recording studio is the focus for all sound sources, as this is where the production process takes place. Figure 5.17 is a simple block diagram of a typical studio set-up, showing the audio pathway from its sources to the speakers.

An overview of a simple audio chain

The audio pathway as indicated in Figure 5.17 starts from the source: this may be an artist singing through a microphone. The microphone is plugged into the mixing desk and the signal is then usually sent to the multitrack recorder where the signal is designated a specific channel. On playback from the multi-track recorder, the vocal may be mixed with other recorded channels such as a piano. These two channels are fed back into the mixing desk for a mixdown. The mixdown allows the engineer or producer to add reverb or other effects to create atmosphere; s/he can pan the signals left, mid or right in the stereo image and adjust the equalisation of the channels individually. The producer monitors the mix through the speakers and headphones. When satisfied with the mix, a final master recording is made onto an appropriate format for the client to review.

Analogue and digital production

Why bother with digital? You can access your material very fast with hard discs, CDs and minidiscs. You can also store vast amounts of information and access this quickly. When we think of digital in terms of the production process, the major benefit is that dubbing or the copying of material is capable without the loss of quality, offering a much wider dynamic range than analogue. The disadvantage of a digital system is that it requires much more sophisticated equipment for editing, but it does allow the user to preview the edit in a non-destructive process, i.e. you are not committed to the decision. Advanced digital processing such as time stretching and pitch shift offers great versatility. Having said this, some people claim that a digital recording is too harsh and prefer the analogue system.

Figure 5.17   *Sources of sound*

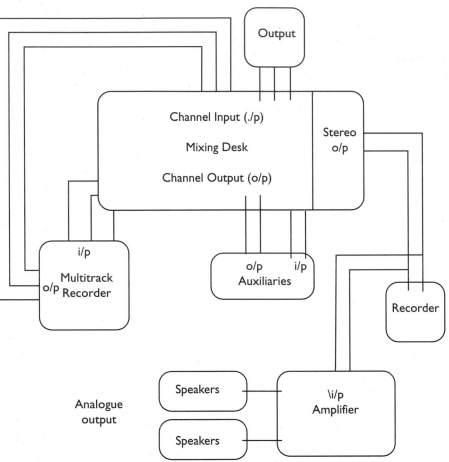

It is important that when producing your product for theatre you decide which system is most cost effective, user friendly and will produce the best results for the production.

Sources

These can be from a variety of digital or analogue sources. One digital source we have not mentioned is Musical Instrument Digital Interface (MIDI). This is the standard communication system for controlling electronic musical instruments, such as keyboards samplers. You can control these via MIDI, using a basic computer and timecode. This gives you the flexibility to edit and manipulate digital information without the loss of any digital audio tracks; this is a powerful ad-dition to any studio, and very common practice.

Other sources could include CDs (useful for sound effects), analogue quarter-inch tape machines to play back location recordings, or minidiscs (a digital portable and studio format). Whatever your source, it is important to record them at the optimum level without distorting, as this will ensure that the original signal remains consistent throughout the recording process. You must select your source materials with care. Audio is a very powerful medium and can change the mood of any situation in a production. It is important at this stage to work closely to the original design brief and have a clear idea of what is to be achieved.

Track sheets

You have selected all your sources and are now ready to record them on the multitrack recorder. You must now consider a track sheet. This will allow you to map out in advance which sound will be assigned to which channel on the recorder. This is very important, especially if you intend to bounce down tracks.

Mixer channels

Your input source or sources now have to follow a route through the mixer prior to the multitrack recorder. This allows you to assign the sources to specific channels as indicated in your track sheet. The mixing desk at this stage is acting as a routine process and level manipulator only. Do not add effects such as reverbs or equalisation at this stage. It is important to record the source signal to the multitrack recorder as faithfully as possible. Any adjustment that needs to be made to the signal should either be rectified at source or on mixdown, but not at the multitrack recording stage; this is because any additions to the signal such as reverb cannot be taken off at a later stage. The mixer assigns buttons, say one to eight (1–8); left panning normally assigns signals to the odd channels and right panning to the even channels, depending on which assign button you select.

Multitrack recorder

Having chosen your channels, it is important to record the signal at its optimum level without clipping or distorting. This will reduce the amount of noise in the system and help greatly during the mixdown in terms of clarity, quality and versatility. Having recorded all your tracks (e.g. 1–8), you now have to route all the channel outputs back to the mixing desk for the mixdown.

Mixing and monitoring

The mixdown is where the benefits of multitrack production become apparent. You now have eight tracks of audio, totally isolated on different channels but relative in time to each other. This is where the producer must use all of his or her creative experience to manipulate the signals. Through the mixing desk it is possible to add effects such as delay and reverb through the auxiliaries, creating atmosphere and dynamics relevant to the production. The equalisation of each individual channel can be altered throughout the dynamic range, to address the high, mid and low frequencies; this adds clarity to the production and avoids clashing frequencies. Panning the channels forms the stereo image and brings the entire recording to life along with the channel volume faders.

Mastering and dubbing

Presuming you are happy with your mix, you are now ready to master your product. You need to choose a suitable format, preferably digital. This will allow you to save the recording in a stereo format and take copies directly from this for the client, without any real degradation in quality. You now have the flexibility to dub onto a suitable format for the client, always keeping your master recording safe. When mixing down, you have the option of using external processors such as compressors to enhance, restrict or expand the stereo image prior to mastering. Remember to record at the optimum level without clipping or distorting the signal.

Review and evaluation

If you are totally confident that your product meets the requirements of the design, you need to arrange a meeting with the client to listen to the finished product. There may be several meetings like this and many remixes until the client is happy, but always refer to the original design brief for clarification of the aims.

Finally, having completed all your recordings for the show, you may be required to log them and place them in a logical order on a suitable format for the sound engineer to play during the production. There are several ways of doing this:

- The easiest way is to dub each individual recording onto minidiscs (assuming the production or venue can arrange the playback facility for minidisc). This will allow you to label each track, search and log the total duration, and have access to instant playback at the touch of a button for cueing. Timing is probably the most important element in any production and the minidisc meets the demands and offers the flexibility and quality required for today's productions.

- However, minidiscs may not be available for your production, so the careful logging and ordering of material becomes more important for cassette and analogue quarter-inch tape. Every audio piece will have to be logged to a tape counter and the operator must cue from the counter display. If you use quarter-inch tape then simple leader can provide a visual separation between audio sections (see reel-to-reel splicing below).

Splicing tape for the reel-to-reel recorder

In order to make a whole sound effects tape, you will need to put the different lengths of tape together. This action is called *splicing*. Cut the magnetic tape at the place where you want the effect to begin or end (this decision will be made either by you or the director during rehearsal) and join it in to the other effects by means of splicing tape. Leader tape (which comes in many different colours) will help you designate which cue is which, so that when you come to the production you will know simply by looking at the tape and cross-referring to your production notes whether you have the

right effect cued in. In fact most modern machines have a lens which stops the machine when it recognises a certain kind of leader tape passing beneath it; your cueing work is mostly done in the studio during the splicing process, when you add this tape in.

Splicing tool kit

- editing block
- reel-to-reel tape recorder
- magnetic tape
- leader tape
- splicing tape
- one-sided razor blade

To splice a tape:

1 Mark the tape at the appropriate point.
2 Cut the tape on the block, getting rid of the unnecessary length.
3 Rejoin the tape, using a coloured piece of leader tape to identify the cue (see Figure 5.18).

Sound cue sheet

The sheet in Figure 5.19 is similar to the lighting cue sheet on page 167, and, when filled in, will be the Bible for the sound operator to work from during the show. If you have more than one tape deck, and/or different types of deck, you will need to reference this in the Tape Deck section. Number off the decks at your disposal, and fill in the numbers at the appropriate cue. The Leader section is for you to denote the colour you have designated your cue, e.g. red. Speaker Select indicates the speakers you wish to use on the cue, Level indicates the volume and Tone indicates the amount of bass or treble you wish to put on the cue. The Masters are usually graded as a percentage of 10, e.g. 6/10. The Action will be a visual/script clue for you, which you will pick up from rehearsals. In the Comments box, you can put in bring-up or fade-out times.

Figure 5.18 *How to splice a tape*

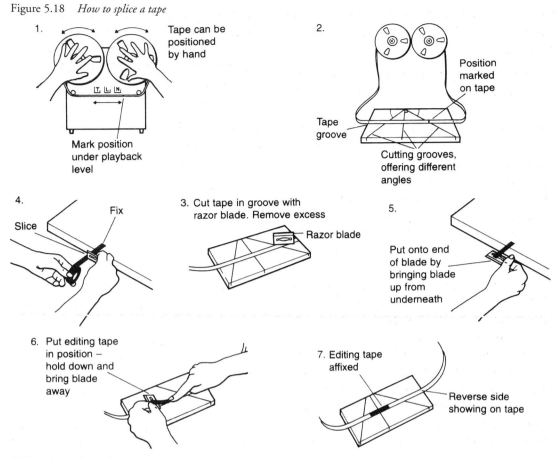

Figure 5.19 *A sound cue sheet*

Cue no.	Tape Deck	Leader	Speaker Select	Level	Tone	Masters	Action/ Subject	Comments
1								
2								
3								
4								
5								
6								
7								
8								

TASK

Create your own cue sheet and sound tape, using the techniques outlined above, for the first two scenes of *Ubu Roi*.

Stage management

The Stage Manager is responsible for the organisation of all the backstage procedures: props setting, getting the actors onto the stage at the right time, the get-in and get-out. In addition, the SM assists the director during rehearsals and fills in any gaps in the personnel. On many smaller shows, members of the stage management team will be involved in the lighting and sound operation and may even take walk-on parts during the performance (hence the term Acting Stage Manger or ASM). The SM assumes complete control of the production from the point of the commencement of the final dress rehearsal. S/he co-ordinates all of the departments – lighting, sound, costume, props and acting company – and attempts to ensure that everything runs smoothly and according to plan.

TASK

During the play, the stage management team set and strike props and items of scenery. In Figure 5.20, you will see a diagram of a Stage Manager's cue sheet, showing the items of scenery that have to be *struck* (taken off the stage) and the items that have to be set, along with a list of the props that need to be set. Create your own diagram for a target piece of text.

You will need to make a note of props and furniture requirements, and of the precise timing and location of their use: see Figures 5.20–5.22.

Figure 5.20   *A Props breakdown list*

PROPS BREAKDOWN LIST

PRODUCTION:

DIRECTOR:

DESIGNER:

PAGE   OF

ITEM	ACT/SCENE	PAGE No.	INFORMATION/NOTES # DENOTES PRIORITY	STOCK	MAKE	BORROW	HIRE	BUY	COST	CONTACT

Figure 5.21   *A Furniture breakdown list*

FURNITURE BREAKDOWN LIST

PRODUCTION:

DIRECTOR:

DESIGNER:

PAGE   OF

ITEM	ACT/SCENE	PAGE No.	INFORMATION/NOTES	STOCK	MAKE	BORROW	HIRE	BUY	COST	CONTACT

Figure 5.22 *A Provisional breakdown list*

PROVISIONAL BREAKDOWN

PRODUCTION:		DIRECTOR:	DESIGNER:	LD:	PAGE OF	PERIOD:
ACT/SCENE	CHARACTERS		LOCATION & TIME		NOTES: SET/FURNITURE/PROPS/SND/SPFX/ETC.	

Costume

Costumes need to be created for your actors, but professional cutting and designing is too complicated for a manual of this kind. Most productions do not generally require professional cutting, but ingenuity and a knowledge of materials are vital. Ralph Oswick, Artistic Director of the *Natural Theatre Company*, is a master at this kind of improvised costume-making. Below are Ralph's notes about the brief, design and manufacture of the costumes for a low-budget children's show, *The Mad Hatter's Tea Party*, written by Andy Pollard. The show was first produced at the Rondo Theatre in Bath in December 1995. If you read through this project outline and the process by which Ralph arrived at the final product, you will be able to see the way to complete your own brief.

The Mad Hatter's Tea Party

The costumes for this show had to be clear-cut characters, easily recognised but retaining a certain Natural Theatre Company originality and style (see Figure 1.4 on page 13). The costumes had to be cheap, colourful but not 'pantoesque', and suitable for a quick-change without a backstage dresser. The author wanted an old-fashioned Englishness, with references to *Alice in Wonderland* without exactly reproducing the characters in that story.

The costume brief was organised into a list with bullet points. As creative ideas came to the surface, they were checked off against this list to see if they fulfilled every requirement:

- Easily recognisable but not stereotypical
- Cheap
- NTC style
- Actors can change out of the costume quickly and alone
- Does the idea refer to *Alice in Wonderland* in some way?
- Do the costumes relate effectively with the set design?

The company decided not to go for sparkly, satin, Christmas-type materials, but to rely on clear silhouettes and crisp simplicity, with any colours in the costumes reflecting the rather odd shades already being used on the set. The set involved a cluttered tea-table and two doors set in a darkly painted hedge. Characters often stood behind the table, so the top halves of their costumes were most important. All the characters had sudden entrances through the doors, or through trapdoors, and this was why clarity/recognition was an important part of the original brief. The success of this tactic was displayed in the paintings and drawings sent in by the young audience after the show. Their illustrations were incredibly detailed and accurate both from the point of view of the set and the costumes.

DRAWINGS

The drawings in Figures 5.23–5.29 were taken from Ralph's margin sketches made in the original script, and were used to help the actors visualise the characters at the first reading. Very few colour drawings were done, as the general colour scheme was already known. On the lower-budget Natural Theatre Company shows, the actors do a certain amount of prop/costume-buying and their choices are verified by the director or designer. This process stems from the street theatre work, in which the performers have almost complete control of their costumes and characters (as long as they fit in with the overall NTC style).

THE DATE-KEEPER

A grey army greatcoat and an 'official' hat were taken from the company store and sprayed in a misty way, with some stencils of moon and stars. Old cans of car-paint were used for this purpose. The coat was useful because it covered up several other costumes which the actor had on underneath (all of the actors had to play several parts). The spraying made the coat appear quite dull, however, so zodiac signs were wired on here and there (glue very rarely works in the long term), along with some random clusters of tiny, sparkling stars. Epaulettes were lifted from another costume, wired on and then sprayed down. Florists soft-wire was used for this purpose. The final effect was that of an officious, celestial 'jobsworth'-type figure.

Figure 5.23 *The Date-keeper*

THE MAD HATTER

It was felt that this costume should look exactly like the original character in the *Alice in Wonderland* book, so the company simply hired the complete outfit. The NTC wardrobe might have provided something suitable, but the hired outfit was exactly the right colour. In addition, top-hats are extremely expensive to buy, and tend to appear very amateurish if made at home. Another important factor to bear in mind in this choice of costume, was that the actor wearing it did not have to worry about changing quickly, because he only had this one character to play. The Mad Hatter was therefore able to indulge himself in a set of spats, an authentic pair of character shoes and a wing collar.

Figure 5.24 *The Mad hatter*

THE MARCH HARE

The character of the March Hare was very different to that of the character in *Alice in Wonderland*, which allowed some room for a little experimentation with the costume. The author (who also played the part) did not like the first, zany, streetwise version (shown in Figure 5.25). He felt the sunglasses would distance him from the children, and was not particularly keen to show his legs. The actor also felt that this look was not really 'English' enough. This drawing was used in the publicity, but in the end the performer used a tweedy suit with breeches. The ears came from a cheap bunny-girl outfit and were fixed to a Sherlock Holmes-style deerhunter. After much discussion the designer banned Balaclava helmets with ears sewn on, along with cutey mittens, which the actors thought helped to express the animal identities of the characters. The hare-lip was carefully painted onto the

Figure 5.25 *The March Hare*

* 181 *

Figure 5.26   *The Dormouse*

actor's face for each show, and very realistic whiskers (made from vinyl) were also glued on. A set of very expensive sticky-out teeth (already used by the company on a previous show) completed the picture.

THE DORMOUSE

The original tweed suit and muffler (based on Rastus Mouse from the *Rupert Bear* story) was eventually rejected, as the character became less of a posh person and more of a yokel/country bumpkin type as the rehearsals proceeded. Eventually, a smock, handkerchief and a straw hat with ears attached were used. In this case, the whiskers were drawn on, so that the actor could change roles quickly.

Figure 5.27   *The Great Teapot*

THE GREAT TEAPOT

This character finally appeared through the face of a huge clock on the stage, so all that was required was a black rollneck sweater with gloves. The teapot itself was quite difficult to achieve, and in the end, one of the company's globe heads was used, held together by velcro. The handle and spout were shown side-on, in silhouette and cut from plywood. A three-dimensional shape would have been much too demanding of the time and resources available, and in any case, the pot-head was only seen from the front, so it was completely convincing. The actor had to use a radio microphone, because the foam lining of the globe head muffled the voice.

Figure 5.28   *The Sheep Lady*

THE SHEEP LADY

This performer was never intended to be a real sheep, so an old raincoat and hat with hundreds of cotton wool balls glued on, were used to delineate a human being with sheep characteristics. This process took a lot of patience and care, but was not as time-consuming as we had originally thought. The cotton wool, however, caught on all the rough surfaces, leaving minute traces of itself everywhere, and drove the cast and crew completely mad. The costume was finally sprayed with clear, matt varnish and odd touches of grey car paint, which made it less than fireproof but a great deal easier to cope with during the show. The shoes were very small and black and helped the performer to walk in a sheep-like manner. Bits started dangling off over the weeks, but this effect actually made the costume appear more authentic, so no repairs had to be made.

THE TRAIN DRIVER

This costume was made up from old police uniforms (which you can obtain from the police force with a little persuasion!) and various train badges. Although the children would be used to seeing a more modern railway uniform, the classic look was chosen to fit in with the 'Englishness' of the production design.

THE CATERPILLAR

The Caterpillar had a kind of keen, 'I know best' outlook on life, and various versions of the costume were attempted to fit in with these characteristics (heating duct, stuffed stockings etc.). Finally, a brilliantly simple solution was arrived at: the fur-lined hood and one sleeve of a green anorak with an orange lining was bound up with dozens of rubber bands. The actor simply put his head through the hood and operated the tapering sleeve with a rod. The result was the world's first train-spotting caterpillar.

NOTES

- These costumes, manufactured with little or no budget, had such clear characteristics that they worked just as well as more elaborate and expensive costumes might have done. Simplicity was the key to their 'cleverness', and an audience appreciates resourcefulness of this kind. Each component was carefully chosen in consultation with the performer. Virtually no sewing was needed, and certainly no time-consuming, difficult dyeing. The glues did not work all the time because they were used to piece together very different materials. A knowledge of paints and glues is very important for this kind of operation.
- The shapes were varied so that it would be difficult for the children to tell who exactly was playing each role at any particular moment during the show. The variety of shapes also helped the actors to assume their different roles.
- For a longer-running show, the cleaning of some of the costumes would have become a problem, particularly that of the Sheep Lady. Cleaning must always be borne in mind when designing costumes, because, over a long run, they can become extremely smelly if not attended to.
- Most of the work was handed out to 'helpers' because the costumes did not require specialist knowledge or skills. This allowed the company to concentrate on the rehearsals.

SUMMARY OF DESIGN PROCESS

- Clarity is of the greatest importance.

Figure 5.29   *The Train Driver*

- Consult with performers at all stages of the design and manufacture.
- Practicality – will the costume take the required paint/glue?
- An observation from reality is often more comic than a fantasy costume.
- Design from the perspective of the text and not from outside it, e.g. the streetwise March Hare did not actually fit with the story line devised by the author.

Here is a list of questions the designer asked the director and performer before designing the Sheep Lady.

1 Is it a known character, or something new to the audience?
Answer: New

2 Is it a sheep or a lady, or a combination of both?
Answer: A combination.

3 Which characteristics do I need to capture?
Answer: Shape of old lady, texture, colour, walk.

4 What are the staging logistics regarding other costumes, quick-change, trap-door entrances?
Answer: Must fit in with the English eccentricity and flavour of the other designs; don't need a quick-change or trap-door entrance so bulk is not a problem.

5 Which cheap materials will convey a 'sheep-look', while also suggesting a 'knitted-look'?
Answer: Not sheepskin! Lint is good, but does not hold together, so the answer has to be cotton wool balls.

6 Where can I get bags of white-only cotton wool balls?
Answer: You can't. Find a willing slave to pick them out!

> ## TASK
>
> Create a costume brief; design and make drawings for the costumes for Ma and Pa Ubu. Base your designs on the materials which you have available, and the information provided on the original designs at the beginning of this chapter. If you have completed a set design for *Ubu Roi*, your costume designs will need to fit in with that concept.

How to make a mask

There are many types of mask, and different ways of making them. When talking about masks we often assume we mean something that covers all or most of the face and attaches around the back of the head. While this is generally true, it is not always so. A mask can be anything that alters or disguises the face: a false nose, a hat, make-up, an elastic band, glasses, a half-mask, a neutral mask, a gas-mask, a cardboard box, a paper bag with eye-holes pushed through it, etc. In theatre work we often experiment with such things without realising that what we are doing is mask-work.

Here, we are going to show you how to make three basic types of mask:

1 a neutral mask
2 a flat character mask
3 traditional half and full face masks.

A NEUTRAL MASK

You can buy plastic white face-masks in many toy and costume shops, but these often have very little life as performance masks. Neutral masks are plain, non-character masks that remove all facial expression and focus attention on the movement of the head and body. We recommend the following basic design, or close variation.

Equipment required:

- thick white card
- scissors
- stanley knife
- elastic
- studs
- hammer
- woodwork bench/cutting board
- pencil.

Method:

Draw the outline onto card, including eyes, nose and mouth. Cut round it with knife, taking care not to cut out entire nose shape. Punch studs through sides of mask with hammer. Tie on elastic tight enough to keep mask on bridge of nose, but light enough so that it does not bend. This mask must be kept facing audience at all times.

A FLAT CHARACTER MASK

The technique is essentially as for above. This time, however, you choose a face from a magazine. If it isn't big enough you can blow it up using a photocopier. Stick the face on card and cut round it (cut eye-holes). These masks don't work well as talkers so a mouth-hole is rarely necessary. Decorate your mask; give it a hat, or a jaunty cigarette, or some jewellery. Try to let the mask tell you what should happen as you go along.

TRADITIONAL HALF AND FULL FACE MASKS

If your mask is going to talk, then the half-face mask, borrowed from Commedia dell'Arte is often the best choice. If you don't need to talk, a full-face may be better. For the half-mask, don't build down over the mouth.

The simplest way to build these masks is onto a base in papier-mache. There are several ways of achieving a good base. To ensure a good fit you should take a cast of your own face. To do this we use gauze impregnated with plaster of paris (modroc).

Modroc face cast

Equipment needed:

- modroc (cut into strips)
- bowl of water

Figure 5.30   *Making a mould*

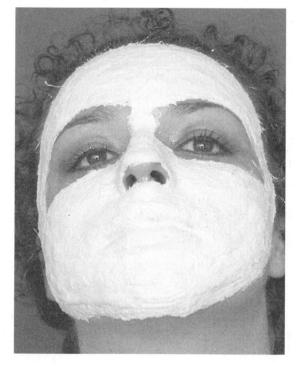

Note: we recommend you avoid using pictures of anyone instantly recognisable or famous, because the audience will see only them and not the mask character you are trying to create.

- petroleum jelly
- cling-film
- soap
- towels
- cotton wool.

Provided a supportive atmosphere is created and certain basic rules are adhered to, this can be a fun experience. Occasionally, someone will find the idea of having their face completely covered too scary. Don't pressurise anyone to have their face cast against their will.

Method:

1 Protect clothing with overalls, towels etc.
2 Give a good covering of petroleum jelly all over face, paying particular attention to eyebrows etc. (any hair can become painfully entangled). It saves on jelly if you use a little cling-film on eye-brows. It is particularly recommended for beards and moustaches.
3 Briefly dip a strip of modroc in the water, lift it up and run your fingers down it to remove excess water and apply it to face.
4 Cover face systematically, leaving the nostrils entirely clear. It is best to use a strip along the bridge of the nose and to line the face with strips along the forehead and jawbone.
5 Build up two or three layers all over for added strength.
6 Wait for modroc to set – it becomes warm to the touch. This usually takes a few minutes.
7 Peel mask off gently, breathing out through mouth.
8 Wash face thoroughly in soap and water.

To make a one-off mask, you can now use this cast as your base. Build features using plas-

Figure 5.31   *The mask mould*

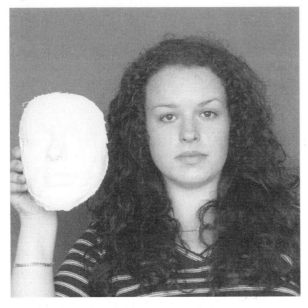

ticine and then cover with papier-mache. To make a permanent plaster positive of your face use the following technique.

Equipment needed:

- modroc cast of face
- quick setting plaster.

Method:

1 Fill in the nostril holes with a little more modroc from the outside. Build up the edges.
2 There should be lots of petroleum jelly still inside the cast, but check to be sure.
3 Prepare the plaster (do not stir), turn cast upside down, pour it in and wait for it to set.
4 Once set, remove from modroc cast. You now have a positive plaster image of your face. Build additional features on with plasticine. You will be able to make many personalised masks from this base.

The modroc technique guarantees a mask that fits you. It is, of course, useful to make masks that fit almost anybody, in which case you can bypass the modroc stage and buy cheap plastic one-size-fits-all masks for use as bases. Simply build features onto them in plasticine before

adding papier-mache. Quicker, but somehow not as satisfying.

Building the features

Equipment needed:

- modelling clay/plasticine

Method:

Whatever you are using as a base, you will now need to build features onto your mask. If building a lot then modelling clay works well. If, however, you are only adding a small amount of features, then plasticine is perfectly adequate. Make sure that you will be able to pull the mask off whatever features you are building (gouging plasticine out of bulbous noses can be a tiresome business!).

Papier-mache

Equipment needed:

- petroleum jelly
- newspaper strips
- tissue strips
- PVA glue
- water
- wallpaper paste.

Method:

1 Cover mask with layer of petroleum jelly.
2 Dilute PVA with a little water to make it go further: about 1 of water to 2 of PVA.
3 Dunk a newspaper strip. Hold it up and run fingers down it to remove excess glue. Lay onto mask, working it gently into features with fingertips.
4 Build up two layers of newspaper before moving onto tissue-paper.
5 Add a couple of layers of tissue-paper, which gives a better finish than newspaper (kitchen roll can be good here too). You can also mush it up with glue and mould features out of it.
6 Leave overnight somewhere dry and warm.
7 Carefully remove mask from base. Leave

again to dry. Wipe out petroleum jelly with kitchen roll.

Preparing the mask to wear

Equipment needed:

- Stanley knife
- scissors
- elastic
- foam
- paints
- superglue.

Method:

1 Trim edges of mask with scissors. Edge these with further strips of papier-mache if necessary.
2 Cut eye-holes with Stanley knife. Keep checking on face and in mirror to get them even.
3 Cut holes 2cm in from sides and attach elastic.
4 Pad mask by glueing in small bits of foam if necessary to make it comfortable to wear.
5 Decorate mask as appropriate.

Theatre terminology

If you have spent some time in professional theatres, you will notice that the staff use all kinds of jargon. Figure 5.32 may help you understand these specific theatrical terms, as it illustrates the different areas of the stage. See page 192 for a full glossary of theatre terminology.

Figure 5.32   *The stage: theatre terminology*

USR	UR of C	USC	UL of C	USL
CSR	R of C	CS	L of C	CSL
DSR	DR of C	DSC	DL of C	DSL

Key

U = Up   D = Down   S = Stage   L = Left   R = Right   C = Centre

Further reading

You are advised to read the following books for further information on production techniques:

Chilver, Peter (1974) *Producing a Play*, Batsford Ltd.

Motley, Cassel & Collier (1976) *Theatre Props*, Macmillan.

Reid, Francis (1978) *The Staging Handbook*, A & C Black.

— (1987) *The Stage Lighting Handbook*, 3rd edn, A & C Black.

— (1989) *Designing for the Theatre*, A & C Black.

Thomas, Terry (1985) *Create your own Stage*, A & C Black.

Tompkins, Julia (1978) *Stage Costumes*, Pitman.

Walne, Graham (1990) *Sound for the Theatre*, A & C Black.

The Costumers Handbook (1980) Prentice-Hall Spectrum Books.

Interview with Greg Ripley-Duggan

How would you describe the work you do?
I work both as a producer and as a theatre production broker on behalf of other producers.

What exactly is a theatre production broker?
Someone who puts together tours for other producers. I liaise between the producers and the theatres that might want to book a touring show, in exactly the same way as you might approach a travel agent to book your holiday. A broker is anyone who sells something somebody else has made. Of course, it's much more fun selling something you made yourself, which is why I also produce my own shows.

What size of theatre do you normally deal with?
It varies enormously. The smallest would be about a 600-seater, which we call middle-scale and the largest would be a 1500-seater, which we call large-scale. I don't personally deal with small-scale venues such as studio theatres and arts centres, which usually seat 100–250.

Who do you deal with at the theatre?
I deal with the theatre manager. Theatres that receive touring companies and do not produce their own work are called 'receiving houses' and do not have Artistic Directors. This is not to say that the people who run them are not interested in 'Art' or are not willing to take risks. Often they will try to balance their programme between shows that are sure-fire hits and will fill the theatre, and plays that are a risk and will not necessarily find an audience; something they feel *should* be seen in their town.

What would be an example of such a play, that was artistically challenging but the risk was taken by receiving houses?

I did the first tour of *Dancing at Lughnasa* by Brian Friel. When we first put it together we thought, this is an Irish play, with a title no-one in England can pronounce, by an all-Irish company; it's going to be difficult. But we managed to persuade regional theatre managers to come to London to see it – they had a very good evening and clearly felt it was the kind of production they should be giving their audiences the chance to see. It then went on to be the most enormous box office hit all over the country. It was vastly successful.

In general, what kind of show goes down well on the touring circuit?
Anything with a star name in it. That's the first criterion a theatre manager would use to assess the box office potential of any production. In some ways it's unfortunate, but inevitable. People go for what they know; they look for a name they recognise. There is also a hierarchy of names. Some stars will automatically fill any theatre in the country, but as the list progresses, it becomes less certain.

Is there any kind of play you know will not succeed?
There was a time when the thriller, the classic, well-made, five-handed Whodunnit, had a definite market place in this country. It still does to a certain extent, but it has declined immensely. There are all kinds of problems with the thriller as a genre. One is that actors simply don't want to do thrillers any more, because they see it as being infra-dig, not real 'Art'. It's a form of theatre that has fallen largely into self-parody. Another thing is that the audience for the thriller has been getting older and older and is gradually ceasing to exist. If you can persuade a famous name to be in a thriller, you could perhaps make it

work. But, in general, I don't think people really want thrillers any more.

What does the audience of the British receiving house really want?
That's the six million dollar question! Increasingly they are deserting drama, which is the saddest thing. The market place for plays is diminishing in this country. There are lots of different reasons for that. One of them is the slow demise of the repertory theatres throughout the country which created an appetite for drama. I think there is another factor, which is that commercial theatre production, on which the receiving houses are becoming increasingly dependent, is becoming a very expensive activity. Artists' fees increase, costs rise astronomically and, consequently, ticket prices that are passed on to the public are very high as well. I think people get to the point where they think 'I'll pay £20 to see a musical, but I won't pay £20 to see a play.' Perhaps in the West End, or at the National Theatre, but not at the local theatre.

Why is that, do you think?
It's largely because of *event status* – a much-vaunted piece of 80s jargon. A musical is simply a bigger undertaking. There are more people on stage; there are people playing music in the pit. It has a kind of event quality that makes it the ideal way to celebrate your anniversary or your birthday. People are much less price-resistant on musicals than they are on plays, sadly.

Why are the repertory houses in such decline?
Oh, quite simply, funding. The government is putting less money through the Arts Council into the regional theatres. This in turn creates difficulties for the big commercial theatres in the West End of London, because the talent they need is not being developed in rep as it used to be. It is very rare for an actor fresh out of drama school to be offered a part in the West End, but where are they to go and play serious, demanding roles in front of live audiences?

What, briefly, is the difference between commercial theatre, repertory theatre and the subsidised sector?
They are terms that often overlap. Theoretically, people in the commercial theatre take no subsidy from anybody. They put on plays with the objective of making a profit, in exactly the same way as anyone in any other line of private business has the primary objective of making a profit.

The regional repertory theatres are subsidised in order to put on plays to satisfy the local audience. There was a time in this country when it was a question of local pride that you had a repertory theatre in your town. It symbolised the town as a cultured, civilised place. And it also allowed local writers to develop who would write appropriate material for the area.

Finally, there is what is loosely called the subsidised sector, companies (largely London-based) established with a specific brief to provide artistically challenging material, to produce classic plays with casts too prohibitively large for anyone else, and to support new writing. Examples are the *Royal Shakespeare Company*, the *Royal National Theatre*, the *Bush Theatre*, the *Almeida*, the *Royal Court* and many more. These theatres receive grants, which they continually re-apply for, from the Arts Council at national level, or from the Regional Arts Boards at regional level.

Nowadays, because of rising costs, commercial producers will often co-produce with subsidised theatres, because it enables them to put shows on more cheaply and increases the likelihood of making a profit. This also, however, has a positive effect on the quality of the work. Productions need careful nurturing in a way the subsidised theatres are accustomed to doing.

What is the average rehearsal time in a repertory theatre?
Three weeks. Ten years ago it used to be four, fifteen years ago it was five, but the funding crisis has slashed it to three. Sometimes, it can even be as little as one or two weeks. The commercial theatre has probably always survived with three weeks or less, but there are certain plays I don't think you *can* rehearse in that time, however good you are. Such a short rehearsal period limits the kind of work you can create artistically; it is probably quite sufficient for a straightforward play that you block in a week and then allow some time to explore character, but it strongly mitigates against ensemble work and detailed exploration of text. In contrast, the national companies have much longer rehearsal periods, often six weeks.

Don't those quality productions with longer rehearsal periods often then tour or transfer to the commercial sector?
Many of them do, yes. Examples are shows such as *Les Miserables* from the *RSC*, and currently, from the *National*, there are shows like *Wind in the Willows* at the Old Vic and *An Inspector Calls* at the Garrick. Then there is a whole raft of smaller subsidised theatres who regularly transfer work. The *Hampstead Theatre Club* created *Dead Funny*, one of the noted successes of recent years, and the *Almeida* created *Medea* with Diana Rigg and *Deep Blue Sea* among others. The

Donmar Warehouse transferred *The Glass Menagerie* which sold out at the Comedy Theatre, and so the list goes on. In a way, the commercial theatre in the West End is terribly dependent on transfers from subsidised theatres (what we would call *subsequent exploitation*), partly because of their own rising costs, and partly because the subsidised theatres are producing hits that commercial producers wish to benefit from.

To what extent does a producer need to be trained in and brought up with the theatre, or is it enough to have a sound business instinct?
What you are asking about is the balance between business skills and theatre skills. In my experience, business people who attempt to work in the theatre tend to fail. The most successful producers are often those who have grown up in the industry and discover that they have business flair; former actors, directors, revue performers who have drifted into production. Ultimately, as a producer, you have to deal with artists, with people who are *not* commercial, and your interpersonal skills are paramount. You have to persuade actors to be in plays, or even to perform in certain theatres. There are many egos to be flattered and massaged in the theatre and it helps if the producer understands where the actors and directors are coming from. Business people tend to see everything in pure commodity terms, but plays are not just cans of baked beans, they don't just 'behave'. Above all they are full of actors who are difficult people; they fall sick, they die, they get lost, they refuse to appear.

What are the main roles of the theatre producer?
You have to buy the rights to the play; persuade named actors to be in it; cast the play; budget the play; organise the press and publicity campaign; negotiate contracts with company and venues, and *capitalise* the play, which means raise the necessary money to put it on.

So what do you do first?
The first thing you do is set a budget for the production, assessing your likely costs in each area – cast, crew, publicity and so on – and then you have to stick to it. Of course, you then need to raise the initial money to pay for your pre-production period, i.e. before you take any money at the box office. Actors and designers all need to be paid long before you see any proceeds from the performances.

Where do you raise the money for a play?
Usually from small investors. It's a notoriously risky business, so the pool of investors is constantly changing. There *are* regular investors, who will often re-

main loyal to one producer who has made some money for them at some point. Others invest because it's glamorous. You can take friends or colleagues to see *your* play. Ultimately there are as many reasons for investing as there are investors. It's my job to find them and persuade them they want to support a particular production.

What do you actually spend most of your time doing?
Negotiating. Endless negotiating: with actors about salaries; with stage management about salaries; with venues about the deal you're going into the theatre on; with printers about payment and delivery time. Endless rounds of being on the telephone trying to persuade people to give you a favour or to give you a very good deal, because, if you get two or three of those wrong, you could lose a lot of money. The deal you negotiate in each case will be more or less than you originally budgeted for, so your budget is constantly changing. If your rehearsal rooms cost more than you had planned, you will have to try to save money somewhere else.

Another primary responsibility is for the publicity. On a large show you would normally pay a fee to a press agent. You are responsible for the print, i.e. the posters and handbills which you have to organise (design, quantities, delivery etc.). You also make contracts with various venues, which have to be negotiated and finalised. You make contracts with the artists. And then a raft of bits and pieces like finding rehearsal rooms at an affordable price, which is virtually impossible in London today. Other than that you need to keep the company happy on a day-to-day basis. Perhaps the designer needs more money because the director is making new demands on the set. Perhaps your star actor is unhappy with their costume, or their billing on the poster. You have to try to predict what every problem is going to be and head it off before it gets too big. A play is a complex organism.

What is your relationship with the director of the play?
The director is crucial, the person who spends the budget and decides on the exact amount of rehearsal time and any extras during the process: extra costume, props etc. Ultimately, the director determines whether the production is going to be any good or not. He or she is responsible for casting and working with the actors. Normally the director will choose the designer as well, because it must be someone they like working with and you are always looking for a winning team.

So does the director choose the producer or the producer choose the director?

Directors often create their own work with their own contacts. They will choose a play and find a few members of the cast, then approach a producer with a package. In other words, the director starts as producer, turns a play into what we call a *project*, meaning it has one or two interested actors and looks commercially viable, and then hands it over so that they can get on with the business of directing it. Normally, however, it happens the other way round. The producer turns a play into a project and then looks around for the right person to direct it. That judgement will be based partly on aesthetics, i.e. whether you like their previous work; partly on other considerations such as whether they can cast a play – some directors are very good at persuading famous actors and actresses to work with them – and, sometimes, on whether they can control money (some directors stop getting work because their productions always run vastly over-budget).

How do the producer and director go about casting a play?
It very much depends on the production. I recently co-produced *Macbeth* with Mark Rylance, where he both directed and played the lead role. One of the key things he was looking for from the cast was the kind of people he could work with, who would adopt his approach to rehearsals, i.e. accept experimentation, not be concerned with star status and fit in well with a company. While that is not the norm, these are still important considerations for many companies. You also have to remember that a cast will have to live in each other's pockets for quite some time and you want to avoid conflict, so it is important to look at the personality underlying the talent.

The more commercial the theatre, the more it will be concerned with an actor's ability to draw an audience. In other words, you want to cast your play with actors the audience wants to see, which nowadays means actors who have established themselves through television work (the most consistent showcase where you can gain a reputation).

Those are the two extremes and, inevitably, most casting processes lie somewhere between the two, balancing up an actor's ability to act, their reputation and their compatibility with director and company.

Do you always use an audition process?
No. Major parts will often be cast without audition, simply through a *Spotlight* search, a telephone call to the agent and then a meeting over coffee. There is a point in their career where an actor no longer expects to be auditioned. Then there are the more junior parts for the less experienced or well-known actors which will generally be offered through an audition process.

Do producers sit in on auditions and do those auditions take place in theatres?
Producers only tend to sit in on auditions when it's a big West End musical. They don't really have any direct responsibility for casting, although they may take a professional interest in it, so there is no need for them to be there. Generally speaking, auditions take place in church halls and rehearsal rooms, even for the West End – renting a theatre is an expensive business!

What are the requirements for audition at professional level?
Exactly the same as you would expect at most drama schools: two contrasting pieces or two songs for a musical. Occasionally you might have a bit of dialogue given to you to see what you could do with it, if they are unsure.

Is it a good idea to choose a speech from the play you are auditioning for?
I wouldn't recommend it, as your choice of speech might suggest which part you wanted and prejudice your chances of getting any other part in the same play.

How important is an actor's CV?
The less an actor is known, the more important it is. Let's say you are casting *Macbeth*, and you are still looking for your Macduff. Once you realise you are not going to get anyone famous into the part, the CV becomes critical. A lot of what you are looking for is who they have worked with and where they have worked, i.e. people who have worked in prestigious establishments with high-class directors. You do look at the parts played, of course, but you are probably less interested in someone who has played King Lear at a very obscure fringe theatre than you are in someone who has played Ross at the National or Macduff at Birmingham Rep. The CV should be short, usually a one-page list of credits.

How imaginative should you be as an actor in the construction of your CV?
Not at all, probably. A casting director simply wants to know what you have done. They don't need to know superfluous facts such as being able to burp on cue; they certainly won't cast you because of it.

To what extent are you casting on age and appearance, and how much on an actor's ability to play a variety of roles?
Both. Ultimately, you're looking for talent. Looking

'right' for a part is important, but it is not necessarily the thing a director looks for most. The basics must be in place, of course; if the play stipulates a character is female, Asian and 35 years old, then the actor cast in that role will probably approximate that description; but directors are not so concerned with this: after all, you're on stage, no-one actually sees you very closely, and huge amounts can be done with costume and make-up. They are much more concerned with innate talent, and there are stage actors who appear dashing and handsome on the stage, when they are often not at all in real life; they are just sufficiently good actors to convey the impression that they look like that.

For the young actor, how much do they need to understand the roles they may be cast in and tailor themselves; i.e. what is your type?
On stage, flexibility is the key and accent is a huge part of that. If you are stuck with one accent, particularly one less in demand such as RP/upper class English, you will be limited. Television, on the contrary, does cast much more according to appearance. Actors who start out in television, however, are not

necessarily successful in making the transition to the stage. The skills are very different.

How important is your choice of agent?
Very important. Imagine buying an actor from a superstore. The first question you would ask is: do you trust the label? Does this actor come from Fortnum & Mason, Sainsbury's or Kwiksave? In an ideal world, an actor would decide what kind of agent or agency best represents the image they wish to project, and would work towards getting on their books.

The central thing about an actor's relationship with their agent is that they must trust each other. But the objectives of an actor and an agent are not the same. An actor expects the agent to find them work. An agent is driven by producers and television companies calling up, looking to cast particular roles. If none of those roles suit client X, then they will not call him. Agents are rarely in the business of saying 'Here is a wonderful actor, where can I find them work?' Ultimately, you are reliant on the quality of an agent's address book.

Glossary of theatre terminology

Anti-pros (US)   See Front-of-House lights.

Apron   Extension of stage beyond the proscenium.

ASM   Assistant stage manager.

Auditorium   Area in which the audience is accommodated during the performance.

Backcloth   Cloth usually painted, suspended from Flies at the rear of the stage.

Backing   (1) Cloth or solid pieces placed behind doorways and other openings on sets to conceal stage machinery and building (2) Financial support for a production.

Bar   Horizontally flown rod (usually metal) from which scenery, lighting and other equipment are suspended.

Bar bells   Bells sounded in all front-of-house areas to warn audience that the performance is

about to continue. Operated from prompt corner, and so usually written into prompt copy.

Barndoor   Adjustable shutters attached to stage lights to control the area of light covered by a particular lamp.

Batten   (1) See Bar (2) Piece of wood attached to flown cloth to straighten it and keep it taut (3) Piece of wood joining two flats (4) A group of stage lights suspended over the stage.

Beam light   A light with no lens, giving a parallel beam.

Beginners   Call given by deputy stage manager to bring those actors who appear first in the play to the stage.

Bifocal spot   Spotlight with additional shutters to allow hard and soft edges.

Black light   Ultra violet light.

Blocking The process of arranging moves to be made by the actor.

Board Lighting control panel.

Book (1) Alternative term for the scripts (2) The prompt copy (3) The part of a musical show conducted in dialogue.

Bookflat Two flats hinged together on the vertical.

Booking Closing a book flat.

Boom A vertical lighting bar.

Boom arch Used to hang a lantern from a boom.

Border Flown scenic piece designed to conceal the upper part of the stage and its machinery or equipment.

Box set Setting which encloses the acting area on three sides. Conventionally in imitation of a room in which the fourth wall has been removed.

Brace Portable support for flats.

Bridge Walkway above the stage used to reach stage equipment.

Call (1) Warning given at intervals to technicians and actors that they are needed on stage (2) Notice of the time at which actors will be required to rehearse a particular scene.

Callboard Notice board on which calls and all other information relevant to the production should be posted.

Cans Headsets used for communication and co-ordination of technical departments during a performance.

Centreline Imaginary line drawn from rear to front of stage and dividing it exactly in half. Marked as CL on stage plans.

Channel A circuit in the lighting or sound system.

Chase A repeated sequence of changing lighting states.

Check To diminish the intensity of light or sound on stage.

Cinemoid A colour medium or filter.

Circuit The means by which a lantern is connected to a dimmer or patch panel.

Clamp C or G clamps are attached to lights to fasten them to bars.

Cleat Fixing on the back of flats to allow them to be laced together (cleated) with a sash line or cleat line. Also a metal fly rail to which ropes are tied.

Clothscene Scene played before downstage drop or tabs, while a major scene changes takes place.

Colour call The list of coloured gels required for a lighting design taken from the plan of the lighting design.

Colourframe Holder for the colour medium or filter in front of the light.

Colour medium Translucent filter material placed in front of lights to give a coloured illumination.

Colour wheel In lighting, a device attached to lamps which, when rotated, charges the colour medium through which the light is shown.

Come down (1) Instruction to actor to move towards the audience (2) Instruction to lower intensity of sound or light (3) End of performance; time when curtain comes down.

Corner plate Triangle of plywood used to reinforce the corners of a flat.

Counterweights Mechanical system used for raising and lowering flown scenery.

Counterweight flying The system of flying scenery, lights, etc. whereby the flown item is balanced by counterweights.

Crossfade The practice of moving to a new lighting or sound effect without intervening darkness or silence: one effect fades out simultaneously with the new one's being brought into play.

Crossover (1) The device on a sound system that routes the sound of the correct pitch to the correct part of the loudspeaker. (2) The space behind the stage through which actors can get from one side of the stage to the other without being seen by the audience.

Cue (1) Verbal or physical signal for an actor to enter or speak a line (2) Point at which an effect is executed or business takes place.

Cue light Box with two lights, red and green, which warn an actor or technician to stand-by (red) and then do (green) whatever is required of them. Ensures greater precision when visibility or audibility is limited.

Cue sheet List of particular effects executed by one department in a production.

Cue-to-cue Rehearsal of technical effects in a production with actors. The scene is rehearsed in sections beginning with a cue for stand-by and concluding when the effect is finished.

Curtain call Process of actors appearing at the end of the play to receive audience applause. Formerly actors were called before the curtain by the audience.

Curtain speech Out of character address to the audience by a cast member or participant.

Curtain up (1) Time at which a play begins. (2) A call given to the company to warn them the performance has begun.

Cut cloth Vertical scenic piece cut to reveal more scenery behind it. Most common in musicals.

Cutting list List of materials required for scenery and set construction together with the correct dimensions of the pieces.

Cyclorama Undecorated backing to a stage, usually semi-circular and creating a sense of space and height. Often some theatres have permanent or standing cycloramas which have actually been built. The term is always abbreviated to cyc.

Dead (1) The point at which a piece of scenery reaches the desired position onstage (2) A redundant production or scenic element.

Decibel dB: the measurement of volume of sound.

Diffusion (colour) Used like a gel but to soften and spread the beam of light rather than to colour it. Also called a frost.

Dim The process of decreasing the intensity of light onstage.

Dimmers The apparatus whereby lights are electrically dimmed.

Dip Small covered hole in stage floor with electric sockets.

Dock Area at side or rear of stage where scenery is stored when not in use.

Downstage Part of stage nearest to audience.

Dress circle Also known as the circle. Area of seating above the stalls and below the balcony.

Dressing Items used to decorate a setting.

Dress parade The final check of costumes before the first dress rehearsal. The cast parade each of their costumes in order before the Director and Costume Designer so that any final alterations can be made.

Drop Suspended cloth flown into stage area.

DSM Deputy stage manager.

Dutchman (US) Thin piece of material used to cover the cracks between two flats.

Elevation A working drawing usually drawn accurately and to scale, showing the side view of the set or lighting arrangement.

Ellipsoidal The type of reflector used in many profile spots.

Entrance (1) Place on a set through which the actor may appear (2) Point in the script at which an actor appears.

Exit (1) The process of leaving the stage (2) Point in the script at which an actor leaves the stage.

Fader A means of controlling the output level of a lantern (lamp) or amplifier.

False proscenium Construction placed behind the real theatre proscenium for decorative or practical purposes.

Fit-up Installation of lighting, technical equipment and scenery onstage when coming into a theatre.

Flash-out System to check whether the lights are functioning properly by putting them on one at a time.

Flat Scenic unit comprised of wood or stretched cloth applied to a timber frame and supported so that it stands vertical to the stage door. Door flats and window flats have these openings in them. Masking flats are placed at the outer edges of the acting area to disguise areas of the stage from the public.

Flies Area above the stage in which scenery, lighting and other equipment are kept. If whole backdrops are to be stored then the flies should be at least twice the height of the stage opening.

Floodlights Also called floods. Lights which give a general fixed spread of light.

Floorcloth Painted canvas sheets placed on the stage floor to give a specific effect.

Floor pocket (US) See dip.

Flown (1) Scenery or equipment which has been suspended above the stage (2) Flown pieces are any scenic elements which will be made to appear to disappear from view in sight of the audience.

Fly The process of bringing scenery in and out of the stage area vertically.

Flying (1) The process of stocking the flies (2) Special effects whereby actors are suspended by wires to create the illusion of flying.

Flyfloor Gallery at either side of the stage from which the flies are operated.

Floats See footlights.

Focusing The process of fixing the exact area to be lit by each light onstage.

FOH Front-of-house. Any part of the theatre in front of the proscenium arch.

Follow spot Light directed at actor which can follow all movements.

Footlights Lights set into the stage at floor level which throw strong general light into performers' faces downstage.

Fourth wall Imaginary wall between audience and actors which completes the naturalistic room.

French brace Support for scenery fixed to stage.

Fresnel Type of spotlight with a fresnel lens which gives an even field of light with soft edges.

Frontcloth See cloth.

Front-of-House lights Lights hung in front of the proscenium arch.

Frost See diffusion.

Gauze Painted cloth screen, opaque when lit from the front, then becomes transparent when lit from behind. Often used at front of stage to diffuse total stage picture.

Gel Colour medium introduced before light to alter colour of beam.

Get-in/out (US) See fit-up process of bringing scenery into or taking it out of the theatre.

Ghost A beam of light which inadvertently leaks from a light and falls where it is not wanted.

Gobo (1) Screen introduced before a stage light to give a particular image onstage (2) Cut out shape that is projected.

Green room General area in which cast and crew wait during performance.

Grid Metal frame from which all flying equipment is suspended.

Groundrow Raised section of scenery usually depicting bushes, rocks, etc.

Grouping (US) See blocking.

Half Half hour call. Warning to company given thirty-five minutes before performance.

Handprop Any prop handled by an actor, such as a handbag, walking stick, umbrella.

Hanging Attaching flying pieces to appropriate bars.

Hook clamp The device that holds a lantern onto a bar.

Hot lining The method by which lanterns, bulbs and cables are checked during rigging.

House (1) Audience (2) In opera, the entire theatre, and by implication, the company.

Impedance A term for the electrical resistance found in a/c circuits, thus affecting the ability of a cable to transmit sound as electrical pulses. Measured in ohms.

In one (US) See clothscene.

Inset A small scene set inside a larger one.

Iris A device within a lantern which allows a circular beam to be altered through a range of sizes.

Iron A fire proof curtain that can be dropped downstage of the tabs in case of fire. Today it is usually made of solid metal and is electrically operated.

Kill Instruction to cease use of particular effect in lighting or sound.

Ladder A ladder-shaped frame used for hanging side lights. It cannot usually be climbed.

Lamp Unit of lighting equipment.

Lantern See lamp.

Left Stage left. That part of the stage to the actor's left when he is facing toward the audience.

Leg Cloth suspended vertically from flies and used to mask sides of stage and small areas within it.

Levels (1) Indicates intensity or volume of light or sound (2) Raised areas onstage used for acting.

Limes Jargon for follow spots and their operators.

Line drawings (US) See technical drawing.

Linnebach projector Used for projecting a picture from a gel or glass slide onto the set. Often used to give a shadow effect.

Load in/out (US) See get in/out.

Lose To turn off lighting or sound, or to remove an article from the set.

Luminaire International term for lighting equipment. Not restricted to theatrical lighting.

Marking (1) In use of props or scenery, the deployment of substitutes for the real object during rehearsal (2) In singing, a means of using the voice with reduced volume and without vocalising extremes of register (3) Any account of a role in which the full powers are not being used by the performer in order to save resources.

Maroon A pyrotechnic giving the effect of a loud explosion.

Mark out The system of lines and objects set

on a rehearsal room floor to indicate the exact position of scenery and furniture. Marking out is the process of doing this.

Mask To hide or conceal unwanted areas or machinery. Also used to describe one actor obscuring another unintentionally.

MD Musical director.

Memory Memory board. An advanced type of lighting control system where the required levels are stored electronically.

Mezzanine Area of seating above the orchestra and below the balcony. When a theatre has only a single balcony, first several rows are frequently designated the mezzanine.

Mixer Sound controls desk, used to mix and adjust levels of sounds from various sources.

Offstage Any backstage area not seen by the audience. Most specifically used to indicate the areas at the actor's right and left.

OP Opposite prompt. Stage Right (US Stage left).

Orchestra (US) See stalls.

Out Flying term for up.

Overture (1) The music which begins a performance (2) A call to the actors and technicians that the performance is about to begin in a musical work.

PA system The public address or any sound amplification system.

Pack A number of flats all stored together.

Pan (1) Movement of lighting from side to side (2) Used to describe water-based stage make-up (pancakes) (3) Term (now nearly obsolete) to describe theatre sound installation.

Parcan Type of lantern which holds a par lamp.

Patch border panel A panel at which the circuits governed by individual lighting dimmers can be changed.

Perch Lighting position concealed behind the proscenium.

Periactus A tall, prism-shaped piece of painted scenery which can be revolved to show various phases.

Pipe (US) See bar.

Places please (US) See beginners.

Platform (US) See rostrum.

Plot (1) Commonly used to describe the action of a play (2) Any list of cues for effects used in the play.

PM Production manager.

Practical Any object which must do onstage the same job that it would in life of any working apparatus, e.g. a light switch or water tap (faucet).

Preset (1) Used to describe an article placed in its working area before the performance commences (2) Also describes a basic lighting state that the audience sees before the action begins.

Projector (US) See floodlight.

Prompt copy Fully annotated copy of the play with all the production details from which the show is run each time it is performed.

Properties Props. Any item or artide used by the actors in performance other than costume and scenery.

Props skip Basket or cupboard in which props are kept when not in use.

Props table Table in convenient offstage area on which all properties are left prior to performance and to which they should be returned when dead.

Pros proscenium arch The arch which stands between stage and auditorium. A pros arch theatre is a conventional theatre with a proscenium arch, usually without a forestage.

PS Prompt side. Conventionally meaning stage left. The term now refers only to the side of the stage in which the prompt corner will be found in the US the PS is generally stage right.

Prompt corner Desk and console at the side of the stage from which the stage manager runs the show.

Pyrotechnics Any chemical effects used on-stage or in wings to create lighting or special effects.

Quarter Back stage pre-show call given 20 minutes before curtain up (i.e. 15 minutes before beginners).

Rail Bottom or top batten of the frame of a flat.

Rake The incline of a stage floor away from the horizontal; a raked stage is higher at the upstage end than at the downstage.

Readthrough Early rehearsal at which the play is read without action. Usually accompanied by discussion.

Reflectors The shiny surfaces in the back of lighting equipment which help intensify the beam.

Rigging The means of fixing lamps to appropriate bars before lighting a production.

Right Stage right. That part of the stage to the actor's right when he is facing the audience.

Risers The vertical part of a stage step.

Rostrum A raised platform sometimes with a collapsible frame used for giving local prominence to certain areas onstage.

Run (1) The number of scheduled performances of a work (2) Abbreviated form of run through.

Runners A pair of curtains parting at the centre and moving horizontally.

Saturation rig An arrangement of lights in which the maximum number of spotlights is placed in every possible position.

Scatter The light outside the main beam of a spot.

Scrim (US) See gauze.

Seque Musical term indicating that one number should go immediately into the next.

Set To prepare the stage for action. To set up is to get ready. To set back is to return to the beginning of a given sequence.

Shutter Device in front of lamp to alter shape of beam.

Single purchase Counterweight flying system where the cradle travels the same distance as the fly bar's travel. The counterweight frame therefore occupies the full height of the side wall of the stage.

Sightlines The angles of visibility from the auditorium.

SM Stage manager.

Snap line Chalk line, chalked piece of string which when stretched tight is used for making straight lines on stage.

Special Piece of lighting equipment whose main function is to perform a particular effect.

Spiking See marking.

Spill Unwanted light onstage.

Spot Spotlight. Light giving a small circle of light, the dimensions of which can be precisely controlled by focusing.

Stagger-run Runthrough at which the production is pieced together, aiming at fluency but allowing for corrective stops.

Stalls Floor level area of seating in the auditorium.

Strike Instruction to remove any redundant or unnecessary object from stage.

Super Non-speaking actor not specifically named in the text.

Swag Curtains or tabs gathered together so they do not hang straight.

Switchboard Board from which lights are controlled.

Tabs Theatre curtains, most usually the House curtain.

Tabtrack Metal track on which the tabs run allowing them to open and close.

Tallescope Extendable ladder on wheels used in rigging and focusing lights and for minor corrections to flown pieces.

Teaser Short flown border used to mask scenery or equipment.

Tech Technical rehearsal at which all technical effects are rehearsed in the context of the whole production.

Theatre in the Round Acting area with audience on all sides.

Throw in lighting The distance between a light source and the object lit.

Thrust stage Type of stage which projects into the auditorium so that the audience can sit on at least three sides.

Tilt The vertical movement of light.

Tonnentor (US) See teaser.

Trap Hole cut in stage and concealed by floor allowing access from below. Grave traps are usually double traps creating the illusion of a grave or pit Once a common part of all theatres, traps are now becoming increasingly rare.

Trapeze Single short hung lighting bar.

Treads The flat part of stage steps.

Truck Movable cradle upon which scenery is placed to facilitate its movement.

Upstage In a proscenium or thrust stage the area furthest away from the audience.

Wagon (US) See truck.

Walk-through Rehearsals at which actors go through entrances, moves and exits to make clear any changes or alterations made necessary through change of cast or venue.

Warning bells (US) See Bar bells.

Ways The maximum number of combinations of channels on a lighting installation.

Wings The sides of the stage concealed from the audience's view.

Work-out In a dance or movement rehearsal, a vigorous session to prepare the body for specific work.

Workshop Any non-performing backstage area of a theatre.

Workshop performance A performance in which maximum effort goes towards acting and interpretation rather than sets or costumes.

chapter six

THE HISTORY AND DEVELOPMENT OF THE THEATRE

Drama and the other performing arts are always to be found at the forefront of any dynamic political and social change. Whether the artists are merely reflecting the change that is already occurring within society, or whether they are leading the change themselves, the nature of the art form is that these artists attract controversy and the attention of the authorities. This places a certain responsibility on the shoulders of performing artists; whether or not they wish to be seen as political, their actions and their work will be seen as such because it is performed in public and is therefore powerful.

As we look at the history of the theatre in this chapter, we have tried to make connections between performances and the contemporary socio-political influences: religion, education, the economy. In this way we hope to make it apparent that no performing artist works in isolation. Whether or not an actor, writer or director believes themselves to be 'apolitical', as a performer they stand in the centre of a complex web of socio-political relationships. An understanding of these relationships aids the perception of changes which are being effected within the world of the performing arts.

In terms of the text itself, this chapter focuses on the range of styles of theatre which have developed over the centuries. There are many cross-references to be made between this chapter and others in the book, because the history of theatre is the core to our understanding of acting, directing and production techniques today. Each description of the period is accompanied by text-based and practical exercises which will help you to explore the period and style in greater depth.

Greek theatre

Athens was the centre of the Greek civilisation for thousands of years, and the works of the Athenian playwrights are still studied today, including writers such as Sophocles, Aristophanes, Euripides, Aeschylus. These writers produced plays as part of a competition, and the competition took place during festivals dedicated to the god Dionysus. There were three festivals per year: the *City Dionysia* in late March/early April, the *Lenaia* in January, and the *Rural Dionysia* in December.

The festivals were not only occasions for theatre productions but also poetry recitation and dancing. Competition was an important element of these proceedings, as it was to Greek society as a whole (the Greeks began the tradition of the Olympic games). One of the greatest honours that Greek society could bestow was to be the winner of the playwriting competition. Compare the significance which modern society today accords playwrights – Greek writers would have been household names; how many modern playwrights can you name? Perhaps the different attitude is based in the fact that these plays were performed as part of a festival in celebration of a god, and that this religious (and political) emphasis made the Greek writers more worthy of respect in the eyes of the population. A look at a programme of the festivals might improve your understanding of the religious and artistic events that took place.

The Athenian festivals

The schedule for the festival of the *City Dionysia*:

DAY 1: PROCESSION ESCORTING THE IMAGE OF DIONYSUS

This was a grand religious procession which celebrated the roots of the cult surrounding the god. The statue of the god was taken out of its shrine, to the town of Eleutherai (a town on the border between Attica and Boetia) and then back to the theatre, where it was placed in a suitable position to witness the competition.

The procession was led by magistrates and priests, and was quite spectacular. The wealthy sponsors of the festival (the *choregoi*) followed the procession with their Chorus. The Chorus supported the main characters in the Greek plays, and were made up of perhaps 20 men, who danced and sang during the play. It was something of a status symbol to be the sponsor of a Chorus (to some extent, this tradition continues today, with wealthy companies sponsoring prestigious companies such as the Royal Shakespeare Company to the tune of many millions of pounds). This process would halt in the market place of Eleutherai and a Chorus would dance and sing before statues of the 12 gods. There then followed a great banquet and, at nightfall, the whole procession turned round and headed back to Athens.

On this day, the performers and dramatists also mounted a special ceremony, called the *proagon*. This served to publicise the plays about to be performed, and took place in the *odeum* (on the Southern slope of the Acropolis). Each dramatist would mount a platform and inform the audience of the subject of the play.

DAY 2 AM: THE PROCESSION OF THE SACRED PRECINCT OF DIONYSUS

Offerings were carried by citizens and any foreign residents (*metics*), who wore scarlet robes. The procession climaxed in the sacrifice of a bull.

DAY 2 PM: THE CONTEST FOR THE DITHYRAMBIC CHORUSES

The *dithyramb* was a hymn sung by 50 men in honour of Dionysus, and was accompanied by a flute. Each of the ten Attic tribes was represented by a Chorus. The dithyramb was performed in a circular motion around the altar.

Note: The dithyrambs are one of the sources of Greek tragedy, evidenced by the important choral element in these plays.

DAYS 3–6: DRAMATIC PERFORMANCES

Each writer offered four plays (a *tetralogy*), which consisted of three tragedies (a *trilogy*) and a satyr-play. The tragedies were not necessarily linked together by plot. Five comic poets also entered into competition with each other.

The combination of religious and artistic events thus combined to produce a festival unlike any other in its time.

TASK

Pick any Greek play and pretend that you are the dramatist. Prepare a speech which will convince an uninformed audience of its merit. Don't forget that this is a competition!

THE PERFORMING SPACE

The theatre was called the *theatron*. The audience sat in the *auditorium*. Over 10,000 people could be seated in the auditorium at the Theatre of Dionysus, so it is highly probable that the whole community attended the performances. The Chorus danced and sang in the circular level area, called the *orchestra* (which means 'dancing place'). Behind the orchestra you could find the *skene* (which is where the word 'scene' comes from).

- *Auditorium*: The auditorium was where the spectators were seated; it was shaped like a bowl and cut into the side of a sloping hillside. The priest of Dionysus was the most important member of the audience and was seated in the middle of the front row. Priests and high officials sat on either side of him. The seats were mostly made of wood, and gangways divided the seats into three bands.

- *Orchestra*: the Chorus was the most important element in early Greek plays, and danced around the altar which could be found in the middle of the orchestra. There were 50 people in the dithyrambic Chorus.

- *Skene*: the skene was the stage building, and in front of this was a raised stage called the *proskenion*. The stage building was a long wooden structure, and scenery was attached to the outside. As the back wall of the stage, the wooden building acted as a kind of 'sounding board' and helped with the projection of the actors' voices and the music around the auditorium. Bits of

Figure 6.1   *The Periclean Theatre*

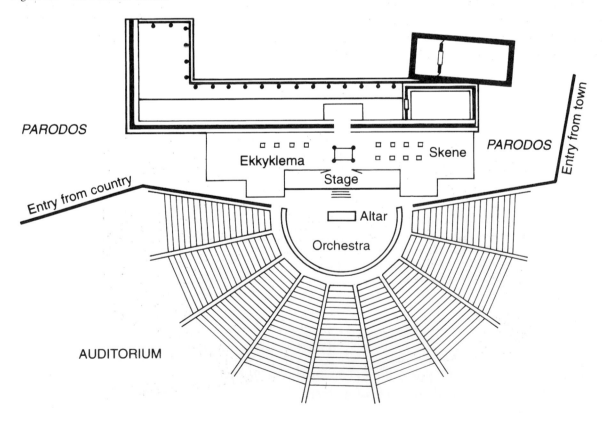

scenery were stored inside the stage building, along with the costumes and masks. Actors were also known to make appearances from the flat roof of the skene.

Dimensions

The distance from the skene (stage building) to the back of the auditorium measured approximately 300 feet. This meant that an actor six feet high would look as if he were about three inches high. The back row of the auditorium was approximately 100 feet above the level of the orchestra. The skene was 105 feet in length, and 12 feet deep. The width between the projecting wings was 45 feet.

Stage equipment and staging

The scenery on the skene could represent a palace, a cliff with a cave or an orchard. Behind the skene was a platform on wheels, called an *ekkyklema*. This would have been pushed out through the central doors from behind the skene when it was needed, and perhaps ran on grooves. The central doors would have been approximately 12 feet wide. The ekkyklema itself might have measured ten feet by six feet. The Greeks used the ekkyklema to prepare important tableaux and then bring them into the view of the audience. A tableau is a static stage 'picture', and the ekkyklema might have been used for significant moments such as the revelation of the bodies of Agamemnon and Kassandra in the play *Agamemnon*; see Figure 6.2.

The Theatre of Dionysus also boasted a wooden crane or *mechane*, which was used for swinging or flying characters through the air. The mechane was equipped with ropes and hooks with which to fly the actor, and he (all the actors were male) would be lifted with this equipment from behind the skene, to the required height, and then swung onto the stage. Occasionally the flying actor would also have been actually lowered onto the stage. The mechane itself could be transformed to represent flying chariots, monsters and other divine entities.

There was also an upper storey called the *theologeion* which was used for the entrance of the gods when they did not arrive by the mechane.

Figure 6.2   *An impression of Agamemnon and Kassandra on an ekkyklema*

Scenery

The scenery would have been very basic, only using the very bare essentials to indicate a setting; e.g. a tent, a statue or a single tree. The set itself would have been made of wood and stored in the skene building. Scenery was also painted on curtains or wooden boards and attached to the skene or the mechane. The scenery, however, did not depict landscapes but buildings in perspective. The Greeks called this art of scene painting *skenographia*.

ARISTOTLE'S POETICS

Aristotle (384–321 BC), a Greek critic and thinker, wrote a work entitled *The Poetics*, in which he discusses the vital points and assets which a tragedy should possess in order to be considered of artistic merit. This work is of critical importance to the development of drama. The medieval poet Chaucer certainly possessed Aristotle's works, and Elizabethan dramatists formulated their own distillation of *The Poetics*, entitled the *Dramatic Unities*.

Read the description of *Oedipus Rex* before looking at each of Aristotle's 'Elements of Tragedy'. (See Chapter 4 for a detailed examination of the play in production.)

Text focus – *Oedipus Rex*, Sophocles

It is important to realise that the original Greek audience would have been very familiar with the story of *Oedipus Rex*. The task of the writer is therefore to engage the audience, notwithstanding their foreknowledge of Oedipus' fate.

Even though the audience knows that Oedipus is certain to kill his father and have sexual relations with his mother, the spectators are constantly gripped by the suspense of finding out 'how' the prophecy is going to be fulfilled. Time and time again, Oedipus' discovery of the truth of the prophecy is delayed by the intervention of subsidiary characters; e.g. the messenger who brings news of Oedipus' adoptive father in Corinth, which leads Oedipus to the false conclusion that the original prophecy was incorrect. These delays and the extent to which each member of the audience identifies with Oedipus and his struggles, combine to produce an intensely moving and powerful climax. A moment of recognition such as when Oedipus realises the awful truth about himself is called *anagnorisis*. The many reversals of fortune that the hero experiences are called *peripeteia*.

Oedipus is also faced with various challenges, such as the Sphinx. Unlike modern films, where such a sequence would be seen as a high-point in the 'action', Sophocles concentrates on the reasons *why* Oedipus takes on the challenge in the first place and the emotions that the mere reporting of such an encounter would arouse. Aristotle commented on the competence of the poet who might achieve a fascinating drama by structuring his pieces well, without the need for what we might now describe as 'Hollywood-style' fast-action sequences.

The way that the hero deals with these challenges demonstrates the Athenian values of intelligence and self-reliance, and encourages the perception that a man can be master of his own destiny. This perception, however, is revealed to be false, when Oedipus realises that his whole life has been controlled by the gods right from the beginning. The effect of the play overall is to encourage the audience to fear that their own individual efforts to control their existence and create their lives, are meaningless in the face of the divine power of the gods. Historical research leads us to believe that Sophocles was an extremely religious man, and that he would have believed that the actions of the gods were correct, no matter how painful the effects of those actions were to the individual human being.

According to Aristotle, there are six main points to the construction of a tragedy. Aristotle based these points on Greek tragedies which already existed.

The plot

Some plots are 'simple' and some 'complex'.

(X)

By this statement, Aristotle meant that the action of the plot might occur with or without an intricate system of reversals and discoveries (*perepeteia* and *anagnorisis*), which altered the fortunes of the central character.

Peripeteia (reversal)

A 'reversal' is a change of the situation into the opposite ... like the man in *Oedipus* who came to cheer Oedipus and rid him of his anxiety about his mother by revealing his parentage and changed the whole situation.

(XI)

Anagnorisis (discovery)

A 'discovery' as the term implies is a change from ignorance to knowledge, producing either friendship or hatred in those who are destined for good fortune or bad. A discovery is most effective when it coincides with reversals, such as that involved by the discovery in the *Oedipus*.

(XI)

Calamity

The third element of a tragic plot according to Aristotle was '*calamity*'.

a destructive or painful occurrence, such as a death on the stage, acute suffering and wounding and so on.

(XI)

(*All quotations are taken from* Art of Aristotle's Poetics, *introduced and annotated by W. Hamilton Fyfe, translated by I. Baywater.*)

All of these elements had to be carefully worked into a plot so that they were seen as necessary, and not simply placed in the play's construction at the whim of the writer.

There were also three kinds of plot to be avoided by the Greek tragedian.

It is obvious to begin with that one should not show worthy men passing from good fortune to bad. That does not arouse pity or fear but shocks our feelings. Nor again wicked people passing from bad fortune to good ... Nor again the passing of a thoroughly bad man from good fortune to bad fortune. Such a structure might satisfy our feelings but it arouses neither pity nor fear.

(XIII)

Aristotle thought that the best kind of plot was one which involved a man who possessed both good and bad qualities. The downfall of this central character, which was a certain and inevitable asset for a tragedy, had to be caused by a great flaw in the character's personality, and not because of an evil act. This is clearly true with Oedipus, who is essentially good but is also arrogant.

Character

Characters must essentially be good (in the moral sense), appropriate, realistic and consistent.

Diction

Under the head of Diction one subject of inquiry is the various modes of speech, the knowledge of which is proper to elocution or to the man who knows the master art ...

(XIX)

Aristotle discusses the value and nature of the language used in plays in some depth in *The Poetics*, but essentially wanted the reader to understand that a valued tragedian must be aware of the intricacies and nuances of language, and be very aware of its grammatical construction in order to be considered an artist.

Thought

Under the head of Thought come all the effects to be produced by the language. Some of these are proof and refutation, the arousing of feelings like pity, fear, anger and so on, and then again exaggeration and depreciation.

(XIX)

Thought is apparent in all the speeches of the characters or in their actions.

Spectacle

Under this heading Aristotle discusses that which actually occurs on the stage between the actors.

Fear and pity sometimes result from what is seen on the stage and are sometimes aroused by the actual arrangement of the incidents, which is preferable and the mark of a better poet. The plot should be so constructed that even without seeing the play anyone hearing of the incidents thrills with fear and pity as a result of what occurs. So would anyone feel who heard the story of Oedipus. To produce this appeal through an appeal to the eye is inartistic and needs adventitious aid, while those who by such means produce an effect which is not fearful but merely monstrous have nothing to do with tragedy.

(XIII)

Aristotle evidently believes that the use of blood, gore and general mayhem is the sign of a bad writer. The key to a good play is the nature of the events themselves, and how these events are placed within the plot's structure, and not their playing out on stage.

Melody

Aristotle fails to discuss the use of music in any great detail in *The Poetics*, other than to describe it as a pleasurable accessory to the drama itself.

TASKS

1 Read Ovid's *Metamorphoses*. In groups, select a myth and stage it.
2 Devise your own tragic tale and stage it, attempting to include all the elements identified by Aristotle. Be sure to include at least one *peripeteia* and *anagnorisis*.
3 Present 1 and/or 2 at your own festival of *City Dionysia*.

Medieval theatre

The medieval period spans 1100–1500 AD. It was preceded by what are known as the 'Dark Ages' (500–1100 AD), which followed the collapse of the Roman Empire under the weight of its own corruption and attacks from Eastern warrior tribes. A great deal of knowledge in all areas of human expertise (the arts, law, medicine, science, philosophy and astrology) was either destroyed or remained lost until the advent of the Italian Renaissance in the late fourteenth century.

European societies gradually built new power structures after these invasions. Monarchies, aristocracies and the Church, ruled by the Papacy in Rome, stepped into the power vacuum created by the dissolution of the Roman empire.

The strong tradition of elegant and philosophical comedies and tragedies developed by the Greeks and continued by the Romans disappeared, and a completely original dramatic form was created, which is now known as medieval theatre.

EDUCATION AND RELIGION

Although there were medieval scholars, these were mainly members of the clergy. The common people were only educated in the teachings of the Bible. Consequently much of the drama formed in this period uses religious stories as its foundation. Unfortunately, because reading and writing skills were such a rare commodity, very few manuscripts of actual plays survive from this period. The few plays that do exist in written form contain very few stage directions, so modern scholars are often reduced to making educated guesses as to how the plays were actually produced. Piecing together a history of medieval theatre is like completing a jigsaw puzzle with half of the pieces missing! From the facts that do exist, however, it is possible to create a flavour of the kinds of performances which were given.

DRAMATIC ROOTS

Medieval drama consists of two main traditions. The first is known as *Latin Liturgical Drama*, which was practised by the priests of the churches and took place within the interior of the church. This form of drama was very closely based on biblical texts and religious ceremony. An excerpt from the extremely detailed stage directions to one such liturgical drama, *Quem Quaeritis*, will give a flavour of the nature of these dramas:

> While the third lesson is being read, four of the brethren shall vest, one of whom, wearing an alb as though for some different purpose, shall enter and go stealthily to the place of the Sepulchre and sit there quietly, holding a palm in his hands. Then while the third psalm is being sung, the other three brethren, vested in copes and holding thuribles (censers) in their hands, shall enter in their turn and go to the place of the sepulchre, step by step as if searching for something. Now these things are done in imitation of the angel seated on the tomb and of the women coming with perfumes to anoint the body of Jesus.
> *Quoted and translated by Karl Young,* The Drama of the Medieval Church, *I, 249 (Oxford 1933)*

The piece is extremely atmospheric but restrained, and there is no attempt to portray real characters, only to symbolise a certain event that took place in biblical history. The monks would intone dialogue at points during the drama and sing hymns. Latin was used during these pieces, as it was during religious services, which it has to be assumed, the common people, with no access to learning, might have found very difficult to understand. Gradually, however, Latin was replaced by the use of the *vernacular* or English (which is very different to the English known and understood today). The use of the vernacular allowed the common people to participate in these liturgical dramas, and then to create their own *secular* drama (outside the control of the church).

Secular drama was devised by the people themselves and practised outside of the church on religious festival days such as *Corpus Christi*. This form contained games and role-playing, and was frequently comic – a dramatic asset completely alien to the liturgical tradition! It is important to note that although these plays were no longer practised within the church itself, all of the dramas found their basis in biblical stories, or were moral tales constructed around religious beliefs.

Although it is highly probable that the powerful church had some controlling influence on the content of the secular drama, the finances for these productions came from the various Merchants Guilds (a group of craftsmen, e.g. shoemakers, tailors or weavers, from a town would group together and form a Guild). Each particular Guild would take responsibility for one element of the dramatic presentation. The same principle can be seen today in the carnival processions which still exist in many British towns, where a particular group sponsors and builds a float for the town carnival.

GENERAL STYLE

Medieval secular drama did not attempt to present real life; it used bold characterisations and symbolic representations of events. The main aim was to *tell the story*. Characters were heavily stylised and easily recognised by the audience because of one or two major character traits.

- Mak, in the Second Shepherd's play (written by a man known to us only as the Wakefield Master – after the cycle of plays of which this version is a part) is an arch-deceiver and a thief; his wife possesses a sharp tongue. The shepherds themselves are portrayed as 'ordinary, honest men'. These shepherds, however, are also capable of great verbal skills when required, for instance, when presenting their gifts to Christ at Bethlehem, and can talk with great authority on the teachings of Christ, which would be completely 'out-of-character' for a common man.

In this kind of rudimentary, broad story-telling technique, there is no room for intricate plots or complex character development. This is because the main function of the drama (heavily influenced by the Church) was to show how religious teachings and morality worked in society. Today we are accustomed to dramatic forms which explore how individuals work, and a much more complex form (Naturalism, page 230) has developed to accommodate this modern preoccupation. Medieval theatre style has much more in common with the broad strokes of Documentary theatre and Agit-prop, than with the subtleties of naturalistic characterisation and plot development.

There are two major forms of play which still exist in written form today: Morality/Miracle plays and the Cycle plays.

MORALITY/MIRACLE PLAYS

The Castel of Perseverance

The Castel of Perseverance would have been performed as 'theatre-in-the-round'. There were a number of different stages or 'mansions' as they were called; in the centre was the Castle of Perseverance itself, and beneath it, Mankind's bed. The theatre was a large enclosure which was dug and then fenced off for the specific purpose of showing this play. The different 'mansions' housed God, Covetousness, the

Flesh, the Devil and others. The audience would have toured around the enclosure, directed by wardens, seeing different parts of the play.

Content

The Morality plays encouraged their audience to reform their 'sinful' behaviour, and characteristically used actors to represent the abstract ideas of Virtue and Vice in the plays themselves. *The Castel of Perseverance* (author unknown but certainly written about 1405) is the longest and the largest-scale surviving example of a morality play. Virtue and Vice battle over the soul of Mankind (symbolically represented by one or a number of actors) from the time of his birth to his death and beyond. The Seven Deadly Sins, the World, the Flesh and the Devil attack and tempt Man. He is rescued by the Good Angel and lodges in the Castel of Perseverance with the Seven Moral Virtues, but after giving into further temptations, dies in a state of sin. Man's pleas for forgiveness persuade God to take Man's soul into Heaven. *Everyman* is perhaps the best known of the English Morality plays, and contains a character who symbolises the whole of mankind; *Everyman* tells the story of a man tempted by sins along the path of his life.

Staging

Each separate sequence would have been performed on what were known as 'pageant wagons'. Although no pictures actually survive of a pageant wagon, and there was certainly more than one type, it can be estimated that they would have looked something like Figure 6.3.

By looking at the various texts in existence, historians have guessed that the pageant wagons must have contained various elements of staging equipment, such as trapdoors, curtains and windlasses to raise and perhaps fly characters in.

The pageant wagons would have been drawn

Figure 6.3 *A pageant wagon*

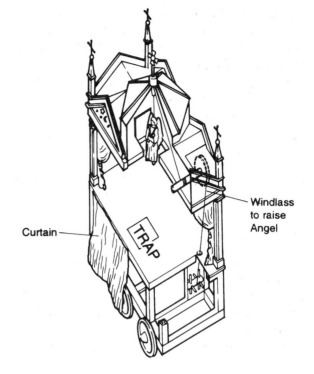

around a number of different 'stations' over the length of the festival. A 'station' was a specific site in the town where a pageant wagon would draw up and perform its scene to the gathered crowd before moving on to the next site. In the York Passion Sequence, for example, there were 12 separate stations spread around the city.

It is important to remember that theatre was still essentially an amateur activity. Although there was a strong sense of competition between the various Guilds, people took on the tasks associated with a production out of a sense of civic pride or perhaps religious devotion. It was not until the Elizabethan age that actors became professionals again, and plays essentially served to entertain a paying public. This shift in emphasis had a number of repercussions for the theatre, which are still relevant today.

CYCLE PLAYS

Content

Most towns in Britain could boast of a Cycle play at least once a year. The plays were performed on public holidays and religious festivals day, such as Whitsuntide. There could be as many as 48 scenes/sequences in each Cycle, and some Cycles were so long that they would begin at 4.30 am and only finish at nightfall. The Cycle would cover a selection of the major events told in the Bible, from the moment of creation through to the day of judgement. Below is a list of the events which would have been covered in the Corpus Christi Cycle.

Old Testament stories
1. The Creation of Angels
2. The Fall of Lucifer
3. Adam and Eve
4. Adam and Eve in the Garden of Eden
5. The Fall of Adam and Eve
6. Cain and Abel
7. Noah and Noah's wife
8. Abraham and Isaac
9. Isaac, Jacob and Esau, Procession of Prophets
10. Procession of Prophets, Moses and the Pharaoh
11. Moses and Pharaoh
12. Balaam and the Ass

New Testament stories
13. Annunciation/Mary and Gabriel
14. Trial of Mary and Joseph
15. Elizabeth and Mary
16. Nativity/Shepherds and Angels
17. Three Kings and Herod
18. Flight into Egypt
19. Slaughter of the Innocents by Herod
20. Death of Herod
21. Christ and the Doctors
22. Baptism/John the Baptist
23. Christ and Satan/The Temptation
24. Transfiguration
25. Woman Taken in Adultery
26. Raising of Lazarus
27. The Passion Sequence
28. Judas
29. Harrowing of Hell
30. Resurrection
31. Ascension
32. Antichrist
33. Day of Judgement

Text focus – *Everyman*

In the late Middle Ages in Europe, people were consistently preoccupied with death and the destruction of the flesh. Gruesome death, from disease, battle or the much earlier onset of old age, was always just around the corner. The dead and the dying were not hidden away in hospitals and mortuaries; death was an everyday experience. This demonstrated itself in a macabre fascination with the processes of dying and decomposition. Many tombs and monuments at the time were surmounted by horrific representations of the decaying body or the skeleton beneath, which was accompanied by an inscription reminding us that we will all die at some point.

In contrast to the rotting of the body, the widely held view of the Christian world in the Middle Ages was that the soul would go either to heaven or to hell. The official religion of England until the Reformation was Roman Catholicism, which held that when we died our good and bad deeds are put in the balance by God to decide which way the soul will go. The Catholic Church also believed that people were essentially sinful, but could meet God provided they confessed to a priest and received absolution before death.

ORIGINS

The play itself shows the central figure of Everyman, representing all of humanity, being called to God (i.e. to die). He tries to take his friends with him, but they all let him down, with the exception of Good-deeds, who accompanies him right into the grave. The play is probably a translation of the late fifteenth century Flemish Morality play *Elckerlijc* which dates *Everyman* at around 1520. Both plays had as their source an oriental folktale called *The Faithful Friend* that would have been used as a story to embellish sermons in church.

THE PLOT OF *EVERYMAN*

- the Messenger acts as prologue and tells the audience they are about to witness Everyman accounting to God for his sins
- God complains that his laws have been forgotten and sends Death to fetch Everyman to make his final account
- Everyman is scared and asks to take his friends – all those who have promised to stand by him through his life
- he goes to Fellowship (friends), but is rejected
- he goes to Kindred and Cousin (family), but is rejected
- he goes to Goods (possessions), who says it was his love of wealth and belongings that put him into trouble in the first place
- Good-deeds lies on the ground, unable to move because of Everyman's sins
- Knowledge tells him he must confess
- Everyman meets Confession and is absolved of his sins; this releases Good-deeds
- Everyman is now ready to die and must say goodbye to his own faculties, here personified as Beauty, Strength, Discretion and Five-wits (the senses)
- he arrives at his graveside and they too abandon him
- only Good-deeds follows him into his grave
- Everyman is taken to God by Angel

- a Doctor speaks as epilogue, warning the audience to learn from the fall of Everyman.

PERSONIFICATION

The technique of embodying concepts or ideas in the form of specific characters is known as *personification* (from the Latin, *persona*, meaning mask). In this way anything can be given a character. The best known personifications which were used throughout medieval Europe are the Seven Virtues and the Seven Deadly Sins (most recently the inspiration for the film, *Seven*).

The Seven Deadly Sins:

- pride
- gluttony
- sloth
- covetousness
- envy
- wrath
- lechery.

The Seven Virtues:

- patience
- hope
- charity
- faith
- love
- generosity
- chastity.

It is always more entertaining to represent evil, than good; consequently, there are few stage representations of the Seven Virtues. The fullest and most entertaining representation of the Seven Deadly Sins comes almost a century later, from the pen of Shakespeare's contemporary, Christopher Marlowe. Here they are as they appear to Dr Faustus:

Faustus:	What art thou, the first?
Pride:	I am Pride. I disdain to have any parents. I am like to Ovid's flea; I can creep into every corner of a wench: sometimes, like a periwig, I sit upon her brow; next, like a necklace, I hang about her neck; then, like a fan of feathers, I kiss her lips; and then, turning myself to a wrought smock, do what I list. But fie, what a smell is here? I'll not speak another word, unless the ground be perfumed and covered with cloth of arras.
Faustus:	Thou art a proud knave indeed. What art thou, the second?
Covetousness:	I am Covetousness, begotten of an old churl in a leather bag; and, might I now obtain my wish, this house, you and all, should turn to gold, that I might lock you safe into my chest. O my sweet gold!
Faustus:	And what art thou, the third?
Envy:	I am Envy, begotten of a chimney-sweeper and an oyster-wife. I cannot read and therefore wish all books were burned. I am lean with seeing others eat. O, that there would come a famine over the world, that all might die, and I live alone! Then thou

	shouldst see how fat I'd be. But must thou sit and I stand? Come down, with a vengeance!
Faustus:	Out, envious wretch! But what art thou, the fourth?
Wrath:	I am Wrath. I had neither father nor mother; I leaped out of a lion's mouth when I was scarce an hour old, and ever since have run up and down the world with this case of rapiers, wounding myself when I could get none to fight withal. I was born in hell.
Faustus:	And what art thou, the fifth?
Gluttony:	I am Gluttony. My parents are all dead, and the devil a penny they have left me but a small pension, and that buys me thirty meals a day and ten bevers – a small trifle to suffice nature. My father was a gammon of bacon and my mother was a hogshead of claret wine ... Now, Faustus ... wilt thou bid me to supper?
Faustus:	No, I'll see thee hanged; thou wilt eat up all my victuals.
Gluttony:	The devil choke thee.
Faustus:	Choke thyself, Glutton! What art thou, the sixth?
Sloth:	Heigh-ho! I am Sloth. I was begotten on a sunny bank, where I have lain ever since; and you have done me great injury to bring me from thence; let me be carried thither again by Gluttony and Lechery. Heigh-ho! I'll not speak a word more for a king's ransom.
Faustus:	And what are you, Mistress Minx, the seventh and last?
Lechery:	Who, I, sir? I am one that loves an inch of raw mutton better than an ell of fried stockfish, and the first letter of my name begins with Lechery.
Lucifer:	Away, to hell, away!

(Extract from Christopher Marlowe:
The Complete Plays *(1969), introduced and annotated by J.B. Sloane, Penguin.)*

TASK

- Cast and perform the scene. Use Marlowe's language, but find your own versions of the characters; e.g. Wrath as a raging football fan with a couple of switch-blades.
- Script and perform your own updated version of the Deadly Sins.

GENDER

It is typical of medieval drama for the only female characters in *Everyman* to be Good-deeds, Knowledge and Angel. All Seven Virtues are also female. The only Deadly Sin that Marlowe characterises as female is Lechery. A stark choice is presented here to women: if they are not chaste and virtuous, they will be seen as whores.

TASK

In groups, determine what we still personify as female, and discuss why this is so.

LANGUAGE

Everyman was written in 'Middle English' by an unknown author. The language is recognisable and reasonably easy to follow once our ear is attuned. Certain words, phrases and grammatical constructions are no longer in use, but the essential vocabulary is not greatly different from the English we speak today. The biggest difficulty is produced by the fact that *Everyman* is written in rhyming couplets. Anyone who has tried writing in rhyming couplets will know how tempting it is to produce awkward sentences in the interests of rhyme. This is made even worse by the fact that it is also a translation (of the Flemish play), and the playwright has sometimes produced deeply contorted sentences in order to find an English rhyme to replace a Dutch one. Look at the following example: these lines in *Elckerlijc*

> Hier in desen aertschen leven
> Die heylighe sacramenten seven ...

literally translate as:

> Here in this earthly life
> The holy sacraments seven ...

but in *Everyman*, become:

> Here in this transitory life, for thee and me,
> The blessed sacraments seven there be ...

– an ugly contortion if ever there was one. However, it is necessitated by the demands of the verse and bears the clear marks of translation. Notice the way it results in the verb going to the end of the sentence: '... seven there be'. This happens several times in the following extract which is near the beginning of the play. Death has just confronted Everyman and told him he must make his way to God to give a final reckoning of all his sins and good deeds. He looks around for friends to help him, and finds Fellowship. The scene is very simple. Fellowship offers to support him in any way he can, but changes his mind as soon as he hears the true nature of Everyman's distress. The writer has made the scene work by making Everyman concerned about being rejected. The more concerned he is, the more Fellowship pounds him on the back and promises absolute allegiance. This makes it all the more poignant when the final rejection comes, as we know it must.

Everyman:	Well met, good Fellowship, and good morrow!
Fellowship:	Everyman, good morrow by this day.
	Sir, why lookest thou so piteously?
	If any thing be amiss, I pray thee, me say,
	That I may help to remedy.
Everyman:	Yea, good Fellowship, yea,
	I am in great jeopardy.
Fellowship:	My true friend, show to me your mind;
	I will not forsake thee, unto my life's end,
	In the way of good company.
Everyman:	That was well spoken, and lovingly.
Fellowship:	Sir, I must needs know your heaviness;
	I have pity to see you in any distress;
	If any have you wronged ye shall revenged be,
	Though I on the ground be slain for thee, –
	Though that I know before that I should die.
Everyman:	Verily, Fellowship, gramercy
Fellowship:	Tush! by thy thanks I set not a straw.
	Show me your grief and say no more.
Everyman:	If I my heart to you break
	And then you to turn your mind from me,
	And would not me comfort, when you hear me speak,
	Then should I ten times sorrier be.
Fellowship:	Sir, I say as I will do in deed.
Everyman:	Then be you a good friend at need:
	I have found you true here before.
Fellowship:	And so ye shall evermore;
	For, in faith, and though go to Hell,
	I will not forsake thee by the way!
Everyman:	Ye speak like a good friend;
	I believe you well;
	I shall deserve it, and I may.
Fellowship:	I speak of no deserving, by this day.
	For he that will say and nothing do
	Is not worthy with good company to go;
	Therefore show me the grief of your mind,

	As to your friend most loving and kind.
Everyman:	I shall show you how it is;
	Commanded I am to go a journey,
	A long way, hard and dangerous,
	And give a strait count without delay
	Before the high judge Adonai
	Wherefore I pray you, bear me company,
	As ye have promised, in this journey.
Fellowship:	This is matter indeed! Promise is duty,
	But, and I should take such a voyage on me,
	I know it well, it should be to my pain:
	Also it make me afeard, certain.
	But let us take counsel here as well we can,
	For your words would fear a strong man.
Everyman:	Why, ye said, if I had need,
	Ye would never forsake, quick nor dead,
	Though it were to hell truly.
Fellowship:	So I said, certainly,
	But such pleasures be set aside, thee sooth to say:
	And also, if we took such a journey,
	When should we come again?
Everyman:	Nay, never again till the day of doom.
Fellowship:	In faith, then will I not come there!
	Who hath you these tidings brought?
Everyman:	Indeed, Death was with me here.
Fellowship:	Now, by God that all hath bought,
	If Death were the messenger,
	For no man that is living to-day
	I will not go that loath journey –
	Nor for the father that begat me!
Everyman:	Ye promised otherwise, pardie
Fellowship:	I wot well I say so truly;
	And yet if thou wilt eat, and drink, and make good cheer,
	Or haunt to women, the lusty company,
	I would not forsake you, while the day is clear,
	Trust me verily!
Everyman:	Yea, thereto ye would be ready,
	To go to mirth, solace, and play,
	Your mind will sooner apply
	Than to bear me company in my long journey.
Fellowship:	Now, in good faith, I will not that way.
	But and thou wilt murder, or any man kill,
	In that I will help thee with a good will!
Everyman:	O that is simple advice indeed!
	Gentle fellow, help me in my necessity;
	We have loved long, and now I need,
	And now, gentle Fellowship, remember me.
Fellowship:	Whether ye have loved me or no,
	By Saint John, I will not with thee go.
Everyman:	Yet I pray thee, take the labour, and do so much for me
	To bring me forward, for saint charity,
	And comfort me till I come without the town.
Fellowship:	Nay, and thou would give me a new gown,
	I would not a foot with thee go;

	But and you had tarried I would not have left thee so,
	And as now, God speed thee in thy journey.
	For from here I will depart as fast as I may.
Everyman:	Whither away, Fellowship? Will you forsake me?
Fellowship:	Yea, by my fay, to God I betake thee.
Everyman:	Farewell, good Fellowship; for this my heart is sore;
	Adieu for ever, I shall see thee no more.
Fellowship:	In faith, Everyman, farewell now at the end;
	For you I will remember that parting is mourning. [*exit*]
Everyman:	Alack! Shall we thus depart indeed?
	Our Lady, help, without any more comfort,
	Lo, Fellowship forsaketh me in my most need:
	For help in this world whither shall I resort?
	Fellowship here before with me would merry make;
	And now little sorrow for me doth he take.
	It is said, in prosperity men friends may find,
	Which in adversity be full unkind.

TASK

In pairs, prepare a reading of the scene. Read the following notes to help understand the characters and the shape of the scene.

Fellowship asks Everyman five times to say what is the trouble, each time making wilder protestations about his loyalty. He makes pompous and empty promises to keep him company till his dying day, to be killed for him or go to hell for him if required. When it turns out that this is precisely what *is* required of him, he immediately backs down. The playwright has made him dig a deeper hole for himself to gain maximum effect from his cowardice. Fellowship describes himself perfectly in the lines

> For he that will say and nothing do
> Is not worthy with good company to go

Fellowship wins Everyman over with his protestations and convinces him to speak out. It is important that Fellowship is played with sincerity, if Everyman is not to appear stupid for believing him at all. At this point we also have no reason to believe that Fellowship is anything but a good man; after all, he says all the right things about loyalty and friendship. It is after Everyman tells him about the real journey he has to undertake, that Fellowship begins to reveal the kind of activity that would inspire his genuine loyalty, and it is precisely the wine, women and song that we know Everyman must now repent for. Fellowship's repeated plea of 'trust me, verily' now appears cowardly and hard-hearted, and the mock sincerity entirely false. He is clearly just a fair-weather friend who only wants to be with Everyman when things are going well.

In his next speech, however, he exposes his true moral bankruptcy by offering to help Everyman commit murder, and 'with a good will!' In response, Everyman calls him 'gentle fellow' and 'gentle Fellowship', still hoping that he will not have to face God alone. The contrast of Everyman's gentle and helpless pleading with Fellowship's criminal bravado adds to the pathos. We feel sorry for Everyman, despite the fact that he has brought the situation on himself and has been, until recently, just like Fellowship himself.

Throughout the second half of the section Everyman persists in reminding Fellowship of his earlier promises and asking for his company. In fact, he does so five times – once for each of Fellowship's opening protestations. Fellowship makes five offers, then changes his mind and makes five refusals. The scene is carefully balanced, ensuring that Fellowship starts out by condemning exactly the sort of friend he turns out to be. Such a friend is not just lacking in positive virtues; in the medieval Christian morality of the play, a man cannot simply be neutral. Where a gap is left by virtue, *vice* will swiftly follow; there is no middle ground.

STAGING *EVERYMAN*

A play like *Everyman* initially appears difficult. The Christian concepts are largely unfamiliar, the language appears archaic and the characters simplistic. Despite this, *Everyman* is still performed. The characters are well drawn and easily come to life in the hands of actors. Like the Deadly Sins, they are vibrant characterisations that are worth the perseverance.

The authors recently performed the play with a group studying on a BTEC First Diploma. We put together a production team and looked for our own versions of these characters. We asked ourselves the simple question, 'What would they be if they were alive today?' Here is a cast list of *Everyman* (in order of appearance) and the characters and costumes we chose:

Cast list	Gender of player	Character
Messenger	F	Clerk of the court
God	F	Supreme Judge
Death	F	Terminator
Everyman	M & F	Joe and Jenny Bloggs
Fellowship	F	Hearty St. Trinian's girl
Cousin/Kindred	F & F	Family women
Goods	M	Arthur Daly
Good-deeds	F	Girl Guide
Knowledge	M	Professor
Confession	F	Priest
Beauty	F	Marilyn Monroe
Strength	M	Gladiator
Discretion	M	Spy
Five-wits	F	Sniffer dog
Angel	F	Angel (minus wings)

In the Middle Ages, the play would have toured around, and as such, props and scenery would have been minimal. A raised platform may have been used for God and for Everyman to ascend to his grave, but little else. We used simple configurations of stage blocks to achieve our different settings.

We decided to keep the whole cast on stage all the time and use them to set the scenes. This was the key to the production. The settings were as follows (refer back to plot summary on page 211):

Characters/Scene	Setting
God	Court room

Figure 6.4   *Everyman and Everywoman*

Everyman	Initially discovered in disco
Fellowship	Prize-giving at St. Trinians. Fellowship receiving prize (from actor playing Knowledge)
Cousin/Kindred	Cast used to establish domestic scene interrupted by Everyman: cooking, watching telly etc.
Goods	Market scene created by cast
Confession	Church and confessional booth
Beauty Strength Discretion Five-wits	Fashion parade of faculties on catwalk
Grave	Catwalk led to grave

TASKS

- Stage *Everyman* creating your own versions of the characters and finding your own settings.
- Take a modern situation (a story from recent headlines, for example) and create your own morality play, complete with personifications. How would you characterise and write for Politics, World War, Poverty, Drugs, Commerce etc.?

Elizabethan theatre

The Renaissance (*renaissance* literally means rebirth) period is considered to have begun in Italy in the fourteenth century, and is characterised by intensified classical scholarship, and geographic and scientific discoveries:

- Columbus discovered the Americas.
- Leonardo Da Vinci drew up plans for flying machines and Vessalius illustrated anatomies of the human body.
- Ancient Greek and Roman texts were rediscovered.
- Secular and commercial activities gradually displaced the religious and contemplative obsessions of the medieval period.
- In Britain, the feudal system was slowly replaced by the birth of capitalistic enterprise. Although the nobility were still extremely powerful, the merchant class had also gained power and exerted great influence both at court and on the new culture.

Education was no longer the sole province of the nobility, and the sons of the new merchant class (Shakespeare was one of these) were also educated at private schools. With the advent of the new printing presses, books and other printed literature, such as pamphlets and songsheets, became much more popular and available. The tuition of young scholars focused on the writings of the ancient Greek and Roman philosophers, dramatists and historians. These influences can be seen very clearly in the new drama, which casts aside the loose, meandering sequences of the Cycle and Morality plays, in favour of the well-structured and sophisticated play-models first conceived by the ancient Greeks. Plays are once again divided into acts and scenes, and we see the re-emergence of plot devices such as *peripeteia* and *anagnorisis* (see page 205). The *Dramatic Unities*, regarded by most of the Elizabethan dramatists as inviolable laws, were a distillation of Aristotle's *Poetics*. These *Unities* were those of Time, Action and Place and were widely held to be binding rules of dramatic construction. The new, professional writers (Shakespeare, Kyd, Marlowe and Jonson, etc.), awakened by access to these great fields of learning, turned away from biblical stories in search of fresh avenues for dramatic enterprise.

The Elizabethan writers picked up the themes of revenge, power, and love that we see in Greek and Roman plays, and used them in contemporary, fictional settings. We no longer see plays about the nativity and judgement day, but instead, dramas concerning financial and sexual corruption in Italian courts, epics on the many international and civil wars, and plays set in fantastic spirit worlds.

STAGING

Prior to the construction of the first theatres, actors were accustomed to travelling around the country in wagons, carrying portable stages which were set up where there was an audience; there is some evidence to suggest the presence of indoor stages as well as those erected in the courtyards of inns.

James Burbage founded the first permanent, dedicated playhouse in 1576. He was a member of a company called the *Earl of Leicester's Men*, so-called because actors and companies only survived the abuse of city corporations who disapproved of theatre on moral and religious grounds, because they were protected by various members of the nobility. It was called

Figure 6.5 *The interior of the Swan Playhouse (Johannes de Witt, 1596)*

the Theatre, and was probably very similar in design to two round, wooden buildings which also existed at this time on the south bank of the Thames, used for 'sports' – bull and bear-baiting.

From the design of Figure 6.5 (interior of the Swan playhouse, another theatre in the same area), you can see that the stage thrusts out beneath a canopy. The canopy was necessary to protect the stage and its properties during downpours of rain, because this theatre and others like it were all constructed without the benefit of a roof. To the rear of the stage are two doors, through which the actors could enter and exit from their 'tiring house' or the backstage area. Above the two doors there is a gallery with windows. The gallery would have been used at different times by musicians, members of the audience and the actors. The stage is skirted by cloth in order to close off the underneath from the 'groundlings' – members of the audience occupying the cheap, standing area (still called the stalls today). This cloth would have been of different colours for different styles of theatre, e.g. black cloth for tragedies.

The Theatre was a financial success for Burbage and his partners in Shoreditch. By 1600 there were a number of playhouses, the majority situated on the south bank of the Thames, near Southwark. The Theatre, which had originally been constructed in Shoreditch, to be accompanied by another playhouse called The Curtain, was pulled down in 1598 and re-built as The Globe in Bankside. The other major playhouses in this area were called The Rose and The Bear Ring.

CONTENT

The Elizabethan and Jacobean age was fertile ground for all manner of dramatic styles. Romantic comedies, satires, tragedies, revenge tragedies, histories, and city comedies were all thriving traditions which attracted huge audiences for the main theatres in London and the travelling players who toured the inns and courtyards throughout the country. A look at each style in turn will tell us a great deal, not only about the kind of entertainment which the Elizabethan audience liked, but also about the social and political preoccupations of a world completely different to our own.

ROMANTIC COMEDIES

This convention is characterised by the presence of the 'idea of romantic love', which lovers struggle to attain, despite obstacles placed in the way by evil intrigues managed by others and by chance. Ballads, music and songs accompany the complicated plots, full of reversals and surprises, and populated by humorous characters. The romantic comedy usually ends happily, with the lovers somehow defeating all impediments to their union.

The tradition has its roots in the medieval stories concerning knights and damsels, but the Elizabethan dramatists developed this tradition into popular drama, by making fun of the lofty values of romantic love and by taking the themes into new and fantasy worlds.

A Midsummer Night's Dream by Shakespeare is an extremely fantastical romantic comedy. The magical fairy world, inhabited by Oberon, Titania and Puck, becomes confused with the 'real' world, and the four lovers' intentions towards each other are twisted and thwarted by the comic antics of Puck. The scenes concerning the plight of the several lovers, who wander about the forest under the influence of spells and potions, are contrasted by the scenes populated by the mechanicals; Bottom, Quince, Snug, Flute, Snout and Starveling. The mechanicals are actors attempting to rehearse a play, and Shakespeare uses these characters to satirise the acting profession, and also to further complicate the plots twisting around the fairy world and the four lovers. The use of such contrasts and the art of exaggeration typify the Elizabethan romantic comedy.

SATIRE AND CITY COMEDY

Ben Jonson was the most prolific and perhaps most proficient of the Elizabethan satirists. John Marston and Chapman also number among accomplished writers of this species of comedy. This kind of play descends from the Greek comedies which accompanied the more respectable tragedies during the competitions, penned by wits such as Aristophanes. Satirists take topical issues, and use irony and ridicule to demonstrate the weakness and stupidity of those involved. Johnson and Marston did this only too well, and both were imprisoned for irritating the powerful people in Elizabethan society.

Satirical comedies depended very much on the use of stock characters; misers, opportunists, hypocritical priests, gluttonous rich people and gullible fools all find their way into Jonson's plays. All characters are treated to a host of misfortunes, and are shamed before each other and the audience because of their moral weaknesses. *The Alchemist* by Jonson concerns a plot hatched by two con-merchants to deceive their 'clients' into believing that they have discovered the secret of making gold. The clients fall in with the scheme because of their greed, but all lose their investments, and are punished in a number of ways. It is interesting to note, however, that the two original schemers escape virtually scot-free, despite being responsible for a criminal deception; Jonson's message seeming to be that the fraudsters are perhaps less guilty than the various hypocrites and fools who fall for their scheme.

Comedies which dealt specifically with London and its society are referred to as *city* comedies. The chief exponents of this form of drama were writers such as Thomas Middleton, Thomas Dekker, Thomas Heywood, Phillip Massinger, and Beaumont and Fletcher. These writers not only satirised the rich and the corrupt, but they also satirised each other in their own plays. Jonson argued with Dekker, Marston and Shakespeare on the grounds of poor writing-practice, and ridiculed all of them directly in his plays. Jonson particularly disliked Shakespeare's work, because his plays did not always obey the *Dramatic Unities,* whereas Jonson's work always attempted to adhere to them. This may provide us with some indication as to the influence which the Greeks and classical civilisation had upon Elizabethan theatre. Who would be criticised today because he or she did not follow a set of guidelines devised several thousand years ago?

TRAGEDY AND REVENGE TRAGEDY

Elizabethan tragedies are typified by their questioning of the order and the beliefs of the society in which they happen to be set. At the centre of the maelstrom of events stands the hero, plagued by doubt, and who, because of a critical error of judgement finds himself treading a path ever-downward toward total disaster. This critical error, or tragic flaw is an Aristotelian idea (see page 205). In addition to the classical influence, there is also a clear link between these plays and the medieval Morality plays. In *Dr Faustus*, by Christopher Marlowe, the proud hero (Dr Faustus) is carried away by his thirst for knowledge, and uses magical powers to call up the Devil. Faustus sells his soul to the Devil in exchange for various material rewards, and ends up roasting in the flames of hell for his unforgivable arrogance. The hero's questioning of the divine order and his interference in the order of his own world has led him into eternal damnation. The medieval Morality plays always ended with the salvation of the central character's soul despite the fact that he had committed many sins; but not so the Elizabethan tragedians. Their vision was much more bleak, and perhaps we can see the influence of the classical dramatist in the harsh and uncompromising conclusion. Like Oedipus, Faustus is condemned to eternal despair in the face of the might of divine forces, which ultimately were always beyond his control, no matter how strongly his pride informed him of the opposite. At the end of *Dr Faustus*, a Chorus enters:

Chorus: Cut is the branch that might have grown full straight,
And burned is Apollo's laurel bough,
That sometime grew within this learned man.
Faustus is gone. Regard his hellish fall
Whose fiendful fortune may exhort the wise
Only to wonder at unlawful things,
Whose deepness doth entice such forward wits,
To practice more than heavenly power permits.

(Epilogue, Dr Faustus, *Christopher Marlowe)*

The Chorus also enter at the end of *Oedipus Rex* and make a similarly uncompromising commentary on the events recently demonstrated to the audience:

Chorus: People of Thebes, my countrymen, look on Oedipus.
He solved the famous riddle with his brilliance,
He rose to power, a man beyond all power.
Who could behold his greatness without envy?
Now that a black sea of terror has overwhelmed him.
Now as we keep our watch and wait the final day,
Count no man happy till he dies, free of pain at last.

(extract from Sophocles, The Three Plays *(1984), trans. Robert Fagles, Penguin Classics)*

Compare the two speeches cited above: the debt which the Elizabethans owed to their Greek forebears quickly becomes apparent, in terms of both the structure, the pessimism and the cosmic proportions of the tragedy. Both Oedipus and Dr Faustus sought to know 'too much', and continued their quests despite much good advice to the contrary. Both heroes paid for their arrogance with a fate far worse than death: Oedipus condemned to a living hell and Faustus burning in the fires of Christian hell for all eternity.

Central to our understanding of Elizabethan tragedy is a comprehension of the kind of thinking which influenced the creation of so many bloodthirsty and criminal villains.

Scholars believe that the writings of Nicolo di Bernardo dei Machiavelli (1469–1527) reached England by 1585 and subsequently had a great deal of influence on the work of tragedians such as Marlowe, and revenge tragedians such as Kyd, Marston, Tourneur and Webster. Machiavelli, however, was somewhat misrepresented because his work was not translated in its entirety from Italian into English. The translation concentrated on the sensational aspects of Machiavelli's work, which stated that man was basically an evil creature, and that cruelty was entirely justifiable to maintain power and order. Machiavelli's statement that the need for a completely fair and just ruler was of the utmost importance for the continued well-being of a state or country, was entirely missed out in the translation. However, the dramatists fully explored and exploited what became known as Machiavelli's law, that the end justifies the means.

Tragedians treat us to portraits of incredibly cruel villains, who act seemingly without compunction or remorse: the Cardinal in *The Duchess of Malfi*, Flamineo in *The White Devil*, Barabas in *The Jew of Malta*, Iago in *Othello*, among many others. Their evil seems

RESEARCH TASKS

- See R. A. Banks, *Drama and Theatre Arts*, pp. 121–129 for more information on the development of tragedy (1985, Hodder & Stoughton).
- How does *Hamlet* differ from the conventional revenge tragedy of the period? Below is a list of Revenge plays you might wish to investigate, with details of recommended editions:
  Tourner, *The Atheists Tragedy* (1959, Ernest Benn Limited)
  — *The Revenger's Tragedy* (1967, Edward Arnold)
  Beaumont and Fletcher, *The Maids Tragedy* (1949, Ernest Benn Limited)
  — *Cupid's Revenge* (1970, Cambridge University Press)
  — *Thierry and Theoderet* (1949, Ernest Benn Limited)
  Shakespeare, *Titus Andronicus* (1992, Ulverscroft)
  Kyd, *The Spanish Tragedy* (1989, A & C Black)
- Find out what a staging convention is and then name the staging conventions which accompanied the playing of Elizabethan revenge tragedies.
- There is a great deal of information available on the Elizabethan theatre which we have only barely touched upon in this short account: the court masques, costume, the boy players, the political perspective of the plays, set design and properties, the attitude of the authorities to the theatre, the nature of the audience. Take one of these topics and do some research in your library.

completely motiveless, and the presence on stage of such motiveless evil is at once disturbing and incredible. This tradition, however, still survives today in innumerable Hollywood films; anti-heroes display apparently fathomless and uncontainable instincts for murder and evil, in much the same way as the villains conduct themselves in revenge tragedies. There is very little room for the psychological development of such characters in revenge tragedies, with the notable exception of Shakespeare's *Hamlet*, which completely breaks that mould. The theme of revenge and the actions that it drives the characters to perform are sufficient for the needs of the majority of playwrights writing in this mode.

Text Focus – *Macbeth*, William Shakespeare

Macbeth has always been one of Shakespeare's richest, best-loved and most accessible plays. The range of issues it touches upon is quite staggering: good and evil, the supernatural, prophecy, the imagination, the psyche, ambition, power, brutality, sexuality, the natural order, social law, tyranny, totalitarian rule, deceit, guilt, espionage, betrayal. Shakespeare uses language which is powerful, evocative and enormously rich in imagery. *Macbeth* has a tightly-written plot that races to its conclusion, and gives the earliest real insight into the mind of a killer – and not only that, but a *pair* of killers. One only has to look at the fascination the entire nation has had with the gruesome crimes of Fred and Rosemary West to understand why the murderous Macbeth and his killer queen still occupy such a prominent position in our hearts and minds today.

The play was probably written in 1605 or 1606, and is based on historical material found in Raphael Holinshed's *Chronicles of England, Scotland and Ireland*, published in 1587. Shakespeare borrowed from history but greatly embellished it, altering key facts in the retelling. The real Macbeth ruled Scotland for 17 years (1040–1057). He did, indeed, take the crown after killing King Duncan, but the real Duncan was killed in battle and not murdered in his bed, as in Shakespeare's play.

SYNOPSIS OF *MACBETH*

The play begins in the thick of battle. Macbeth and Banquo, generals in King Duncan's army, are victorious over rebel forces. Returning from battle across barren moorland, Macbeth and Banquo meet three 'weird sisters' who prophesy that Macbeth will become Thane of Cawdor and then King. Part of the prophecy comes true as Duncan rewards Macbeth with the title of Thane of Cawdor for his bravery.

Duncan visits the castle of Macbeth and Lady Macbeth. Together, they plot to kill him. Macduff, the Thane of Fife, arrives and finds the body. Suspicion falls on the king's sons, Malcolm and Donalbain, who have fled for their lives. In their absence, Macbeth is crowned.

Having heard the witches' prophecies, Banquo becomes suspicious of Macbeth. Macbeth hires two assassins to murder him, but Banquo's ghost returns to haunt Macbeth at his coronation banquet.

Macbeth visits the witches again. They prophesy, warning him against Macduff. He learns that Macduff has fled to England, and arranges for assassins to massacre Lady Macduff and their children. Macduff, in England with Malcolm, hears the news and swears revenge.

Consumed with guilt, Lady Macbeth becomes steadily mad, and dies. Malcolm and Macduff lead an army from England, and after a dramatic confrontation, Macbeth is slain.

Note: *Macbeth* was written in the early years of James I's reign, who succeeded Elizabeth I to the throne. The Latin translation of his name is 'Jacobus', which is why we refer to plays from this period as Elizabethan-Jacobean drama.

TASK

1 Find out about the real witches of the Middle Ages. Who were they, why were they so feared, and what happened to them?
2 Is there a modern-day equivalent of a witch? How does this suggest the witches might be played in a modern production of *Macbeth*?

Shakespeare was writing at the end of the medieval period, and his work shares many of the same concerns with works such as *Everyman*: the moral order, death and repentance. There is a new freedom, however. The author of *Everyman* could never have portrayed witches on a stage. This is because the huge growth of trade and colonisation in the sixteenth century prompted a move away from the old certainties of the medieval Church. Elizabethan and Jacobean society saw the emergence of the individual, and of psychological studies of individual personalities. There is a spirit of real questioning in the language and structure of the drama of the time. In Macbeth, we see a character engaged in a struggle to understand the baffling forces of his own imagination, held in balance between the existing Christian moral order and the older belief in witchcraft and prophecy. This is what he says after the initial encounter with the weird sisters:

Act I, Scene III

Macbeth: [*Aside*] This supernatural soliciting
Cannot be ill; cannot be good. If ill,
Why hath it given me earnest of success,
Commencing in truth? I am Thane of Cawdor.
If good, why do I yield to that suggestion
Whose horrid image doth unfix my hair
And make my seated heart knock at my ribs
Against the use of nature? Present fears
Are less than horrible imaginings.
My thought, whose murder yet is but fantastical,
Shakes to my single state of man that function
Is smothered in surmise, and nothing is
But what is not.

Macbeth enters a world of moral uncertainty, as murky as the moorland sisters themselves. The witches chant:

Fair is foul and foul is fair
Hover through the fog and filthy air. (*Act I, Scene I*)

If the witches are evil, Macbeth argues, why are they able to prophecy the truth? If they are good, however, why is his mind already fantasising about killing Duncan, because that is surely what the 'horrid suggestion' is. Unlike the recent bloodshed on the battlefield, however, the thought of *this* kind of killing makes his hair stand on end; it is 'against the use of nature'. We see a mind prey to horrible imaginings, to grotesque fantasies that seem to take firm hold at the merest suggestion of the witches. They only foretold the future; the way to achieve it is in Macbeth's mind. The idea takes root, however, because the witches seem real; after all, Banquo has seen them too. They would be believable to an Elizabethan Jacobean audience as they were part of the folklore of the time, of the collective experience of the supernatural in a world caught between the pagan and the Christian. Macbeth's imaginings, however, are his alone. The mere thinking of them isolates him from his comrades, and he becomes an agent in a world where 'nothing is but what is not'. Alone, he might never have acted upon his thought's 'fantastical murder'.

His wife plays a vital role in using all her powers of persuasion on Macbeth. She accuses him of being unmanly in his cowardice, and claims that killing is just a thing a man should be able to do. Much of the imagery of the play is about the triumph of the aggressive and 'masculine' over the gentle and 'feminine'. Listen to Lady Macbeth as she prepares herself for evil by calling for the destruction of her natural self, of her femininity:

Act I, Scene V

Lady M.:   Come you spirits
That tend on mortal thoughts, unsex me here,
And fill me from the crown to the toe, top-full
Of direst cruelty! make thick my blood;
Stop up the access and passage to remorse,
That no compunctious visitings of nature
Shake my fell purpose, nor keep peace between
The effect and it. Come to my women's breasts,
And take my milk for gall, you murdering ministers,
Wherever in your sightless substances
You wait on nature's mischief! Come, thick night,
And pall thee in the dunnest smoke of hell,
That my keen knife see not the wound it makes,
Nor heaven peep through the blanket of the dark
To cry 'Hold, hold!'

It is an extraordinary speech, in which the natural world is again subverted. Nature itself is no longer allowed to break through the shroud of hellish smoke that blots out the heavens. Lady Macbeth imagines herself surrounded by spirits who virtually unsex her.

TASK

1 Research into women who kill. Do they 'unsex' themselves? Can a woman kill and still be 'feminine'? Have notions of gender behaviour changed dramatically since Shakespeare's time?

2 Take the speech and divide it up. Each learn a snippet:
   • as a group, use the speech and devise your own ritual for conjuring spirits.
   • blindfold yourself and stand or sit in the middle of the group who whisper the lines at you.

3 Learn the whole speech and perform it blindfold. Believe in the spirits and what you are asking them to do to you.

Note: it is so much more powerful if the speech is delivered, not simply as rhetoric, but as something that will actually happen. Try it out – enjoy the short, passionate energy of 'make thick my blood', 'take my milk for gall', and 'come thick night'.

When Macbeth himself arrives, Lady Macbeth is primed and ready to kill. She will stop at nothing, but Macbeth has misgivings. In the following scene, Macbeth has left the banquet held in Duncan's honour, and Lady Macbeth has come to find him.

Act I, Scene VII

[*Enter Lady Macbeth*]

Macbeth: How now! What news?
Lady M.:   He has almost supp'd. Why have you left the chamber?
Macbeth: Hath he asked for me?
Lady M.:   Know you not he has?
Macbeth: We will proceed no further in this business.
He hath honoured me of late; and I have bought
Golden opinions from all sorts of people,
Which would be worn now in their newest gloss,
Not cast aside so soon.
Lady M.:   Was the hope drunk
Wherein you dressed yourself? hath it slept since,
And wakes it now to look so green and pale
At what it did so freely? From this time,
Such I account thy love. Art thou afeard
To be the same in thine own act and valour
As thou art in desire? Letting 'I dare not' wait upon 'I would'
Like the poor cat i'th'adage?
Macbeth: Prithee, peace;
I dare do all that may become a man;
Who dares do more is none.
Lady M.:   What beast was't then
That made you break this enterprise to me?
When you durst do it, then you were a man;
And to be more than what you were, you would
Be so much more the man. Nor time nor place
Did then adhere, and yet you would make both;
They have made themselves, and that their fitness now
Does unmake you. I have given suck, and know
How tender 'tis to love the babe that milks me –
I would, while it was smiling in my face,
Have plucked my nipple from his boneless gums,
And dash'd the brains out, had I so sworn
As you have done to this.
Macbeth: If we should fail?
Lady M.:   We fail!
But screw your courage to the sticking place,
And we'll not fail. When Duncan is asleep –
Whereto the rather shall his day's hard journey
Soundly invite him – his two chamberlains
Will I with wine and wassail so convince
That memory, the warder of the brain,
Shall be a fume, and the receipt of reason
A limbec only. When in swinish sleep
Their drenchèd natures lie as in a death,
What cannot you and I perform upon
Th' unguarded Duncan? what not put upon
His spongy officers who shall bear the guilt
Of our great quell?
Macbeth: Bring forth men-children only;
For thy undaunted mettle should compose
Nothing but males. Will it not be receiv'd

When we have mark'd with blood those sleepy two
Of his chamber, and us'd their very daggers,
That they have done't?

Lady M.:   Who dares receive it other,
As we shall make our griefs and clamours roar
Upon his death?

Macbeth: I am settled, and bend up
Each corporal agent to this terrible feat.
Away, and mock the time with fairest show;
False face must hide what the false heart doth know.

Note the way in which Lady Macbeth uses each of Macbeth's remarks, turning the imagery to her own advantage. Read the passage though a few times and then complete the following tasks.

TASK

1 Translate the scene into modern English. Find appropriate equivalents for anything that seems particularly Elizabethan.
2 List the tactics used by Lady Macbeth to persuade Macbeth to commit murder.
3 Improvise the scene in your own words. Try out as many methods of persuasion as you can. What proves most effective? Try it also independently of the story; e.g. Jill tries to persuade Jack to steal for her.
4 Now learn the words. Use all you have discovered about persuasion to prepare a playing of the scene. Both characters shift from anger and resentment, to mutual celebration, and to grim determination. Chart this journey accurately for each character. It's a great scene, so enjoy!

Restoration theatre

HISTORICAL CONTEXT

In 1642, Charles I raised his standard at Nottingham, and the English Civil War began. For the next 18 years, the theatre was practically non-existent, firstly because of the Civil War, and then, after the peace, because of the influence of the Puritans.

The Puritans consisted of a number of religious sects that held a similar outlook, even if they did not always share the same aims. They were stern, solemn and religious people who believed in worshipping God and avoiding pleasure. While they held influence under the protection of Oliver Cromwell, fairs, theatres and even Christmas celebrations were banned.

In 1659, Oliver Cromwell died, and his son Richard became Lord Protector. In 1660, the people were dissatisfied with this government, and Charles II was invited to reclaim the throne. He was welcomed back to England with much pomp and ceremony, and things changed dramatically as people threw off the old, stifling morality of the Puritans and had some fun.

At first there was a shortage of theatres and actors, but in 1663, Charles granted royal patents to Thomas Killigrew and Richard Davenant for the theatres at Drury Lane and Covent Garden, giving them a monopoly on theatrical performance; Londoners once again thrilled to nights at the theatre.

INNOVATIONS

During his time in exile, Charles II had become accustomed to theatre in the continental style; soon these innovations were incorporated into English theatre to please the King and the courtiers.

At first, old tennis courts were used for performances, but when new theatres were built, they were rectangular buildings with fanned seating, raised stages framed by a proscenium arch, and hand-painted scenery, rather than the round buildings of the Elizabethan age, or the rectangular halls which were patronised by the wealthy before the Civil War. A small apron stage protruded in front of the proscenium, and two doors on each side of the stage allowed the actors to enter and exit.

But the biggest innovation of Restoration theatre was the introduction of actresses! Before the Restoration, women's parts were played by boys. Now these parts could be played by beautiful and talented women. These were the first real superstars of the theatre. One of these new actresses, Nell Gwynn, is probably more famous for being the mistress of Charles II than for her acting talents, although at the time she was very popular with audiences for her acting in comedy.

Ironically, these actresses were required to play 'breeches' roles; i.e. they had to dress up as men! This allowed the plot to be complicated by mistaken identity, and showed off the actresses' figures better than the female costumes of the day. The tradition still survives in modern day pantomime.

Figure 6.6 *A Restoration actress*

THE PLAYS

Although some fine tragedies were written in the Restoration period, such as *All for Love* by John Dryden (the Poet Laureate), and *Venice Preserved* by Thomas Ottway, this era is best known for its comedies.

Restoration comedy was quite a departure from previous types of comic plays. Most importantly, the plays are contemporary. Rather than writing about Roman emperors, Greek heroes or dead kings and queens, the

Restoration playwrights wrote about the issues of their own age. The plays are set in the *beau monde* of people of wealth, rank and fashion, and the dominant subject is love and marriage.

It must be remembered that during this period, marriages among the gentry were arranged to secure wealth and property, the woman bringing a dowry to her husband upon marriage. With death or desertion being the only ways to escape unhappy marriages, it may be understood that getting married was not necessarily the happiest event in a couple's life.

The plays have certain conventions which are common to most:

1 The characters have names which fit their characters, e.g. Constant, Petulant, Wilful.

2 The plots are very complicated, full of tricks and mistaken identities.

3 The plots are usually concerned with love and marriage.

4 The up-and-coming middle classes (merchants, squires etc.) and country people (usually from Shropshire) are the butt of many jokes.

5 The plays are full of wit, shown in the sparkling *repartee* and guile of the main characters.

To illustrate this, there follows a synopsis of the events in perhaps the greatest Restoration comedy, *The Way of the World* by William Congreve. (Note: the women are known by surname alone.)

Text focus – *The Way of the World*

ACT I

Edward Mirabell, a London gentleman, is in love with Millamont. Unfortunately he has offended her aunt, Lady Wishfort, who has legal control of half of Millamont's money. Mirabell pretends to woo Lady Wishfort, to hide the fact that he is in love with her niece. Mrs Marwood, who wants Mirabell for herself, kindly tells Lady Wishfort all about it.

Mirabell arranges a secret marriage between his servant, Waitwell, and Lady Wishfort's maid, Foible. He hears from two of his foppish friends, Anthony Witwoud and Petulant, that Sir Wilful Witwoud, Anthony's half-brother and Lady Wishfort's nephew, has arrived in town from Shropshire, and Lady Wishfort plans that *he* should marry Millamont.

ACT II

Mrs Fainall, Lady Wishfort's daughter, meets Mrs Marwood in St. James Park, and they talk about how loathsome men are. When Mrs Fainall leaves to converse with Mirabell, who was formerly her lover, we discover that Mr Fainall and Mrs Marwood are lovers.

When Mrs Fainall and Mirabell return, we learn that she dislikes her husband, and also that Mirabell has ordered Waitwell to disguise himself as Mirabell's rich uncle, Sir Rowland, and in this guise to woo and marry Lady Wishfort. Mirabell will then reveal Sir Rowland's true identity, and thus force Lady Wishfort to permit his marriage to Millamont.

ACT III

Lady Wishfort, who is already eager to meet Sir Rowland, is even more determined to prevent Mirabell's marriage to Millamont, when Foible, who is working for Mirabell in this intrigue, tells her of some (fictional) insults that Mirabell made about her. She decides to marry Sir Rowland, and then persuades him to disinherit Mirabell.

Sir Wilful arrives, and is mocked and teased by his half-brother (Anthony) and Petulant. Fainall and Mrs Marwood send Lady Wishfort an anonymous letter exposing 'Sir Rowland'.

ACT IV

Sir Wilful and Mirabell woo Millamont separately. Sir Wilful becomes drunk and Millamont refuses his suit, bringing her into conflict with her aunt who insists that she accepts, or lose her inheritance.

'Sir Rowland' arrives and courts Lady Wishfort. They decide on a quick marriage to cause Mirabell problems. When the anonymous letter arrives, 'Sir Rowland' convinces Lady Wishfort that it was written by Mirabell, so she ignores it.

ACT V

Fainall and Mrs Marwood spill the beans to Lady Wishfort. Fainall tries to bully her to agree not to marry anybody, and to sign Millamont's money over to his wife (and therefore to him) as she has forfeited her right to it by refusing to marry Sir Wilful.

Just as Lady Wishfort is poised to give in, to avoid a scandal, Mirabell appears, reveals the Fainall-Marwood affair, and produces a long-held document which gives him control over Mrs Fainall's estate.

Sir Wilful withdraws his proposal of marriage, and Lady Wishfort agrees to a wedding between Mirabell and Millamont.

This all sounds rather complicated, and it is! The best way to get used to it all is to read the plays. The selection listed below are all available in modern annotated editions.

- Ariadne – *She Ventures and He Wins*
- Behn – *The Feigned Courtesans, The Rover*
- Centelivre – *The Basset Table, The Busybody*
- Congreve – *The Double Dealer, Lover For Love, The Way of the World*
- Ethridge – *The Man of Mode*
- Farquhar – *The Beaux Strategem, The Recruiting Officer*
- Pix – *The Beaux Defeated*
- Vanbrugh – *The Provoked Wife, The Relapse*
- Wycherley – *The Country Wife, The Plain Dealer*

THE PLAYWRIGHTS

At this time, playwriting was precarious employment. The author's payment was the box office receipts of the third night. If a play was successful, an author would make some money, but equally, if it closed on the second night, the poor author didn't get a penny.

Some authors, like Congreve and Ethridge were already rich and so did not depend on the theatre for their livelihood; others like Ottway and Farquhar died in poverty.

In writing, too, women took a major part for the first time, with Aphra Behn, a former government spy and a close friend of the Earl of Rochester, being the first woman to earn her living as a playwright. There were also others, such as Mrs Pix, Susan Centrelivre and others who wrote successful plays and were able to provide a female view of the battle of the sexes

BACKLASH

If Restoration comedy was a reaction against the repression of Puritan England, then it too became the focus of critics, when some people felt that things had become too liberal and unrestrained.

In 1698, Jeremy Collier, a non-conformist priest wrote and published a pamphlet called *A Short View of the Immorality and Profaneness of the English Stage*. This attacked the morality of the Restoration plays, some of which were indeed quite bawdy. This provoked a pamphlet war, with both sides taking up the cudgels in print to argue their case, Congreve and Vanbrugh appearing for the playwrights. Collier published his last pamphlet on the subject in 1707, and this effectively saw the end of the Restoration period in the theatre. Whatever the rights or wrongs of the case, it undoubtedly introduced great changes in British plays, and prepared the way for the mawkishly sentimental plays of the later eighteenth century. The next theatrical explosion did not happen until over a century later.

Modern European theatre

Towards the end of the nineteenth century, the theatre began a period of rapid development. For over a century, audiences had been watching costume dramas, melodramas and light comedies, but now certain historical factors combined to bring about a sustained period of experimentation with theatrical form and content.

- There was much political upheaval, with unrest in Europe and Russian, and colonial wars in the British Empire. It was a time when many people were questioning the old accepted order and this was reflected in the arts.
- New ideas, notably those of Darwin on evolution and Freud on psychology, changed people's perceptions of themselves and challenged the orthodox ideas of God and religion and the human race's place in the structure of the world.
- This period saw the beginning of the great age of communication. The printed word was already widely available, and inventions like the telegraph, moving pictures, and radio, meant that ideas could travel much more quickly than in the past.
- In the spirit of experimentation, artists

crossed mediums to find new means of expression. Surrealists, for example, showed an early interest in film, not as an alternative to painting, but as another artistic form.

Small theatres, such as the Théâtre Libre in Paris and the Moscow Art Theatre, were privately funded, and undertook whole seasons of new and challenging works of drama which often received vitriolic criticism in the press, and even caused riots.

In this section we will look at some of these theatrical movements, but this should only be a starting point for your own research into the subject. It should also be remembered that many of these movements existed at the same time. Expressionism did not replace Naturalism and then give way in its turn to Surrealism – there was much overlap.

The new ideas did not replace the old ideas overnight, if at all. For every avant-garde production, there were probably 99 in the old style, just as today the West End is crammed with long-running musicals and revivals of classic plays.

Naturalism

Naturalism has been a dominant theatrical practice since its advent at the end of the nineteenth century. Its influence has pervaded theatrical culture since that time, and is also the dominant mode of production in film and television. As such, it is a form with which we are very familiar, more due to our exposure to these mass media than through theatre. But what is Naturalism? Unfortunately, there is no set form for a naturalistic play. We can identify certain characteristics which such a play might have, but very few, if any, will exhibit all of them. Below are some of the major elements associated with theatrical Naturalism:

- *A slice of life* – the naturalistic play originally expressed a new awareness of social relationships. The industrial revolution and burgeoning class consciousness in the middle of the last century fostered a spirit of inquiry into the social forces acting on human beings to make them what they are. It attempted to answer questions such as, what makes people violent? what determines class? or culture? This meant that plays could no longer afford to deal with gods, kings and heroes. They had to deal with the real world as ordinary people experienced it. As a result, plays strove to create the illusion that what the audience is seeing is really happening before their eyes; as if a slice of life has been placed under the microscope for detailed examination by the spectator. This meant a return to the classical Unity of time favoured by Aristotle, but so often broken by Shakespeare, among others. Action had to be sequential, i.e. the story had to start at the beginning and end at the end. This may sound obvious, but some narrative techniques such as flashbacks could not be used as they would spoil the illusion that the action was happening there and then.

- *Sequential action and narrative* – this simply means that the story starts at the beginning and ends at the end. This may sound obvious, but some narrative techniques such as flashbacks cannot be used, as they would spoil the illusion that the action is actually happening on stage.

- *The fourth wall* – the set is a very important part of a naturalistic play. It is the environment where the characters live, and the place where the story is played out. It is usually very detailed and includes all of the furniture and clutter that you would expect to find in the type of place that the play is set in, usually the home of the main character. The set shows three walls of the room, but the fourth wall which looks out onto the auditorium is imaginary so the audience can see in. The actors behave as if the audience is not there. The classic 'box' set is the best known example of this kind of illusionist drama, where all elements are reproduced to convince the audience that they are looking at a 'real' room.

- *Identifiable characters* – the characters in

Figure 6.7   *A naturalistic set design (a) the set (b) a ground plan of the set*

(a)

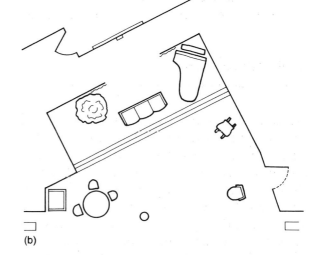

(b)

the play are contemporary to the time that the play was written. They believe in believable and recognisable ways and are psychologically developed and fully rounded. They reflect the environment in which we see them, and are, in fact, shaped by it.

The problem of watching the original naturalistic dramas today, is that they are now around a hundred years old, so we are unable to relate to them in the same way as their original audiences did. But if you compare the criteria above with a current soap opera then you will begin to see how it all works.

Historically, Naturalism had existed in art for many years and was taken up in literary circles, notably by the French author, Emile Zola. In 1873, Zola adapted his novel, *Therese Raquin* for the stage and had some success, but the names most closely related to Naturalism are Ibsen, Stanislavski and Chekhov.

HENRIK IBSEN

Henrik Ibsen was a Norwegian playwright who wrote a number of historical dramas and verse plays, before he turned to what is now termed Naturalism, at the age of 49. Ibsen had strong political and social beliefs, and he developed this form to deal with social issues which tended to be avoided or ignored at the time. His main plays from this period were:

Pillars of Society   (1877)
A Doll's House   (1879)
Ghosts   (1881)
An Enemy of the People   (1882)

A Doll's House deals with domestic conflict between a husband and wife, which leads to the wife leaving her husband and children to regain her freedom. *Ghosts* looks at the destructiveness of secrets within a family, and addresses such topics as incest and venereal disease. This now seems rather tame and ordinary to us, being very much province of the daily soaps, but in the 1880s it was deeply shocking. *Ghosts* was banned in Germany by order of the police, and when it was first performed in London, it received terrible reviews, with one critic comparing it to an open drain.

STANISLAVSKI AND THE SYSTEM

Naturalism became enshrined as the predominant acting style as a result of the work of the great Russian director and actor-trainer Stanislavski (1863–1938). He spent his early years observing the great actors of the day and figuring out what enabled them to produce such powerful and convincing performances. What he observed was that the best actors radiated an aura on stage that reached across the footlights to the audience. They were relaxed, concentrated and filled with energy; the kind of energy found when a child is engrossed in building a sand-castle or someone in love is writing a letter. Stanislavski knew that everyone has heightened moments of experience when they are totally at one with what they are doing; when they feel relaxed, creative and conscious of their own power. He also knew that for most of us such moments are rare. He called it *The Creative State of Mind* (CSM) and dedicated himself to helping actors find and recreate it at will.

To do this, he developed a series of exercises which would enable actors to achieve the relaxation and concentration necessary to achieve the Creative State of Mind. These exercises now form the basis of most professional actor training in Europe and America. In 1898 he founded the Moscow Art Theatre (MAT) and began developing his system of actor training to enable all actors to reach the height of their ability.

Stanislavski's background

He was born Konstantin Sergeyevich Alexeyev, the son of a wealthy manufacturing family. He had eight brothers and sisters and was of a sickly disposition, living in mortal fear of infection throughout his life (something for which he was severely lampooned by the writer Bulgakov in his novel *Black Snow* about his time with Stanislavski). The Alexeyev family regularly staged amateur performances in a purpose-built small theatre on their estate, and the young *Kostya* was an enthusiastic participant. Very early on he began the lifelong habit of keeping detailed notebooks of his theatrical explorations. His fascination with detail lead him to puppetry, where he created elaborate sets and costumes to tackle grandiose themes such as Don Juan's descent into hell.

Konstantin grew up in a Russia where the theatre was lacking in any naturalness or subtlety of characterisation. Sets and costumes were more or less whatever was to hand and actors had the habit of standing stage centre and declaiming straight out to the audience. His own experiments on the family estate had shown him that much greater reality could be achieved if there was attention to detail and the actors were guided and pushed by a director.

Stanislavski disliked the theatre of the time for the following reasons:

- it lacked seriousness and integrity
- the 'star' system
- its neglect of training for actors
- its neglect of the rehearsal process
- its boring repertoire (cheap French and German farces).

The Saxe-Meiningen Company

Stanislavski was very impressed by the work of the touring company of The Duke of Saxe-Meininge from Germany, whom he first saw in 1890. They were already experimenting with a much more realistic approach to acting, using authentic properties and costumes to create a convincing world on stage. This was particularly noticeable in their ensemble crowd work, where they would place actors spreading out and off the stage to create the illusion of far greater numbers. The crowd members would have individualised responses to the main stage action. In addition to this, the company was run with military precision; lateness and sloppiness were simply not tolerated. This appealed to the young actor and director, who had, by now, adopted the stage name Stanislavski.

The Society for Art and Literature

This was founded by Stanislavski with some friends. He took charge of its associated theatre group and, from 1890, began to carve out his reputation as an innovative young director. His research and attention to detail were unparalleled. He even went to Venice to research for a production of *Othello* in which he was playing the lead. This production opened to critical acclaim in 1896, where he was praised for the naturalness he had brought to the role.

Moscow Art Theatre

In 1897, Stanislavski made two important associations that were to shape the future of western theatre. Firstly he met with the dramaturg Nemirovich-Danchenko (known as Nemirovich), who asked him to form a theatre company. They created the Moscow Art Theatre (MAT). In the same year he met the playwright Anton Chekhov, whose play *The Seagull* would be the new theatre's first production. The Seagull became the company logo.

Stanislavski's main interest was in the actor,

and in particular how he or she could attain a truthful, convincing performance. He evolved what became known as his System, or The Method which, he said, was not something new but something that successful actors had always done. It drew together an approach for the non-genius actor who could not and should not rely on inspiration alone to create a satisfactory performance. The main aim of The System was to help the actor create an illusion of actuality on stage; to convince the audience that the actor was playing a real person and that their thoughts and feelings were those of the character being embodied.

Stanislavski elaborated on *The System* in three books:

1 *An Actor Prepares* (1937). Here he attempted to systematise the *psychological* and *emotional* preparation an actor needed for personal development and the creation of a particular role.

2 *Building A Character* (1949). This dealt with the *physical* and *vocal* training needed to communicate the different aspects of a role.

3 *Creating A Role* (1961). This book gave detailed examples of the application of The System to various roles. It also contained modifications to The System and theories, reached through the author's greater experience of them in application.

(For The System in practice, See Chapter 2, page 73.)

ANTON CHEKHOV

Anton Pavlovich Chekhov (1860–1904) became one of Russia's best-known and best-loved authors. His early career was spent writing pithy and powerful short stories that were full of pathos and humour despite their apparently undramatic themes. He honed this to a fine art in his dramatic work, where plays consisted of detailed character studies of late-Imperial Russians from the upper-middle classes, struggling to come to terms with the changing world around them and their failure to achieve what they wanted in life. Examples of this are *The Three Sisters*, who live in the country and want to return to Moscow. Throughout the play it is clear that they never will. Characters fall in love but are unable to express how they feel to the one they love. In the plays of Chekhov we enter a world of disillusionment and failure of communication.

Chekhov himself insisted that his plays were comedies. They are certainly not comedies in the way we now understand them. The audience would be unlikely to find itself rolling in the aisles at the grim display of human failure on the stage before them. And yet the characters are drawn with such depth and understanding that, with careful playing, the most dire of human disillusions can be seen as something we all share. As we recognise ourselves in the characters, so we can laugh at ourselves in them.

Here, then, is the main difficulty in playing Chekhov. The characters are very much products of their own time and culture. They are glum philosophisers, but also quick to feel emotion. Characters are often crying with happiness or sadness, but are dry-eyed a moment later. This is an aspect of the Russian temperament that the more phlegmatic English find it difficult to identify with. Mike Alfreds, founding Director of Shared Experience, argues that we have to replace 'our Anglo-Saxon mode of emotional expression by a more extrovert, Slavic one. For English people, the main way of handling emotion is to underplay, to understate – to withhold and repress. With Russians, emotional release is more available. It is not a matter of one nationality being capable of more or less feeling than the other, but of how an emotion is expressed' (quoted by David Allen in *New Theatre Quarterly*, II, 8, November 1986).

Interview with Debbie Isitt of the *Snarling Beasties*

Debbie is one of Britain's foremost female playwrights with such titles as *Punch and Judy*, *The Woman who Cooked her Husband*, and the award-winning *Nasty Neighbours*.

What qualities do you look for in a performer?
Charisma, energy, style, commitment, truth, vulnerability, relaxation, confidence, emotional expression, physical expression, an earthy quality, good breathing, a risk taker.

What motivates you as a writer?
The need to explore an idea. The idea may develop from a variety of different sources – but once a seed is planted I often feel compelled to feed it until it hopefully grows into an exciting play. Sometimes there is something in me that needs to connect with someone else's emotional journey. Creating a character allows me to discover things about myself and this I find cathartic. Sometimes I am motivated by an injustice or a political viewpoint that has stirred me into action – anger is a great motivator.

Is there a contradiction between your comic style and your serious subjects (e.g. sexual violence)?
To me wherever there is tragedy there is comedy; wherever there is genius there is madness; wherever there is truth there are lies. I believe my kind of theatre is about finding one's own subjective view of the world and expressing it. I never set out to make a comic piece, but in following the harsh reality of a situation, I often find that there is a funny side. I believe that the 'truth' of any situation often throws up this paradox.

How do you see the relationship between naturalism and stylisation in your work?
They are as much a part of each other as the comic and tragic elements of the work. I interpret naturalism as an acting style, based on the Stanislavski method. Stylisation is the thing that takes over when the naturalism is at its height. Basically, stylisation helps heighten the naturalism or 'truth' of the moment. The line between the two is fine, the crossover often invisible; it is more a fusion of the two.

I also fuse naturalism and stylisation in design. People often comment that the visual and physical removal from reality that this fusion brings helps them deal with the sometimes disturbing nature of the content; humour works in the same way.

How do you start writing something?
Often by sketching out ideas, then taking the ideas, characters and themes I want to explore into a workshop situation and improvising around them with actors. Sometimes I start writing as soon as I have an idea and find that I have written a draft without any workshop influence. Sometimes I begin by researching the theme or subject that I am writing about; holding interviews, reading, collecting information, making notes; then using these as the basis for my writing.

How do you create convincing dialogue?
I think this is something that depends on my ear. I am a very absorbent sort of person – I take a lot in when I listen. I can often hear the characters arguing or chatting, then I just write it down.

How do you build a storyline?
By following the emotional journeys of the characters to their logical, often awful, conclusions.

How do you create convincing characters?
Characters are usually a combination of people I know, myself and the actors who are playing them. They grow with the writing process. You hope that by the end they are convincing.

What role does improvisation play in the writing and production of a piece?
I have mentioned that I sometimes hold improvisational workshops to explore the themes and develop the characters when I write. This is a wonderful process if you have actors that are open and patient. It allows the writer to 'play' with the ideas in an energetic and collaborative way. It is a confidence-building exercise as much as anything, a support network, a playground. But there is always the cut-off point where you have to be alone and just write. In rehearsal, improvisation is a crucial part of the

process. It helps you work out the character's emotional journey; it allows you to dig away at the subtext. In performance it is brilliant when you forget your lines!

What is your most memorable experience of live performance?
The Wizard of Oz at the Birmingham Rep in 1976; a Brazilian production of *Garbo* at the 1988 Edinburgh Festival; Gloria's *Sarrasine* at the 1990 Edinburgh Festival.

What was your biggest learning experience in the theatre?
Discovering that you never stop learning about theatre. And that, if you want to, you can actually produce theatre anywhere; the only resources you can rely on are those of the artists themselves.

What advice would you give a young aspiring writer?
Write what you feel strongly about, or think you might feel strongly about; take risks; dig deep within; get your work performed; involve actors; don't put it away in a drawer and *don't* give up on it.

Do you run workshops exploring your technique?
Occasionally, yes. Usually, these are on request.

Any other thoughts for the would-be Beastie?
Understand your relationship with the work you want to do. Ask yourself why you are interested in a given role, play or company. If the answers are 'because it pays well' or 'it'll be good for my CV', don't bother! Your work is a part of you: it *is* you. Look after it, but learn to take risks too. You can learn about yourself through your work.

Expressionism

This movement also started in the art world. The artist August Herve coined the term to show his opposition to Impressionist painting.

In 1907, an Austrian artist, Oskar Kokoshka wrote the first expressionist play, *Murder, Hope of Women*, a short play lasting about three pages, which for many years was thought to be unstageable due to the nature of the content.

Directly after the First World War, the whole of Europe was consumed by political conflict. The Russian Revolution had taken place in 1917, and many people had been influenced by the ideas of Marx, Lenin and Trotsky. Europe as a continent had lost 40 million people in a war which was perceived by many of the workers and intellectuals as being of potential benefit only to the ruling classes and the arms manufacturers (British weapons had been sold to the Germans, and vice versa). How could European theatre reflect or give voice to the trauma that this huge event in its history had caused?

The Expressionist movement is perhaps one of the most interesting in the history of theatre, because of its attempt to voice on stage the inner turbulence of the human spirit. Expressionists attempted to make the world see themselves in terms of their inner selves. How did they interpret such a vague term as the 'soul'? – in psychological terms, as in *The Cabinet of Dr Caligari*, and as a vocalisation of pure, raw emotional energy such as can be seen from one of the most famous Expressionist paintings, *The Scream*, by Münch.

The style of Expressionist drama is unnatural, or possibly supernatural. It tends to use sound and colour to express the emotions of the characters as much as words, and this can be seen in the design of lighting, set, costume and make-up.

Text focus – *Woyzeck*, George Buchner

The Expressionist movement gained momentum in Germany between 1900 and 1925, but its theatrical roots can be traced back to the play, *Woyzeck*, written by George Büchner, and unfinished at his death in 1837. Although written many years before, in another period of social upheaval, *Woyzeck* gives a dramatic representation of the isolation of the individual, which so many people felt in the 1920s. It received its first production in 1913, and was adapted into an opera in 1925. Not only did the play influence the Expressionists, but also other influential theatre practitioners such as Brecht and Artaud.

THE PLOT

Essentially, the story is a simple one of a man who discovers that this wife has been unfaithful to him. He is gradually driven mad by this knowledge, murders her and then kills himself. So far it is similar to many conventional plays, e.g. *Othello*, but what we are more interested in is how it all happens.

All of the characters who are in positions of authority are two-dimensional. They are designated by their titles – The Captain, The Doctor, The Drum-Major – and all of them treat Woyzeck abominably in different ways. The Captain patronises him, the Doctor uses him for scientific purposes and all of the other characters who are meant to be on his side either betray him or do nothing to help him. In addition, there are two ambiguous and unsettling characters who seem to express Woyzeck's dilemma: the Showman with his performing Astronomical Horse, and the story-telling Grandmother.

The message is: Man, be natural. You were fashioned out of dust, out of sand, out of mud – would you be anything more than dust, sand, mud?
Look here, how about this for the power of reason? The astronomical hors c'n calculate, but he can't count on his fingers. Why's that? Because he can't express himself, can't explain – in fact, he's a human being translated!

(The Showman)

Once upon a time there was a poor little boy who had no father and mother; everything was dead and there was no-one left in the whole world. Everything was quite dead, so he went off, whimpering. All day and all night. And since there was no-one left on earth he decided to go up to heaven where the moon shone down so kind. But when he got to the moon it was a lump of rotten wood. Then he went to the sun, but when he got there it was a withered-up sunflower. And when he got to the stars they were little spangled midges stuck there, like the ones shrikes stick on blackthorns. So he went back to the earth, but the earth was an overturned pot. He was completely alone, and he sat down and cried. He's sitting there still, all alone.

(The Story-telling Grandmother)

Both these speeches show the loneliness and alienation that Woyzeck feels, his inability to communicate meaningfully with other people. It is not surprising that it should strike a chord in a Europe falling towards war.

Antonin Artaud

Artaud has left a very different theatrical legacy to those left by Stanislavski and Brecht. His disturbing, radical writings on the world of the theatre have inspired a generation of theatre practitioners along the path of experimentation and innovation. If you are looking for an alternative to the rational worlds presented in the works of Brecht and Stanislavski, then start with *The Theatre and Its Double* by Artaud. This extract below will give you an insight into the mind of this theatrical revolutionary.

Our longstanding habit of seeking diversions has made us forget the slightest idea of serious theatre which upsets all our preconceptions, inspiring us with fiery, magnetic imagery and finally reacting on us after the manner of unforgettable soul therapy.
Everything that acts is cruelty. Theatre must rebuild itself on a concept of this drastic action pushed to the limit.
Infused with the idea that the masses think with their senses first and foremost and that it is ridiculous to appeal primar-

ily to our understanding as we do in everyday psychological theatre, the Theatre of Cruelty proposes to resort to mass theatre, thereby rediscovering a little of the poetry in the ferment of great agitated crowds hurled against one another, sensations only too rare nowadays, when masses of holiday crowds throng the streets.

Artaud is perhaps one of the most often misunderstood practitioners, and it is perhaps easy to see why after reading his texts. He writes in a disjointed and seemingly irrational manner. Take his work section by section, paragraph by paragraph, and start to make your own sense of the text.

Note that 'Cruelty' is reinterpreted as a drastic action pushed to the limit. Imagine the most extreme effect possible onstage and then imagine an entire performance of such actions. Also note that the final paragraph talks about people's sensations as a collective entity. This is the most common denomination of any theatrical performance, but how many other practitioners considered this element of the performance? Where Stanislavski and Brecht contented themselves with an examination of acting and directing techniques, Artaud perceived the theatre in its entirety.

Artaud believed in a popular, inspirational form of theatre which placed an equal emphasis on all of the five human senses. The Artaudian theatre is one which creates a environment around the performers and the audience; it is a total experience of light, sound and text.

TASK

Create a performance using the extract from *The Theatre and its Double*, above. Turn your space into a complete theatrical environment, which pulses with the dangerous rhythms of this text. Use lights, costume, sound and any effects you can think of to create this environment. The audience should feel totally encapsulated by the piece, and not merely have their attention drawn to it.

Text focus – *The Cenci*

The following is an extract from Artaud's *The Cenci*. The play is based upon the true story of Count Francesco Cenci, born in Rome in 1527, who devoted himself to a life of debauchery and corruption. Infatuated with his 16-year-old daughter, Lucretia, he attempts to rape her and so she conspires with her brothers Orsino and Giacomo to assassinate him. The brothers in turn hire two assassins to aid them. Below is Artaud's version of the first unsuccessful attempt by the two brothers to assassinate their father. In italics you can read Artaud's stage directions, and in bold, how a group of students actually interpreted the text.

This section of text lasted approximately 20 minutes in total and was performed in a small studio theatre by 16 students. The performers all wore black clothes with black and white face make-up. The audience was split into various sections throughout the entire space.

But I remember two miles from the castle, a path comes to a kind of chasm – deep down, a black torrent of water frothing and eddying ceaselessly through rocky caverns – and at that point a bridge spans the chasm.

It is unclear from Artaud's surviving text how the above lines are delivered.

Audience entered the darkened, smoke-filled theatre, greeted by some performers who guide them wordlessly to various places to sit in the theatre. A strange series of sound effects with the theme of time (bells, chimes, mechanical whirrs) plays on a sound tape. One

performer speaks the lines above. Blackness, and then lights slowly come up on an image of a giant ticking clock created by the bodies of all the performers. The curtain rises. The smoke is turned off. Thunder rolls. Special time gobo comes up on the tableau after thunder roll is complete. Loud rave music replaces the time-theme effects. The performers arrange themselves on the set, forming a tableau of a clock DSC. The tableau dissolves. The two blocks move aside and an actor in a white dress sits alone DSC. Other performers descend from the blocks. The time gobo fades out. Dancers rotate around performer in a white dress. Strobe comes on. Rotation around performer in white dress ceases. Strobe turns off.

General cover comes up and the colour chase starts around the auditorium. Two performers smear paint over face of performer in white dress.

All performers shout 'Cenci'. Performers freeze. Pause for three seconds. The rave music fades out. Fade lights to blackout.

Dusk. The scene follows the last one without interruption. A fearful storm breaks out. Several claps of thunder explode at close intervals. Immediately, Orsino can be seen entering, followed by his two assassins. They are struggling against a violent wind. Orsino posts his assassins.

Soundscape. Bring up backlights. The performers create shapes on the floor of the stage and begin incantation noises. An actor is now sitting on the blocks USL. Red special comes up to illuminate this actor. This performer speaks occasional lines into the radio mike over the chanting of the soundscape. The chanting rises to a pitch where they are all screaming. At this point, the performers gradually begin whispering the word 'Cenci'. When they have all joined in the chant, it begins to fade into whispers, and the lights fade to blackout. Pause for ten seconds. General cover comes up to light Orsino and Giacomo who start crawling forward from USL and USR.

Orsino: Yes, you understand well enough. We ourselves are the hurricane, so scream your lungs out if you wish.

Giacomo: Do you think they know how to go about it? Just tell them to strike their man down, don't confuse them by telling them to match their silent throats with the screech of the hurricane.

Three thunderclaps reverberate. Several armour-clad men appear moving slowly, like figures on the great clock of Strasbourg cathedral. Repeated peals of thunder.

Sound storm effects increase. G and O fall to the floor at the front of the stage as if looking for something. Music is heard, a track which starts softly but quickly becomes manic. The performers on the blocks start dancing and then move in to attack the two brothers. The other performers lift the brothers above their heads and carry them to the rear of the stage.

Orsino: Calm yourself. Everything is all right. Each of the two knows the part he has to play.

Giacomo: My fear is that they may overplay their parts and no longer be capable of doing anything real.

When the performers have all reached the USC, the lights black out. Five second pause as the performers make a tableau. General cover up again to reveal the tableau for five seconds. Blackout for eight seconds as the performers move to centre stage to create another tableau. General cover up again for five seconds. Blackout for eight seconds as the group move downstage to create another tableau. General cover up again for five seconds as the performers make their final tableau. Blackout for ten seconds as the performers move into next position.

Quiet, atmospheric music comes up slowly. The follow-spot comes up USL on the four strangers who walk slowly in a diagonal across the stage to SDR and then walk off.

The jerky tramping of feet can be heard again. Lucretia, Bernardo, Beatrice appear, walking at the same statue-like pace, and very far behind them, bringing up the rear, is Count Cenci. The storm rages with increasing fury, and mingled with the wind, one can hear voices repeating the name, 'Cenci', first in a single, prolonged high-pitched tone, then like the pendulum of a clock: Cenci, Cenci, Cenci.

At moments all the names blend together at one point in the sky, like countless birds whose individual flights have converged together. Then the voices grow and pass by like a flight of birds very close at hand.

Backlights come up as Cenci appears USC. Cenci walks down to CS, pushes two performers aside and shouts, 'What, then?'. Backlights are cross-faded with the special above Cenci. She stands alone CS. The music 'Jane's Addiction' is brought up. The strobe is turned on. Performers attack the Cenci in pairs until all lie defeated on the floor and she stands alone CS, omnipotent.

Cenci: [*facing the voices, shouts into the storm*] What then!!

Immediately the outlines of the assassins can be seen surging forth, spinning like tops and meeting, and passing each other in the illumination of a flash of lightning. At the same time, the roar of two pistol shots is heard. Night has fallen, the lightning flashes cease. Everything vanishes.

Giacomo: What, failed?

Orsino: Failed!

Curtain.

Strobe is turned off. Music is faded out. The light above Cenci is faded out. Cenci and all the other performers snake their way to the front of the stage and kneel facing outwards. One performer is lying USC on top of the white block. She is lit by a special coming up slowly and says, 'WHAT FAILED?'. Lights fade out over ten seconds to blackout.

Performers begin to chant. 'Cenci, Cenci, Cenci'. Chant fades. Lights fade to blackout. Curtain.

TASK

Read the above and discuss the themes raised by the text and both sets of production notes. What might you add or change to the adapted production of the play? Would you use a completely different approach? Design and workshop your ideas. Try out as many different ways of staging the piece as possible. Don't be afraid to experiment – everything is permitted!

Suggested reading

Artaud, *The Cenci* (1989) Calder & Boyars.
Brecht, *Baal* (1994) Methuen Drama.
Büchner, *Woyzeck* (1994) Methuen.
Capek, *R.U.R. (Rossum's Universal Robots)* (1930) Oxford University Press.

O'Neill, *The Hairy Ape* (1994) Royal National Theatre.
Toller, *Masses and Man* (1934) Bodley Head.
— *Hoppla! Such is Life* (1995) Harwood Academic.
— *The Machine Wreckers* (1995) Nick Hern Books.

Epic theatre

The name was coined to describe the political theatre style of Erwin Piscator and Bertolt Brecht in the Germany of the 1920s. Like Stanislavski in Russia, Brecht and Piscator were opposed to the opulent, spectacular bourgeois theatre of their day and sought to inject commitment and realism into their work. Unlike Stanislavski, however, their intent was political, and the techniques they used were far removed from the detailed Naturalism of the Moscow Arts Theatre's early experiments.

GERMANY IN THE 1920S

Germany in the 1920s and 30s was an extraordinary place. It had just lost the First World War and was required to make crippling war reparations under the terms of the Treaty of Versailles. Its attempts to become a democracy resulted in the Weimar Republic in 1919, which produced a confusing array of political parties, from the communist left to the fascist right. As early as 1923, Adolf Hitler's National Socialist party made an abortive attempt to take power in Bavaria (the Munich Putsch). The arts world was thriving, with extraordinary experiments in architecture, painting and theatre. Inflation, however was rampant. Archive film footage shows people taking a suitcase of money to buy bread. Depression set in during the early 1930s, requiring a desperate solution: in 1933, Hitler was elected Chancellor.

THE ORIGINS OF EPIC THEATRE

The word 'epic' is normally associated with lengthy stories that range across time and contain numerous episodes; for example, Homer's tale of *The Odyssey*. In modern times this role has been fulfilled by the novel. In each case the author tells the story, bringing in incidental characters when needed and offering their own comments on the action as it goes along. In naturalistic drama, however, the dramatist can speak to us only through the words of the characters.

To Brecht and Piscator, the 'epic' structure seemed to offer new possibilities for a more objective theatre; a theatre that would encourage the audience to think about the way that society worked, rather than simply providing a piece of entertainment which was forgotten as soon as the final curtain came down.

They developed a number of techniques to encourage the audience to think. The techniques were devised to remind the audience that they were in a theatre, being presented with a performance by actors; and so the spectacle and illusion of the classic German stage was stripped away.

The stage design was made up only of those items and props that were absolutely necessary to the telling of the story. The props themselves were symbolic, rather than representations of real objects. There were no conventional pieces of scenery, leaving the stage a bare, empty space in which the story could be acted out. Any set changes would be made in full view of the audience.

Lighting was as simple as possible. The lights themselves could be plainly seen from the auditorium, as could the operators. This was to ensure that the audience perceived the actors as being in the same world as themselves. Light would be bright throughout the play, with minimal changes which were intended to show something, and were not for mood or atmospheric effect. For example, in *The Caucasian Chalk Circle*, the lights would go down when Grusha rescues the baby: to show the passage of time, to indicate that she takes all night to decide to take him, and to stop the audience feeling sentimental about babies. Brecht's model for the lighting was the boxing ring. Harsh lighting there increased rather than decreased the audience's participation. It was also a highly popular form of entertainment.

Music was not to provide an accompaniment to the action, but rather to comment on or conflict with the action on stage. Brecht made much use of songs in his plays, but stressed that they should be clearly marked out from the rest of the performance. There would be no smooth transition from speech to song to heighten emotion. Brecht's model for this was the Music Hall, a traditional form of popular entertainment for the working class audience he wanted to reach.

Structure: in theory, all of the elements of the epic play are capable of operating independently of each other. In other words, each scene and song is capable of telling its own story and carrying its own message. In practice this was more difficult to achieve, and Brecht's later work differed less and less from the mainstream dramatic tradition.

Suspense had no place in Epic theatre. The point was not, will A deceive B, but how will A deceive B and why. As a result, each scene was introduced by a written title (often projected on a giant screen), or brief song, which would inform the audience of what was to come. The models for this were myths and folk-tales where we already know the story but want to hear it again. Such stories often have teaching messages for their audience.

In many ways, Brecht was not attempting anything new. He was using techniques that predated Naturalism by thousands of years, and simply applying them to a society in crisis as tools for analysis and instruction. In the Elizabethan, medieval and Greek theatres, the audience witnessed all the stage mechanics; there was no illusionist lighting and the effects were stylised in dance and movement or heightened language. In the oral tradition of the folk-tale, the storyteller is always set apart – the audience never believes the teller *is* the character.

The actor as storyteller: the epic performer wants to show their character rather than live it. Brecht devised a number of rehearsal techniques to help the actors fashion this kind of performance including:

- actors speaking in the third person
- actors speaking in the past tense
- actors articulating the stage directions.

This was all to enable the actor to be clear about what they were presenting to the audience. In performance, however, this would not happen unless it was written into the text. For example, in *The Caucasian Chalk Circle*, the wooing scene between Grusha and Simon is spoken in a formal third person which serves to show the innocence and uncertainty of the two characters, but also prevents us from just being sentimental and makes us consider the practical nature of their decision to marry under such circumstances.

Brecht himself tries to explain this in the following poem, *Showing has to be Shown*:

Show that you are showing! Among all the varied attitudes
Which you show when showing how men play their parts
The attitude of showing must never be forgotten.
All attitudes must be based on the attitude of showing
This is how to practise: before you show the way
A man betrays someone, or is seized by jealousy
Or concludes a deal, first look
At the audience, as if you wished to say:
'Now take note, this man is now betraying someone and this is how he does it,
This is what he is like when jealousy seizes him, and this
Is how he deals when dealing.' In this way
Your showing will keep the attitude of showing
Of putting forward what has been made ready, of finishing off
Of continually going further. So show

That what you show is something you show every night, have often shown before
And your playing will resemble a weaver's weaving, the work of a
Craftsman. And all that goes with showing
Like your continual concern to
Make watching simpler, always to ensure the best
View of every episode – that too you should make visible. Then
All this betraying and dealing and
Being seized by jealousy will be as it were
Imbued with something of the quality of a
Daily operation, for instance of eating, saying Good Morning and
Doing one's work. (For you are working, aren't you?)
And behind your stage parts you yourself must still be visible
As those who are playing them.

(trans J. Willett (1980) Methuen)

All these techniques were designed to stimulate thought in the audience rather than to excite the emotions. They do not deny emotion, or spectacle, or laughter, but prioritise the creation of a thinking, critical audience. Together, the techniques are generally called the *alienation effect*, also known as *V-effekt* from the German world *Verfremdungseffekt* (which literally means distancing effect). Brecht suggests the playing of an adult by a child as the clearest example of alienation. An excellent example in modern theatre is in Peter Weiss's *Marat/Sade*, where the inmates of an asylum re-enact the murder of the French revolutionary, Jean-Paul Marat (see page 251).

TASK

Experiment with alienation. Establish a scene played by both male and female performers where gender roles are clearly established; for example, chatting-up scenes. Run through them, observing carefully the different behaviour of each gender. Now repeat the scene, this time reversing roles. Female characters should be played by the male actors and vice versa. Make sure that you show the characteristics of the opposite sex, not just for fun, but so that you *understand* them. Discuss why men and women behave as they do.

A good example of this kind of gender alienation is Caryl Churchill's *Cloud 9*. The translation into English as alienation is perhaps unfortunate and has contributed to the misunderstanding of Brecht as being anti-emotion. He was not opposed to emotion in itself but to washes of sentimentality that paid no attention to the social reasons why a person was suffering.

Compare the epic model with the Aristotelian model of Greek drama in Sophocles' *Oedipus* *the King*. The play gives no reasons for Oedipus being cursed other than 'the will of the gods'. We are presented with a man's inexorable fall, in which we pity him and fear that Fate might deal us such a blow. Our emotions are purged and we are grateful that our lot is not as bad as his. In other words, the play serves to make us accept the hand that Fate, or life, has dealt us. To Brecht the Marxist, this implies that the oppressed must stay oppressed, which is precisely what he wanted to change.

Brecht himself attempted to explain the differences between the dramatic (Aristotelian) theatre and the Epic theatre in the following table:

Dramatic Theatre	Epic Theatre
● plot	● narrative
● implicates the spectator in a stage situation	● turns the spectator into an observer
● wears down his/her capacity for action	● arouses his/her capacity for action
● provides him/her with sensations	● forces him/her to take decisions
● the spectator is involved in something	● the spectator is made to face something
● suggestion	● argument
● the spectator shares the experience	● the spectator stands outside, studies
● the human being is taken for granted	● the human being is the object of the inquiry
● the human being is unalterable	● the human being is alterable and able to alter
● eyes on the finish	● eyes on the course
● one scene makes another	● each scene for itself
● growth	● montage
● the human being as a fixed point	● the human being as a process
● thought determines being	● social being determines thought
● feeling	● reason

These statements are by no means all simple opposites (antitheses). They show a shift of emphasis from indulging in the human experience to being able to change it.

TASK

Find out where you stand. How many of your group think that war, poverty, sexual violence etc. are an inevitable and unavoidable part of the human condition, and how many think that it is possible to change behaviour and attitudes to make things better? The central question is: does society make us or do we make society? What do you think?

Now turn it into a piece of theatre to prove your point.

If it is possible for human beings to change their behaviour, does theatre have a role to play? Certainly, Brecht and Piscator wanted it to have a role, as did the British political theatre companies of the 1970s.

The influence of Brecht

Brecht has, in many ways, had a huge influence on what we see in British theatre today. Firstly, his plays have now reached the status of being classics and are performed by big companies. For example, in 1995/6 The National Theatre staged *Mother Courage*, with Diana Rigg in the lead role – a part originally played by Helene Weigel, Brecht's second wife; the Donmar Warehouse staged an adaptation of the *Threepenny Opera* in 1995; the Orange Tree Theatre in Richmond staged a promenade performance of *The Good Person of Setzuan*, etc. Despite the difficulty in staging them, the plays remain popular, though they are rarely performed on the commercial stage. The main influence Brecht has had however, is that so many of the stylistic changes he introduced into the theatre are now commonplace. We are not shocked to see the lights, we accept a scaffolding set as representing a living room or a battlefield and we are familiar with actors changing parts within a play. These things do not deter us from being involved in the play, or accepting it as real in stage terms. In other words, the conventions have changed (see Raymond Williams quoted on page 83).

TASK

Compare Brecht's thoughts to the theatrical aims of Augusto Boal's Forum theatre (see Chapter 1, page 23). List the similarities and differences in their approach. How does Boal implicate the spectator in the action *and* the solution?

TASK

Look at the structure of *The Caucasian Chalk Circle* below. Now choose your own fable or folk-tale and write it as an epic play, paying attention to the following elements:

- Politics – what aspect of oppression are you examining?
- Stage design – no illusion, essential props only
- Lighting – full white light, not used for atmosphere
- Music and song – to comment on the stage action
- Structure – no suspense, scenes introduced by placard
- Actor as storyteller – show costume changes; actors address audience if necessary; acting as demonstration; have a narrator
- V-effekt – all of the above and any ways you can think of to invite objective, critical thought.

Text focus – *The Caucasian Chalk Circle*

Brecht wrote *The Caucasian Chalk Circle* in 1944 while in exile from Nazi Germany in the United States. It is a complex, beautifully written *epic* play, requiring great delicacy in its staging. The play is divided into a prologue and six scenes. It explores the theme of justice and ownership by telling the story of a noble child abandoned by his mother during a civil war. The child is brought up by a peasant woman, who grows to love him. A court finally awards the child to his adoptive mother rather than the natural mother who left him to his fate. The play concludes that things should 'belong' to those who need them and will care for them, as in the final lines:

What there is shall belong to those who are
  good for it, thus
The children to the maternal, that they thrive;
The carriages to good drivers, that they are
  driven well;
And the valley to the waterers, that it shall
  bear fruit ...

WHY IS THE STRUCTURE EPIC?

According to Brecht, epic involves a montage of scenes that inform each other but do not grow from each other. This is true of *The Caucasian Chalk Circle* in that it has two source stories, both involving a dis-

TASK

Think of an example of someone who owns something but treats it badly, when you know that someone else who doesn't, or couldn't, own it would treat it far better. What would happen if someone suggested that the two people swap, or the owner should give the item up? Could you present a convincing case? Share your stories in small groups. Pick one and write or improvise it as a short court-room drama.

pute over a child, which mirror the dispute over land in the prologue. There are also two sections to the play, in addition to the prologue. Both start on Easter Day of the same year, but have different characters. The final scene of the play brings both halves together. We have broken the play down into its component scenes, showing how Brecht's techniques work. Every scene is created in order to reveal human nature more clearly, to show us in the act of constructing ourselves; not to show character development.

Plot	Epic structure
Scene 1: The struggle for the valley* Delegates from two collective farming villages (known as *kolchos*) met with an expert to sort out a dispute*: The goat-breeders who farmed a certain piece of land before the war agree to hand the land over to enable the fruit-growers to develop a much-needed irrigation project. Legal entitlement gives way to greater need. To celebrate the settling of the dispute, a well-known folk-singer, Arkady Cheidze, is to tell an old story that is set in modern times*. He uses the fruit-farmers as actors*.	* The prologue serves no *narrative* function i.e. it does not forward a story. It establishes the themes of justice and ownership, and ensures that the audience watches the rest of the play with real people, situations and disputes in mind. * The dispute is idealised. This is how people in a pure, communist society would sort out their problems. * The story to be enacted is a folk-tale. Quite literally, it begins 'Once upon a time'. The existence of the prologue means we cannot simply *escape* into the story. It has already been set in a critical context. * As we watch we are constantly reminded that the characters are being portrayed by the farmers. This is one of the many techniques of the Epic theatre to make the audience watch in a detached way. Often, productions will show the peasants getting changed on stage. Half-masks and full-masks are used, adding to the distance.
Scene 2: The noble child In the city of Nukha, the wealthy governor is overthrown and killed in a palace coup. The Grand Duke flees. A soldier, Simon, proposes to the kitchen-maid, Grusha. She accepts. The governor's wife abandons her baby Michael and escapes. Simon must go with her. Grusha, against her better judgement, takes the baby into the mountains*.	* The singer acts as *Chorus*, telling the story but also commenting on the actions and dilemmas of the characters. We are shown the essential selfishness of all actions. Grusha's sympathy for the baby is seen as humane but foolish.
Scene 3: The Flight into the Northern Mountains* Grusha and the baby are pursued by two ironshirts (soldiers). She tries to get food and shelter but is denied at every turn. The Ironshirts catch her trying to give the child away to a peasant woman. She clubs one of them on the head and escapes with the child by crossing a dangerous rope-bridge. She decides to be the child's mother*.	* The scene shows Grusha facing a variety of practical difficulties and overcoming them. The demands of the situation teach her cunning and self-reliance. She moves from a naive kitchen girl to a young woman capable of harsh choices and even violence. * Brecht is keen to show that keeping Michael is not just sentimental. It is also practical. Grusha's humanity will not let her leave him to die.

Plot	Epic structure
Scene 4: In the Northern Mountains Grusha, half-dead, arrives at her brother's farm*. He persuades her to make the child safe by marrying an invalid peasant who turns out to be feigning illness to avoid the army*. Time passes. The winter thaw brings danger of discovery. Simon finds her and learns she is married with a child*. She tries to explain. Ironshirts arrive and take the boy away. Grusha must face trial for abduction.	* In the peasant community of the Northern Mountains everyone is out for their own gain. Again we see Grusha confronted by practical necessities involving harsh decisions. * Circumstances force her to break her promise to Simon, the soldier. There is a comic wedding scene. * Simon's dramatic function is to arrive after two years and show us how far Grusha has moved.
*Scene 5: The story of the judge** The story goes back to the day of the palace coup when the Grand Duke escaped*. In disguise he is harboured by a drunken poacher, Azdak. The Ironshirts have just hung the old judge, but are not quite sure which side they are supporting. To spite the new rulers, they elect Azdak as judge in his place*. Azdak is selfish and drunken, but he is a revolutionary and many of his judgements are in favour of the poor*. At the end of two years of such rulings the Grand Duke is reinstated. Azdak fears for his life.	* Occurring second in stage time, this story actually takes place at the same time as scene 2. (Both start on Easter Day.) * Playing with the time sequence is not usual in naturalistic drama. In epic, however, the storytelling style makes this possible. * In a world where the courts, established by the rich, favour the rich, a character like Azdak would not become a judge. This scene demonstrates the bizarre events that would need to occur for a person who might actually help the poor, to become a judge. * Azdak's judgements are demonstrated in a number of brief, representational scenes. We never meet the characters again. Masks and doubling up are techniques generally used.
Scene 6: The chalk circle Azdak is to be hanged, but is reprieved by the Grand Duke for sheltering him two years before. Grusha arrives in court to face Michael's mother, Natella Abashvili*. Azdak hears the evidence and gives them the test of the chalk circle. The child is placed in the middle of the circle to be tugged out by the 'true' mother. Grusha lets go, unable to hurt Michael. She is awarded the child. Natella's estate is turned into a park for children and Azdak disappears, in true fairy-tale style, never to be seen again*.	* The separate stories of Grusha and Azdak come together. Both are poor but intelligent, and find their own justice in an unjust world. * The play itself has two source stories which also come together. The first is a thirteenth century Chinese fable by Li Hsing Dao called *The Chalk Circle* (translated into German in 1925 by Brecht's friend Klabund). This involves a disputed child being returned to its rightful parent by a wise emperor. The second is the judgement of Solomon from the Old Testament in which two new mothers dispute the only living baby. Solomon offers to cut the baby in half with a sword until the real mother relinquishes her claim and is awarded the child. Here the legend is subverted in that Azdak awards the child to the adoptive mother.

Brecht was a Marxist and believed that we are products of our environment. We should cease to believe in gods and princes who do not have our interests at heart and create the world as we want it. Azdak and Grusha are seen as doing so.

STAGING *THE CAUCASIAN CHALK CIRCLE*

In 1953 Karl von Appen was commissioned to design the set, costumes and masks for the Berliner Ensemble production:

Appen first sketched the groupings for each scene, and from this a basic layout was developed. The stage was enclosed by a semi-circular white backcloth known as a cyclorama, in front of which hung a changeable drop-cloth, or 'flag' as Brecht termed it, painted in the style of Chinese ink-drawings. Behind this, pieces of scenery could be erected on the revolving stage. During the 'Flight to the Northern Mountains', for example, Grusha plodded with the child on her back against the revolve, and the set for each episode emerged from behind the 'flag', travelled towards her and stopped for her to play the scene. This fluid, mobile staging enabled the many scenes to flow into one another without any waste of time.

The painted drop-cloths and pieces of scenery Appen called 'quotations', because they printed a selected part which stood for the whole. On the drop-cloth for scene 2 a wedge-shaped beehive of houses represented the city of Nukha, and a miniaturised façade on the stage represented the church. While these 'quotations' were part of Brecht's anti-illusionistic, alienating technique, the chosen settlements of reality had to have a feel of solid authenticity.

(Hugh Rorrison, Introduction to Caucasian Chalk
Circle, Methuen)

Despite the simplicity of the design, it is clear from this description that a huge effort went into creating it. Brecht wanted exactly the right amount of set needed to tell each section of story, and for it to be beautifully made; his was not lazy or cheap-skate

theatre. He made enormous demands on himself, his designer and his actors.

Brecht was heavily influenced by the theatre, visual art and literature of China. The primary source for this play was a Chinese folk-tale, and he wanted the drop-cloths painted in the style of Chinese ink-drawings. He found particular resonance in the descriptive style of Chinese acting, where an action would be described by a narrator and enacted simultaneously by a performer. Brecht saw an immediate connection in this simple 'folk' style with the qualities of demonstration he required of his own actors.

Look at the following passage from the play, from the end of scene two, after the palace coup. The Governor has just been beheaded and we have heard the new leader, The Fat Prince, offer 1,000 Piastres reward for the Governor's baby, whom he assumes has been taken by the escaping mother. We then return to Grusha who is sitting with the abandoned baby. She must escape for her own protection, but still she waits. The baby will be killed if she leaves it. *She* will be killed if she takes it. In order to show us the processes by which she makes her decision to rescue Michael, the singer delivers her thoughts, and the questions she feels the baby is asking of her. This has a distancing effect, yet it is lyrical, quite beautiful and full of human feeling. The stage directions tell the actor what she must do.

Figure 6.8   *Our production of* The Caucasian Chalk Circle

As Grusha enters cautiously through the doorway, the fat prince and the Ironshirts leave. Trampling of horses' hooves again. Carrying a bundle, Grusha walks towards the gateway. At the last moment, she turns to see if the child is there. Promptly the singer begins to sing. She stands rooted to the spot.

The Singer:
As she was standing between courtyard and gate, she heard
Or thought she heard, a low voice. The child
Called to her, not whining but calling quite sensibly:
At least so it seemed to her: 'Woman', it said, 'Help me'.
Went on calling not whining but calling quite sensibly:
'Don't you know, woman, that she who does not listen to a cry for help
But passes by shutting her ears, will never hear
The gentle call of a lover
Nor the blackbird at dawn, nor the happy
Sigh of an exhausted grape-picker at the sound of the Angelus.'
Hearing this

Grusha walks a few steps towards the child and bends over it.

         she went back to the child
Just for one more look, just to sit with it
For a moment or two till someone should come
its mother, perhaps, or someone else –

She sits down opposite the child, and leans against a trunk.

Just for a moment before she left, for now the danger was too great
The city full of flame and grief.

The light grows dimmer as though evening and night were falling,
Grusha has gone into the palace and fetched a lamp and some milk, which she gives the child to drink.

The Singer [*loudly*]:
Terrible is the temptation to do good!

Grusha now settles down to keep watch over the child through the night. Once she lights a small lamp to look at it. Once, she tucks it in with a brocade coat. Now and again she listens and looks up to see if someone is coming.

For a long time she sat with the child.
Evening came, night came, dawn came.
Too long she sat, too long she watched
The soft breathing, the little fists
Till towards morning the temptation grew too strong.
She rose, she leaned over, she sighed, she lifted the child
She carried it off.

She does what the singer says as he describes it.

Like booty she took it for herself
Like a thief she sneaked away.

At each point Grusha makes a conscious decision to involve herself a little further. She was on her way out, but turns to check if the child is there. When she imagines the child speaking to her, she goes to it 'just for one more look'. Her intention is still to leave. After all, the child is not her responsibility. Someone must be looking after it, 'Its mother perhaps, or someone else.' Brecht is using dramatic irony: the audience knows, although Grusha does not, that the mother and servants have all gone. Logically, then, Grusha must wait until it is absolutely clear that no-one is coming for him, i.e. all night.

Here, Grusha's natural concern for the child's welfare contrasts drastically with the actions of the real mother, who was more concerned with getting the right pair of slippers to go with her expensive dresses. To his mother, Michael was a possession. In the haste of the escape she had to prioritise her possessions and Michael lost out. To Grusha, who has no possessions besides the small bundle she is carrying, Michael is a human being asking quietly for help.

There is a high price to pay for taking the child, which might be her life. But the price of not taking him is also high: if she is deaf to his plea, the singer suggests, she would be deaf to everything else, every beautiful sound. This openness and inability to close her ears, or heart, is Grusha's downfall. As a result she is hounded by Ironshirts, throws herself on the mercy of her weak brother, marries a sham invalid and breaks her promise to the man she has promised to marry.

In real life, she would probably have been caught and killed, as would the child. It is, in many ways, stupid of her not also to think of the dangers. Grusha is no idealised, class-conscious fighter. She is naive and exploitable. She fondly imagines that everyone else will want to help, which, of course, they do not.

This, however, is a folk-tale, a fairy-tale of sorts. It even begins with the words, 'Once upon a time'. As such, miraculous things can happen. She escapes from the Ironshirts across a rickety bridge, and when she comes to trial, the only man who could possibly have found in her favour is in the judge's chair. When he has awarded Grusha the child, Azdak disappears, never to be seen again.

For the actor, the objectives/intentions are being given by the singer and so simple acting is required. She can take her motivation directly from the singer's words. Try it out with someone reading the text. Who follows whom?

TASK

In pairs, choose your own scenario, which must:

- show someone engaged in an action
- show someone at the very point of making a rational decision under difficult circumstances.

Improvise, prepare, script and perform it. It should last no longer than two minutes. The piece should:

- show that being human involves difficult choices
- show that it is the combination of intellect and emotion that makes us human
- show that no action is entirely selfless.

Note: One person narrating another's actions is a standard comedy impro, and a very good one, because you can exploit deliberate differences between the words and the action. Here you are trying to create a very different mood, so it is important to resist the temptation for the quick gag.

Text Focus – *Marat/Sade* by Peter Weiss (trans. Geoffrey Skelton; verse adaptation by Adrian Mitchell)

Note: Before reading this section, we advise you to familiarise yourself with Epic theatre (page 240) and Theatre of Cruelty (page 240).

Marat/Sade is a history lesson as well as an exploration of the human condition seen through a society in conflict and a soul in torment. When it was first performed in England by the RSC in 1964 it was a ground-breaking piece of non-naturalistic theatre. Nothing since has quite managed the extraordinary combination of styles and theatrical images Peter Weiss achieves in this play. In the words of its director, Peter Brook:

> Weiss not only uses total theatre, that time-honoured notion of getting all the elements of the stage to serve the play. His force is not only in the quantity of instruments he uses; it is above all in the jangle produced by the clash of styles. Everything is put in its place by its neighbour – the serious side by the comic, the noble by the popular, the literary by the crude, the intellectual by the physical: the abstraction is vivified by the stage image, the violence illuminated by the cool flow of thought. The strands of meaning of the play pass to and fro through its structure . . .

HISTORICAL BACKGROUND

Prior to the 1789 revolution, France operated on a feudal basis. Huge power was vested in the aristocracy, who, in many ways, had more influence than the king (Louis XVI). The vast majority of the population were peasants who lived in poverty. The population grew and attempts were made to tax landowning gentry from the emerging bourgeoisie. In addition, in 1788, a bad harvest led to widespread discontent among the peasantry and political crisis ensued.

- *1789*: the Estates-General were convened for the first time in over a hundred years. (The Estates-General were a kind of parliament convened by the king during times of crisis and divided into three estates: the First Estate = the church; the Second Estate = the nobility; the Third Estate = the middle-class commoners.) This time, however, the members of the Third Estate (the Commons) took the revolutionary step of declaring *their* assembly to be the National Assembly. The Estates-General were destroyed. During the same year, angry peasants attacked the properties of the aristocracy. This became known as *La Grande Peur* (the big fear).

- *14 July 1789*: The Bastille (a prison in Paris) was stormed for its stored munitions. The date became a symbol of the revolution and is still celebrated today.
  The new National Assembly created a Declaration of Rights reducing the power of the king and bringing about a constitutional monarchy (as in Britain today). This, and the rule of the National Assembly, lasted until 1791.

- *1792*: Austria and Prussia invaded France. There were riots in Paris. The king was imprisoned by the self-declared *Paris Commune*.
  A republic was established on the 22 September.

- *1793*: The king was sent to the guillotine on 21 January. Two revolutionary factions then fought it out: the Montagnards and the Girondists. The Montagnards won, and this heralded the beginning of the *Reign of Terror*. Figures such as Danton and Robespierre were in power. Thousands were sent to the guillotine, including the revolutionary Girondists.
  Eventually, even close friends of the revolution went to the guillotine, including Robespierre. No-one was safe. Jean-Paul Marat was assassinated on 13 July (see below).

- *1795*: A new constitution was declared, providing some stability.

- The Consulate was established in *1799* with Napoleon Bonaparte as first consul. His control spread until he declared the first French Empire of *1804*, bringing the revolutionary period to a close.

- *1808*: The fictional date of the play *Marat/Sade*, 15 years after the death of Marat. Napoleon had already been Emperor for four years.

JEAN-PAUL MARAT (1743–1793)

Marat trained as a doctor. From 1789, he ran a newspaper, *L'Ami du Peuple*, in which he wrote savage attacks on the corruption of those in power, and called for a temporary dictatorship. His political sympathies were with the radical Jacobins. His enemies in the National Assembly were the moderate Girondists who had him tried for treason and anti-patriotic behaviour. He was acquitted, but was stabbed to death in his bath by Charlotte Corday, a Girondist sympathiser, on 13 July 1793 (the day before Bastille day).

Marat was very popular with the people. He was seen as pure and incorruptible. His political faction, however, was responsible for sending thousands to the guillotine.

While running illegal printing presses, Marat was forced to go into hiding in the sewers of Paris, where he contracted a debilitating skin disease. This required him to sit in a bath-tub and have damp cloths on his body. He was in his bath when Corday stabbed him.

MARQUIS DE SADE (1740–1814)

An aristocrat, a soldier and a writer. De Sade wrote poems, novels and plays which explored and expounded his theory that pain and cruelty are an integral part of nature and should be enjoyed as such, hence the word 'sadism'. Many of his works feature the systematic sexual degradation of their subjects and were largely banned. He himself was imprisoned for his sexual behaviour and spent 27 years in prisons and asylums.

He was briefly a judge in the revolutionary tribunals, but was unable to sentence anyone to death.

CONTENT AND STYLE

The play's title has been shortened to *Marat/Sade* for simplicity, but is in full: *The Persecution and Assassination of Marat as Performed by the Inmates of the Asylum of Charenton under the Direction of the Marquis de Sade.*

The Marquis de Sade was genuinely an inmate of the Asylum of Charenton. He wrote many plays which the liberal director of the institution allowed him to stage. It was fashionable for the well-to-do of Paris to watch the notorious de Sade's performances. This is the opening premise of the piece. We, the audience, are treated to a performance of a play written by the Marquis de Sade and performed by the inmates. (As with *The Caucasian Chalk Circle* (see page 245) we are presented with a play within a play.)

The play features a debate between Sade and Marat. (In real life the two never met face-to-face; the encounter in the play is pure fiction.) Both are revolutionaries. Each seeks social change, but each takes a radically different approach to achieving it. Sade sits on a dais on one side of the stage and Marat sits in his bath-tub on a dais on the other. The debating chamber is set. But there can be no clear, objective debate here, since all the lines spoken by Marat have been written by Sade. And, of course, the audience knows that both, including Sade's lines, have been written by a twentieth century German playwright, called Peter Weiss. We are always seeing through a particular lens. The very structure of the play questions the objectivity of history.

To complicate things further, all the roles (with the exception of the director Coulmier, his family, and Sade himself) are played by inmates of the asylum; they are subject to a range of psychological disorders, each carefully chosen for the light it sheds on the historical figure being portrayed.

- The part of Marat is played by a 'lucky paranoic'. The real Marat ended his days denouncing traitors whom he perceived to be all around him, and was a *political* paranoic.
- The part of Charlotte Corday, his assassin, is played by a girl with sleeping sickness and melancholia. The comic properties of an assassin who keeps falling asleep are fairly apparent, but it works best on stage in relation to her lover and Girondist Deputy, Duperret. Who better to play a lover than an erotomaniac? Accordingly, Duperret takes every opportunity to grope Charlotte, particularly when she obligingly falls asleep from time to time. Clinically, the sleeping sickness results from the mind shutting down from reality, from the intensity of the melancholia. The figure of Corday in the play is portrayed as an innocent bourgeois abroad in the brutal and terrifying world of Paris during The Terror. Her shutting down and sleeping symbolises the bourgeois inability to stomach the violence necessary to change society, i.e. she wants to do it nicely. As a result, Duperret and Corday are made to discuss love and human freedom in the form of an operatic aria (scene 22), exposing their political philosophy as bourgeois fantasy.

The key to the piece is the central conceit of having historical figures enacted by asylum patients. The style of the patients' performance is that of little children performing in a nativity play; i.e. the performers do not necessarily understand the words they are speaking. The delight in watching them comes largely from our own sense of greater knowledge. We feel superior: they look both cute and silly in their costumes. They are playing at being grown-ups like us. And yet, of course, in the Marat/Sade they are poking fun at us, the audience, the whole time. (Compare this with the discussion of Bouffon in the interview with Ewan Marshall of The Graeae on page 108.) In other words, the whole piece is an elaborate exercise in dramatic irony, in that the audience always seems to know and understand more than the 'simple' performers. And yet the irony is on us, because those same performers, by the very act of doing the play, are asking philosophical and political questions of the utmost complexity and are continually exposing the inadequacies of their bourgeois audience.

TASK

Research into schizophrenia. Particularly interesting are the theories of R. D. Laing who suggested that we are all on a continuum, one end of which is something society defines as madness. Report back and compare your findings.

The different performance styles tumble over themselves in the piece. Like the opera sequence, each offers a different lens through which to perceive reality. Inevitably, we get a different reading of an event if it is staged as a song, or a mime, or a dance. Here we get them all, some deriving from the epic theatre tradition, and some exploring the ritualistic theatre proposed by Antonin Artaud. Below, we have listed the main features of the play's structure and dramatic methods and have suggested where their origin might lie. Look out for them as you read the extracts below.

EPIC FEATURES

- division of play into 33 independent scenes
- narrative function of the Herald. Statement of intent i.e. no suspense, we know *what* will happen and are interested in *how* and *why*
- use of titles for scenes
- use of song to tell story and to comment upon action

- direct address to audience
- historical figures played by inmates of an asylum. We see them being prepared for their role. There is no illusion
- naive acting style
- use of tableaux.

ARTAUDIAN FEATURES

- clash of styles
- ritual
- rhythm
- cacophony
- madness
- naive, primitive performance style.

The extract below is near the beginning of the play, when Charlotte Corday first attempts to gain entry to Marat's house. Note that the scene is announced by the Herald and Corday's entry is accompanied by her musical theme, both effects combining to give the sense of a ritual act:

9 *Corday's first visit*

Herald: Corday's first visit
            [*Orchestra plays the Corday theme*]
Corday: I have come to speak to Citizen Marat
            I have an important message for him
            about the situation in Caen my home
            where his enemies are gathering
Simonne: We don't want any visitors
            We want a bit of peace
            If you've got anything to say to Marat
            put it in writing
Corday: What I have to say cannot be said in writing
            I want to stand in front of him and look at him
            [*amorously*]
            I want to see his body tremble and his forehead bubble with sweat
            I want to thrust right between his ribs the dagger
            which I carry between my breasts
            [*obsessively*]
            I shall take the dagger in both hands
            and push it through his flesh
            and then I will hear
            [*approaches Marat*]
            what he has got to say to me

[*She stands directly in front of the bath.*
She raises the dagger and is poised to strike.
Simonne stands paralysed.
Sade rises from his seat.]

Sade: Not yet Corday
         You have to come to his door three times
         [*Corday stops short, hides the dagger and withdraws to her bench.*
         The sisters and Duperret follow her as she leaves.]

Corday does not get into the house on this occasion and yet we see her approach Marat, dagger raised, stating overtly what she wants to do to him. This is typical of the games played by Weiss throughout. The style allows us to see Corday almost commit the murder. The patient playing Corday becomes highly charged during the erotic speech written for her by Sade. This builds to a climax and is then interrupted with a bland statement of fact by Sade, whose apparent disinterest contrasts starkly with the intense passion of the words he has written. It is as if the play was going horribly wrong, with the patient playing Corday getting carried away, propelled out of control by the words she is speaking. If this were the case, however, Sade would be concerned. After all, she has a knife. He is not, and so we assume that Sade himself has engineered this moment. There are numerous points in the play where patients seem to lose control of their stage persona, and yet each point makes good structural sense and, as such, is deliberate. The audience is never quite sure, however; a point underlined by the continual concern of the institution's Director, Monsieur Coulmier.

Note the repetition of Corday's 'I want'. Three times she says it: 'I want ... I want ... I want ... I shall ...' and it is three times that she will approach the door wanting to kill, and on the third time she will succeed. This pattern is reminiscent of stories throughout myth and fable, from the three little pigs, to Jesus being denied three times by Peter. All the ingredients of the classic story are here.

And so the central action is set and interrupted. In fact, the whole play is one interrupted action. (In this sense, the patients' play fulfils Aristotle's requirement of 'one complete action'.) Corday finally raises her dagger on her third visit in scene 30. Even then it is stopped for a musical, historical interlude, itself jokingly called *Interruptus*. In one sense, Weiss is doing no more than exploiting suspense, just as a thriller writer might do, only here, the suspense has added purpose.

Having established this central, interrupted action, the story moves back and shows us Corday's preparations for the murder, under the title: *10. Song and mime of Corday's arrival in Paris*. A song describes Corday arriving in Paris and purchasing the knife to kill Marat. The music goes from sweet and lyrical to rough and rhythmic over these lines, sung by the Four Singers:

> Charlotte Corday walked alone
> Paris birds sang sugar calls
> Charlotte walked down lanes of stone
> through the haze from perfume stalls
> Charlotte smelt the dead's gangrene
> Heard the singing guillotine

Here the patients form a procession, making its way towards the guillotine. They are pulling a cart, or *tumbrel*, filled with those about to die. The rhythm is monotonous and builds into a 'dance of death' with the patients making 'ecstatic and contorted movements'. She then speaks these lines:

Corday: [*in front of the arena, turned to the public. Behind her the stamping continues*]
           What kind of town is this
           The sun can hardly pierce the haze
           not a haze made out of rain and fog
           but steaming thick and hot
           like the mist in a slaughterhouse
           Why are they howling
           What are they dragging through the streets
           They carry stakes but what's impaled on those stakes
           Why do they hop what they are dancing for
           Why are they racked with laughter

Why do the children scream
What are those heaps they fight over
those heaps with eyes and mouths
What kind of town is this
hacked buttocks lying in the street
What are all these faces
    [*Behind her the dance of death takes place.*
    The Four Singers join the dancers.
    The cart is turned into a place of execution. Two Patients represent the guillotine. The execution is
    prepared in gruesome detail.
    Corday sits slumped at the foremost edge of the arena.]
Soon these faces will close around me
These eyes and mouths will call me to join them

Again, we are introduced to the scene, this time by the singers, who paint a picture of the innocent Charlotte in a gruesome, murderous Paris. Her words conjure up a grotesque image of children fighting over piles of bodies, her description mirroring the contorted and ecstatic movements of the dance of death we see on stage. Her words now reach beyond the murder she intends and predict her own death, when she will join those going to the guillotine.

TASK

1 Note the rhythmic repetition of the questions: why, what, why, why, why, what, what, what ...? Try this speech out, one at a time while the others stamp and clap the rhythm. Try saying it louder as you go through, but also try it staying level, or being spoken more explosively. Experiment with the language for maximum effect. What happens if you switch from screaming it almost unintelligibly, to delivering it in a melancholic monotone? Discuss the effects of your findings.
2 Create your own dance of death. Create a crashing rhythm using objects and voices. Let your imaginations go into the rhythm and the movement. It is perfectly controlled, but may not appear so to an outsider. Find the ecstatic contortions.
3 Combine 1 and 2 above in a staging of this moment.

Marat then launches an attack from his bath-tub. He refers directly to the sacrificed lives of the dying aristocrats whom we see being executed in dumb-show:

Marat: ...
        So what is this sacrifice
        compared with the sacrifices the people made
        to keep you fat
        What are a few looted mansions
        compared with their looted lives
        You don't care
        if the foreign armies with whom you're making secret deals
        march in and massacre the people
        You hope the people will be wiped out so you can flourish
        and when they are wiped out not a muscle will twitch in your puffy bourgeois faces

which are now all twisted up with anger and disgust

[*Coulmier rises. The head falls off. Triumphant screams. The Patients play ball with the head.*]

Coulmier: Monsieur de Sade
we can't allow this
you really cannot call this education
It isn't making my patients any better
they're all becoming over-excited
After all we invited the public here
to show them that our patients
are not all social lepers

[*Sade does not react. He gazes with a mocking smile across the stage and cues the Herald.*]

Herald: [*tapping his staff before Coulmier has finished speaking*]
We only show these people massacred
because this indisputably occurred
Please calmly watch these barbarous displays
which could not happen nowadays
The men of that time mostly now demised
were primitive we are more civilised

[*Herald points with his staff at the execution scene.*
Trumpet call.
Procession of nobles forms quickly, lining up for execution.]

Corday: [*rising*]
Up there on the scaffold
you stand completely still and stare
farther than your executioners eyes can see
That is how I will stand
when it's all over
[*she closes her eyes and appears to be sleeping*]

Sade: Look at them Marat
these men who once owned everything
See how they turn their defeat into victory
Now that their pleasures have been taken away
the guillotine saves them from endless boredom
Gaily they offer their heads as if for coronation
is not that the pinnacle of perversion

[*The victims kneel in front of the execution block. Sade gestures to the whole group to retreat.*
The Patients withdraw. The cart is taken away. Corday is led to her bench. A curtain is drawn to
hide the Patients.]

Sade smiles at Coulmier's interruption, as if he knew that the image produced would offend his sensibilities. In fact, he has already written and rehearsed the Herald's pacifying response. This is the danger of the drama. It gives freedom of speech to those normally denied it. This is terrifying for those who wish to control. As here, their reactions are often predictable. We know we are controlled, because we always know exactly when we have stepped over the boundaries. This sense of danger is inherent in both epic theatre and the theatre of Artaud.

TASK

Continue your staging. How will you create the guillotine? What will you use as a cart? or costumes? Cast the parts of Sade, Marat, Coulmier and Herald and perform.

At times the play's effects cross the boundaries between the two types of theatre, despite their differences. Like Sade and Marat, Brecht and Artaud both wanted to attack bourgeois values. Also like them, Brecht and Artaud had different methods; the one seeking objectivity and critical detachment, and the other wanting the audience to suspend judgement and surrender itself to rhythm. But they *could* combine. An example of this in *Marat/Sade* is the use of verse; heightened, formal language that is self-consciously patterned and rhythmic. This suits the purpose of Epic by continually exposing the language as artificial. We are constantly reminded that each speech is constructed by the playwright. The verse also suits the Theatre of Cruelty in that it enables the building of energy through rhythm and repetition that sweeps us along, like a mantra or a football chant. What Weiss achieves is to have the full power of the chant and suddenly snatch it away from us to examine the underlying issue.

The scene above questions the rationality of a mass slaughter that is hypocritically condemned by those who directly benefit from it. In this case it is Coulmier and the bourgeois audience who came to power in the revolution, but who cannot bear to hear about the violence that brought them that power. They wish to distance themselves and blame that behaviour on others. As the Herald says with heavy irony, they were primitive, 'we are more civilised'.

TASK

A modern example of this hypocrisy might be a government defending companies who sell weapons or torture equipment to foreign powers, while simultaneously condemning those other countries for brutality. Brainstorm other examples, choose one and devise a brief play that incorporates both Epic and Artaudian techniques.

SUMMARY

Experimental work in any discipline often plays with the idea of authorship. It *questions convention* and challenges the audience to be conscious of the mind that produced it. It does not pretend to be 'timeless'. *Marat/Sade* is one of the greatest examples of such a play. It *is* difficult, but practical attempts at staging this hugely entertaining text are highly rewarding.

Documentary and political theatre

AGIT-PROP

The USSR

Agit-prop is short for agitation and propaganda, and originated in the USSR after the 1917 revolution. News bulletins were transmitted to the towns by telegraph and read out through megaphones; the aim was not merely to inform the audience but to excite it with political (Communist) fervour. The bulletins were therefore combined with political exhortations, and rounded off with the Communist anthem. Soon music began to be added to arouse appropriate emotions or underline certain points, and the news-readers would use bodily movements to emphasise what they were saying.

It was therefore a very short step to turn a factual news bulletin into a theatrical performance; the first regular Agit-prop troupe called Blue Blouse was founded by the National Institute of Journalists in Moscow in 1923. They presented a montage of current events in a review format of songs and sketches. Naturally these events were presented with a definite Marxist ideological bias. They also acted out examples of behaviour or personal characteristics that the Communist Party had designated as harmful. They satirised and caricatured these aspects of behaviour (i.e. made them look ridiculous).

It was quickly realised how powerful and effective theatre could be, as a medium of social control. The Trades Union Council of the Moscow Department of Culture created a formula for a 'Living Newspaper' production that other productions should imitate. It was as follows:

- a parade/march in
- a lecture, illustrated by the performance of short scenes
- a commentator who linked the scenes, summed up the action and made the political meaning absolutely clear at the end of the performance.

Europe

Meanwhile, in the rest of Europe (especially in Germany in the wake of the Great War), the naturalistic domestic dramas for and about the middle classes seemed irrelevant. Actors and other theatre practitioners saw an opportunity to develop an exciting new theatre form aimed at a working class audience, which would reflect the barbarity of human nature and point to social injustice. The audience would be required to sit up and think, rather than relax and passively watch.

In Russia the new political theatre was a way of maintaining the newly established status quo. In Europe it was the opposite: a call to revolution. One such revolutionary was Erwin Piscator.

THE THEATRE OF ERWIN PISCATOR (1893–1966)

The play on the stage should act as an advance-guard action in the proletarian war of liberation … the theatre of the proletariat must be a theatre of class – of class-warfare.

(Edwin Piscator)

Although Piscator claimed to appeal to the proletariat, his early work was in fact simplistic and emotive propaganda. He believed that a simple presentation of the true facts about social injustice would be enough 'to kindle the flame of social revolution among the workers'. These facts were actually presented in a highly subjective way. One of his first productions, *Russia's Day*, illustrates his early style.

Text focus – *Russia's Day*, Piscator

This play is a melodrama, calling for mutiny and murder as an answer to military repression in Hungary. The set is a backdrop of a map of Europe.

- The working classes are portrayed as real people while the representatives of the establishment are caricatured: a diplomat, priest and an army officer are all comically presented as the servants of a character called 'World Capital', who is a large money bag wearing a stockbroker's hat and addressed as 'Your Majesty'.
- The 'War Widowed' and the 'War Wounded' enter to blame Capitalism for their sufferings in a simple formula of questions and answers.
- A voice through a megaphone representing the

Russian Revolution exhorts the Germans to destroy Capitalism by violence.
- A dying Hungarian describes thousands of fathers massacred, mothers imprisoned and sisters and wives raped, and dies with the cry of 'Comrades, don't let Russia be beaten down!'

The play ends with this stage direction:

A roaring chorus represents a battle cry. Masses appear on the stage … from every direction … with cries of 'Brothers, Comrades unite!' The German Worker recites the first verse of the International, the chorus on stage join in as do the audience.

DOCUMENTARY THEATRE

Piscator's later works

Despite the simplistic nature of his original productions, Piscator was a theatrical visionary who, according to Bertolt Brecht, 'broke nearly all theatrical conventions'. He staged some remarkable productions with his company at the *Theater am Nollendorfplatz* in Berlin.

Piscator began to incorporate technology into his productions, using large projectors to show newsreel and photographs of real people and events. The juxtaposition of factual material and dramatic action became a regular feature, and remains an essential element of contemporary documentary theatre. A piece of film or a photograph can be used to emphasise what is happening on the stage or to contrast with it: to highlight hypocrisy and injustice.

Many of his plays used heavy machinery in order to reflect the industrial technological nature of modern society. *The Merchant of Berlin* was acted on hydraulic lifts and motorised bridges.

Although Piscator became more sophisticated, he never lost his revolutionary intentions. To this end his search was always for 'totality, immediacy and authenticity'; in other words, for a dramatic form which involved and aroused the audience to political action through the representation of an 'objective' reality. This search led him first to the revue form (which

TASK

Create a piece of documentary theatre, noting the following points:

- Documentary theatre is the theatre of fact. Its purpose might be educational or political; it often aims to make its audience aware of a particular problem or injustice.
- Your challenge will be how to turn factual evidence and statistics into theatre that makes people sit up and listen: the piece must be entertaining and grab the audience's attention.
- Suitable subjects include:
  homelessness
  teenage pregnancy
  sexual harassment.
- Your piece of documentary theatre should contain at least some of the following:
  songs
  poems
  news reports
  quotes: from politicians, experts, the general public etc.
  newsreel or film footage
  dramatised reconstructions of real or possible events (these can be rehearsed improvisations)
  dance
  music
  statistics.
  Everything you include should be an integral part of the presentation.
- You may use suitable costumes or props.

has remained the format for much of modern documentary theatre) and then to the development of Epic theatre.

Documentary Theatre is theatre that wishes to educate and elucidate.
It can be on any subject that is socially or politically relevant to its audience.
It uses a mixture of techniques to make its point: songs; comedy sketches; Com-media dell'Arte; caricatures of real figures; serious drama; slides and film. The options are endless.
It mixes fact and fiction, real incidents with imagined ones.
Its aim is to change opinion or inform.
It is often, but not always political.
(Living Newspaper, in 1930s America)

The Theatre of the Absurd

The theatre of the absurd is as difficult to define as any other style of theatre, in the sense that it is extremely varied in form, and its contributors differ greatly in terms of artistic and social background; Pinter, Beckett, Ionesco, Adamov, Albee and Arrabal have all been described as absurdist writers, and of these, only Pinter and Beckett bear any comparison. The one common strand to all of these writers is the *essence* of this form of theatre: the sense that life, with all of its mores, social customs and beliefs, is absurd. Any attempt to communicate or succeed in this absurd world is doomed to failure; hope for improvement is futile.

However, this form of theatre has just as strong a link with religion as do the Morality plays of the medieval era. The very basis of the theatre of the absurd is the existentialist philosophy, which (in simplistic terms) described religious belief as irrational. But if there is no God, what is the meaning of existence? By which rules do we live? What are our values? What's the point? Absurdist writers were variously seen, in their times, as violent, negative and humorous.

An early form of absurdist theatre are the Ubu plays by Alfred Jarry (see Chapter 5, page 154 for a text focus and tasks on *Ubu Roi*). The theatrical surrealists (e.g. Appollinaire who wrote the *Breasts of Tireasias*) might be seen as the less-intellectual and more aggressive relations of the absurdists; their first aim was to shock the audience and, in terms of form, to overturn as many of the conventions of the naturalistic theatre as possible. In its time, surrealist exhibitions and performances caused riots and sparked off lawsuits and general public outcry. *Monty Python* is perhaps the most popular corollary of the surrealist movement in today's modern media.

> ★ *hot tip*
>
> For an investigation into black comedy, watch the film *Dr Strangelove* directed by Stanley Kubrick (who also directed *The Shining*), starring Peter Sellers.

TASK

Balloon debate: Each person has to justify their continued existence in turn. Allow each person two minutes each. Only those that can convince the audience that their lives have meaning can stay on board the balloon.

Absurdist writers

Arthur Adamov (Russian-born French): *Ping Pong*, 1959, John Calder.

Fernando Arrabal (French): *The Architect and the Emperor of Assyria*, 1967, John Calder.

Eugene Ionesco (Rumanian-born French): *Rhinoceros* (1959, John Calder), *The Chairs* (1954, John Calder), *The Lesson* (1958, John Calder).

Samuel Beckett (Irish but wrote in French): *Endgame* (1958, Faber & Faber), *Waiting for Godot* (1992, Macmillan).

Alfred Jarry (French): *Ubu Plays*, 1968, trans. C. Connolly and S. Watson Taylor, Methuen and Co. (see text focus in Chapter 5, page 154).

Harold Pinter (British): *The Birthday Party* (1991, Faber & Faber), *The Dumb Waiter* (1960, French), *The Caretaker* (1991, Faber & Faber).

Edward Albee (American): *The American Dream* (1995, Penguin), *Zoo Story* (1959, French).

Sam Shepherd (American): *Curse of the Starving Class*, from *Seven Plays*, 1985, Faber & Faber.

chapter seven

FINDING WORK IN THE THEATRE

It is a widely accepted truth that the acting profession is one of the most difficult in which to find work: 75 per cent of actors are unemployed 75 per cent of the time, as the saying goes. The daily grind of unemployment and searching for work is enough to put even the most dedicated and talented people off acting as a career. There is no such thing as a 'lucky' break. The people who seem to get 'lucky' are generally the actors that work the hardest at trying to find work. Of course, as in any profession, there is a lot of nepotism/favouritism, and if you are fortunate enough to have the right connections, you are more likely to find an audience before many of your contemporaries. If you do not have connections but are still determined to get on, then the best piece of advice is to equip yourself with another skill (e.g. typing, bricklaying etc.) which will help you to find temporary work, and thus stay sane while you wait for your career to develop.

In this chapter, you will find some useful information and tips to help you in your search for work.

Equity

Equity (the British Actors Equity Association) is the name of the independent trade union which represents 45,000 performers, actors, stage managers, theatre designers and directors, choreographers, dancers, singers, stunt performers, puppeteers, announcers and professional broadcasters within the entertainment's industry. The union sets rates of pay and all the working conditions which employees must abide by if they are employing actors under Equity contracts. The union provides useful protection in a profession whose members are extremely vulnerable to exploitation, because of the shortage of the work available.

- Equity is run by a council of 67 members who are elected every two years by a postal ballot.
- Membership costs from £30 a year up to a maximum of around £1,200 a year, depending on how much you earn.

It used to be against the law to work in the theatre without first acquiring an Equity card. This piece of legislation was, however, overturned while Margaret Thatcher was Prime Minister. In theory, this meant that employers would now be able to hire actors without Equity cards and thus at any rate of pay. This strategy has generally failed, because most reputable theatre companies and television companies still abide by Equity contracts; agencies and prospective employers still regard an Equity card as a sign of an actor's professionalism and commitment, and it is an invaluable asset in finding employment. At the very least, an Equity contract will provide a civilised rate of pay and decent conditions of work.

How do you obtain an Equity card?

You can either be admitted to Equity as a provisional or a full member. The usual method is to gain access to the union as a provisional member, for which you need to prove that you have worked for approximately eight full weeks as a professional performer. 'Professional' in this case means to have been paid the equivalent of the current Equity rate of pay (you could telephone Equity on the telephone number given on page 264, to find out how much this is). Don't panic if you are working on a day-to-day basis, i.e. as a children's entertainer or as a singer, because you can claim for the individual days or nights you have worked, provided you have a contract from your employer to prove it. If you are working in this way, it is a good idea to take along your own contract which the employer can easily sign on the spot for you; Figure 7.1 shows a specimen contract.

Figure 7.1   *A specimen contract for performers*

CONTRACT FOR PERFORMERS

The following constitutes a formal agreement.

Date:

Between:

[Employer's name and address]

[Your name] (hereby referred to as 'the artiste')

_____

[Employer's name] hereby agrees to engage the artiste to perform the following duties:
Performance of _____ duration as singer/children's entertainer
The engagement shall commence on _____/_____/_____ and end
on _____/_____/_____

[Employer's name] shall pay the artiste the sum of £_____

[Employer's name]   [Your name]

Signature   Signature

When you have received six of these contracts (for the fee of £100 for one day's work), in combination with five other contracts from more established employers such as the *Natural Theatre Company* for longer periods of work, you will gain access to Equity's provisional status. Once you have got your card, you can start branching out. Find more work of a similar nature to that which you found before you got your card, and start applying to agencies for representation.

In order to get a full Equity card, you need to amass evidence of 30 weeks' full-time paid employment at the minimum Equity rate. If you are extremely lucky, you will find these 30 weeks of work straight away, but this is unlikely. If you have to compile a variety of contracts, they will all need to have been signed within one year.

Contact Equity at the following addresses for more information, if you are considering making an application for membership.

London area:
Equity
Guild House
Upper St. Martin's Lane
London
WC2H 9EG
Tel: 0171 379 6000
Fax: 0171 379 7001

Scotland:
Equity
65 Bath Street
Glasgow
G2 2BX
Tel: 0141 332 1669

North of England:
Equity
Coavon Court
12 Blackfriars Street
Salford
M3 5BQ
Tel: 0161 832 3183

Wales and South West:
Equity
Transport House
1 Cathedral Street
Cardiff
Tel: 01222 397971

The Independent Theatre Council

The Independent Theatre Council (ITC) is an organisation which provides information and support in a similar way to Equity, but mainly to the employers of the acting profession. Just as actors must qualify for Equity membership, so companies must also qualify for membership of ITC. Equity and ITC, however, do negotiate between them, and if you are an Equity member working under an ITC contract, you stand an extremely good chance of earning a good wage, with access to arbitration if necessary.

ITC also offers excellent information and workshops for those in the position to employ others and seeking to employ them fairly, and for companies just starting out. ITC will provide you with vital information concerning funding, booking a tour, marketing, being an employer, insurance, contracts, the charitable status of your company, and working and legal structures. You can contact the ITC at the following address:

Independent Theatre Council
4 Baden Place
Crosby Row
London
SE1 1YW
0171 403 1727

Further training

There are various options available upon leaving school: Colleges of Further Education, Sixth Form or straight into practical performance training. After this you will be able to either go onto Higher Education, an accredited drama school or to work! Of course you might find full-time, promising work at the age of 16, but this would be quite exceptional. For the majority of performers, Further and/or Higher Education in addition to postgraduate education or training is the usual route into the theatre. Stage Managers can also train at accredited drama schools, but most stage management personnel work their way up through the ranks of Assistant and Deputy Stage Manager, and gain their experience on the job.

A book entitled *Contacts* will be very useful when considering further, professional training. The training section contains all of the addresses of current practising teaching establishments for performers. You can buy *Contacts* from:
    The Spotlight
    7 Leicester Place
    London
    WC2H 7BP
    Tel: 0171 437 7631
    Fax: 0171 437 5881

★ *hot tip*

Contacts is an essential purchase for anyone involved in the performing arts, as it provides an up-to-date directory of drama schools, agents, photographers, theatres, theatre companies and properties companies.

Whether or not you are still at college, you should be doing your utmost to equip yourself with as many skills as possible. It is only by diversifying and mastering skills as varied as stage management to playing the piano, that you will be able to stay in the performing arts. Money spent on private lessons is a worthwhile investment, as your acquired skills may repay you a hundred times in professional life.

For in-depth information on degree courses, you should go to your nearest career centre or library. Look out for Careers Research and Advisory Centre (CRAC) publications. These are generally the most comprehensive and approachable guides, but you will find plenty of other information in a well-stocked main library.

Agencies

Finding a good agent is often a difficult and expensive process. Unless you are lucky enough to be 'spotted' in a show and then approached by an agent, you will have to write many letters to stand any chance of finding one. In addition, some agents will be only too keen to take substantial amounts of money from you (in the form of joiner's fees and photographer's fees), and perhaps do very little in return for it. If you do not know an actor who can recommend an agent whom you might approach, then apply to some of the agencies listed in *Contacts*.

● If you want to be accepted in a good actor's agency, you will need at least some professional experience and an Equity card, or to have graduated from one of the accredited drama schools.

Collective agencies offer an alternative to the conventional agencies. A collective agency will also charge some kind of joiner's fee, and will usually ask for ten per cent of your earnings. You will be expected to take part in the running of the agency (answering the telephone, completing forms, etc.), and will gain much experience. The essential problem with collective agencies is that there is no permanent contact for the prospective employers to talk to, and this sometimes makes it difficult for the agency to attract work of any great quality. All agencies are different, however, and if you are fortunate enough to be auditioned, go along and check it out. Ask about the sort of work recently offered to members of the agency, and what kinds of contacts they have managed to establish.

Joining an agency is, however, only one facet of your career-search. You also need to be writing letters and sending off CVs on your own behalf. Intensive effort will bring rewards in the form of work and contacts, but these rewards may not be immediate or on a grand scale. Have no illusions: letter-writing is a time-consuming and arduous process and you may not receive one positive reply from 100 letters (although if this does happen you may need to re-examine your technique). In the following section you will find some ideas and advice about the kind of letters you need to write and the appropriate style, but there is no substitute for your own imagination and initiative. Creativity is the key to attract interest from your prospective employers, but at the same time, try not to let your enthusiasm carry you away. *Always* maintain a professional stance.

Setting up a theatre company

There are very few areas in the performing arts profession where you are guaranteed to make money, but by setting up your own company, you can virtually guarantee that you will *lose* money and that, at best, you will always be struggling to break even. Very few companies can expect to grow from small company status and survive for long enough to be able to win grants from the Arts Council and other funding sources. You *can* make a living from live theatre, but the road is long, and you will need to acquire many administrative and communication skills to negotiate this path successfully. If you do not care about the financial side, there is nothing more exciting for a performing artist to do, than being part of an original company. You will be fortunate enough if you can manage to find regular work for other

companies, but for people with initiative and vision, this can be frustrating in the long-run. If you want to devise your own work, or put on new, innovative plays, then you will have little choice but to set up your own company.

Step 1

Firstly you need to arrive at a decision-making process. Is one person going to make all of the decisions, like the conventional theatre director, or are you going to institute a more democratic process and perhaps vote on important decisions concerning the direction which your company is going to take. How often is the company going to meet? Agendas and minutes should be arranged and taken. These kinds of records will help both you and any potential funders.

Step 2

Decide upon a mission statement which will define your company. It may read something like this:

The Bonkers Theatre Company has been set up to perform new plays by previously unperformed writers. Its mission is to take these plays to as wide an audience as possible in the Midlands area.

Or:

The Big Boots Theatre-in-Education Company has been set up to provide a wide range of dramatic provision in the Kent area. The company intends to perform plays concerning social and political issues. Its mission is to raise awareness of contemporary politics in the adolescent population of the South-Eastern region, through a range of innovative techniques, namely that of Forum theatre.

This statement will help you to focus on what you have set out to do. It will also be useful when you are applying for funding or talking to the press.

Step 3

How are you going to break even? – by performing plays that people want to see. This is a question of pitching your material carefully, and choosing a suitable venue. In the case of the *Bonkers Theatre Company*, this will be an uphill task. The best option would be to produce a new play in conjunction with something more established, maybe something by Shakespeare, or to produce it in a venue which is renowned for the quality of its new writing.

Producing a new play in conjunction with a more celebrated piece is a tactic frequently employed at the Edinburgh Festival, by both new and established companies. Most companies manage to break even in this way. The *Big Boots Theatre Company* should manage to break even, and will probably make money, once it has established itself in the locality. If a theatre-in-education (TIE) company performs material which schools can afford (and which is based on books, plays or on subjects which are part of the National Curriculum or on 'A' Level courses) and market themselves effectively, they may earn a living. Well-established local businesses also like to fund TIE projects because the material is 'safe' and will serve to raise the profile of the business within the community. Smaller businesses are also usually happy to lend properties or materials for this kind of enterprise.

In the case of all companies, efficient and effective marketing and organisation, as well as your originality and talent, are the keys to longevity.

TASK

Send a questionnaire out to the local business community. Ask whether they would be willing to help fund a theatre company, and if so, what kind, and when would be the best time of year to apply for the money? Stamped addressed envelopes should be enclosed to encourage a reply.

Step 4

Find a base for your company. This may be someone's home, a semi-permanent rehearsal space or even a local school. The latter is certainly a good idea if you are a TIE company, and is an option which many TIE companies have chosen in the past. You will need a telephone, an answering machine, and if you can afford it, a fax machine.

Step 5

Decide upon your play, and start marketing. The marketing and administration of the exercise should start well before the play goes into rehearsal.

- If you are devising a piece, send out a description of the material you are intending to devise. Emphasise the themes you are working with, rather than the style you think the finished product may exhibit.
- Where you direct your marketing efforts will depend upon the kind of theatre you are intending to produce. TIE companies will want to direct their efforts to all Heads of Drama in local schools and colleges.
- Send letters of enquiry to schools or theatres in the immediate area; keep a record of letters sent out and those returned. Follow up by telephone all of your letters a week after posting, and keep telephoning until you get a reply. If this initial mail-out fails to get enough work, follow it up with another which reaches a wider area.
- Remember that the further you have to travel, the higher your transport costs will be, so budget and estimate carefully before quoting a price to your venue.
- How much you charge depends upon the length of the show and its quality. Make sure that you are working on the premise that you at least break even.
- In the case of TIE in schools, you will charge a flat fee. You may also charge theatres a flat fee, but if you are a new company, it is much more likely that the theatre management will offer you a box office split, which means that you take a percentage cut of the ticket money. This kind of arrangement works to the advantage of the theatre in the case of new work, because there is a strong possibility that a large amount of seats will remain unsold.
- You will need to make a budget. Add up all of your expenditure, from the amount spent on stationery, to that spent on the actors' wages. This will tell you how much money you need to earn on your tour, and so how much money you will need to charge and how many performances you will have to complete.

Step 6

Once you have established yourselves, you may start to apply for state funding. In order for the Arts Council to consider approving a grant, they will need to have seen at least two shows, prior to your first application. Alternatively, the work of one or more members of the company needs to be already known to them.

You will be applying through the Arts Council's Projects and Small-Scale Touring grant systems. The Arts Council assesses the work of companies through the work of various drama projects officers. These officers work on a voluntary basis, and there is no absolute guarantee that any of your shows will be seen by them. To increase your chances, full information about your performance (dates, times, box office details) must reach the drama projects section of the Arts Council by the 10th of the month, one month in advance of the performance itself. The attending officer will then write an assessment of your piece.

Apply to the Arts Council for full information on making applications for funding:

Arts Council of England
14 Great Peter Street
London
SW1P 3NQ
Tel: 0171 333 0100
Fax: 0171 973 6590

Scottish Arts Council
12 Manor Place
Edinburgh
EH3 7DD
Tel: 0131 226 6051
Fax: 0131 225 9833

Arts Council of Wales
Holst House
Museum Place
Cardiff
CF1 3NX
Tel: 01222 394711
Fax: 01222 221447

Arts Council of Northern Ireland
181a Stranmillis Road
Belfast
BT9 5DU
Tel: 01232 381591
Fax: 01232 661715

Touring a show

The following section will draw upon information gathered during a visit to the Fringe of the Edinburgh Festival during 1995, and material used in a production of *Situation Dog* which played at the Hill Street Theatre. *Situation Dog* encountered a great many difficulties during its two-week production span at the Fringe. Problems concerned:

- sponsorship
- the press
- publicity
- the venue
- the production.

Many of these problems could have been overcome with better preparation (and a more in-depth reading of the Fringe's own guidelines for performers new to the Fringe). If you take the time to read through this account, you could save yourself some money and a lot of wasted time.

Situation Dog at the Edinburgh Fringe

SPONSORSHIP

It is fairly unlikely that you will receive any sponsorship if yours is a new company, unless you are acquainted with a member of the Board of a wealthy company. Your chances increase if you approach potential sponsors well before the production date; if your company is known in its local area and has mounted previous productions; and if the play's content has a worthy message or is, in some sense, a 'community' production.

A sponsor's first question is likely to be, 'What is my company going to get out of this?' If the play is new, avant-garde and perceived as 'arty' or 'controversial' then sponsorship from a small, local company is unlikely, unless they too like to be seen as 'arty' or 'controversial'. A 'worthy' community play is a much better option for such businesses, because it will raise their profile, when the Edinburgh trip is advertised in the local media. An untested, innovative piece of drama, threatens any sponsor with bringing them into disrepute and attracting controversy.

So, you have to pitch yourself and your image correctly if you are serious about raising money, and you have to do it before the start of the financial year (April). In fact, many shows make provisional bookings to attend the Fringe, and then drop out in the May/June period because they have been unable to find the necessary funding.

Situation Dog managed to attract £500 worth of sponsorship by June, and needed to find at least another £1,000 by September if it was to stand any chance of breaking even. The best decision from a financial point of view at this time, would have been to cancel the production. In the event the show went on, and some money was lost. The loss is worth taking if you are confident of winning an award and being able to book your show into provincial or London venues.

Figure 7.2 shows a copy of the letter which was sent out to every business in the local area, and to businesses with which any member of the company had ever had any dealings in the past.

Figure 7.2   *A specimen letter to raise sponsorship*

SHIFTY THEATRE COMPANY
Director: Ian Reade
12 Oak Road, Eastgate, Essex, SS3 1AB
Tel. (01789) 123456

To   Mr R Kelly
Manager
Midland Bank
1 High Street
Eastgate
SS1 2BC

21 July 1995

Dear Mr Kelly

I would like to interest you in the work of the *Shifty Theatre Company,* with a view to setting up some species of sponsorship arrangement, between the Midland Bank and ourselves. In this letter I shall endeavour to give you as much information as possible about the company, its members, current and future projects, and also the rationale behind the funding that we are seeking.

The company
The *Shifty Theatre Company* was set up in April of this year in order to satisfy the needs of several people in full-time employment, who are committed to practising theatre. The essential idea was that the company would perform the works of new writers and other rarely performed plays. The founders of the company feel that performing new work and exploring innovative plays, is vital to both the theatre world and to the local community.

Company members
The company is made up of people who have trained and/or work together:

Ian Reade BA (Hons.): Writer/Director
Trained at Kent University in Drama and Theatre Studies. Member of the *Natural Theatre Company* for three years, and toured the world, performing comedies. First piece, *Little Plaything* performed at The Railway, Southend, in 1995. *Situation Dog* to go to Edinburgh Fringe 1995. Also full-time lecturer in Performing Arts at South East Essex College.

Brian McDivot: Actor
Trained at South East Essex College on the course for entry into performing arts. Brian has won the LAMDA Gold award, and has been working at the Palace Theatre as a performer throughout the summer.

Dave Robert BA (Hons.): Press Officer
Trained at Kent University in Drama and Theatre Studies, and at the LeCoq School of Mime in Paris. Now a part-time lecturer in Performing Arts.

Martin Green BA (Hons.): Publicity
Trained at Dartington in Drama and Theatre Studies, and is soon to be commencing an MA in Theatre Studies at Leeds University.

John Churchill BA (Hons.): Stage Manager/Writer
Trained at Reading University in Drama and Film, and is now a part-time lecturer in Performing Arts.

Lucy Reade: Assistant Stage Manager
At present training in Drama and Film at Reading University.

Current and future projects
The company is planning to take *Situation Dog* by Ian Reade, to the Edinburgh Festival, with the possibility of touring it to further venues in the South East at a later date. Please find poster and publicity material for the Edinburgh production enclosed with this letter.

The company are planning to produce a play by David Gale (ex-*Lumiere and Son*), which has not yet been decided, either just before or just after Christmas and to be performed in Southend and the locality.

The company are continually engaged in writing and reviewing their own pieces and those of other interested parties, and it is hoped that the company can find another suitable piece within the next few months with the aim of producing it in Edinburgh 1996.

Funding rationale
The figures for the current production of *Situation Dog* are given below.

Fringe Membership Fee		£250
Accommodation	(5 × £50 × 2 weeks)	£500
Theatre Rent	(Guarantee)	£500
Publicity	(Poster, leaflets, video)	£200
Administrator	(Telephone, stationery)	£100
Travel	(5 × £96)	£480
Costumes/Props		£200
TOTAL		£2230

We are approaching other local businesses and funding bodies but resources are very thin on the ground. Abacus Insurance Services in Colchester and Southend Borough Arts Council have both expressed a strong interest in the project. The company believes that there is a good possibility that Abacus will fund the props and costumes costs, and that the Arts Council will guarantee the rent of the theatre. We would be very grateful if you could find sufficient to principally cover the accommodation (and/or any of the other items listed above!).

I hope you will agree with us that this is an exciting and worthwhile project which, at the very least, will secure some representation for Southend at the Festival, and with a bit of luck bring back the Fringe First award! Should you be interested in sponsoring the project, your company logo will be prominently displayed on any advertising material, such as programmes and posters, and you will of course receive thanks in any interviews given to both the local and the national press. The *Shifty Theatre Company* has already received some exposure in the local papers, and we are co-ordinating a wider campaign in the run-up to the Festival. Incidentally, there is a preview production of the play in Southend at the Dixon Studio, Palace Theatre, 20 and 21 July, 8.30 pm to 9.30 pm, if you would like to come.

Should you require any further information, do not hesitate to contact the company at the above address.

Yours sincerely

Ian Reade
Shifty Theatre Company

PRESS

A press release (see Figure 7.3) accompanied the applications for sponsorship. The press release tries to sell itself on the 'unusual' nature of the play's content and its potentiality to shock the audience, tied in with a sense of humour. This press release was sent to local businesses and to more exceptional sponsors like *Winalot* and other companies who might be interested in sponsoring the play for the novelty value which such an association might bring. In hindsight, it might have been better to have prepared a different press release for the two different targets.

Figure 7.3   *Press release for* Situation Dog

---

press pack press release press pack

SITUATION DOG
By Ian Reade

17 August–2 September (not 21, 28) 12.15 am (1.10 am)
Hill Street Theatre (venue 41) 19 Hill Street
Tickets: £5.00 (£4.00) Box Office 0131 226 6522

Shifty Theatre Company spark controversy on first Festival visit

Situation Dog is the latest play from the controversial Shifty Theatre Company on their first visit to the Fringe Festival

CONTROVERSY

The play concerns Mr Pitch, a dog-killing psychopath, containing violent scenes that explore the most effective, yet painful, ways of disposing of our four-legged friends. No dog is safe from the attentions of Mr Pitch.

MUTTS, MURDER, MONGRELS AND MAYHEM

Modern society has brought the need for cleanliness. It has imbued within us a deep-seated desire for an inner oasis of sterility. A need arising from the encounter between mankind and the hygiene of modern, technological society. Mr Pitch is an ordinary man, a Sunday driver on the road of life, transformed into a dog-hating maniac by a chain of unfortunate coincidences. This piece describes, in highly physical and intelligent terms, the short and tragic history of Mr Pitch, a man in search of a clean pavement.

Adults only. Bring dogs at own risk
For further information and photos contact:
David Robert Press Office 01227 772297
Ian Reade Director 01702 611785

Shifty Theatre Company, 12 Oak Road, Eastgate, Essex SS3 1AB

press pack press release press pack

The press release was also sent to all of the major newspapers, radio and television stations, along with the poster (see Figure 7.4). One television station and three newspapers contacted the company. The quality of this publicity is crucial.

The press release and handbill (see Figure 7.5) must be presented on glossy finished paper. The press release should be sent in a pack of well-finished materials which should also include photographs and reviews if you have them. The design of these materials is all-important, and if you do not know a designer personally you will easily be able to find one training at your local college who would be glad to use this project as part of his/her portfolio.

PUBLICITY

Handbills were also produced on coloured paper (red) with the poster design on the front and an edited version of the press release on the back (see Figure 7.5). Thousands of these were printed and handed out on the streets during the Festival, by a man dressed in a suit wearing a dog's head (loaned by the *Natural Theatre* and built by Aardvark productions). This was the most effective piece of publicity, and succeeded in attracting more people than any of the other means of advertising.

Figure 7.4   *Poster for* Situation Dog

Figure 7.5   *Handbill for* Situation Dog

Situation Dog is the latest play from the Shifty Theatre Company on their first visit to the Fringe Festival

MUTTS, MONGRELS

The play concerns Mr Pitch, a Sunday driver on the road of life, transformed into a dog-killing psychopath by a chain of unfortunate coincidences. Wronged man in search of rightful retribution, or a misogynist who receives his just desserts? Decide for yourselves as you observe this tortured, hilarious account of a man in search of a clean pavement, at the most compelling, blackly-humorous show on the Fringe.

MURDER AND MAYHEM

Modern society has brought the need for cleanliness. It has imbued within us a deep-seated desire for an inner oasis of sterility. A need arising from the encounter between mankind and the hygiene of modern, technological society. What tortured, desperate lengths will a human being not go to in order to satisfy this need?

<u>Adults only. Dogs at owner's risk</u>

Although this handbill was quite effective, we saw some truly excellent ones. The European Production House (sponsored by Mars Confectionery) gave out a handout for a play called *Treats*, with a mini-Mars bar attached: see Figure 7.6. The leaflet was also very professionally designed. The whole package was a good example of sponsorship, play and image-design combining together to produce a clear image.

You will also notice a small sticky label, which advertises the fact that the play has received a good review. These labels are essential additions as soon as you receive a decent review, because the public places a great deal of (often misplaced) faith in critiques.

The Shifty Theatre also postered heavily around the town. You can glue your posters to walls, pillars and lamp-posts all around Edinburgh. Although the City Council threatens to take action against fly-posting every year, legislation has yet to be introduced to prevent this activity. You will need to re-poster every day, and try not to lose your temper at people who glue over your posters. Card is very useful for providing backing to posters which can then be tied onto railings. You will also need a billboard upon which to make a display near your theatre. You can pay a company to do this operation for you, and some venue agencies take on this work (for a fee of course).

THE VENUE

The best kinds of venue in Edinburgh are near the centre of the town. Of course, these venues are more expensive, and you have to weigh up the odds between your outlay and likely returns. Price also depends upon your time-slot, early- to mid-evening being the most expensive. Late slots are almost impossible to sell tickets for, although I met an American company performing a horror show, based

Figure 7.6   *Think about why this playbill is attractive and effective*

Figure 7.7   *You may also want to take your show to the Edinburgh Festival*

on a cult television series, at 11.30 pm which was sold out several nights running. This is quite exceptional.

Some venues are also quite inhospitable, with poor facilities. This makes it hard for you to sell your show, because people cannot relax. If you have the luxury of being able to go to Edinburgh a year in advance of your show, then look for a venue with pleasant bars and eating facilities, and accommodating staff. Customers may go from one show to the next in such venues, and are more likely to return at a later date. Apply to the agency running the venue at the earliest opportunity, to ensure your chosen slot. This may not be possible in the first year, because companies often book from one year to the next.

THE PRODUCTION

If you are intent on performing a new play, but are equally sure that you do not want to lose money, then you will also need to put on something like a Shakespeare play or a children's show. Either of these are guaranteed to bring in an audience, and will make enough money to cover your overheads.

In 1995, physical theatre was the audience's favourite, but by far the biggest sellers at the Fringe are the comedy and children's shows. It is difficult to sell new work anyway, but at Edinburgh, your difficulties are accentuated by the competition. The kind of people most attracted to seeing new work, tend to be those with the least money, so competition for this audience is tough.

Selling yourself

When applying for a post you will need to complete a Curriculum Vitae (CV) and a covering letter. Both take a good deal of time to prepare in the first instance, but will become easier with some experience and practice.

hot tip

This may sound obvious, but it is much better to use a computer than a typewriter for the purposes of compiling CVs and covering letters. Mistakes can be easily rectified with the aid of a computer, and you will need to constantly update your CV as your experience increases.

CURRICULUM VITAE

There are many variations in the format of the CV, and the one you eventually choose will largely depend upon the particular purpose for which you need the document.

In this chapter you will find two CVs, one for work experience (Figure 7.8, page 276) and one belonging to a professional actor (see Figure 7.11, page 282). The first is such that you might use to find a work experience placement or, with some modification, acting work if accompanied by a 5" × 4" or 10" × 8" black and white photograph. The second example is a very specific kind of CV which some agencies and drama schools use to advertise their actors. You may wish to imitate this format, although

it is a difficult type of CV to perfect, unless you can afford to hire professional help (you will no doubt need to hire a professional photographer in the case of either CV).

When modifying the following examples to suit your own needs, bear in mind the following points:

● Try to keep the length of the CV down to one page.
● Take care to include all the experience you have of the job or area of work you are seeking (whether paid or unpaid), but beware of cramming the page so that the CV cannot be easily read. Most Artistic/

Casting Directors will have to sift through thousands of applications for every single job, and will throw a 'difficult' one straight in the bin.

- Make sure the information is accurate. You will be questioned about it if called to audition or interview, and may be asked for evidence.

- Try not to leave any large, empty spaces on the page: it looks as if you have nothing to say for yourself.

- Make absolutely sure that your spelling and punctuation is correct. Presentation is everything at this stage. Your CV is doing all of your talking for you, so try to make sure that it is speaking the 'Queen's English'.

Figure 7.8   *A sample Curriculum Vitae, suitable for a work experience appliction or general enquiry*

Curriculum Vitae

Name: Rip Thorn
Address: 11 Livingstone Close, West Hampstead, W3 45W
Telephone: (0171) 987 6543
Date of birth: 14/4/80
Seeking position of: Work Experience Placement

Education & Qualifications

1993–1996	Newquay Secondary Modern	GCSEs
		English Literature B
		English Language B
		Drama A
		German C
		History C
1996–present day	Frome VIth Form College	BTEC National Diploma
1996	LAMDA	Bronze

Employment

11/95–present day	Lacrew's Pet Shop	Counter Assistant
06/94–11/95	Sid's Newsagents	Counter Assistant

Skills

- Computer literate (Word/Claris Works/Pagemaker)
- Musician – guitar, piano, baritone

Interests

Visiting the theatre, sports, acrobatics and gymnastics, computer programming

Referees

Ned Sherrin	Pierre Lacrew	Sydney Greenstreet
Lecturer in	TC Drama School	Sid's Newsagents
Performing Arts	9 The Mall	56–58 Bug Lane
Bright's College	High Street	Beckington
21 Onion Passage	Frome	Somerset
Bath	Somerset	BA1 21Z
Somerset	BA9 3PG	(0134) 678432
BA1 6SX	(01373) 896754	
(01225) 456732		

COVERING LETTER

The importance of good research cannot be underestimated when writing your covering letter. Remember, there may be thousands of people applying for the same job as yourself. You can only hope to impress your potential employer with your commitment and suitability for the post by understanding the kind of work they do. Ideally, you should have visited the theatre/theatre company and be familiar with its work, or have at least read some material. A quick telephone call to the company administrator may be one way of finding out some valuable information. There are also numerous publications/directories available in bookshops and libraries which will help you in this task. The following directories are the main sources of such information.

British Alternative Theatre Directory
  Rebecca Books
  Ivor House
  1 Bridge Street
  Cardiff
  CF1 2TH
  Tel: 01222 378452

British Performing Arts Yearbook
Irish Performing Arts Yearbook
Performing Arts Yearbook for Europe
  Rhinegold Publishing Ltd
  241 Shaftesbury Avenue
  London
  WC2 8EH
  Tel: 0171 240 5749

The Original British Theatre Directory
  Richmond House Publishing Co. Ltd
  1 Richmond Mews
  London
  W1V 5AG
  Tel: 0171 437 9556

Figure 7.9 on page 278 is an example of a covering letter. It is important to note that the applicant seems extremely interested and committed, without being ingratiating. A potential employer is looking for your suitability for the part or company, and not how well you can flatter them.

Life in the theatre

The two interviews below should give you some ideas about the reality of finding work and earning your living in the theatre.

Interview with Claire Marshall – actress with *Forced Entertainment*

How did you manage to get a job with Forced Entertainment
Serendipity. Tim and Terry had met me a couple of times – they had done a workshop at my university and also seen our final year shows – and my graduating coincided with the company looking for two extra performers. They asked me if I'd like to join them for *Some Confusions in the Law about Love* (1989); the show was about two months into development and there were specific 'roles' that Fred McVittie and

I stepped into – two hopeless skeletons who spoke the language of ancient Japanese love poetry. I think my genuine bewilderment was a great asset – I remember Richard saying that I was very good at looking confused – and I just stayed on (nobody asked me to leave). Although I knew virtually nothing about the company or indeed the field of practice, working with them felt familiar. They were doing what I'd previously been unable to define or describe.

[continued on page 279]

Figure 7.9   *A specimen covering letter*

From: A.N. Actor
        11 Logdale Road
        Wolverhampton
        West Midlands
        WV3 4AW
        Tel: 01902 543783

To: A.N. Gifted
        Artistic Director
        Bonkers Theatre Company
        56 Bullring
        Birmingham
        B6W 7ER

6 June 1996

Dear Mr Gifted

I have been following the work of the Bonkers Theatre Company for several years, and am very interested in the unusual and eccentric style in which the plays are performed. I saw your work both at the Birmingham Rep. and at the Glasgow Garden festival in 1993.

I am a performer, and would very much like to work on pieces of this nature. Together with a few friends, I have already performed several pieces (one at the Leeds Amateur Festival, and one at the opening of the Custard Factory) of a similar nature to Bonkers Theatre. Our group has difficulties, however, with performing all year round because of other commitments, and I am keen to find other work in this area. Would it be possible for me to meet you, perhaps with a view to becoming involved in your next project? Alternatively, if you are holding workshops or auditions in the near future, would you please consider inviting me along?

Please look at the enclosed Curriculum Vitae for more details of my previous work and training. I have also enclosed photos of our company in action.

I look forward to hearing from you in the near future.

Yours sincerely

A.N. Actor

Encs. CV and photos.

Figure 7.10   *Claire Marshall, Forced Entertainment* – Marina and Lee

Fred went on to work with his own company, *Pants Performance.*

How long do you spend devising each piece?
The three month period before opening a show in late September is probably the most important time in our year, in terms of generating ideas and material that we'll feed off for the rest of the year. It's a kind of laboratory time. By the time a show is up and touring, we're thinking about the next piece; perhaps as a development of the touring show or a reaction against it. (After the grim sparseness of *Speak Bitterness* (1995), we started yearning for dancing trees and flashing lights!). We tour until Christmas, then try to fit in some more research and development time – maybe in late January – with an eye to the next touring show; this is becoming very difficult as we take on more and more projects and extend our touring. Our process and lifestyle tends to mean that one project bleeds into the next – a theatre show may generate a gallery installation; an idea that didn't make it out of the rehearsal room might end up in a photographic collaboration with Hugo Glendinning or be the seed for a weekend of teaching. (That teaching may then inform and infect a site-specific performance.) It can take two or three (or more!) projects to satisfy our investigations into, or our obsessions with an idea – so in this way, I think each large scale project probably has a development time of about six months.

What sort of activities do you engage in during the devising process?
Improvising, talking, watching bits of films, more talking. We tend to start a project with a rag-bag of ideas – a piece of costume, some dialogue found in a cowboy novel, an interest in forensic investigations, a scene from a favourite film. (A scene that somebody once glimpsed while channel-hopping one night – a woman taped to a chair – became the central image for *Club of No Regrets* in 1993.) Generally the first thing we do is make a set (overseen by Richard Lowden) from bits and pieces of old sets, or things we've found in the car park at the back of our building, and then we play in it. Tim (Etchells) churns out text, and in the early days it's just left lying around for anyone to try out. As textures and mood begin to emerge, Tim will write more specifically, and that set will be refined. John Avery (composer) will come to watch us, and will write bits of music for us to work

with. Throughout this period, everything is up for grabs – sometimes other members of the company will write a bit of text or come up with a design idea.

A lot of our time is spent talking, trying to work out why things go together. We can talk for a week about a five minute section – hammering away until it makes sense, or sometimes we'll send Terry, Richard and Tim off to make a pragmatic decision.

Are you enjoying working with the company? Is there anything you dislike?
I don't like being poor, but then that's my choice. It's difficult to do other work because of the amount of work we generate for ourselves; to chase a second career in adverts and voice-overs demands time and energy that our schedule doesn't really allow – but again, I guess that's my choice. The constant financial insecurity the company has to operate under is a big pressure.

Describe your favourite piece by Forced Entertainment, *and say why you particularly enjoyed it.*
I don't really have a 'favourite'. I suppose *Marina and Lee* (1990) is special to me because it was the first show I was involved in right from the beginning [see Figure 7.10]; it's like a marker for a decision I made, i.e. to stay in Sheffield. *Nights in this City* (1995) feels 'significant' because it was made specially for Sheffield. As it was based on a coach-trip, the whole devising process mostly took place in a crowded estate car at dusk. We spent many weeks just driving around Sheffield, rediscovering it for ourselves. Remembering past shows is as much about remembering that year, that time and all that happened then; who you met and

who you lost, what your favourite outfit was, as much as it is about the merits or 'success' of the show.

As an actress, are there any roles you dream of playing?
I've always wanted to be in *The Bill*, as an acid-tongued lawyer or maybe a middle-class junkie who is part of Carver's past (suggested, of course, just by eye-brow acting and paper shuffling). I'd like to be in any of the American cop-shows of the *NYPD Blue* type – suppressed emotional agony and sudden displays of fury at an unfair world. Any kind of action film would do; David Lunch's work looks good fun because of all the secrets and obsessions.

I don't really fantasise about 'great roles for women' in the sense of playing 'strong yet vulnerable', but if I were a film or television actor, I'd like the same opportunities for ambiguity, self-parody, cruelty and strangeness that men have access to.

Have you got any advice for people interested in devising innovative performances?
I think people often copy what they like until their own stuff comes through, and that seems like a fine system to me. You have to be prepared to explain what you do and why you do it – and you have to develop a good relationship with promoters, funders and other practitioners. Once you're at a venue, make friends with technicians and publicity; that sounds like 'run around bestowing flowers and kisses' – I just mean that technical and administrative support is invaluable. It's also a good idea to give the people at the box office a few pithy sentences to describe the show – something a bit more chatty than what's on your publicity material.

Interview with Pavel Douglas

How did you go about getting your Equity card?
I started acting when I was still at school, and was naive enough not to think about such things, even when I worked unpaid at the original Traverse Theatre. I say 'unpaid' because there was no contract involved, and if there is no contract you cannot claim for that period when applying for your Equity card. Every subsequent job was denied to me on the grounds that I didn't have an Equity card, usually with the words 'We suggest you go to drama school like everybody else. You'll stand a better chance of getting a card when you get out.' so I joined the Lindsay Kemp Troupe who didn't care about Equity. Eventually, of course, I did go to drama school, and on coming out, started 'at the bottom' again, as ASM

at Pitlochry. This meant, however, that by the end of their 40-week run I was a full Equity member.

How did you find an agent?
When I was working at the Traverse, I was employed on a production with the late Libby Glen. Years later, she gave up acting to become an agent and so I wrote to her. I owe her and Arlington Associates a great deal for giving me a chance. If finding an agent seems a difficult task, finding the right agent is even more problematic.

How do you spend your time when you're not working?
By working of course! This is not meant to sound pretentious, but you get nowhere by standing still. I

also think it's important to work within the industry in any capacity, so that you keep learning. I've been in stage management, set construction, lighting, dressing, you name it. Now I'm lucky enough to be in great demand as a voice-over. This keeps me fed and available for castings etc. The important thing is never to consider yourself as between jobs. If there isn't any work, then make it for yourself: use the 'down' time, sleep if you must, but not to your cost. I've know actors who've made a career out of resting, but it's not for me.

Which kind of work do you prefer doing? And which job would you most like to get in the future?
If I could direct theatre, and act on film for the rest of my life, I'd be very happy. Don't get me wrong – I adore stage acting, and for me the occasional stage play is essential for 'getting my bottle back'. If I can't do this then I do stand-up comedy or compère work, in order to maintain a live audience—performer relationship. However, as I get old I find that the theatre is very hard work for very little remuneration. This is why I concentrate on getting film and television work. Acting to camera is my passion. It requires a completely different discipline and enormous concentration. I also enjoy directing plays because it enables me to use every skill that I have learned. Directing also only occupies an average of three weeks per production and that money is (usually) proportionate to the workload.

What are the essential qualities for an actor?
Pride and humility. By that I mean, enough of an ego to survive, but not so much that you are a pain in the neck.

Did you go to drama school, and was the training useful to you in your career?

I spent two years at East 15 Acting School, between 1970 and 1972. I was taken on by Maggie Bury (the Principal) without a grant, and worked as a bar-man and technician in the school theatre to pay my way. I enjoyed the school, for about half of the time. A good thing about drama school is that it allows you to practise without having to face the struggle of finding work; that comes afterwards.

How has the acting profession changed since you started?
I'm not sure that it has changed that much. It is possibly less closeted than it used to be, and there are certainly more actors then ever before. Now everyone seems to think that they can be an actor. Castings are full of models with great bone structure but little talent. There are countless outlets for work, but there is not enough money to do anything of real value. Standards (generally) are not as high as they should be. You have to be prepared to compromise a bit more, and talent still doesn't guarantee work or connections.

What advice would you give to young performers just starting on their careers?
Diversify into as many areas as possible, and thus increase your chances of staying in work. And if you want to do something, then go ahead and do it. There's nothing worse than saying you're going to do something and looking back and thinking, 'If only I had tried ...' Above all, never work on anything stronger than an aspirin, eat properly, stay fit and do your homework before an audition.
Preparation is 80 per cent of the job. Also, don't allow yourself to be crushed by disappointment. However you look at it, you can't possibly be right for every job, even though you may think you are.

Figure 7.11   *An example of a professional actor's Curriculum Vitae*

CV – PAVEL DOUGLAS

FILM AND TELEVISION credits to end of 1995 from 1985

Title	Character	Production Co.		
The Bruce	Comyn the Red	Cromwell Productions	FF	G/S
Nelsons Column 2	Richard	BBC	Sitcom	
GoldenEye	French Warship Captain	EON/UIP	FF	16th
Driven	Doc	TTTV	FF	C/S
Heartbreak Hotel	Sven	BBC	VT	C/S
Lovejoy Series 5	Lord Alexander Felsham	BBC/Witzend	F	R
Passport to Murder	Charles Devon	NBC (Film of the Month)	F	G/S
Tattle Tale	Edouard Astier	Canal+/Movie Channel	F	G/S
Intrigues (in French)	The Director	TF1 (France)	VT	C/S
Riviera	Lord Edward Covington	ECTV/TF1/Granada Int.	VT	R
Lovejoy Series 3	Lord Felsham	BBC/Witzend	F	R
Runaway Bay	McCoy	Lifetime/Ellipse	F	G
Shelf of London	Two Cameos	Universal Pictures	F	G
Lovejoy Series 2	Alexander	BBC/Witzend	F	R
Capital City	Gregorcz	Euston Films	F	G
Chronicles of Narnia	Lord Berne	BBC	F	G
Bergerac	De Lavarre	BBC	F	–
EastEnders	Gregory Mantel	BBC	VT	R
Making News	John Keats	Thames	VT	–
Hannay	Porter	Thames	VT	–
Reasonable Force	Radio Reporter	BBC	F	–
Clem	Paul	Channel Four	VT	G
Robin of Sherwood 1 & 2	Captain (Sheriff's Guard)	HTV	F	–
Menace Unseen	TV Reporter	Anglia	F	–
First Among Equals	Viscount Rupert Seymour	Granada	VT	G
Lovejoy Series 1	Lord Alexander Felsham	BBC	F	R
The Master of Ballantrae	Bonnie Prince Charlie	HTV International	F	–
Jamaica Inn	The Hon James Barton	HTV International	F	–
Widows Series 2	Det. Sgt Reynolds	Euston Films	F	–
Function Rooms	The Landlord	HTV	VT	G
Into the Labyrinth	Mordred	HTV	VT	G

(Other 'small-roles' have not been included.)

Key:
FF: Feature Film   F: Film for Television   VT: Multi-camera for Television
C/S: Co-Star (Main Titles)   G/S: Guest-Star (Single Card)   R: Regular (Multi Episodic)
G: Guest.

FEATURE FILM DETAILS:

The Bruce	Directed by Bob Carruthers for Cromwell Productions Ltd, UK.
GoldenEye	Directed by Martin Campbell for EON Productions Ltd, London.
Driven	Directed by Bharat Nalluri for Pilgrim Pictures, Newcastle.
Passport to Murder	Directed by David Hemmings for FTM Productions, Los Angeles.
Tattle Tale	Directed by Baz Taylor for Chrysalide Films, Paris.

THEATRE

As Director

The British are Coming	Natural Theatre Company
The Jekyll and Hyde Follies	Natural Theatre Company
Largo Desolato	Bristol Old Vic Company
Spy Society	Natural Theatre Company
Prairie Oysters	Natural Theatre Company
Blood Weekend	Natural Theatre Company

As an Actor

The Natural Theatre Company
Bristol Old Vic Company
Sheffield Crucible
The Citizens Theatre Company
Attic Theatre Company
The Lindsay Kemp Troupe
Pitlochry Festival Company
Traverse Theatre Company
(This section also includes Production Management/Lighting/Set Design & Construction Stage Fight Direction/and Lecturing at The Actors' Studio – Houston Texas.)

UK TELEVISION COMMERCIALS

Volvo 740
Quick Fit Euro
Fiat Punto
VW/Skoda Favorit

RADIO DRAMA/DUBBING/VOICE-OVERS (Advertising & Corporate)
CORPORATE & TRAINING FILMS/FILM NARRATION/PRESENTATION TO
CAMERA

This section is too long and detailed to be included, but can be supplied on request.

CORPORATE THEATRE/LIVE PRESENTATION

Xerox	The Journey Continues
GEC/Plessey	Voice '95
Kenco	'Carte Noire' Launch
British Youth Olympics	(Master of Ceremonies)
3M	TMA '94
Kwick Fit	On Trial

INDEX